Windows 95

PROGRAMMING WITH

CUSTOM CONTROLS

Windows 95

PROGRAMMING WITH
CUSTOM CONTROLS

Paul Cilwa

THE CORIOLIS GROUP

Publisher	Keith Weiskamp
Editor	Mira Fosse
Proofreader	Diane Green Cook
Cover Design	Bradley Grannis
Cover Artist	Gary Smith
Layout Production	Michelle Stroup
Indexer	Diane Green Cook

The Coriolis Group
7339 E. Acoma Drive, Suite 7
Scottsdale, AZ 85260
Phone: (602) 483-0192
Fax: (602) 483-0193
Web address: www.coriolis.com

ISBN 1-883577-73-X : $39.99

Printed in the United States of America

10 9 8 7 6 5 4 3 2 1

Contents

Introduction   xv

Part 1   The Secret Life of Component Software   1

Chapter 1   The Power of Software Components   3

The Birth of Reusable Code   4
Enter the VBX   5

Here Comes the OCX   6

The Modern Control Freak   6

Take One Encapsulation and Call Me in the Morning   7
Where Do We Go from Here?   8

Ten Reasons Why VBXs Aren't Dead Yet   8
#1:   Your Clients Want Applications Now   9
#2:   Windows 95 Supports Existing 16-Bit Code   10
#3:   The VBX Standard Is Well-Defined   14
#4:   VBXs Are Easy to Design and Write   14
#5:   VBXs Can Be Written on Top of Existing Windows   16
#6:   VBXs Teach Object-Oriented Discipline   17
#7:   VBXs Add Objects to Visual Basic 3   18
#8:   VBXs Provide a Good Point-of-Control for Data-Less Objects   19

v

#9:   VBXs Can Be Written to Triple Standards   19
#10: OCXs Can Be Easily Derived from VBXs   21

Chapter 2   OCXs: The Wave of the Future?   23

Big Waves and COMmon Breakers   24

Control Freaks   25

Surf's Up!   27

Chapter 3   A VBX Skeleton Revisited   29

Inside the VBX   30

A Look at INTERNAL.H   31
A Look at VISUAL.C   32
VBXHELP.C   43
MAIN.RC   47
MAIN.DEF   48

The Skeleton Walked   48

Part 2   A VBX Class Library   49

Chapter 4   Creating a Vendor-Free GDI Class Library   51

C Disadvantages   52

C++ Advantages   53

The Goal   54

Facing a Dilemma   54

Creating a Vendor-Free Windows Class Library   55

Classes and Style   56

GDI Basics   57

The Baggage Department   58

Your Point of Departure   59

Coding the Constructors and Operators   60
Defining the size Class   62
Introducing the rectangle Class   62

With Flying Colors   65
Creating Color Component Classes   67

A Brush with Death   73

Don't Forget Your Pen!   76

An Airborne Device   78
Creating the paintcontext Class   83
Creating the clientcontext Class   84

Test Flight   85

Additional Airlines   85

Chapter 5   Creating a Vendor-Free text Class   87

Creating the text Class   88
Defining the Header File   89
Secret Origins of a text Object   90
Safely Stored in the Fortress of Solitude   93
A Hero's Assignment   95
So, Who's Faster...Flash or Superman?   96
The Hero's Sidekick   98
Elastic Lad to the Rescue!   100
Metallo, The Villain without a Heart   102
Triplicate Girl Surrounds the Villains   103
Revealing That Secret Identity   104
Divide and Conquer   106

Testing Your New Powers   108

The Dust Clears   110

Chapter 6   Implementing the VBX++ Class Library   111

Using VBX++: A Preview   112

Implementing VBX++   114

Microsoft Visual C++ Compiler Options   115
Borland C++ Compiler Options   116
Creating the model Class   117

Handling Methods   136

The control Class   139

Property Classes   142

boolproperty   150
colorproperty   152
enumproperty   152
textproperty   153
pictureproperty   155
floatproperty   156

A List of Properties   156

Special Events...and Ordinary Ones   158

Just Do It   162

Part 3   A VBX Generator   167

Chapter 7   Introducing the VBX Genie   169

The Design of a Code Generator   170

The Code Template   171
The Code Generator   172
The User Interface   172

Choosing an Implementation Language   173

Chapter 8   Creating the User Interface   177

Creating the Main Form—the Prime Directive   178

Coding Prime   179
Wiring in the Tab Control   181

Supporting the Project Page   183

Supporting the Version Page   184

Introducing the Listable Classes   187

Supporting Collections   189

Introducing the Property Functions   191
Finishing the Initialization   193

Supporting the Model Page   196

Wrapping Up the Model Page   201

Supporting the Properties Page   201

Supporting Custom Properties   207

Supporting the Events Page   214

Supporting Custom Events   216

Adding the Methods Page   220

Chapter 9   Generating Code   223

Attaching the Code Script   224

Creating the Code Scripts   225
Generating Code   226

Chapter 10   Self-Installing IDE Tools   235

Bottling the Genie   236

Hand Me That Hammer   236

Installing to MSVC 1.5x   242

Creating a Brand-New MSVC Project   243

Installing VBX Genie as a Borland C++ Tool   249

Creating a Brand-New Borland C++ Project   255

Chapter 11   Creating a Setup Program for VBX Genie   261

The VBX Genie Setup Chronicles   262

Platforms or Sandbars?   262

What Does Setup Wizard Actually Do?   264
A Closer Look at the Setup Problem   265

Creating Our Plan of Attack   267

Creating the Pre-Setup Program   268

Building the Generic Genie   271

Adding the Reusable About Box   274

Creating the Setup Wizard Workaround Installer   276
Coding the Reusable ProgressBarClass   278
Expanding the Win31 Files   281

Updating SWDEPEND.INI   282

Installing PRESETUP   284

Installing the Workaround   284

The Setup Wizard Workaround   285

Loading the Bus and Heading on Home   295

Chapter 12   A VBX for the Find and Replace Dialogs   297

The Dialog Dilemma   298

The Find and Replace Dialogs   300

Generating the FindReplace Control Skeleton   303

Storing and Accessing the FINDREPLACE Structure   306

Supporting Context-Sensitive, Online Help   313

Distributing the Control   315

Testing the FindReplace Control   315

Chapter 13   Adding Tool Tips to Standard Controls   317

A Sign of the Times   318

A Signpost Up Ahead... 318

Sign Language 319
Coding the Methods 322
Going to the Head of the Subclass 324
Setting Properties 327
System Colors in VB 329
Signs and Portents 335

The Tip Window 338

Using the Tips Control 342

Part 4 Microsoft's OLE Control Wizard 345

Chapter 14 What Is This Thing Called COM? 347

Introducing the Common Object Model 350

Introducing the IUnknown Interface 351

Introducing OLE Automation 353

OLE Controls 354

Memory Lights the Corners 355

Property Types 356

Stock Properties 356
Extended Properties 356
Ambient Properties 357

Stock Methods 358

Events 358

The VBX/OCX Face-off 361

Chapter 15 Creating a Simple OCX 365

Creating a 16-bit OCX 367

Checking and Changing the Control Settings 371

Creating a 32-bit OCX 372

Examining the Code   378
Supporting Property Pages   384
Supporting the Registration Database   385

Chapter 16   Working With OCX Stock Properties   391

Designing a Better Listbox   393

Taking TabList for a Dry Run   395

A Glimpse of a Hidden Control   396

Setting Default Property Values   398
Choosing a Tissue Color   402

Using the Stock Font Property   406

Setting Up the Property Pages   407

Moving Along   409

Chapter 17   Custom OCX Properties   411

Introducing Custom Properties   412

Starting with the Roots   413
Implementing Enumerated Properties   418

Sending Down Shoots   424

Seed Properties   427

Strings and Things   429

One Tree, Many Branches   430

You Say You Want to Derive a Control...?   434

The Appearance Property   435

Paddling On   436

Chapter 18 Custom Methods and Events 437

Specializing the TabList Control 438

Specializing the ImageList Control 443

Implementing Custom Events 450

Caught In the Thicket 454

Appendix A A Few Notes on the Tools 455

Appendix B Combination VBX/OCXs 459

Appendix C Using the Companion CD-ROM 461

Index 465

Introduction

A N OLD CHINESE CURSE GOES, "May you live in interesting times." In a sense, we are all cursed because few times in history have been as interesting as these. As programmers we are particularly cursed because our work is what is *driving* many of the changes that *make* these times so interesting! And we are not immune; the very tools we use to create these changes are themselves changing; sometimes, much faster than we can keep up.

A case in point is the VBX (an acronym for **V**isual **B**asic **E**xtension). The VBX has grown past its humble Visual Basic beginnings and is used by many other application development environments and tools, including Microsoft Visual C++, Borland C++, Delphi, PowerBuilder, and others. And yet the VBX, barely four years old itself, is already considered obsolete and replaced by the *OCX* (OLE Control Extension), whose standards are quickly evolving.

In the old (mainframe) days, you could count on library routines you wrote to be useful for at least a few years. Now you are lucky if they are still useful in a few months. In early 1994, I published a book with The Coriolis Group titled *Windows Programming Power with Custom Controls*. This book showed C/C++ programmers how to leverage their investment in the then current standard Windows controls by using them to build combination standard control/VBXs in single DLLs (Dynamic Link Libraries). This book also introduced a useful VBX skeleton that allowed programmers to concentrate on the features that made their controls special, instead of the housekeeping chores every VBX requires.

At the time I wrote the book, the VBX standards were in quite a state of flux, especially in terms of the way they were supported by different compiler platforms, such as Visual C++, Borland C++, and so on. Fortunately, I received valuable feedback from numerous programmers around the world who were using the code and techniques presented in the book to develop their own custom controls and applications.

With the emergence of OCXs and the newer platforms including Visual Basic 4, Visual C++ 4, and Delphi 2 (32-bit), I decided it was time to take the concepts of software component creation much further and show how to take advantage of the power of the newer control technology for Windows development.

Software Components—The Next Generation

Most applications you come across these days (especially those developed with the popular visual development environments) are likely to have been developed with the aid of custom controls. As I'm sure you're aware, custom controls have introduced hundreds of thousands of developers to the art of creating software with custom components.

Who Needs This Book

If you're the kind of person who would rather spend your extra time rafting through the Grand Canyon, fly fishing in Colorado, trekking in the Himalayas, or simply getting bombed at the local "hang out" joint during happy hour, instead of coding up yet another Windows development tool, then this book is for you. My main goal is to help you save time by showing you how you can create your own software components that you can use over and over.

To follow along, you'll need some experience programming for Windows in C and C++. The custom control code presented was written with both. In addition, some exposure to Visual Basic is helpful since that is still the primary consumer of VBX-style software components—and the first environment in which OCXs could be used.

What You'll Need

In order to compile a VBX, you must have a C/C++ compiler that will generate 16-bit code. If you are a Microsoft aficionado, that means Microsoft Visual C++ version 1.52 or earlier. A *later* compiler will not do, since Microsoft compilers version 2.0 and better generate *only* 32-bit code. On the other hand, any Borland C/C++ compiler capable of generating Windows code will do (although Borland C++ 4.0 through 4.02 had *serious* bugs; if you still own one of those versions, you should request an update).

To run or test a VBX, you'll need Visual Basic version 3, or the 16-bit version of Visual Basic 4 Professional Edition. (The other editions of VB4 do not include a 16-bit version.) The other platforms that use VBXs actually run version 1.0 VBXs. If you can accept the limitations of a VBX written to the version 1.0 specifications, you can use any of those platforms.

In order to create an OCX in the Microsoft environment, you'll need to install the Control Wizard. This comes on the same CD-ROM as Visual C++, but requires a separate setup step. To create an OCX in the Borland C++ environment will require Borland C++ 5.0.

Keep in mind that at the time of this writing, not all platforms make use of OCXs. To run or test an OCX in any meaningful way will require Visual Basic 4, Visual C++ 4, Borland C++ 5, or Delphi 32-bit.

I've tried to make this book work with as many tools as possible. But, frankly, with two major vendors shipping updates every few months—Borland alone released five versions of their C++ environment last year—it's impossible to keep up. So, rather than giving cookbook directions for compiling, I'll try to make it clear *why* various compiler switches were set, and so on, so *you* can make intelligent decisions regarding your own development tools.

How to Use This Book

This book is *not* your typical, book-by-the-pound exhaustive treatise on every single bit of trivia and arcana to be found on the subject of programming (although you'll find plenty of trivia inside). It's also not just a manual for creating VBXs or OCXs (although it does present that information). It's intended to be a journey through the 1996 world of component software, and a way not only to thread yourself through the needle of the transition to 32-bit code, but to learn how to handle future such transitions on your own.

VBXs and OCXs are just the excuse: What you'll be learning is how to write component-style code that is tight, bullet-proof, and truly reusable. Along the way you'll learn object-oriented coding techniques that work in C as well as C++, how to make C++ overloaded operators really work for you, how to get the most from the new Visual Basic classes, and how to design DLLs that can be used for more than one related purpose.

If you are, and wish to remain, a one-trick pony—your trick being a single computer language—this book may *not* be for you. Neither may be these times. Currently, the preferred method of rapid application development among many of the country's Fortune 500 (whom I teach) is to create tools in C or C++—or both—and to use platforms like Visual Basic or Delphi as the "glue" to bind the tools together. While it is possible for one programmer to write the tool and another to apply the glue, you can be much *more* valuable if you can do both—as your paycheck will show.

This book is intended to be fun to read, and the code it describes is intended to be fun to write and work with. As usual, I'll be tossing in bits of programming and design advice along with the code. This advice is based on over 15 years of professional programming and design experience, most of it with Windows; my readers and students generally find it useful.

So crank up that vibrating mat on your executive-backed swivel chair, boot up the computer, and start reading. (If you are running Windows 95, you should have time to get through most of the first chapter before the boot sequence completes!)

How to Use the Code

Accompanying this book is a useful CD-ROM jam-packed with the source code from this book, custom controls, and resources to help you roll your own OCX controls. Some people *like* to key in every line from a book; they feel it helps them meditate on the code and grok some kind of fullness from it. Well, that's how they used to teach music; so maybe there's something to it. But for those of you who prefer studying and using to typing, all of the source code is available in electronic form.

The directories on the CD-ROM are organized by chapter. Each chapter subdirectory—excuse me, I guess they're called *folders* now—contains the files as they should appear *at the end* of the chapter. That way, you can start at any point and add the things you find in the next chapter. Since this is a "group" project, feel free to modify anything here to meet your own needs ... and to live with the consequences.

In its desire to force the industry into its favored direction (OCXs), Microsoft has offered an OLE Control Wizard add-on for Visual C++, but no such tool for creating VBXs. Yet, most tools in which you'd *like* to use software components don't yet understand the OCX interface. So this book provides you with an intermediate tool: a *VBX Genie* that will generate the house-keeping code of my VBX skeleton. The VBX Genie will generate this code in your choice of C or C++; either way, the code will easily tie in to the OLE Control Wizard's generated code, allowing you to produce combination DLLs with a minimum of fuss and *no* maintenance nightmares.

And since just throwing such a code generator at you would waste an incredible opportunity to understand how such a generator is written, I won't do that. Instead, we'll build VBX Genie together, in the neutral Visual Basic language, which will give us a chance to look at sophisticated coding techniques in all of Visual Basic, C and C++. (But if you simply want to use it, it's there on the CD-ROM, ready to install.)

In addition, the CD-ROM contains a few giveaways. One is the Programmer's File Editor, a freeware Windows application that is better than Notepad at editing code for which your IDE (Integrated Development Environment) is unsuitable for any reason.

What's Inside

This book is divided into four major sections, or parts. In the first part, we'll look in general terms at what a VBX is for, how one is made, and why you might want one. Then we'll examine OCXs the same way. We'll close part one by revisiting the VBX skeleton from my earlier book, simplified for these days when no one uses the older "standard" custom controls any more.

In the next part, we'll break new ground by creating a C++ class library for VBXs. This library, to be useful, must not be married to either Borland or Microsoft development environments. That's what I call a "vendor-free" class library, and in order to write one for VBXs, we'll have to do up little class libraries for Windows GDI components as well. By the time you get done with this part, you should have a good feel for how easy it is to create a usable class library, and be ready to run off and do one of your own, just for fun!

In Part III we'll switch languages for a bit. Are you tired of manually copying code for every repetitive coding task? Code generators are easy and fun to write, especially with the tools that fall out of this part's project: a VBX Genie that can generate the code we developed earlier in the book automatically, and to specification.

The next part examines OCXs in-depth. How do they differ from VBXs? How are they the same? We'll go ahead and create an OCX or two as we study them; you may find the OCX controls useful in and of themselves.

Contacting Me

If you bought my other book, you know what a pain in the butt it can be to get some of the code to run. The poor folks at The Coriolis Group had to answer the phone at all hours of the day to try to handle tech support problems. Well, heck, I've changed my ways. Now you can reach me any time of the day or night. I've purchased a beeper and a cell-phone so that you easily track me down. Just call: 1-900 Bug Paul

No longer will you have to worry about how to install the software or get the Skeleton control to compile. This is the way all computer book authors should make the bulk of their income. Hey, it worked for Microsoft!

Seriously, the Coriolis Group has a World-Wide Web page devoted to its books, including this one. I've made every effort to see that the code runs on all the development environments I can, but let's face it—I haven't tried any of it on *your* computer. If you do have trouble, odds are you won't be the first with that particular problem; and if the solution isn't already there, I'll do my best to post one there as soon as possible.

On Your Way

The Chinese also say, "The longest journey begins with a single step." I believe in lots of small, easy steps (rather than a few, staggering, giant ones) so the sooner you start the first chapter, the sooner you'll complete this particular journey. Wear soft shoes! It'll be fun.

PART 1

The Secret Life of Component Software

The Power of Software Components   3

OCXs: The Wave of the Future?   23

A VBX Skeleton Revisited   29

The Power of Software Components

I N 1869, JOHN WESLEY POWELL led the first expedition down the Grand Canyon. This really was the first expedition; there is no evidence that Native Americans ever navigated the Colorado through the Canyon (although they certainly lived within its walls). So when Powell and his men made their trip, they were truly going where no human had gone before.

Powell started out with nine other men and four heavy wooden boats. These wide-bottomed boats were Powell's best hope of running the rapids he was pretty sure his expedition would encounter along the way. Nevertheless, before the trip was over, Powell lost two of the boats and four of his men. (The four men deserted; three of them were never seen again.) The adventure of a lifetime had taken him over three months.

Last year, I spent 17 days rafting the Grand Canyon ... *for fun.* We put in at Lee's Ferry, just like Powell, and left at Lake Meade not far from Powell's take out point. We ate gourmet meals along the way, slept comfortably, and had time to hike into numerous side canyons and to go for dips in the Little Colorado and Deer Creek tributaries.

What happened?

In two words, incremental development. The first step was Powell's *proving it could be done.*

> *It's amazing how securely you can attempt something you know can be accomplished, because someone else has already done it.*

The next step was the development in World War II of the rubber, inflatable raft. (This step also built on previous steps, such as the inventions of vulcanized rubber and the pneumatic pump.)

The next step, a stroke of genius, occurred when the legendary Georgie White put the sale of war surplus rubber rafts and her love of the Canyon together, and started the first commercially-priced rafting trips down the Colorado. Passenger trips had been taken before but they were made in wooden dories and subject to flips in the wilder rapids. Georgie's rubber rafts simply bulldozed through the waves, scaring everyone and getting them wet, but keeping them safe.

The Birth of Reusable Code

While a 70-year-old Georgie White was still leading expeditions down the Canyon, I was busily working on Tandem mainframe computers (we called them "minis" at the time), programming in the proprietary language TAL. I quickly realized that I tended to write the same pieces of code over and over; and since TAL is a block-structured language (like C), I learned to place all my code in small, focused functions and procedures that could easily be reused. I also did something very few programmers do: I *fully documented* my library. By the end of a year I had over 400 functions, ranging in complexity from a little routine that converted binary values into ASCII, to a set of procedures that implemented a fully-functional report writer.

I constantly amazed my managers and coworkers with my ability to produce a month's worth of work in an afternoon. I could do this because I no longer did much programming; I simply *assembled* new programs from invocations of functions I'd already written. Four more years passed by and that library was constantly used.

It's been a long time since I was able to write a tool I could reuse for four years.

Enter the VBX

But then came Visual Basic. Part of VB's charm—and almost certainly the reason for its success—was its custom controls, called *VBXs*. These controls allowed us programmers to extend the programming environment. VBXs did what Microsoft Windows' standard controls had never quite managed to pull off: Produce a cottage industry of third-party, reusable, packaged, programming components. The age of the software component had arrived.

The third-party VBX market poured over the programming scene like the Colorado through a Class 10 rapid. Hundreds of companies got into the act and over a thousand controls quickly emerged. Software development using ready-to-wear components really came of age as programmers had a wide selection of controls to choose from including database access, multimedia control, network and Internet communications, animation and graphics, user interface tools, grids and spreadsheets, word processors, text editors, and spell checkers, real-time controllers, and even components as exotic as expert systems. Magazines, books, and seminars on Visual Basic and other visual languages quickly changed their focus to emphasize the flexibility, power, and down-right time savings of building Windows applications with VBXs.

> *VBXs were responsible for changing the landscape of Windows development more so than any other software development tool or technique introduced in the early 90s. Why? They were the first practical implementation of a software component that could plug into a development platform and make itself available to any application that needs it.*

However, like a sulky child that has gotten his or her way and then decided that's not what he or she wanted after all, Microsoft almost immediately declared the VBX to be obsolete. While Visual Basic, Microsoft's own product, was using version 3.0 VBXs, its other programming environment, Visual C++, could only utilize version 1.0! At the time of this writing, the 32-bit versions of Visual C++ can't use them at all.

Microsoft explained that the VBX standard's shortcoming was its inability to work in the 32-bit world. Now, please understand, *this shortcoming is manu-*

factured. There is no reason that a marshaling layer cannot be written to convert 32-bit parameters to 16-bit; after all, that's what Microsoft has already done with other Windows code, to allow 16-bit DLLs of other types to function in 32-bit operating systems like Windows 95 and Windows NT.

Here Comes the OCX

Microsoft's newest vision is one in which everything is part of the OLE (**O**bject **L**inking and **E**mbedding, although the acronym is no longer descriptive) world. While VBXs could probably have been forced to fit into this picture, Microsoft decided to abandon them, replacing them with OLE controls. These are commonly called *OCXs*, although the "acronym" doesn't really mean anything.

I'll have more to say about OCXs in the next chapter, as well as some detailed stuff in the last two parts of this book. For now, let's just say that OCXs are functional equivalents to VBXs, in that they are drop-in software components—but, like so much Microsoft has done lately, they require anywhere from twice to ten times the system resources of their VBX predecessors while providing little additional value to the programmer.

The Modern Control Freak

As a Windows user—you must be one, right?—you are familiar with controls; they are the things you point at, click, and drag to work on your data. Once upon a time these features would have been hardware controls on a card-sorting machine or typewriter; now they are mere pictures on a screen. But they respond to keystrokes and mouse clicks and we love 'em.

As a Windows programmer, you're probably familiar with the back side of controls: The fact that every control is a Windows window, with a window procedure, receiving and sending messages to and from other windows, notifying its parent window when the user points, clicks, or drags. As the programmer of VBXs, you may be aware that there is an additional layer on top of the standard Windows window that hooks the control into the Visual Basic, Delphi, PowerBuilder, or Borland C++ development environment. This layer supplies the picture of the control for the toolbox; it supplies the names of "properties" and "events" that make the control useful, and converts references to the properties and events into Windows messages sent to the underlying control.

The OCX standard also builds on the Windows window; but while in many ways it duplicates the abilities of the VBX, it does so in ways so complex and arcane that until Microsoft hid this complexity in a C++ class library, practically no one understood it or was able to make it work. In fact, the author of the first published book on OLE 2 programming has declared *he* didn't understand it while he was *writing the book!*

However, Microsoft's class library does give us the ability to write OCXs. Just pray to whatever deity you worship that you don't discover a bug that requires diving into Microsoft's code to fix. Personally, I'd rather flip a raft.

One of the nice things about any well-written custom control is that it fully encapsulates whatever functions it's supposed to perform. To make this clearer, let's compare a custom control to your TV set. You know that the inside of the TV set is filled with wires, circuit boards, hot things, and electrical things. You also know better than to open up the back and mess in there. You *also* know that *you don't have to.* All the controls that concern *you* are conveniently located on the front, back, or side of the set, or in the remote control.

> *A well-written custom control should also offer a clean, streamlined appearance to the programmer. There are things the programmer can and should manipulate (properties, events, and methods), but anything the programmer doesn't need should be hidden away inside the control, out of the programmer's reach.*

Using this model, you can put just about *anything* useful in a custom control. It doesn't have to be a control the end user will use or see; it can be a "back-panel" control there for the convenience of the programmer. For example, Visual Basic's Timer control isn't visible at run-time; it simply encapsulates timing functions for the convenience of the programmer.

Take One Encapsulation and Call Me in the Morning

You encapsulate a standard Windows control by making sure that Windows messages are the only way to communicate with it programmatically. No global variables there, folks!

When building a VBX or OCX on top of a standard Windows control, you define your own properties (VBXs and OCXs) and methods (OCXs only) for the control, and when those properties and methods are exercised, you pass the appropriate Windows messages on to the underlying Windows window. You also define events, which are triggered when the underlying window sends a notification message to the VBX or OCX layer (which it thinks is its "parent" window).

The main reason, I think, that custom controls of the standard Windows window type never took off is that back then, Windows programs were written only in C; and C programmers are notorious for never using anyone else's code. They didn't *like* encapsulated controls; they prefer their TV sets with the cases removed and the picture tubes unscrewed from the chassis. But when they found themselves out-competed by Visual Basic programmers, they took another look. Or, perhaps, that old-style C programmer has simply become extinct in a Darwinian battle of the fittest. Today's programmer must be fluent in several languages, afraid of none, and able to produce using a variety of tools. He or she must be a walking catalog of available components, and able to create new components when—and *only* when—suitable ones cannot be found.

Where Do We Go from Here?

So, what do you do—write VBXs knowing their days are numbered? Write OCXs that currently are usable in just a few situations? Give up programming and become a Grand Canyon river guide? If I had to choose, I'd go with the river. However, there is another, fourth choice.

> *It is possible to write a VBX that can do double-duty as an OCX.*

This is only feasible if *you really* understand the requirements of both VBXs and OCXs, and if you very carefully adhere to a structured style of programming that produces small, tightly focused functions. Let's next examine more closely why VBXs will be around long enough to make this effort worthwhile, and why VBXs provide a firm foundation for OCX programming.

Ten Reasons Why VBXs Aren't Dead Yet

In addition to writing and rafting, I teach Visual Basic, Visual C++, and Borland C++ programming. Because all three of these environments claim support for VBXs, the question inevitably comes up in each class: "Must I learn to write VBXs?" This is immediately followed by another question: "But aren't VBXs obsolete?"

The rumor that VBXs are, or will soon become, obsolete, stems from the fact that VBXs are written to a 16-bit standard, but the current version of Windows runs in 32 bits, as Windows NT has all along. Since VBXs run in 16-bit code segments, the fear is that they will not adapt to the new environments. This fear is encouraged by Microsoft, who has refused to extend the VBX standard to 32 bits, and has instead offered yet another new standard, the OCX, to replace it.

So what's a developer to do? Continue to write tools that may become obsolete any moment? Throw out all the previously written and purchased tools—yet again? How many times must we do this, anyway? It seems whenever we start to stockpile genuinely reusable code, Microsoft pulls the rug out from under us. It's no wonder we programmers live on Mylanta.

But take heart. Things aren't as bad as they seem. While you'll want to learn to write OCXs soon (and in fact will be doing so by the time you complete this book!) that doesn't mean all your skill in developing or using VBXs is now at the bottom of the river. There are several reasons that the death of VBXs, to paraphrase Mark Twain, has been greatly exaggerated.

#1: Your Clients Want Applications Now

It's easy to miss a little thing like this, but, hey—guess what—Windows 95 was originally supposed to be released at *least one year before it come out*. See, Microsoft gets into trouble when they throw out all their old tools, too. Your clients aren't *about* to throw out everything they've purchased—at least not all at once. Some may still be running Windows 3.1. Visual Basic 3.0 development will continue for a while. And Microsoft does know this, and builds enough backward compatibility to allow it.

But your clients have needs *now*. We can't all wait until some mythical day arrives when the platforms on which we develop these applications achieve some pinnacle of perfection, never needing another release. And guess what, folks—that day ain't comin'. The driving force behind new releases isn't a reach for perfection; it's a reach for higher profits. As long as users are willing to upgrade their operating systems, operating systems suppliers will be willing to supply upgrades. It's that simple.

So what are your tools for speedy application development? The same as last week: Visual Basic, Visual C++, Borland C++, Borland Delphi, and so on. And the components you can use to help speed development further? You guessed it: VBXs.

Now, it's true that if you *were* to write an OCX today, you could plug it into a VB 4 application. You could also fit it into a Visual C++ 4 app and a Delphi 32-bit app as well. But do you know *how* to write an OCX today? No? I didn't think so. Yes, you must learn to do so eventually, and this book will help you achieve that goal. But meanwhile, you gotta eat ... and VBXs can help pay the food bill. Besides, the effort you spend writing VBXs today will not be totally wasted, because...

#2: Windows 95 Supports Existing 16-Bit Code

Remember what I said earlier: New versions of operating systems are released as long as people are willing to buy them. People will *not* buy them if it means throwing out all their existing applications. Those apps cost too much to replace all at once. (In fact, my clients are starting to grumble over the frequency with which they must replace the applications themselves. Few of them felt the dockable toolbars without genuine functional improvements made the expense of upgrading the Microsoft Office applications worthwhile, for instance.) So, just as Windows 3.1 fully supported applications written for Windows 3.0, Windows 95 had to support Windows 3.1 applications. Many of those applications were written in Visual Basic or native C and a simple recompile will *not* upgrade them to 32 bits. So, what else could be done?

To understand how this trick is pulled off, you have to know a little bit about the Intel 80x86 chips at the heart of virtually all IBM-compatible PCs. (The PowerPC chip mimics the Intel chips when running Intel-compatible operating systems, so what I'm about to say applies there as well.)

Real mode, as you probably know, is how MS-DOS programs normally run. The *real* refers to the fact that the addresses in the program are the *real* addresses being accessed—that is, address 0000:0000 is *really* the *very first* address in RAM. Address 0000:0001 is the next byte, and so on as shown in Figure 1.1. Since real mode programs are expected to run just one at a time, there's no need to provide

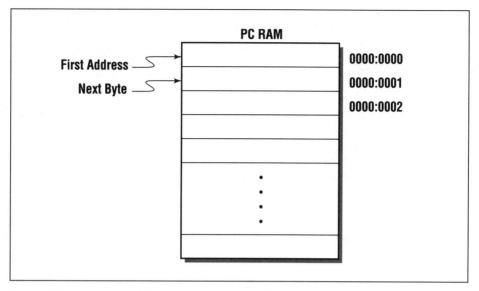

Figure 1.1 Accessing PC memory in real mode.

protection against accidentally writing into another program's memory space, as could happen if a pointer got trashed or the programmer forgot to initialize it to a meaningful value.

In protected mode, a level of protection is potentially provided. Each block of memory requested by an application is defined by a *descriptor*, and the index of the descriptor is kept in the most significant 13 bits of the 32-bit address. As Figure 1.2 illustrates, a level of indirection is used here, but it's okay, because the CPU itself handles it automatically at chip-level speeds. The descriptor provides all kinds of useful information, such as whether the memory block it points to is code or data, whether or not it can be written to, its size, and so on.

At least one table of descriptors is available the whole time the CPU is running in protected mode. This table is called the *global descriptor table* or *GDT*. But Windows doesn't make much use of the GDT. Instead, each running task can use a *local descriptor table (LDT)*. The LDTs of different tasks can have entirely separate sets of descriptors, pointing to separate and isolated blocks of RAM. This *configuration* provides the "protection" in "protected mode" as shown in Figure 1.3.

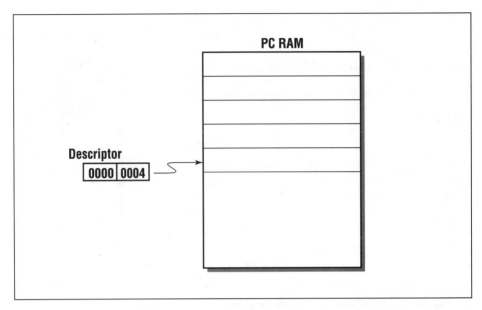

Figure 1.2 Accessing PC memory in protected mode using a descriptor.

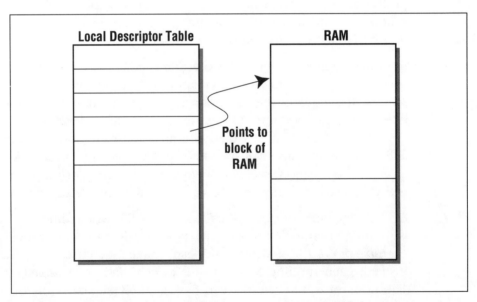

Figure 1.3 The local descriptor table used to set up protection for protected mode.

However, Windows 3.1 didn't make good use of this scheme. While DOS programs each run as separate tasks with their own LDTs, all Windows apps running concurrently share the same LDT. That's why it was still possible for a crashing Windows app to leave behind an "unstable" environment. When users called with "weird" problems, our first response was usually, "Try restarting Windows and see if the problem doesn't go away."

In Windows 95 and NT, 32-bit applications do *not* share LDTs. That's one reason that Windows is now more inherently stable than it used to be. However, to support existing 16-bit applications, Microsoft compromised this ideal setup, and all 16-bit apps run together in a single, 16-bit task, using the same LDT. So they are no more stable (with regard to each other) than they were in Windows 3.1. It is still possible to make that 16-bit task unstable if a 16-bit app crashes or doesn't clean up after itself properly. While the 32-bit apps running can continue to do so safely, the only way to restore stability to that 16-bit task is—you guessed it—restart Windows.

> *Remember the descriptors in the LDT I mentioned? I said they contained a lot of useful information, including whether the segment being described was code or data. Well, if the segment is a code segment, the descriptor also states whether it is 16- or 32-bit code! Thus, much of the work is already done.*

In fact, the only reason there's a problem at all is that when Windows went to 32 bits, almost all of the standard parameters were also altered from 16 to 32 bits. These days window handles are 32 bits, not 16 bits like they used to be. So are atoms. So are brush handles, pen handles, handles to device contexts, and so on. Even the *wParam* parameter to each window procedure has been expanded to 32 bits! So letting the CPU switch to 16-bit code processing is not enough. Practically all the parameters to nearly every procedure must undergo a translation as well.

The OLE 2 standard requires support of both 16- and 32-bit code. The parameter translations are done at a single interface and allow the application to run without *too* much of a performance penalty. (That penalty is just enough to encourage users to upgrade to the new, "faster" 32-bit versions as soon as possible. Note that the new versions need not be *actually* faster under Windows 95 than their predecessors were under Windows 3.1, for people to *perceive* an improvement!) This translation mechanism is called *marshaling*.

So, here's the bottom line: While VBXs may not port directly to a 32-bit environment, the applications that use them *will continue to be supported. You may therefore continue to write and use VBXs as required, knowing that an upgrade to Windows 95 will not require an* immediate *upgrade of your application.*

You can then eventually upgrade your controls to a 32-bit OCX version, which we'll cover later in this book. And that *eventual* upgrade ... well, if you benefit from Microsoft's strategy, too, what's the harm in that?

Besides, the alternative would be to write OCXs now, and to develop client applications in one of the few available development environments that understands them. And, in comparison to the OCX standard...

#3: The VBX Standard Is Well-Defined

The VBX standard is easy to follow partly because it has been around (relatively speaking) for so long. In fact, in spite of the addition of many built-in properties, events, and methods since Visual Basic 1.0, the structure itself is essentially unchanged. This is fortunate because only version 1.0 VBXs can be used by some versions of Visual C++ or Borland C++ applications (actually, the limitation is in Microsoft Foundation Classes and ObjectWindows, not the compilers themselves).

Compare this to the OCX "standard," which is not yet truly a standard at all. Sure, Control Wizard (and other tools) can produce a skeleton OCX; we'll be doing that later in this book. But Control Wizard works by generating C++ classes that are derived from other C++ classes that actually make OLE 2 work—and these classes are poorly documented. Microsoft is free to fiddle with OLE 2's innards all they want; and, until they manage to get some real performance out of it, who knows which of their changes might affect your control adversely? While the OLE 2 underpinnings aren't likely to change *very much*, they *are* likely to change somewhat. You'll want to learn OCXs today, but only so you'll be *ready* for them *tomorrow*. For today's applications, you still need to write VBXs, so it's fortunate that...

#4: VBXs Are Easy to Design and Write

While VBXs seem very different from "standard" Windows child controls, they are not *that* different, and the differences are well defined.

The most obvious difference is that the programmer interface to a VBX is built into the VBX itself. That is, the names of properties and events—the strings themselves—are usually hard-coded into the VBX. At first this seems to violate the Windows ideal of easy internationalization. But, you'll quickly realize that only the internationalization of the *tool* is affected: The application itself can be sent to France, or Upper Volta, or wherever, because the property names in the VBX itself will never be seen by the end user.

(Besides, if you are concerned with internationalizing the tool itself, you can always store the property names as resource strings, and substitute internationalized resources, as Windows programmers have traditionally done for years. Beware, though, that this technique can have serious repercussions—a subject we'd best tackle in another book. For now, it might be best to remember that, while the VBX standard is not yet obsolete, it will be soon enough; and I am not necessarily recommending you use it to write new shrink-wrapped tools—just to get out your current assignments in a timely manner.)

The standard itself is defined in the *Control Development Kit*, included with Visual Basic 3 Professional Edition. (The CDK is *not* included with Visual Basic 4!) Each of the standard properties and events is documented with the number of the version that introduced it, so it is possible to write a version 1.0 VBX if you wish. Of course, all the really *cool* properties were added after version 1.0! But you do what you have to do.

> *VBX-style controls are normally implemented on top of underlying, standard windows. In fact, only with version 3.0 VBXs was it possible to create a special kind of control (called a* graphical *control) that has no underlying window at all! The VBX control structure is superimposed on the underlying window.*

In the next chapter we'll examine a skeleton custom control suitable for deriving your own useful controls. The skeleton exhibits the basic format of a VBX. First, initialized structures define each custom property. Then, an array is declared and initialized to each supported standard and custom property. This pattern is repeated for standard and custom events. Finally, a message switch is implemented that is *very* reminiscent of a window procedure. However, it is called a *control procedure* and has an additional parameter—a handle to the "control."

This whole mechanism, like the original Windows scheme of encapsulating code within a window, allows the programmer to practice object-oriented programming techniques even when not using an object-oriented language (for example, C).

When you are writing a VBX that bears no resemblance to any known standard window class, you get one by default even if you don't specify one. What you get is a generic window that doesn't do much except placidly allow the VBX message-redirecting mechanism to do its thing. However...

#5: VBXs Can Be Written on Top of Existing Windows

Many times what you want to implement is a VBX version of some standard window class that you or someone you know wrote long ago. You might even have in mind an improvement of a standard Windows class, like a VBX'ed owner-draw list box or a numeric-only edit control. This is certainly the Royal Road to VBXs! You needn't worry how the original window functions internally; you only have to know its API, just as you would if you were using the control in a standard Windows application. Your biggest task is to translate the control's Windows API into a VB interface that VB programmers will find intuitive. You'll want to keep track of the "standard" property and event names that have evolved, so you can borrow them whenever appropriate. For example, if your new VBX will contain any kind of list of things, you'll almost certainly want to provide a *List* array property and a *ListCount* property, analogous to the properties of the same name supported by both the Listbox and Combobox VBXs. When you have to extend beyond the universe of pre-existing property names—perhaps you need to allow access to two completely different *kinds* of lists—still try and stick as closely to the model as you can; for example, *NameList* and *NameListCount* and *CityList* and *CityListCount*.

Also, be sensitive to the flags you set for each property. You have a lot of control: A property can be read or written only; accessible at design-time, run-time, or both; applicable before or after the underlying window has been created. Choose wisely.

The whole point is to take what hopefully was designed as a black box—a standard Windows control—and wrap it inside a new black box.

If you do the job right, you'll have an easy-to-use control that *won't* require the programmer eventually using it to make much (or any!) reference to the documentation. Designing a tool in this way means that you'll learn object-oriented techniques even if you haven't yet gotten involved with C++, because ...

#6: VBXs Teach Object-Oriented Discipline

I don't care how deeply you dig in your heels; you have two choices: Learn object-oriented programming or find a new career. Fortunately, object-oriented programming is a lot easier to learn than you may have been led to believe, especially if you were unwise enough to let someone with a computer science degree explain it to you. The whole point to object-oriented programming is that *we*, human beings, are *already hard-wired to understand objects*. Object-oriented programming techniques simply take what we already know how to do, and apply those abilities to the solving of computer problems. And no, Virginia, you do *not* need an "object-oriented language" (such as C++) to do object-oriented programming.

The essence of OOP is to focus on the program piece on which you are currently working. Here's an example C programmers will find homey: one of the set of file manipulation functions in the C standard library. These are the ones that use the **FILE typedef**, as in:

```
FILE * MyFile = fopen ("MYFILE.DAT", "w");
fwrite ("This is some text", 1, 25, MyFile);
fclose (MyFile);
```

As you know if you've bothered to look up the **FILE typedef**, *MyFile* is just a pointer to a structure. What's in the structure? Who cares!— and that's the point. You don't have to know the internal workings of *fopen(), fwrite(),* and *fclose()* for them to operate correctly. *That's object-oriented programming* (at least the encapsulation aspect). You can do the very same thing; just break your programming project into small pieces and, as you code each piece, do so using a "control block" or structure like **FILE** to hide the data required to make this piece work. In object-oriented terms, the structure contains your "properties" and the functions that operate on those properties are "methods."

In point of fact, I usually prefer C to C++ for writing VBXs because you can't easily include either Foundation Classes or ObjectWindows classes in your VBX if you want to use it in an environment that was not built using the class library you chose—like, oh say, Visual Basic. And without a good class library to work with, C++ provides little benefit over C. However, I have written a C++ class library for VBXs, and that does help when we finally get around to writing OCXs, because the OCX Development Kit includes handy classes for simplifying that job. But in the meantime, C will probably be your language of choice. Just remember, you *can* write object-oriented code in a non-object-oriented language. And there's a double benefit there, because...

7: VBXs Add Objects to Visual Basic 3

While it's possible to write object-oriented code in Visual Basic using the technique just outlined, it's annoying to have to do so because Visual Basic 3 *has* objects—it just won't let the VB programmer make any of his or her own. Visual Basic 4 does, but if you can't upgrade to that version yet for any reason, and you're a VB programmer who also knows C, writing a VBX is the one way we have of adding an object to the Visual Basic 3 environment.

You can put this to work as soon as you remind yourself that VBXs *do not have to be visible controls.* The Timer control is a perfect example of this, as is the CmDialog control. Neither of these is a control at all, in the traditional sense; the end user can't see or manipulate them in any way (at least, not directly). However, they take advantage of the fact that controls in Visual Basic are *objects*, with properties, events, and methods. You can do the same. Suppose, for example, you want to encapsulate a logical function—a ZIP code lookup machine, for example—so that the programmer doesn't need to concern him or herself with the mechanism of the machine. By writing an invisible-at-runtime VBX, you can make it so that setting the *ZipCode* property to a valid ZIP code allows a subsequent read of the *City* and *State* properties to return the locality to which that ZIP code is assigned. Likewise, setting *City, State,* and *Address* will allow reading the correct *ZipCode* directly from the property. No muss, no fuss, and the programmer probably won't even have to refer to the online help to figure out how to work the control. Behind the scenes, of course, huge amounts of things are happening: database lookups, and so on. But the control is simple to *use*, and that's what counts. The complexity is all internal, all hidden.

What's more, even when data is not involved...

#8: VBXs Provide a Good Point-of-Control for Data-Less Objects

The Comm control is another invisible control. It does not represent any data, although it may serve as a conduit through which data can travel. What it does (and well!) is encapsulate the various *things* that have to be done in order to perform serial I/O on a PC. Some things it does for you; some you have to specify, but all specifications are neatly laid out and documented and, all in all, the Comm control (which Microsoft did *not* write) serves as an excellent example of using a VBX to encapsulate a device or set of related functions.

So, is the CmDialog control a way to provide access to the Common Dialog DLL to VB programmers. Of course, they had that access already since Visual Basic allows the invocation of functions in DLLs. But such access was very un-Visual Basic-like; and so the CmDialog control is greatly appreciated.

Inexplicably missing from CmDialog, though, is access to the Find and Replace dialogs that are also resident in the Common Dialog control. A VBX that wrapped up those controls in a VB-friendly manner would also be a good idea. (Don't start writing tonight, though, unless you need this control in a hurry; such a control is the subject of a subsequent chapter in this book!)

The whole point of creating these "objects" for Visual Basic is an extension of what Windows was originally supposed to be; each "window" in Windows was originally supposed to be an object in an object-oriented sense. That's why it's so cool that...

#9: VBXs Can Be Written to Triple Standards

VBXs are commonly written to be VBXs and nothing more, but there's no reason this should be so. Sure, the original VB controls (the ones that reside in VBRUN300.DLL) are all based on standard Windows controls and so add nothing but the VB interface. And the VBXs distributed with Visual Basic all add functionality to Visual Basic (and other environments capable of using them, like MFC and ObjectWindows) but not to "standard" Windows applications. But that doesn't mean you have to restrict yourself to this somewhat limited view of things.

Remember, VBXs can be built on any underlying "standard" window—and that includes a standard window written by you, especially for the occasion. That means that, in a single DLL (remember, VBXs *are* DLLs) you can include the code and even the Borland Resource Workshop hooks for a standard control, then add the Visual programmer's interface and VBX hooks on top of that. This may sound like a lot of overhead but it really isn't. The same work is being done as before; it's just being redistributed a little.

Moreover, if you restrict yourself to small, focused functions, you can add your VBX-handling code to an OLE-Control-Wizard-generated OCX and make it work in *all three* environments!

The key is to keep thinking object-oriented all the way, and to always be true to the paradigm in which you are working. When you are designing the "standard" control, think in terms of Windows messages, both for setting and retrieving properties—I mean, data—and for triggering actions (methods). WM_COMMAND messages sent by the control to its parent window are the equivalent of "events." Provide a nice header file for C and C++ programmers to **#include** in their application files and the standard layer is complete.

The hooks for Borland Resource Workshop are optional; if you include them, your application programmers will be able to plug the new control into that environment just like it belonged there, complete with toolbox icon—the same as in Visual Basic. If any of your programmers is still using Microsoft's Dialog Editor (which came with the old Windows SDK) the controls will work there, as well. Unfortunately, Microsoft chose to abandon the standard they created; App Studio does not provide convenient access to standard-style custom controls.

When you add the Visual layer on top of the standard layer, you simply specify your new class as the underlying window class when filling in the MODEL structure. Then plan for properties and events that mirror the messages and WM_COMMAND notifications of that underlying class. If you have a "method" implemented in the underlying window but there is no matching standard method name (you can make up names for properties and events, but not for methods) use the same trick as the CmDialog and Ole2 controls: an *Action* property. Assign it a number (be sure to provide constants for the VB programmer, please!) and, internally, translate the number to the appropriate message sent to the underlying window. Piece of cake!

And then, when you're finally ready...

#10: OCXs Can Be Easily Derived from VBXs

Yes, the OCX standard may still be a closely guarded secret hidden in a C++ class library but, beyond that, OCXs are very similar in form to VBXs. OCXs also have properties, events, and methods. Best of all, from a developer's standpoint, OCXs allow custom-named methods: the most annoying void in the VBX Control Development Kit.

Anyway, and especially if you write VBXs based on custom underlying windows, where the Visual section is only an interface to the underlying window, it should be very simple to convert VBXs to OCXs. And that means, of course, that you may put away your fear of writing instantly-obsolete tools for good.

OCXs: The Wave of the Future?

O NCE UPON A TIME, Microsoft gave us a new, exciting view of the future. It was a new technology, something that naturally built on the vision initiated by Microsoft Windows, something that would allow applications to talk amongst themselves, to control one another, and to share data. This technology would someday allow an application running on one computer to share data and control with an application running on another computer. It was designed to be the wave of the future, and we developers were encouraged to build it into our applications at the risk of releasing software that was obsolete before it reached the shelves. Now, this wouldn't be easy; the new technology was built on an ill-defined specification that most programmers couldn't interpret. But we struggled and fought with it and, sure enough, many applications were released using it.

I am, of course, referring to DDE (Dynamic Data Exchange).

Now, if you thought I was speaking of OLE (the original OLE—what we now refer to as OLE 1), you can certainly be forgiven. After all, Microsoft used *exactly* the same story to sell us OLE 1.

And if you think OLE 1 has *anything* in common with OLE 2, other than the name, you haven't studied the respective APIs. I suspect the only reason this new technology was called OLE at all, was simply to disguise the fact that Microsoft had pulled the rug out from under us developers, once again. (Its *real* name, in any case, is COM—standing for *Common Object Model.*)

Does that mean you shouldn't produce OLE-compliant applications? Not at all. This *is* an important technology. And the problem it attempts to solve—getting computer programs to talk to each other—is even more significant. But, unless you enjoy doing this sort of thing for pleasure, I can't advise you to spend time wrestling with the underlying mechanism with which OLE 2 is implemented. The *useful* interface is the one presented by MFC (Microsoft Foundation Classes). And any other class library offered by some third party is likely to make the technology equally accessible. But the underlying mechanism is just too complex and over-designed, much like DDE was before the DDE Management Library was introduced, to make it worth the average developer's time studying it. After all, given the past history, can "OLE 3" be long in coming to replace it?

Big Waves and COMmon Breakers

OLE 2 is based on a protocol called COM, an acronym *for Common Object Model.* The idea was to come up with a means of representing objects—programming objects, specifically—in a way that would be language, computer, and even platform independent. COM was intended to be a binary standard, and it's supposed to be possible to implement COM objects in any computer language. The end result? True, reusable software components, varying in complexity and power from a simple push button to an entire word processor or spreadsheet.

VBXs are reusable because their properties, events, and methods are "exposed"—that is, a containing application can learn what they are, simply by asking. COM objects, at their core, are supposed to be simpler than VBXs, to support the machine and language independence. So they expose "interfaces," each a collection of functions that the object makes available to a containing application.

An interface is supposed to be a list of function headers, including argument types, without an implementation. Obviously, there must be an implementation *somewhere*; but in true object-oriented fashion, that implementation is not the concern of anyone making use of a COM object. The list of functions is supposed to be language-independent; but in reality, C++ is the only language well-suited to describing it, because all the functions are what C++ calls *virtual functions.*

Originally, there were supposed to be a relatively small number of these interfaces, and each would be published and used by any COM object for which that interface would be useful. In order for an application to know where to start, one interface must be implemented by *every* COM object: *IUnknown.* Starting with this interface, a COM container can find out what other interfaces are available.

Unfortunately, you can't just *ask* a COM object what interfaces it supports, the way you can ask a VBX control for its list of properties. Instead, a COM container shotguns a list of desired interfaces at the object until it gets a positive response. "Can you do this? No? Well, how about that? No? Then, how about this other thing?" This means that it is possible to create a COM object that is usable only by COM containers from the same company, if its designers choose to not publish its interfaces...which kind of defeats the purpose.

Another problem that's come along is that the original interfaces often don't turn out to have all the abilities needed. For example, once you've identified a COM object you like, you have to create an *instance* of it in order to use one. This was supposed to be done using the *IClassFactory* interface. However, the designers of the *IClassFactory* interface didn't take licensing into account—creators of an OLE control might want to require a license file to be present to support design-time use of the control. So a new interface, *IClassFactory2,* was introduced to support licensing. So, now, a COM container must first request a pointer to the *IClassFactory2* interface, and request the *IClassFactory* interface only if the first request fails. I shudder at the prospect of container code someday working its way from *IClassFactory47* down, until it finds an interface that will actually let it create the desired COM object.

Control Freaks

OLE 1 was all about creating compound documents. OLE 2 is intended to address the same need, but adds the ability to create compound *applications.* And so we come to OLE 2 controls, commonly called *OCXs.*

OCXs would seem like an exciting idea to anyone who has never seen a VBX. A compact, reusable, reliable bundle of functionality that can be dropped into any application is a *great* idea. The idea works with VBXs because they expose their properties, events, and methods to the application for the asking.

OCXs also expose their properties, events, and methods; they do it through the *IDispatch* interface. Thus, huge amounts of code later, OLE 2 objects achieve what VBXs had been doing for years...and without the need for four DLLs occupying nearly one megabyte of disk space. Granted, you only need these DLLs once per system...but *every* application using them must distribute them, in case they haven't yet been loaded on the target machine; that's one extra floppy disk for *every* installation set.

Unlike VBXs, which can be queried as to their own capabilities, the public definition of a COM object has been moved to the System Registry (called the Registration Database in previous versions of Windows). This is a turnaround of normal object-oriented practice; and if you've ever had to reinstall Windows and all your applications because of a trashed Registration Database, you'll join me in doubting the wisdom of this move. However, OCXs (and other OLE 2 objects) take so long to load, relatively speaking, that it was necessary to move this information into a more easily accessible location. A common problem among early OLE 2 objects was their inability to be moved: A simple renaming of a subdirectory or addition of a new hard disk could make your compound documents unusable until the component had been re-installed or the Registry manually modified. However, OLE 2 objects written in MFC are normally self-registering—a technique I invented in my book, *Borland Pascal 7.0 Insider*—so simply running or loading an instance of the object in its new location is enough to re-register it.

A VBX can load much more quickly than an OCX; but in exchange the OCX provides support for something we've long wished for in VBXs: *user-defined methods*. Think of it: no more *Action* properties to simulate them, without parameters!

At the time of this writing, MFC is the only class library available for writing OCXs. The 32-bit version of Borland Delphi was once rumored to support standard 16-bit VBXs something Microsoft claimed was impossible, as part of their justification of abandoning the VBX standard for OCXs. It seems Microsoft was right; because the release version of Delphi 2 did not include this feature.

Writing OCXs in MFC is a straightforward affair, assuming you are familiar with MFC to start with. Access comes via Microsoft Visual C++ versions 1.52, 2.2, and 4.0 or better. You create the project with Control Wizard instead of App Wizard, and then use Class Wizard to add properties, events and methods. The actual *code* for these entities is supplied by you, of course.

Beware of OCXs produced by versions of Visual C++ other than those described above. There was a Control Wizard released with Visual C++ 1.5/ 2.0, but the specification for COM changed between that version and later ones, and the controls generated by those first Control Wizards don't actually work with real containers.

Since Visual C++ 1.52 produces only 16-bit code, and Visual C++ 2.2/4.0 produces only 32-bit code, you'll need to use both if you want to enable both 16- and 32-bit developers access to your OCX. Fortunately, you don't have to change your code in between; many developers use the more advanced 2.2 or 4.0 versions of Visual C++ to develop the control, then compile the 16-bit version separately. A marshaling layer to enable 32-bit applications to use 16-bit OCXs, and vice versa, was part of the original promise of OLE 2, but so far we haven't seen it.

Surf's Up!

Microsoft has a way of declaring each new component of its "vision" as if it were inevitable and right. As developers, we obviously cannot ignore these new components. And, when practical, we should certainly make use of these new technologies! But let's try to keep things in perspective. As any surfer knows, there is never *one* "wave of the future"—every wave, no matter how big or impressive—or *otherwise*—is always followed by another.

3

A VBX Skeleton Revisited

IN MY BOOK *Windows Programming Power with Custom Controls*, I developed a VBX skeleton that could be used as a base from which to quickly develop new VBXs. Like any skeleton, it had certain strengths and weaknesses. On the plus side, it showed you how to create a single DLL (VBXs *are* DLLs) that implemented a control usable as a VBX *or* a standard Windows control. It presented a *good* example of structured code, as opposed to the usual book examples that are simplified to demonstrate a technique at the expense of maintainability.

On the minus side, it only showed how to make version 3.0 VBXs. This is fine for Visual Basic, but Microsoft Visual C++ and Borland C++ could only use version 1.0 VBXs at the time. (When I wrote the book, both Visual C++ and Borland C++ were in beta test, and the documentation of both platforms didn't point out this limitation.) And, while Microsoft was already making OLE control noises, there was no hint as to how easy or difficult it would be to convert a VBX to an OCX.

In this chapter I'll re-present a VBX skeleton, but with a few modifications. This presentation is designed to review the structure of a VBX. However, this is by necessity an abbreviated presentation. For a fuller understanding of the nuances of VBX internals, refer to the earlier book (or struggle with the Microsoft documentation bundled with the Control Development Kit).

Inside the VBX

At its core, a VBX is a DLL with certain "hooks" that enable an IDE to recognize it for what it is. These hooks take the form of functions with known names and calling sequences. The two functions are *VBINITCC()* and *VBTERMCC()*. A VBX-aware IDE, such as Visual Basic, will attempt to call *VBINITCC()* when loading the DLL. That function, in turn, must call the CDK (Control Development Kit) function *VBRegisterModel()* for each custom control the VBX supports.

> *The "hook" functions* VBINITCC() *and* VBTERMCC() *are what makes a DLL a VBX—not the file extension. However, nearly all VBXs have a .VBX extension for the convenience of the user.*

Figure 3.1 presents a schematic of the usual structure of a VBX implementing one control.

As shown, the busiest component is VISUAL.C. In my original skeleton, I provided an additional component named MAIN.C. This module contained *LibMain()* (the required entry point for any DLL) and the window procedure for the underlying standard Windows window. Since most VBXs are *not* based on an underlying window any more, I have omitted this component.

VBXHELP.C hasn't changed since my original implementation. We will go over the code but it's cookbook stuff. You don't ever need to modify any of it. MAIN.RC, which used to contain the dialog boxes for "standard" controls, but no longer does. It does contain the bitmaps used to represent the control in the IDE's toolboxes, and an About Box dialog template.

Let's look at the contents of each of these files closely, starting with the most important one—the module that drives all the others.

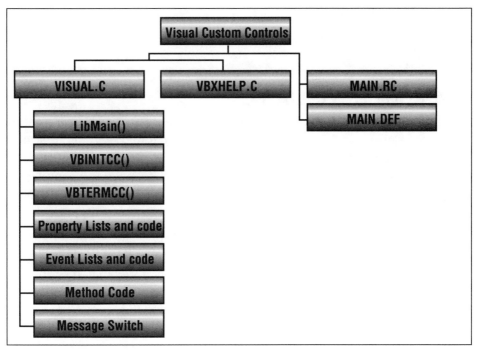

Figure 3.1 The structure of a VBX containing one control.

A Look at INTERNAL.H

Like the woman who is supposed to be behind every successful man, INTERNAL.H is a header file that doesn't show up in the schematic but nevertheless is **#include**d by each of the C modules that do. It provides a common list of other header files that must be **#include**d; it houses the declarations for functions parked in subsidiary files, and it declares the one global variable used by the module:

```
#include <windows.h>
#include <vbapi.h>
#include <stdlib.h>

extern HINSTANCE LibInstance;

HSZ far pascal GetAboutPropertyString (HCTL Control);
HWND far pascal PopupAbout (void);
void far pascal RegisterVbPopups (void);
void far pascal UnregisterVbPopups (void);
LPSTR far pascal HelpFileName (void);

BOOL far pascal OnHelp
    (
    HWND Window,
```

```
BYTE HelpType,
BYTE i,
PPROPINFO Properties[],
PEVENTINFO Events[]
);
```

A Look at VISUAL.C

Because C was originally designed for a one-pass compiler, it's generally more convenient to place structures and functions *before* other structures and functions that reference them, giving C code modules an upside-down appearance. Consequently, I'm going to describe the contents of the VISUAL.C file starting from the bottom. Table 3.1 shows the set of functions that are included.

The last function in VISUAL.C is W*EP()*. *WEP* stands for *Windows Exit Procedure*. This function, which is invoked by Windows when the DLL is unloaded, is required by all DLLs; however, a default version will be supplied if *WEP()* is omitted. This is often done. However, the following function must be invoked when the DLL is unloaded:

```
int far pascal _export WEP (int ExitType)
  {
  UnregisterVbPopups ();
  }
```

The next required routine is *LibMain()*. It is passed a handle to the library instance which we need to save. This function was stored in MAIN.C in the earlier version of the skeleton, but MAIN.C wound up having almost nothing

Table 3.1 The Functions Defined in VISUAL.C

Function	Description
LibMain()	The entry point of the DLL. All DLLs have this function. It is called once when the DLL is loaded.
VBINITCC()	The entry point of the VBX. It is called by each VBX consumer, such as Visual Basic, to request the VBX to register its controls with that consumer.
CtlProc()	The consumer procedure. It is analogous to a window procedure; there must be one for each control in the VBX.
VBTERMCC()	The exit point of the VBX. It is called by each VBX consumer, such as Visual Basic, to request the VBX to clean up and release any resources prior to being unloaded.
WEP()	The exit point of the DLL. All DLLs have this function. It is called once, when the DLL is unloaded.

else in it. In addition to storing the library instance handle, the function registers the popup window the VBX needs by calling *RegisterVbPopups()* (which is actually implemented in VBXHELP.C):

```
HINSTANCE LibInstance = 0;

int far pascal LibMain
    (
    HINSTANCE hInstance,
    WORD DataSeg,
    WORD HeapSize,
    LPSTR CommandLine
    )
    {
    if (HeapSize > 0)
      UnlockData (0);
    LibInstance = hInstance;
    RegisterVbPopups ();
    return TRUE;
    }
```

VBTERMCC() is invoked by the IDE *or* the custom control consumer just before the VBX is unloaded. It therefore has the job of undoing anything "done" during initialization. Even if there's nothing for it to do, the function must be supplied:

```
VOID FAR PASCAL _export VBTERMCC (void)
    {
    }
```

VBINITCC() appears to be a simple function with one executable statement:

```
BOOL far pascal _export VBINITCC (USHORT Version, BOOL Runtime)
    {
    return VBRegisterModel (LibInstance, &Model);
    }
```

The call to *VBRegisterModel()* is deceptive; we pass it the address of a *MODEL* structure but that structure is the key to *everything*. Figure 3.2 shows the schematic of what's actually taking place here.

As shown, the *MODEL* structure contains pointers to two lists: a list of properties and a list of events. Each of these lists is actually a list of pointers, although the pointers to the standard properties and events are pre-defined. In addition, the *MODEL* structure contains a pointer to the control procedure (analogous to a window procedure) and a number of flags that further describe how the control is to be displayed and how it is to act.

I simply store the *Model* variable in the control's data segment so no machine time or code space has to be wasted initializing it. Its definition looks like this:

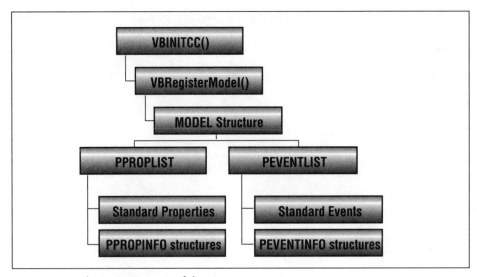

Figure 3.2 The organization of the MODEL structure.

```
MODEL Model =
    {
    VB300_VERSION,
    MODEL_fArrows | MODEL_fFocusOk,
    (PCTLPROC) CtlProc,
    CS_DBLCLKS,
    WS_BORDER,
    sizeof (VBDATA),
    8000,
    "Skeleton",
    "Skeleton",
    NULL,
    Properties,
    Events,
    0,
    0,
    (BYTE) -1,
    93
    };
```

Each field is significant, of course; but I'll defer a discussion of the fields until Chapter 6, when VBX Genie needs to supply values for each one. For now, note the two occurrences of the string "Skeleton." They should be replaced when the skeleton is copied with the name of the new control. Also note fields two, four, and five; these are *MODEL*, class, and window flags, respectively. If you use this skeleton directly, you'll probably want to alter these flags. (VBX Genie would fill in these and the other fields, according to your specifications.)

Field number three provides the address of the control procedure, *CtlProc()*. Of course, this procedure can be named whatever you like. In fact, if you house more than one control in a single VBX, you'll have to be more creative than this. The procedure itself is very similar to a regular window procedure; it receives the same messages (plus some new ones) and has *Window, Message, wParam,* and *lParam* parameters. However, it *also* has an *additional* parameter: *Control.* This is a handle to the control itself; as with a standard window, there can be many instances of a control and this is the way each can tell itself from the others.

ADDING THE CONTROL PROCEDURE

It is common in published sample code to write window and control procedures with all the code in-line. I find this practice appalling. Control procedures are message switches, nothing more. Each incoming message should be identified, its parameters converted to appropriate data types, and the correct handler invoked to do the actual work. Since there are so many Windows and VB messages, a control procedure *still* winds up being longer than the ideal; but the code is simple because each **case** of the **switch** statement is similar:

```
long far pascal _export CtlProc
    (
    HCTL Control,
    HWND Window,
    USHORT Msg,
    USHORT wParam,
    long lParam
    )
  {
  long Error = 0;
  switch (Msg)
    {
    case WM_NCCREATE:
      OnNcCreate (Control, (LPCREATESTRUCT) lParam);
      break;
    case VBM_METHOD:
      return OnMethod (Control, Window,
        wParam, (void far *) lParam);
    case VBN_COMMAND:
      switch (HIWORD (lParam))
        {
        default:
          break;
        }
      break;
    case VBM_SETPROPERTY:
      if (OnSetProperty (Control, Window,
        wParam, lParam, &Error))
```

```
        return Error;
      break;
    case VBM_CHECKPROPERTY:
      if (OnCheckProperty (Control, Window,
          wParam, lParam, &Error))
        return Error;
      break;
    case VBM_GETPROPERTY:
      if (OnGetProperty (Control, Window,
          wParam, (LPVOID) lParam, &Error))
        return Error;
      break;
    case VBM_LOADPROPERTY:
      if (OnLoadProperty (Control, Window,
          wParam, (HFORMFILE) lParam, &Error))
        return Error;
      break;
    case VBM_SAVEPROPERTY:
      if (OnSaveProperty (Control, Window,
          wParam, (HFORMFILE) lParam, &Error))
        return Error;
      break;
    case VBM_GETPROPERTYHSZ:
      if (OnGetStringProperty (Control, Window,
          wParam, (HSZ far *) lParam))
        return 0;
      else
        break;
    case VBM_INITPROPPOPUP:
      switch (wParam)
        {
        case IPROPINFO_About:
          return PopupAbout ();
        }
      break;
    case VBM_HELP:
      if (OnHelp (Window,
          LOBYTE (wParam),
          HIBYTE (wParam),
          Properties, Events))
        return 0;
      break;
    case WM_DESTROY:
      WinHelp (Window, HelpFileName (), HELP_QUIT, 0);
      break;
    case WM_NCDESTROY:
      OnNcDestroy (Control);
      break;
    }
  return VBDefControlProc (Control, Window, Msg, wParam, lParam);
  }
```

As with a window procedure, there's a default handler for messages: *VBDefControlProc()*. Those of you who are familiar with Microsoft Foundation Classes will recognize the names of the handlers; I "borrowed" them from the MFC message handlers.

STARTING BACK AT THE TOP

At this point I'm going to stop working from the bottom up and jump to the top of the file; we'll meet here in the middle. The file starts with a **#include** of INTERNAL.H, the one header file used by all modules in this project. (This facilitates the use of pre-compiled headers.) This is followed by a few **#define**s and a variable to help out in the subsequent code:

```
#include "internal.h"

#define _segment(p) \
    ( (HANDLE) (((unsigned long) (void far *) (p)) >> 16L))
#define _offsetin(struc, fld) ((USHORT)&(((struc *)0)->fld))
#define VBERR_BADINDEX 381

static long Boolean[2] = { 0, -1 };
```

The *segment()* **#define** has changed slightly from its counterpart in the previous implementation of this skeleton. I had copied the code from Microsoft's CDK code samples but never actually *used* the thing. Since the first skeleton was published, I had the occasion to use *segment()* and was nonplussed to discover any use of it as it was originally coded, would not work! This version does.

The *Boolean* array makes it easy to convert between the C definitions of *TRUE* (1) and *FALSE* (0) and Visual Basic's definitions (-1 and 0, respectively).

Next is a skeleton **struct** intended to store control-specific data—in other words, the internal representations of properties. In the skeleton, there is only a placeholder instead of a real member variable:

```
typedef struct
  {
  UINT : 16;
  } VBDATA, far * LPVBDATA;
```

Next come the custom property structures. In the skeleton there is only one, for the "(About)" property:

```
PROPINFO Property_About =
  {
  "(About)",
  DT_HSZ | PF_fGetMsg | PF_fNoRuntimeW | PF_fGetHszMsg,
  0, 0, 0, NULL, 0
  };
```

Other structures would follow if any more custom properties were needed (and generally are). The pointers to all the custom property structures, and the pre-defined values for desired standard properties, are used to initialize an array of those pointers—the same array whose address was included in the *Model* **struct**:

```
PPROPINFO Properties[] =
    {
    PPROPINFO_STD_NAME,
    PPROPINFO_STD_INDEX,
    PPROPINFO_STD_ENABLED,
    PPROPINFO_STD_HELPCONTEXTID,
    PPROPINFO_STD_LEFT,
    PPROPINFO_STD_TOP,
    PPROPINFO_STD_WIDTH,
    PPROPINFO_STD_HEIGHT,
    PPROPINFO_STD_PARENT,
    PPROPINFO_STD_LAST,
    &Property_About,
    // Add your additional PROPINFO addresses here
    NULL
    };
```

The *NULL* as the last item terminates the list.

Meaningful identifiers for indexes into this list will be helpful. In the old days **#define**s would have been used, with all the attendant problems: The debugger wouldn't recognize them; adding a property would probably mean manually editing all the **#define**s, and so on. Fortunately, some unnamed but brilliant person hit on the technique of using an anonymous **enum** to do the job:

```
typedef enum
    {
    IPROPINFO_STD_NAME,
    IPROPINFO_STD_INDEX,
    IPROPINFO_STD_ENABLED,
    IPROPINFO_STD_HELPCONTEXTID,
    IPROPINFO_STD_LEFT,
    IPROPINFO_STD_TOP,
    IPROPINFO_STD_WIDTH,
    IPROPINFO_STD_HEIGHT,
    IPROPINFO_STD_PARENT,
    IPROPINFO_STD_LAST,
    IPROPINFO_About,
    // Add your additional property indexes here
    IPROPINFO_End
    };
```

IPROPINFO_End is not required but makes it easy to note how many properties you have. It also makes it easy to add properties to the end of the list without having to worry about whether they should end in a comma or not.

SUPPORTING EVENTS, METHODS, AND PROPERTIES

At this point in the narrative, if you had any custom events, you would
initialize *EVENTINFO* structures. Following them is the array of pointers to
these structures and the identifiers for the standard events, and the **enum**
indexes for the events:

```
// Define custom events here

PEVENTINFO Events[] =
   {
   PEVENTINFO_STD_CLICK,
   PEVENTINFO_STD_DBLCLICK,
   PEVENTINFO_STD_LAST,
   // Add your additional EVENTINFO addresses here
   NULL
   };

typedef enum
   {
   IEVENTINFO_STD_CLICK,
   IEVENTINFO_STD_DBLCLICK,
   IEVENTINFO_STD_LAST,
   // Add your additional event indexes here
   IEVENTINFO_End
   } EVENTSIX;
```

Note that you'll probably want to alter the list of standard events.

OnNcCreate() and *OnNcDestroy()* allocate and release, respectively, any
resources the control will need to retain throughout its lifetime:

```
static void near pascal OnNcCreate
    (
    HCTL Control,
    LPCREATESTRUCT Create
    )
   {
   LPVBDATA VbData = (LPVBDATA) VBDerefControl (Control);

   // Allocate any memory blocks or system resources here

   }

static void near pascal OnNcDestroy
    (
    HCTL Control
    )
   {
   LPVBDATA VbData = (LPVBDATA) VBDerefControl (Control);
```

```
// Deallocate any memory blocks or system resources here

}
```

Any standard method—there are no custom methods in VBXs—that the VBX consumer invokes, will generate a *VBM_METHOD* message. The skeleton passes any of these on to the default handler:

```
static long near pascal OnMethod
    (
    HCTL Control,
    HWND Window,
    USHORT Method,
    void far * Args
    )
{
LRESULT Result = 0;
switch (Method)
    {
    default:
        Result = VBDefControlProc (Control, Window,
          VBM_METHOD, Method, (long) Args);
    }
return Result;
}
```

Depending on which flags you supply to the *PROPINFO* structure, properties can either be set automatically or via messages; the same is independently true for *retrieving* property values. In the skeleton we can just supply a framework for doing the job:

```
static BOOL near pascal OnSetProperty
    (
    HCTL Control,
    HWND Window,
    USHORT PropertyIX,
    long Value,
    long far * Error
    )
{
LPVBDATA VbData = (LPVBDATA) VBDerefControl (Control);
switch (PropertyIX)
    {

    default:
        return FALSE;
    }
}

static BOOL near pascal OnGetProperty
    (
```

```
    HCTL Control,
    HWND Window,
    USHORT PropertyIX,
    LPVOID Value,
    long far * Error
    )
{
LPVBDATA VbData = (LPVBDATA) VBDerefControl (Control);
switch (PropertyIX)
    {

    default:
       return FALSE;
    }
}
```

In addition to being set or retrieved, properties can be verified *before* setting:

```
static BOOL near pascal OnCheckProperty
    (
    HCTL Control,
    HWND Window,
    USHORT PropertyIX,
    long Value,
    long far * Error
    )
{
LPVBDATA VbData = (LPVBDATA) VBDerefControl (Control);
switch (PropertyIX)
    {

    default:
       return FALSE;
    }
}
```

Some properties, such as colors, may need a string representation so they can appear in the IDE's properties window. The "(About)" property, which is only a pretend property after all, is one of these. (Clicking on the "(About)" property brings up the control's About box.) The request for such a string is handled by this function:

```
static BOOL near pascal OnGetStringProperty
    (
    HCTL Control,
    HWND Window,
    USHORT PropertyIX,
    HSZ far * Value
    )
```

```
   {
LPVBDATA VbData = (LPVBDATA) VBDerefControl (Control);
switch (PropertyIX)
   {
   case IPROPINFO_About:
      *Value = GetAboutPropertyString (Control);
      break;

   default:
      return FALSE;
   }
return TRUE;
}
```

Finally, properties may be loaded from and/or stored to disk. That's handled by these functions:

```
static BOOL near pascal OnLoadProperty
   (
   HCTL Control,
   HWND Window,
   USHORT PropertyIX,
   HFORMFILE FormFile,
   long far * Error
   )
   {
LPVBDATA VbData = (LPVBDATA) VBDerefControl (Control);
switch (PropertyIX)
   {

   default:
      return FALSE;
   }
   }


static BOOL near pascal OnSaveProperty
   (
   HCTL Control,
   HWND Window,
   USHORT PropertyIX,
   HFORMFILE FormFile,
   long far * Error
   )
   {
LPVBDATA VbData = (LPVBDATA) VBDerefControl (Control);
switch (PropertyIX)
   {

   default:
      return FALSE;
   }
   }
```

VBXHELP.C

This file is a natural for a skeleton, because it never has to be changed. It begins with the **#include**:

```
#include "internal.h"
```

Next is the little function that returns an appropriate string for the "(About)" property, as invoked in response to the VBM-GETPROPERTYHSZ message. The *VBCreateHsz()* CDK function accepts a C-style string and returns a handle to one of the two types of VB string:

```
HSZ far pascal GetAboutPropertyString (HCTL Control)
   {
   return VBCreateHsz (_segment (Control),
     "Click here for About->");
   }
```

The dialog procedure for the About box looks normal enough:

```
BOOL _export FAR PASCAL AboutDlgProc
    (
    HWND    Dialog,
    WORD    msg,
    WORD    wParam,
    long    lParam
    )
  {
  switch (msg)
    {
    case WM_INITDIALOG:
      break;
    case WM_COMMAND:
      switch (wParam)
        {
        case IDOK:
          EndDialog (Dialog, IDOK);
          break;
        default:
          return FALSE;
        }
      break;
    default:
      return FALSE;
    }
  return TRUE;
  }
```

However, for some inadequately explored reason, you cannot directly invoke the *DialogBox()* Windows function from a VBX. Instead, you have to create an invisible popup window and run the dialog box from *it*. That means, you need a window procedure for the popup window:

```
LONG _export FAR PASCAL AboutPopupWndProc
    (
    HWND   Window,
    USHORT Message,
    USHORT wParam,
    LONG   lParam
    )
    {
    switch (Message)
       {
       case WM_SHOWWINDOW:
          if (wParam)
             {
             ShowWindow (Window, SW_HIDE);
             PostMessage (Window, WM_USER, 0, 0);
             return 0;
             }
          break;
       case WM_USER:
          VBDialogBoxParam (LibInstance, "About",
             AboutDlgProc, NULL);
          return 0;
       }
    return DefWindowProc (Window, Message, wParam, lParam);
    }
```

At least, thanks to advances in compiler design, we no longer have to obtain "procedure instances" of the dialog procedure; we can pass its address directly.

Causing the About box to actually display, then, involves invoking the *PopupAbout()* function, which creates the popup window, which runs the About dialog box:

```
static char AboutPopupClass[] = "AboutPopup";

HWND far pascal PopupAbout (void)
   {
   return CreateWindow
      (
      AboutPopupClass,
      NULL,
      WS_POPUP,
      0, 0, 0, 0,
      NULL,
```

```
      NULL,
      LibInstance,
      NULL
      );
   }
```

You'll remember the *RegisterVbPopups()* function called from *VBINITCC()*? Well, here's its definition:

```
static WNDCLASS Class =
   {
   0,
   (WNDPROC) AboutPopupWndProc,
   0,
   0,
   0,
   NULL,
   NULL,
   NULL,
   NULL,
   NULL
   };

void far pascal RegisterVbPopups (void)
   {
   Class.hInstance = LibInstance;
   Class.lpszClassName = AboutPopupClass;
   RegisterClass (&Class);
   }
```

Starting with the pre-initialized *WNDCLASS* structure, we just fill in the instance and class name and register the class.

As we have seen, when *WEP()* is invoked, the popup window needs to be *unregistered*:

```
void far pascal UnregisterVbPopups (void)
   {
   UnregisterClass (AboutPopupClass, LibInstance);
   }
```

The assumption that the name of a VBX's help file will be derived from the VBX's name (with a .HLP extension replacing .VBX) is almost always valid. So the *HelpFileName()* provides a programmatic way of deriving this with no maintenance effort on your part:

```
LPSTR far pascal HelpFileName (void)
   {
   static char Pathname[_MAX_PATH] = { 0 };
```

```
    if (! Pathname[0])
      {
      char Drive[_MAX_DRIVE];
      char Dir[_MAX_DIR];
      char FName[_MAX_FNAME];
      char Ext[_MAX_EXT];
      GetModuleFileName (LibInstance, Pathname, _MAX_PATH);
      _splitpath (Pathname, Drive, Dir, FName, Ext);
      _makepath (Pathname, Drive, Dir, FName, ".HLP");
      }
    return Pathname;
    }
```

The *VBM_HELP* message is passed to the control procedure when the VBX consumer requests help either from the IDE's menu or by pressing the F1 key. Here's the handler:

```
BOOL far pascal OnHelp
    (
    HWND Window,
    BYTE HelpType,
    BYTE i,
    PPROPINFO Properties[],
    PEVENTINFO Events[]
    )
    {
    BOOL Result = FALSE;
    switch (HelpType)
      {
      case VBHELP_PROP:
        if (Properties[i] < PPROPINFO_STD_LAST)
          {
          WinHelp (Window, HelpFileName (), HELP_KEY,
            (DWORD) (LPSTR) Properties[i]->npszName);
          Result = TRUE;
          }
        break;
      case VBHELP_EVT:
        if (Events[i] < PEVENTINFO_STD_LAST)
          {
          WinHelp (Window, HelpFileName (), HELP_KEY,
            (DWORD) (LPSTR) Events[i]->npszName);
          Result = TRUE;
          }
        break;
      case VBHELP_CTL:
        WinHelp (Window, HelpFileName (), HELP_CONTENTS, 0);
        Result = TRUE;
        break;
      }
    return Result;
    }
```

This routine provides context-sensitive help automatically, as long as your help file provides topics that match the names of your control's properties and events ... as it should.

MAIN.RC

The resource script file provides four kinds of resources: the bitmaps for the toolbox buttons, the template for the About dialog, an icon for the About dialog, and a VERSIONINFO resource. The bitmaps themselves must be stored as additional .BMP files. Although you wouldn't write this from scratch as a script—you'd use App Studio or Resource Workshop to do it— here's the script, anyway:

```
#include <windows.h>
#include <ver.h>

8000 BITMAP MOVEABLE PURE "8000.BMP"
8001 BITMAP MOVEABLE PURE "8001.BMP"
8003 BITMAP MOVEABLE PURE "8003.BMP"
8006 BITMAP MOVEABLE PURE "8006.BMP"

ABOUT DIALOG 41, 45, 192, 125
STYLE DS_MODALFRAME | WS_POPUP | WS_CAPTION
CAPTION "About Skeleton Custom Control"
FONT 8, "MS Sans Serif"
BEGIN
    CONTROL "Skeleton Custom Control", 0, "STATIC", SS_CENTER | WS_CHILD | _
      WS_VISIBLE, 0, 8, 190, 8
    CONTROL "by Paul S. Cilwa", 0, "STATIC", SS_CENTER | WS_CHILD | WS_VISIBLE,
0, 16, 190, 8
    CONTROL "MAIN", 0, "STATIC", SS_ICON | WS_CHILD | WS_VISIBLE, 87, 29, 18, 20
    CONTROL "Version 1.0.0.0", 0, "STATIC", SS_CENTER | WS_CHILD | WS_VISIBLE,
0, 59, 190, 8
    CONTROL "©1995 Paul S. Cilwa All Rights Reserved", 0, "STATIC", SS_CENTER | _
      WS_CHILD | WS_VISIBLE, 0, 79, 190, 24
    CONTROL "OK", IDOK, "BUTTON", BS_PUSHBUTTON | WS_CHILD | WS_VISIBLE | _
      WS_TABSTOP, 74, 102, 45, 15
END

MAIN ICON "MAIN.ICO"

1 VERSIONINFO LOADONCALL MOVEABLE DISCARDABLE
FILEVERSION 1,0,0,0
PRODUCTVERSION 1,0,0,0
FILEOS VOS__WINDOWS16
FILETYPE VFT_DLL
BEGIN
  BLOCK "StringFileInfo"
  BEGIN
    BLOCK "040904E4"
```

```
    BEGIN
      VALUE "CompanyName", "The Coriolis Group\000"
      VALUE "FileDescription", "Skeleton Custom Control for Visual Basic \000"
      VALUE "FileVersion", "1.0.0.0\000"
      VALUE "InternalName", "Skeleton\000"
      VALUE "LegalCopyright", "©1996 Paul S. Cilwa All Rights Reserved\000"
      VALUE "OriginalFilename", "skeleton.vbx\000"
      VALUE "ProductName", "Skeleton Custom Control\000"
      VALUE "ProductVersion", "1.0.0.0\000"
      VALUE "Comments", "\000"
    END
  END
END
```

MAIN.DEF

Finally, we have the module definition file:

```
LIBRARY Skeleton
DESCRIPTION  "©1996 Paul S. Cilwa All Rights Reserved"
EXETYPE WINDOWS
CODE PRELOAD MOVEABLE DISCARDABLE
DATA PRELOAD MOVEABLE SINGLE
HEAPSIZE   2048
```

If you are using a Microsoft linker and wish to do so, you can add the following lines:

```
EXPORTS
  WEP   RESIDENTNAME
```

The RESIDENTNAME option guarantees the name of the *WEP()* function will be available at all times. However, the Borland linker doesn't recognize this keyword, and it doesn't seem to hurt anything if it isn't there.

The Skeleton Walked

That is a brief look at the skeleton. I have purposely glossed over many details, especially the contents of the various structures and meanings of flags they use, because I wanted to convey to you the general structure of a VBX. As we proceed we'll be spiraling in closer and closer to those details; but, as we do, you'll find them not at all intimidating because they'll *already* look familiar. (That's a trick, but it works!)

In the next chapter we'll look at a VBX structure from an entirely different viewpoint. What you've learned in this chapter will make it possible to understand it. Let's go!

PART 2

A VBX Class Library

Creating a Vendor-Free GDI
Class Library   51

Creating a Vendor-Free text Class   87

Implementing the VBX++ Class Library   111

Creating a Vendor-Free GDI Class Library

4

IN AUGUST I TOOK A JOURNEY around Canada's beautiful Gaspè peninsula with my mother, my daughter, and my ex-wife. (Don't ask. Some things are better left unexplored.) As part of Quèbec province, people in Gaspè speak French. I, on the other hand, do not. However, I gave it a good effort and managed to learn a few words: enough to not appear unspeakably rude (*bonjour, bonsoir, pardón moi*) and to read a menu. (If you know *oeuf, fromage*, and *jambon*, you can get them to make you something awfully close to an Egg McMuffin.) Actually, I was pretty proud of myself until the third morning on the road, when we stopped at a pretty roadside *cantine* for breakfast. The word *patisserie* was on the sign, so I knew they'd have homemade bread. I attempted to order scrambled eggs with cheese and ham, but there was another word on the menu I didn't know. It looked a little like "rotisserie" so I figured it must mean "scramble." Now, I'd been having trouble making the *Quebecois* understand that "chopped" isn't the same as scrambled; so I made sure to say this word several times. I also made a lot of hand motions. The waitress looked incredulous, but I've grown used to this expression from non-English-speaking people to whom I am mangling their native tongue. I just kept smiling and saying, "*Oui! Oui!*" to convince her I meant what I said.

The next thing I knew, the waitress brought out everyone else's breakfasts. Fine, I thought, she's not trying to carry four meals at once. But, on her next visit, she arrived with five plates of toasted homemade bread and placed them all before me. She then left, and returned with five more plates. By now my jaw had dropped and my traveling companions were laughing helplessly. On her last trip, in addition to the remaining plateful of toast I had apparently ordered, was my egg—over easy, *not* scrambled—with ham and a slice of cheese on the side.

> *Amazing, isn't it, how a simple change of language can alter a familiar situation into a funhouse of surprises.*

In the previous chapters, I reviewed some of the basics of creating custom controls in C and we explored the useful skeleton for creating VBX custom controls. Now, we're going to begin the switch to C++. If you're thinking this will be a no-brainer conversion, may I suggest you *not* try to visit a foreign country without first learning their language. Or, at least, if you insist on doing so, refrain from ordering breakfast.

C Disadvantages

You are entitled to ask one question before we even start: Why bother creating custom controls in C++, anyway? Were we having that much trouble writing them in C?

Well, no, we weren't. I wasn't having any trouble ordering breakfast at home in New Hampshire, either. But there are a few things that can get in the way of swiftly throwing together a dynamite, knock-'em-dead VBX in C. For example, the CDK structures have many fields, and these fields are prone to misuse. Granted, starting off with a skeleton can minimize this problem. Still, the enhanced type checking of C++ could prevent it from ever *being* a problem.

Likewise, much CDK code is repetitious. While copying a skeleton is the traditional C way of dealing with such a situation, as you should know, C++ provides a better way: encapsulating the repetitive code in a base class so you inherit it, rather than having to copy it.

Besides, a true skeleton should already implement handlers for every possible message. But, in addition to the 160+ Windows messages, VB adds 41 messages of its own. That's a *lot* of message handlers, and most of them would have to be deleted from each real-life VBX derived from the skeleton. With a C++ class, the handlers can all be implemented in the *base* class, from which you inherit the ones you don't need special handling for, and override the rest.

C++ Advantages

Well, if there are *dis*advantages to writing a custom control in C, are there *advantages* to writing them in C++?

As a matter of fact, there are. For one thing, the CDK structures lend themselves to refinement as C++ classes. As you should know, any C struct can be a base class for a C++ class. The CDK includes sets of functions, nearly all of which take one or the other structure as a first parameter. Thus, the functions are easily and intuitively divided into member functions for classes derived from the structure those functions take as a first parameter.

Then there's all that repetitious code. When it's hidden in a base class, you don't have to worry about it. Just code your exceptions and you're done! In fact, that's probably the biggest advantage and therefore worth repeating. With C++ you can concentrate on dealing with the exceptions instead of the drudgery!

No—that's the *second* biggest advantage.

The first biggest is that OCXs (OLE Controls) must, for all practical purposes, be written in C++. By writing our VBXs in C++, we'll find ourselves in a good position to leverage our code and make it do double-duty—as a VBX and an OCX.

The Goal

In any case, writing a VBX should be a small effort, not a chore. You don't want to wind up having to wade through a lot of generated code in order to find the places to add your own. And, of course, there is always the possibility of accidentally deleting some of that generated code.

Adding custom C++ components to a Visual Basic app should be a practical option. You should be able to say, while working on a VB application, "Hey—this set of functions that I'm about to write would be *perfect* for a custom control!" and then *do* it—because it's *easier* to do it right.

A programmer should get a working VBX in a minimum amount of time. A VBX C++ class makes that possible. And when you add the ability to VBX Genie to further assist by generating the skeleton declarations and methods for your new derived classes, it becomes even less effort! (And then, when it turns out the code you wrote for the new classes doubles as code for an OLE custom control as well—then, we're there! True software components!)

Facing a Dilemma

Oddly, one of the first design decisions that must be made for a generic project like this is: Do we aim at ObjectWindows or Microsoft Foundation Classes? The new class library should ideally be independent of either one. But there are also stylistic issues: For example, do we call the method *OnPaint()* or *EvPaint()*? Do we use proper C++ style and pass reference parameters in most cases, or do we mimic MFC and use the older C style of passing pointers? Whichever style, ObjectWindows or MFC, that we follow, users of the other class library will find our conventions strange.

In the end, I've decided to follow my own philosophy and interpretation of what constitutes good C++ code. The result may appear to be a pastiche of MFC and ObjectWindows, but that's just coincidental. Regarding the two points just specified, I find *On...()* to be a clearer name for event handlers. On the other hand, nearly all parameters in a C++ class *should* be reference parameters, and I won't back away from that just because the writers of MFC apparently weren't comfortable with C++ conventions.

It's possible to go too far in the other direction, too. Borland dragged multiple inheritance to its illogical conclusion, so that practically every class in ObjectWindows is related to every other class, resulting in a hierarchy chart that looks more like an Ozark family tree.

And then there's the naming question: Should class names begin with "C" (as in MFC) or "T" (as in ObjectWindows)? Originally, Borland's ObjectWindows was written for Turbo Pascal for Windows. In Turbo Pascal, objects are declared using a **Type** statement; so objects were considered "types" and a prefixed "T" identified them as such. When ObjectWindows was converted to C++, that convention was retained.

Since MFC started as a C++ library, and C++ classes are declared using the **class** statement, the more obvious "C" was chosen. However, with the advent of OLE and its interface classes, some classes are now given an "I" prefix.

The original C++ convention was to prefix no letters at all; thus we have *iostream* and so on. Now, if you think about it, data types begin with lowercase letters. The advantage of following the C++ convention is that class names then have a visual similarity to the built-in C data types like **int, float**, and **char**. I rather like that, since I always "fully implement" my classes, making as much use as possible of overloaded operators, including cast operators. So that's what I'm going to do here.

There is one other problem that must be faced. We will need to use two classes that are supplied by both MFC and ObjectWindows: a string class and a GDI class sub-library. Fortunately I have such vendor non-specific classes already written, so I can just pop them into the project. But you wouldn't want to miss out on how *they* are designed; after all, they are an integral part of the class library you're going to be betting your career on! So, before we can get started on the VBX++ Class Library proper, we'll take a short detour into the wonderful world of Windows' GDI.

Creating a Vendor-Free Windows Class Library

I travel a *lot*. In the past year I've been to New York and San Francisco, Seattle and Key West, Canada and, on four *different* occasions, the Grand Canyon.

Virtually all of this travel is by air. So I'm familiar with Delta, American, TWA, America West, US Air, and the rest. While each of these airlines would probably disagree, let's face it: They are all pretty much the same. And this is a good thing. Who'd want to have to learn a new set of rules for each airline? If your overnight bag fits in the overhead bin of a Delta jet, you know it will also fit in the bin when you are flying TWA. (Nothing fits in the bin on America West but it doesn't matter, because they usually leave my luggage behind anyway.)

The *reason* I travel is to teach Windows programming. However, there I do *not* have the privilege of working by just one set of rules, because some of my students buy courses in programming Microsoft Foundation Classes, while others prefer programming in Borland ObjectWindows ... and, while the two class libraries are certainly *philosophical* twins, there are too many lexical differences between them to say they are interchangeable. And that's a shame, because the first question my students ask—all of them!—is how can they leverage their Windows code so it doesn't rely on one vendor or the other.

This came to mind, of course, when I set out to write a class library for VBXs. Should I write it to depend on the great amount of work already done for MFC? If so, Borland programmers couldn't use it ... but if I wrote it using ObjectWindows, Visual C++ programmers would be left out.

Wouldn't it be nice if there were a vendor-free Windows class library? One, perhaps, that combined the strengths of the two vendor libraries and omitted their glaring faults?

In this chapter we'll make a strong start in this direction by introducing a Portable GDI class library. The Windows GDI (graphics device interface) is the subsystem that MFC is weakest in, with OWL not giving a much better showing. The individual classes that we'll create are listed in Table 4.1. Notice that this table lists the name of each class as well as the file where each class is defined.

Classes and Style

The biggest problem presented by the existing GDI classes is that each of these sets is inextricably tied in with their respective class libraries. That means, if for some reason you cannot use MFC or OWL in your project, you also cannot use the GDI subset. This problem must be solved before writing a C++ class library for VBXs. Although Microsoft claims MFC can be compiled for use in a stand-alone DLL (VBXs are implemented as DLLs), the instructions for doing so are so complex I've never talked to anyone, including the Microsoft techie giving me the instructions, who'd actually done it!

So I bit the bullet, and put together a GDI class library. I did *not* repeat the shallow encapsulation that Microsoft and Borland have already done so

Table 4.1   The Classes Used to Implement the Portable GDI Library

Class Name	Defined In	Description
point	POINT.CPP	Provides the internal structures and functions for representing a coordinate point.
size	POINT.CPP	Used for representing the extents of rectangle objects.
rectangle	POINT.CPP	Provides the internal structures and functions for representing rectangles.
colorbyte	COLOR.CPP	Stores the required information need to represent the red, green, and blue components for a color.
color	COLOR.CPP	Provides all of the structures and functions to let programmers easily set individual color component values.
brush	BRUSH.CPP	Provides the functions to implement a custom brush for painting solid colors and custom hatch patterns.
pen	PEN.CPP	Provides the functions to implement a custom pen.
devicecontext	DEVICE.CPP	Provides all of the support structures and functions needed to set up the device independence for the Portable GDI Library.
paintcontext	DEVICE.CPP	Sets up a class to control device independent painting.
clientcontext	DEVICE.CPP	Sets up a class to control drawing on client areas.

well. Although it is not a complete implementation—who has time?—what it *does* implement, is from the standpoint of *improving* the Windows SDK, not just making C++ classes out of it. After all, if you don't get an actual benefit from C++, what's the point?

GDI Basics

The Windows GDI is composed of a number of object types. At the core of it all is the *device context*, accessed in Windows C code through a handle that is usually abbreviated "hdc." The device context *represents* one of any number of things your application might like to "draw" on: the client area of the application window, an entire screen, a page in the printer, or even a bitmap or block of memory. Although the manner of *obtaining* a device context varies with the *type* of device context you want, the technique of drawing on it never changes. That means that code written to draw on the screen can also draw on a printer page, given that the drawing function receives a device context as a parameter.

The device context "contains," at all times, one each of three types of tools: a brush, a pen, and a font. When you first obtain the device context, it already contains one of each of these. It has been reported in nearly all Windows documentation that, when you return the device context to the system, you *must* first restore the original pen, brush, and font, if you replaced any of them. *This is not so!* However, you must not return a device context with a specially-created pen, brush, or font. It's all right to return one with any stock objects, however.

> *Pens, brushes, and fonts can be created to specification, or "borrowed" from a "stockroom" of commonly used items such as a black pen or system font. Each is managed in the Windows SDK by a unique type of handle, and each should be represented by a distinct C++ class. Although not all device contexts have associated bitmaps, you can add a bitmap to a device context the same as a pen or brush; so bitmaps need a representing class, as well.*

Finally, although not strictly part of the GDI, basic components such as colors, points, and rectangles are best represented as classes. Because the other classes make reference to these rudimentary ones, we'll start our flight with the Portable GDI class library there.

The Baggage Department

When I write a class, I usually package it in a pair of files. The declaration will be in the header file, of course, along with **inline** definitions; while the compiled definitions are in the .CPP file. However, ideally this library should be packaged as two files: PORTAGDI.H and PORTAGDI.LIB.

(At first I had some trouble convincing both Borland C++ 4.5 or Microsoft Visual C++ 1.52 to link the libraries they created with a test application. But it turned out to be my own fault! I had accidentally compiled the library for medium model, but the test app for large. Watch out for this gotcha!)

As we go through the code I'll try to mention when we switch from the header file to the code file; but it should be obvious: If it's not a **class** statement or an **inline** function, you must be looking at a .CPP file.

Also, I use a trick—one I did *not* make up—to avoid any chance of **#include**-ing a header file more than once. I bracket the header file with the following preprocessor directives:

```
#ifndef _MYFILE_H_
#define _MYFILE_H_

  /
  /

#endif
```

where "_MYFILE_H_" is actually a string derived from the name of the file. I also make sure each header file has embedded **#include** directives for any other header file it references. That way, a programmer using my class libraries *never* has to worry about getting the **#include** directives in any particular order, and none of them has any non-obvious requirements.

(When I questioned a Microsoft instructor on why App Wizard generates positionally-dependent header files, I was told "it was too hard" to do it right!)

Your Point of Departure

The first classes in the Portable GDI Library are those concerned with the coordinate system. These are points, sizes, and rectangles, and are implemented in POINT.CPP. For ease of use with other SDK, MFC, and OWL functions, the classes are derived from the standard *POINT* and *SIZE* classes. We'll start by defining the *point* class and implementing its constructors and operator functions. Then, we'll move on and create the *size* and *rectangle* classes.

Here is the complete definition for *point*:

```
class size;

class point : public tagPOINT
  {
  public:
    point (int X = 0, int Y = 0) { x = X; y =Y; }
    point (LPARAM lParam);
    point (const point & Original);
    BOOL operator== (const point & Test) const;
    BOOL operator!= (const point & Test) const;
    point & operator= (const point & Original);
    point & operator+= (const size Size);
    point & operator-= (const size Size);
    friend point operator+ (const point Point, const size Size);
    friend point operator- (const point Point, const size Size);
    size operator- (const point Point) const;
  };
```

The Microsoft compiler complains unless we actually derive from the tagname (rather than the **struct** name), thus we use name *tagPOINT* in the class definition. Note also the pre-declaration of *size*, which is necessary because some of the *point* methods take parameters, or return, *size* objects. We'll be defining the *size* class a little later.

Again, this class is rudimentary; if you need more arithmetic operators—and you probably will, some day—by all means, add them. I supplied operators that correspond to those in ObjectWindows' *TPoint* class.

When deciding what operators to include with a class and what those operators should mean, don't hesitate to put yourself at the boarding gate of the programmer who will eventually use these classes. Try and anticipate what that person will guess. In this case, adding two points produces a rectangle, not a *point*, so that operator is implemented in the *rectangle* class, here. On the other hand, adding a *size* to a *point* logically (to me, anyway!) produces a new *point* offset from the first; subtracting one *point* from another produces a size. So that's the way I've implemented the class.

Coding the Constructors and Operators

The three constructors (two are implemented in POINT.CPP) cannot initialize x and *y* in the member initialization area because these two properties are *inherited* from the base class. Instead, standard assignment statements must be used:

```
point::point (LPARAM lParam)
   {
   x = LOWORD (lParam);
   y = HIWORD (lParam);
   }

point::point (const point & Original)
   {
   x = Original.x;
   y = Original.y;
   }
```

The test for equivalence is straightforward; and the test for *non*-equivalence simply invokes the test for equivalence:

```
BOOL point::operator== (const point & Test) const
   {
   return ((x == Test.x) && (y == Test.y));
   }
```

```
BOOL point::operator!= (const point & Test) const
    {
    return ! (*this == Test);
    }
```

The three assignment operators—one is a plain, vanilla assignment, and the
other two are arithmetic assignments—follow the required pattern, which is
to say, they each return *this*, a reference to the object itself:

```
point & point::operator= (const point & Original)
    {
    x = Original.x;
    y = Original.y;
    return *this;
    }

point & point::operator+= (const size Size)
    {
    x += Size.cx;
    y += Size.cy;
    return *this;
    }

point & point::operator-= (const size Size)
    {
    x -= Size.cx;
    y -= Size.cy;
    return *this;
    }
```

Two global (**friend**) operators create a temporary object to return; the
arithmetic assignment operators are applied to the temporary so the logic of
adding and subtracting need not be repeated:

```
point operator+ (const point Point, const size Size)
    {
    return point (Point) += Size;
    }

point operator- (const point Point, const size Size)
    {
    return point (Point) -= Size;
    }
```

The remaining operator allows the subtraction of one point from another,
returning a *size* :

```
size point::operator- (const point Point) const
    {
    return size (x - Point.x, y - Point.y);
    }
```

Defining the size Class

The *size* class, similar in its complexity to the *point* class, was pre-declared because some *point* member functions either used or returned *size*s. Here's its full declaration:

```
class size : public tagSIZE
   {
   public:
      size (int CX = 0, int CY = 0) { cx =CX; cy =CY; }
      size (LPARAM lParam);
      size (const size & Original);
      BOOL operator== (const size & Test) const;
      BOOL operator!= (const size & Test) const;
      size & operator= (const size & Original);
      size & operator+= (const size Size);
      size & operator-= (const size Size);
      size operator+ (const size Size) const;
      size operator- (const size Size) const;
   };
```

I won't bore you with the code; it's on the companion CD-ROM and anyway it's so similar to *point* you'd think you were looking at twin flight attendants. Keep in mind that the difference between a *point* and *size* is more conceptual than anything else. The resulting classes will be handy because they let you work with points and sizes in a way that concentrates on the problem you're trying to solve, rather than the implementations of points or sizes. And that, you'll excuse me for saying, is the "point" of object-oriented programming.

Introducing the rectangle Class

The *rectangle* class inherits four properties instead of two (from *tagRECT*):

```
class rectangle : public tagRECT
   {
   public:
      rectangle (int aLeft = 0, int aTop = 0,
         int aRight = 0, int aBottom = 0);
      rectangle (point TopLeft, point BottomRight);
      rectangle (point Point, size Size);
      rectangle (RECT Rect);
      int GetWidth (void) const;
      int GetHeight (void) const;
      long GetArea (void) const;
      point GetTopLeft (void) const;
      point GetBottomRight (void) const;
      BOOL IsEmpty (void) const
         { return IsRectEmpty (this); }
```

```
BOOL operator== (const rectangle & Rect) const;
BOOL operator!= (const rectangle & Rect) const;
BOOL IsIn (const rectangle & Rect) const;
BOOL Contains (const rectangle & Rect) const;
BOOL Contains (const point & Point) const;
rectangle & operator= (const rectangle & Original);
rectangle & operator+= (const rectangle & Rect);
rectangle & operator+= (const size & Size);
rectangle & operator-= (const size & Size);
};
```

Given that the four properties are *left, right, top,* and *bottom,* it won't surprise you that three of the constructors simply make the required assignments—for example:

```
rectangle::rectangle (int aLeft, int aTop,
    int aRight, int aBottom)
  {
  left = aLeft;
  top = aTop;
  right = aRight;
  bottom = aBottom;
  }
```

However, the copy constructor may surprise you:

```
rectangle::rectangle (RECT Rect)
  {
  CopyRect (this, &Rect);
  }
```

"*CopyRect,*" you ask. "Where did *that* come from? If it's a member function, I didn't see it in the declaration."

Well, in a way, it *is* a member function ... an inherited one. "But isn't *tagRECT* a **struct**?"

Well, yes. But, in C (where *tagRECT* is used) the closest you can come to object-oriented programming is to write related functions that operate on a data structure. If you look up "rectangle functions" in the online help for the Windows API, you see that Microsoft supplied us with several functions ready-made to work with rectangles (or, rather, *tagRECT*s); we may as well use them.

So the tests for equivalence and non-equivalence are able to make use of another Windows API call, to *EqualRect()*:

```
BOOL rectangle::operator== (const rectangle & Rect) const
  {
  return EqualRect (this, &Rect);
  }
```

```
BOOL rectangle::operator!= (const rectangle & Rect) const
   {
   return ! EqualRect (this, &Rect);
   }
```

The member functions *GetTopLeft()* and *GetBottomRight()*, which return *points*, are implemented as you would expect them to be. The main reason for writing them was to implement a version of *Contains()* that returns *TRUE* if a *rectangle* being tested lies entirely within the *rectangle* doing the testing:

```
BOOL rectangle::Contains (const rectangle & Rect) const
   {
   return Contains (Rect.GetTopLeft()) &&
      Contains (Rect.GetBottomRight());
   }
```

That function invokes the version of *Contains()* that tests whether a given *point* lies within the *rectangle*; and *that* function is able to use another Windows API call to actually perform the test:

```
BOOL rectangle::Contains (const point & Point) const
   {
   return PtInRect (this, Point);
   }
```

The arithmetic assignment operator that "adds" two *rectangles* expands the original *rectangle*, if necessary, so that it encompasses both its former self and the additional *rectangle*

```
rectangle & rectangle::operator+= (const rectangle & Rect)
   {
   UnionRect (this, this, &Rect);
   return *this;
   }
```

while adding a *size* to a *rectangle* simply inflates it ... and *that's* already got a Windows API function, too!

```
rectangle & rectangle::operator+= (const size & Size)
   {
   InflateRect (this, Size.cx, Size.cy);
   return *this;
   }
```

On the other hand, there is no existing routine called "DeflateRect()," so we have to write that ourselves. The idea is to not allow a rectangle to invert; so if you subtract a size from it that is larger than the rectangle itself, the rectangle simply reduces to zero width or height:

```
rectangle & rectangle::operator-= (const size & Size)
   {
   right -= Size.cx;
   bottom -= Size.cy;
   if (right < left)
      right = left;
   if (bottom < top)
      bottom = top;
   return *this;
   }
```

With Flying Colors

The *color* classes designed for PORTAGDI are actually borrowed, more or less, from the *TXColor* class (and associated classes) I designed for my book, *Borland C++ Insider* (John Wiley & Sons). However, those classes were derived from ObjectWindows' *TColor* class and *color* is not derived from anything, as is appropriate for a portable class library. *color* is implemented in COLOR.CPP.

As you know, colors are stored in Windows as *COLORREF* values. A *COLORREF* is simply a four-byte value in which the three least significant bytes store red, green, and blue values. (The most significant byte is not used.)

When designing the *color* class, I wanted the programmer to be able to use it in ways such as the following:

```
color MyColor (color::Red);
MyColor += green (64);
MyColor /= 2;
```

The first statement declares and defines *MyColor*, initialized to a red. The second statement adds a dark green to the color (but does not affect the red or blue components); the third statement causes the entire color to darken— that is, become half as bright as it was.

In order to pull this off, before we can actually create the *color* class, we need to create a *colorbyte* class. This class serves as a base class for *red, green,* and *blue*. Its declaration looks like this:

```
class colorbyte
   {
   public:
      colorbyte (BYTE aValue)
         : Value (aValue) {}
      colorbyte (colorbyte & aColorbyte)
         : Value (aColorbyte.Value) {}
      colorbyte & operator= (BYTE aValue)
```

```
        { Value = aValue; return *this; }
    colorbyte & operator= (colorbyte & aColorbyte)
        { Value = aColorbyte.Value; return *this;
    colorbyte & operator+= (int aValue);
    colorbyte & operator+= (colorbyte & aColorbyte)
        { return *this += aColorbyte.Value; }
    colorbyte & operator-= (int aValue);
    colorbyte & operator-= (colorbyte & aColorbyte)
        { return *this += aColorbyte.Value; }
    colorbyte & operator*= (int aValue);
    colorbyte & operator/= (int aValue);
    colorbyte operator+ (int aValue) const
        { return colorbyte (*this) += aValue; }
    colorbyte operator+ (colorbyte aColorbyte) const
        { return colorbyte (*this) += aColorbyte; }
    colorbyte operator- (int aValue) const
        { return colorbyte (*this) -= aValue; }
    colorbyte operator- (colorbyte aColorbyte) const
        { return colorbyte (*this) -= aColorbyte; }
    colorbyte operator* (int aValue) const
        { return colorbyte (*this) *= aValue; }
    colorbyte operator/ (int aValue)const
        { return colorbyte (*this) /= aValue; }
    operator BYTE () const { return Value; }
protected:
    BYTE Value;
};
```

The only difference between a *colorbyte* and a regular **unsigned char** is that the value of a *colorbyte* does not "roll over" when an arithmetic calculation tries to make it exceed 255, or decrease beyond zero. Instead, it simply remains at its maximum or minimum value. Policing this is the job of *Normalize()*, a helper function hidden in COLOR.CPP:

```
static BYTE near Normalize (int Test)
    {
    if (Test > 255)
        return 255;
    else if (Test < 0)
        return 0;
    else
        return (BYTE) Test;
    }
```

That makes it possible to implement each of the arithmetic operators for the *colorbyte* class. As usual, I've made the arithmetic assignment operators the ones that actually do the work:

```
colorbyte & colorbyte::operator+= (int aValue)
    {
    Value = Normalize ((int) Value + aValue);
```

```
    return *this;
    }

colorbyte & colorbyte::operator-= (int aValue)
    {
    Value = Normalize ((int) Value - aValue);
    return *this;
    }

colorbyte & colorbyte::operator*= (int aValue)
    {
    Value = Normalize ((int) Value * aValue);
    return *this;
    }

colorbyte & colorbyte::operator/= (int aValue)
    {
    Value = Normalize ((int) Value / aValue);
    return *this;
    }
```

As shown in the declaration, the non-assignment arithmetic operators are implemented by **inline** definitions; they simply construct temporary objects and perform the appropriate arithmetic assignment operators on them.

Creating Color Component Classes

Our next task is to derive the specific color component classes from *colorbyte*. We will need classes to represent *red, green,* and *blue* values. Except for their names, these classes will be identical. That makes them prime prospects for the C++ template facility. Unfortunately, not all compilers support templates yet—Microsoft Visual C++ 1.5x being one of the holdouts. (MSVC 2.0 does support templates, but will not produce 16-bit code, sometimes a requirement in these days of transition between Windows 3.1 and Windows 95.)

So we have to use the poor man's substitute for templates, the **#define**:

```
#define DECLARE_COLORBYTE_CLASS(COLORNAME) \
class COLORNAME : public colorbyte \
    { \
    public: \
        COLORNAME (COLORNAME & V) : colorbyte (V.Value) {} \
        COLORNAME (BYTE aValue = 0) : colorbyte (aValue) {} \
        COLORNAME & operator= (BYTE aValue) \
            { return (COLORNAME &) ((colorbyte &) *this = aValue); } \
        COLORNAME & operator= (COLORNAME & V) \
            { return ((COLORNAME &) ((colorbyte &) *this = V)); } \
        COLORNAME & operator+= (int aValue) \
            { return ((COLORNAME &) ((colorbyte &) *this += aValue)); } \
        COLORNAME & operator+= (COLORNAME & V) \
```

```
            { return ((COLORNAME &) ((colorbyte &) *this += V)); } \
        COLORNAME & operator-= (int aValue) \
            { return ((COLORNAME &) ((colorbyte &) *this -= aValue)); } \
        COLORNAME & operator-= (COLORNAME & V) \
            { return ((COLORNAME &) ((colorbyte &) *this += V)); } \
        COLORNAME & operator*= (int aValue) \
            { return ((COLORNAME &) ((colorbyte &) *this *= aValue)); } \
        COLORNAME & operator/= (int aValue) \
            { return ((COLORNAME &) ((colorbyte &) *this /= aValue)); } \
    }

DECLARE_COLORBYTE_CLASS (red);
DECLARE_COLORBYTE_CLASS (green);
DECLARE_COLORBYTE_CLASS (blue);
```

Notice how I made it possible to invoke the macro with a natural-looking semi-colon terminator: I simply omitted the semi-colon from the end of the macro class declaration. And Microsoft said it couldn't be done in MFC!

Anyway, now that we have our *colorbyte*-derived classes declared (and defined; all methods are **inline**), we can get to the actual *color* class:

```
class color
    {
    public:
        color ()
            : RValue (0), GValue (0), BValue (0) {}
        color (red R, green G, blue B)
            : RValue (R), GValue (G), BValue (B) {}
        color (COLORREF aValue) { *this = aValue; }
        enum systemcolor
            {
            Scrollbar = COLOR_SCROLLBAR,
            Background = COLOR_BACKGROUND,
            ActiveCaption = COLOR_ACTIVECAPTION,
            InactiveCaption = COLOR_INACTIVECAPTION,
            Menu = COLOR_MENU,
            Window = COLOR_WINDOW,
            WindowFrame = COLOR_WINDOWFRAME,
            MenuText = COLOR_MENUTEXT,
            WindowText = COLOR_WINDOWTEXT,
            CaptionText = COLOR_CAPTIONTEXT,
            ActiveBorder = COLOR_ACTIVEBORDER,
            InactiveBorder = COLOR_INACTIVEBORDER,
            AppWorkspace = COLOR_APPWORKSPACE,
            Highlight = COLOR_HIGHLIGHT,
            HighlightText = COLOR_HIGHLIGHTTEXT,
```

```
     ButtonFace = COLOR_BTNFACE,
     ButtonShadow = COLOR_BTNSHADOW,
     GrayText = COLOR_GRAYTEXT,
     ButtonText = COLOR_BTNTEXT,
     InactiveCaptionText = COLOR_INACTIVECAPTIONTEXT,
     ButtonHighlight = COLOR_BTNHIGHLIGHT
     };
color (systemcolor anIndex) { *this = anIndex; }
color & operator= (COLORREF aValue);
color & operator= (systemcolor anIndex);
color & operator= (red R);
color & operator= (green G);
color & operator= (blue B);
short operator== (const color & aColor) const;
short operator== (COLORREF aValue) const
   { return (*this == color (aValue)); }
color & operator+= (color aColor);
color & operator+= (red R);
color & operator+= (green G);
color & operator+= (blue B);
color operator+ (color aColor) const
   { return color (*this) += aColor; }
color operator+ (red R) const
   { return color (*this) += R; }
color operator+ (green G) const
   { return color (*this) += G; }
color operator+ (blue B) const
   { return color (*this) += B; }
color & operator-= (color aColor);
color & operator-= (red R);
color & operator-= (green G);
color & operator-= (blue B);
color operator- (color aColor) const
   { return color (*this) -= aColor; }
color operator- (red R) const
   { return color (*this) -= R; }
color operator- (green G) const
   { return color (*this) -= G; }
color operator- (blue B) const
   { return color (*this) -= B; }
color & operator*= (int aValue);
color operator* (int aValue) const
   { return color (*this) *=aValue; }
color & operator/= (int aValue);
color operator/ (int aValue) const
   { return color (*this) /=aValue; }
color & operator>>= (int Shift);
color operator>> (int Shift) const
   { return color (*this) >>= Shift; }
color & operator<<= (int Shift);
color operator<< (int Shift) const
   { return color (*this) <<= Shift; }
operator COLORREF () const
```

```
        { return RGB (RValue, GValue, BValue); }
    operator red () const
        { return RValue; }
    operator green () const
        { return GValue; }
    operator blue () const
        { return BValue; }
    static const color Red;
    static const color Green;
    static const color Blue;
    static const color Yellow;
    static const color Violet;
    static const color White;
    static const color Black;
private:
    red RValue;
    green GValue;
    blue BValue;
};
```

> *Looking first at the **inline** functions, you'll see that all the really simple stuff—most constructors, and non-assignment arithmetic operators—are implemented this way. That's my way of cutting down on function overhead when implementing a class: Let the compiler, not the run-time computer, do it.*

You'll notice that two of the constructors, the ones that construct a *color* from a *COLORREF* and from a *systemcolor,* defer their implementation to the assignment operator. To construct a *COLORREF*, one should invoke the Windows API macros that do the job:

```
color & color::operator= (COLORREF Value)
    {
    RValue = GetRValue (Value);
    GValue = GetGValue (Value);
    BValue = GetBValue (Value);
    return *this;
    }
```

(Don't you just love the way Microsoft programmers consistently named all their macros in all upper case?—Well, except for these and a few others?)

The constructor that accepts a *systemcolor* has an entirely different job. The *systemcolor* is actually one of the user-set colors used for various components of the Windows GUI, like menus, menu text, and so on. The Windows API has a function, *GetSysColor(),* that retrieves these colors. Of course, it is possible to send that function an invalid color index. By accepting as an argument a *systemcolor*, one of the predefined values in the anonymous **enum**, we guarantee an invalid color cannot be requested:

```
color & color::operator= (systemcolor anIndex)
    {
    return *this = GetSysColor (anIndex);
    }
```

The constructor can then be used in this fashion:

```
color MyColor (color::Window);
```

Each of the assignment operators that accepts just one of the *colorbyte* values, automatically (thanks to C++!) passes on the value to the desired data member; for example:

```
color & color::operator= (red R)
    {
    RValue = R;
    return *this;
    }
```

This allows the programmer to easily set individual color component values:

```
color MyColor;
MyColor = green (128);
MyColor = blue (64);
```

The test for equivalence is obvious enough:

```
short color::operator== (const color & aColor) const
    {
    return ((RValue == aColor.RValue) &&
      (GValue == aColor.GValue) &&
      (BValue == aColor.BValue));
    }
```

You might want to add additional equivalence operators for each of the primary colors; I thought about it but decided the code invoking them would look too confusing.

If you add one color to another, *each* of the components is added individually:

```
color & color::operator+= (color aColor)
    {
    RValue += aColor.RValue;
    GValue += aColor.GValue;
    BValue += aColor.BValue;
    return *this;
    }
```

This allows you to write code adding equal amounts of red and green to get yellow:

```
color MyColor (color::Red);
color Green (color::Green);
MyColor += Green; // MyColor now contains yellow
```

Adding individual colors, however, only affects *that color*... and remember, the *colorbyte* class handles the overflow problem automatically:

```
color & color::operator+= (red R)
    {
    RValue += R;
    return *this;
    }
```

Similarly, the multiply and divide operators are interpreted to refer to changes of intensity; and these changes are passed on to the individual color components:

```
color & color::operator*= (int aValue)
    {
    RValue *= aValue;
    GValue *= aValue;
    BValue *= aValue;
    return *this;
    }
```

I had to give a little thought to what the right and left shift operators might mean. I suppose you could argue with me, but I finally decided the color components themselves should shift: A right shift of one, for example, rotates the red component to green, the green to blue, and the blue to red:

```
color & color::operator>>= (int Shift)
    {
    Shift %= 3;
    while (Shift > 0)
        {
        colorbyte Temp (BValue);
        BValue = GValue;
        GValue = RValue;
        RValue = Temp;
        -Shift;
        }
    return *this;
    }
```

The left shift operator works identically, but in the other direction. That leaves just one more block of code in the implementation file: the definitions of the pre-defined colors:

```
const color color::Red = RGB (255, 0, 0);
const color color::Green = RGB (0, 255, 0);
const color color::Blue = RGB (0, 0, 255);
const color color::Yellow = RGB (255, 255, 0);
const color color::Violet = RGB (255, 0, 255);
const color color::White = RGB (255, 255, 255);
const color color::Black = RGB (0, 0, 0);
```

I had one reader of Borland C++ Insider *suggest that every hue known to man be included as constants. Apparently colors such as mauve, teal, and puce have had precise RGB values defined! But, as Mary Poppins replied to the suggestion that "supercalifragilisticexpialidocious" could be pronounced backwards, that's going a bit too far, don't you think?*

A Brush with Death

Finally, we get to an actual GDI object! The *brush* is our first, implemented in BRUSH.CPP. Every device context arrives in your application with a brush. By default, that is a "white brush." You can replace it, however, with a brush of your own design; and that's where the *brush* class comes in:

```
class brush
    {
    Friend class devicecontext;
    public:
        enum stockbrushes
            {
            White = WHITE_BRUSH,
            LightGray = LTGRAY_BRUSH,
            Gray = GRAY_BRUSH,
            DarkGray = DKGRAY_BRUSH,
            Black = BLACK_BRUSH,
            Invisible = HOLLOW_BRUSH
            };
        brush (stockbrushes StockBrush);
        enum hatchbrushes
            {
            Horizontal = HS_HORIZONTAL,
            Vertical = HS_VERTICAL,
            ForewardDiagonal = HS_FDIAGONAL,
            BackwardDiagonal = HS_BDIAGONAL,
            Cross = HS_CROSS,
            DiagonalCross = HS_DIAGCROSS
            };
        brush (color aColor, hatchbrushes Style);
```

```
    brush (HBITMAP aBitmap);
    brush (color aColor);
    ~brush ();
    operator HBRUSH (void) { return Handle; }
private:
    BOOL StockObject;
    HBRUSH Handle;
    devicecontext * pDC;
};
```

Like all GDI objects, the Windows API brush is represented by a *HANDLE* (specifically, an *HBRUSH*). You could make a point for a constructor that allows a *brush* object to be constructed from a *HBRUSH*; but I think that sort of thing encourages half-object-oriented programming. I do, however, supply a cast to *HBRUSH* so that a *brush* object can be used anywhere an *HBRUSH* can be.

One way brushes can be obtained is from the Windows "stockroom." An **enum**, *stockbrushes*, supplies identifiers for the various stock brushes. The values are the same as the analogous Windows API **#define**s, but by using the **enum** we let the C++ compiler prevent the programmer from accidentally trying to create a brush with an inappropriate value (like, say, *BLACK_PEN*). To obtain a brush from Windows' store of stock objects, the Windows API function *GetStockObject()* is called. Since it returns a generic *HANDLE*, its return value must be cast:

```
brush::brush (stockbrushes StockBrush)
   : Handle ((HBRUSH) GetStockObject (StockBrush)),
     StockObject (TRUE), pDC (NULL)
   {
   }
```

Another type of brush is the *hatch brush*. This is one in which the brushed area is filled in with colored lines, rather than a solid color. Such a brush is often used when the output device is a plotter, since plotters often smear solid colors. There are several styles of hatching; and the **enum** *hatchstyles* supplies the identifiers. Figure 4.1 provides a quick look at the available styles.

GetHatchBrush() is the Windows API function that must be invoked. Notice, too, that the argument sequence has been reversed for this constructor; I did that so that the color of the brush would always come first—it's less confusing to the programmer that way:

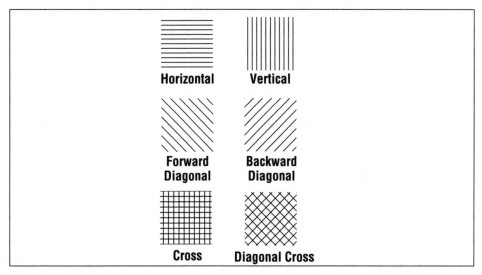

Figure 4.1 The six hatch styles.

```
brush::brush (color aColor, hatchstyles Style)
   : Handle (CreateHatchBrush (Style, aColor)),
     StockObject (FALSE), pDC (NULL)
   {
   }
```

If you have a handy 8x8 pixel bitmap, you can use it to create a brush. Such a thing is called a "patterned brush"; *CreatePatternBrush()* is the Windows API function that creates one:

```
brush::brush (HBITMAP aBitmap)
   : Handle (CreatePatternBrush (aBitmap)),
     StockObject (FALSE), pDC (NULL)
   {
   }
```

By the way, if the bitmap you supply is monochrome, the brush will use the device context's current text and background colors to render itself. Also, if the bitmap is larger than 8x8 pixels, only the top left 8x8 will be used.

We've saved the most common brush for last: the solid color:

```
brush::brush (color aColor)
   : Handle (CreateSolidBrush (aColor)),
```

```
    StockObject (FALSE), pDC (NULL)
{
}
```

Now, even though we *call* this a solid color, you should be aware that most people are not using a 16-million color driver for their monitor; and therefore not every color you request can *be* rendered as a "solid" color. In that case, Windows will automatically supply a dithered brush. In spite of what you may have heard, "dithering" is not a new invention of the current Administration. It is, in fact, an old printer's term that describes using small dots of various primary colors to render a non-primary color (such as brown or chartreuse).

What if you specifically want the nearest, truly solid color the current Windows driver can render? The Windows API has a function, *GetNearestColor()*. It takes a handle to a device context, and a *COLORREF*. Use its return value to specify your brush color:

```
color MyColor (233, 21, 28);
devicecontext MyDC (Window);
brush MyBrush (GetNearestColor (MyDC, MyColor));
```

Created brushes must be deleted, but stock objects must *not* be. This is handled in the destructor:

```
brush::~brush ()
   {
   if (pDC)
     pDC->RestoreBrush ();
   if (! StockObject)
     DeleteObject (Handle);
   }
```

You may remember in the class declaration, that *devicecontext* was said to be a **friend** class. It's vitally important that a brush not be deleted while it is still selected into a device context. The call to *RestoreBrush()*, a method of *devicecontext*, will ensure that. (We'll look at the *devicecontext* class in just a couple of pages.)

Don't Forget Your Pen!

pen objects, implemented in PEN.CPP, are very similar to *brush* objects. A default pen also comes with a device context; there are also stock pens, and pens can also be created to order.

Here's the declaration for the *pen* class:

```
class pen
   friend class devicecontext;
   {
   friend class devicecontext;
   public:
      enum penstyle
         {
         Solid = PS_SOLID,
         Dashed = PS_DASH,
         Dotted = PS_DOT,
         DashDot = PS_DASHDOT,
         DashDotDot = PS_DASHDOTDOT,
         InsideFrame = PS_INSIDEFRAME
         };
      pen (color Color, int Width = 0, penstyle Style = Solid);
      enum stockpens
         {
         White = WHITE_PEN,
         Black = BLACK_PEN,
         Invisible = NULL_PEN
         };
      pen (stockpens StockPen = Black);
      ~pen ();
      operator HPEN (void) { return Handle; }
   private:
      BOOL StockObject;
      HPEN Handle;
       devicecontext * pDC;
   };
```

GetStockObject() can return a stock pen from the "stockroom," just as it
returns stock brushes (and, for that matter, fonts). As with *brush* we have to
cast its return value. This is the default constructor, by the way, since its one
parameter has a default value—that of the stock black pen:

```
pen::pen (stockpens StockPen)
   : Handle ((HPEN) GetStockObject (StockPen)),
     StockObject (TRUE), pDC (NULL)
   {
   }
```

*pen*s can be constructed by specifying a color; you can also specify a
thickness and a style. In the Windows API, all those options must be
specified; but thanks to the magic of default parameters, this constructor
doesn't require anything but color. The *CreatePen()* function of the Windows API does the work:

```
pen::pen (color Color, int Width, penstyle Style)
   : Handle (CreatePen (Style, Width, Color)),
     StockObject (FALSE), pDC (NULL)
   {
   }
```

As with *brush,* the destructor only actually destroys the *pen* if it is not a stock object:

```
pen::~pen ()
   {
   if (pDC)
     pDC->RestorePen ();
   if (! StockObject)
     DeleteObject (Handle);
   }
```

An Airborne Device

The *devicecontext* class is the root of the whole GDI system. It's defined in DEVICE.CPP. The device context is Windows' way of maintaining device independence. It's actually pretty ingenious. The exact same functions are used to draw on any device, be it a printer or a monitor; and the device can be queried as to its capabilities (in most cases).

> *Now, that was the good news. The bad news, for C programmers, is that there are several different kinds of device context and they are all created and destroyed differently...and no normal human can remember which is which.*

But we aren't C programmers. We can hide those discrepancies by putting the bulk of GDI functionality into a base class, and handle the differences in derived classes.

Here's the declaration for the base class, *devicecontext*:

```
class devicecontext
   {
   public:
     devicecontext (HDC aHandle);
     virtual ~devicecontext ();
     operator const HDC (void) { return Handle; }
     devicecontext & operator= (brush & Brush);
     devicecontext & operator= (pen & Pen);
```

```
      devicecontext & operator= (color Color);
      void RestoreBrush (void);
      void RestorePen (void);
      virtual rectangle GetWindowRect (void) const = 0;
      virtual rectangle GetClientRect (void) const = 0;
      virtual rectangle GetClipRect (void) const = 0;
      void SetBackgroundColor (color Color);
      void SetTabStops (int aTabStops) { TabStops = aTabStops; }
      enum drawmode
         {
         Transparent = TRANSPARENT,
         Opaque = OPAQUE
         };
      void SetBackgroundDrawMode (drawmode DrawMode);
      void DrawRectangle (rectangle Rectangle);
      void DrawEllipse (rectangle Rectangle);
      void DrawFocusRectangle (rectangle Rectangle);
      void DrawText (point Point, const char * Text);
      enum alignment
         {
         TopLeft = DT_LEFT,
         MiddleLeft = DT_LEFT | DT_VCENTER | DT_SINGLELINE,
         BottomLeft = DT_LEFT | DT_BOTTOM | DT_SINGLELINE,
         TopCenter = DT_CENTER,
         MiddleCenter = DT_CENTER | DT_VCENTER | DT_SINGLELINE,
         BottomCenter = DT_CENTER | DT_BOTTOM | DT_SINGLELINE,
         TopRight = DT_RIGHT,
         MiddleRight = DT_RIGHT | DT_VCENTER | DT_SINGLELINE,
         BottomRight = DT_RIGHT | DT_BOTTOM | DT_SINGLELINE
         };
      void DrawText (rectangle Rectangle,
         const char * Text, alignment Alignment = MiddleCenter);
   protected:
      HDC Handle;
      void Restore (void);
   private:
      int TabStops;
      HBRUSH OldBrush;
      brush * CurrentBrush;
      HPEN OldPen;
      pen * CurrentPen;
      int OldBkMode;
   };
```

You'll note that I haven't attempted to duplicate *all* drawing functionality in this class. In reality everything you can do with the Windows API should be there; but, as an instructional tool, that many methods hide the core of the class. I encourage you to add any additional methods you need; doing so will be a trivial task. And everything we used for our VBX class library project is here.

The constructor to this base class requires a handle to an existing device context:

```
devicecontext::devicecontext (HDC aHandle)
  :   Handle (aHandle),
      TabStops (4),
        OldBrush (NULL), CurrentBrush (NULL),
        OldPen (NULL), CurrentPen (NULL)
    {
    }
```

The destructor doesn't do anything; but it is **virtual**, a proper setup for a base class—even though you aren't likely to have a container of various *devicecontext* objects, it's still good practice:

```
devicecontext::~devicecontext ()
    {
    }
```

Remember how odd you originally thought the *SelectObject()* function of the Windows API was? It could take a pen, a brush, a font, or other object, and somehow knew what to do with them. Why would anyone want to duplicate this madness into a GDI class library? (You needn't answer, Microsoft and Borland; that was a rhetorical question.) In *devicecontext*, such operations are performed with the addition assignment operator. When the object on the right of the operator is a *brush* or a *pen*, sure enough a *SelectObject()* call results; but at least the programmer doesn't have to be aware of it:

```
devicecontext & devicecontext::operator= (brush & Brush)
    {
    HBRUSH PreviousBrush = (HBRUSH) ::SelectObject (Handle, Brush);
    if (CurrentBrush)
      CurrentBrush->pDC = NULL;
    if (! Old Brush)
      OldBrush = PreviousBrush;
    CurrentBrush = &Brush;
    Brush.pDC = this;
    return *this;
    }

devicecontext & devicecontext::operator= (pen & Pen)
    {
    HPEN PreviousPen = (HPEN) ::SelectObject (Handle, Pen);
    if (CurrentPen)
      Current->pDC = NULL;
    if (! OldPen)
      OldPen = PreviousPen;
    CurrentPen = &Pen;
    Pen.pDC = this;
    return *this;
    }
```

The manipulations of the *CurrentBrush* and *CurrentPen* properties make sure that the current brush and pen *know* they are in use—they use this information, as seen earlier, to detach themselves from the device context if they are destroyed before the device context object is, by invoking the *RestoreBrush()* and *RestorePens()* methods, respectively:

```
void devicecontext::RestoreBrush (void)
  {
  if (OldBrush)
    {
    ::SelectObject (Handle, OldBrush):
    CurrentBrush->pDC = NULL;
    CurrentBrush = NULL;
    }
  }

void devicecontext::RestorePen (void)
  {
  if (OldPen)
    {
    ::SelectObject (Handle, OldPen);
    CurrentPen->pDC = NULL;
    CurrentPen = NULL;
    }
  }
```

When the object on the right is a *color*, the text color is changed.

```
devicecontext & devicecontext::operator= (color Color)
  {
  :SetTextColor (Handle, Color);
  return *this;
  }
```

I was *very* tempted to use the subtraction assignment for setting the background color. However, that seemed pretty obscure, even to me. So I used regular named methods—however, I *did* name them reasonably, instead of using those odd abbreviations the Microsoft programmers love so well:

```
inline void devicecontext::SetBackgroundColor (color Color)
  {
  ::SetBkColor (Handle, Color);
  }

inline void devicecontext::SetBackgroundDrawMode (drawmode DrawMode)
  {
  ::SetBkMode (Handle, DrawMode);
  }
```

(Note that these **inline** functions are found in the header file.)

The three pure, **virtual** functions *GetWindowRect(), GetClientRect(),* and *GetClipRect()* guarantee a drawing function can query the *devicecontext* for location information regardless of the *kind* of *devicecontext* it is.

My versions of *Rectangle(), Ellipse()* and *DrawFocusRect()* have clearer names:

```
void devicecontext::DrawRectangle (rectangle Rectangle)
   {
   ::Rectangle (Handle,
     Rectangle.left, Rectangle.top,
     Rectangle.right, Rectangle.bottom);
   }

void devicecontext::DrawEllipse (rectangle Rectangle)
   {
   ::Ellipse (Handle,
     Rectangle.left, Rectangle.top,
     Rectangle.right, Rectangle.bottom);
   }

void devicecontext::DrawFocusRectangle (rectangle Rectangle)
   {
   ::DrawFocusRect (Handle, &Rectangle);
   }
```

The Windows API has an embarrassment of ways to place text on the device context: *TextOut(), ExtTextOut(), TabbedTextOut(), DrawText()*...it is rapidly becoming a lexical nightmare the equal of the standard C library. In the *devicecontext* class, all functions that draw objects on the device context begin with "Draw"; so the various text functions are selected by choosing the overloaded *DrawText()* that has the parameter list you need. For example, if all you have is a *point* and a string:

```
void devicecontext::DrawText (point Point, const char * Text)
   {
   ::TextOut (Handle,
     Point.x, Point.y,
     Text, strlen (Text));
   }
```

On the other hand, if you wish to place the text within a rectangle—aligned however you like—use this version:

```
void devicecontext::DrawText (rectangle Rectangle,
     const char * Text, alignment Alignment)
   {
   ::DrawText (Handle, Text, -1, &Rectangle,
     (Alignment | DT_EXPANDTABS | DT_TABSTOP) + (TabStops << 8));
   }
```

The last method for us to inspect is *Restore()*. This method is **protected** and it just calls *RestoreBrush()* and *RestorePen()*. It will be used by derived classes to make sure the original GDI objects are restored before the device context is returned:

```
void devicecontext::Restore (void)
  {
  RestoreBrush ();
  RestorePen ();
  }
```

Creating the paintcontext Class

Most drawing in Windows takes place in response to a *WM_PAINT* message; the programmer gets the handle to the device context by invoking the Windows API function *BeginPaint()*. In the Portable GDI Library, the class that represents this type of device context is called *paintcontext*:

```
class paintcontext : public devicecontext
  {
  public:
    paintcontext (HWND aWindow);
    ~paintcontext ();
    paintcontext & operator= (brush & Brush);
    paintcontext & operator= (pen & Pen);
    virtual rectangle GetWindowRect (void) const;
    BOOL ShouldRedrawBackground (void) const
      { return ps.fErase; }
    virtual rectangle GetWindowRect (void) const;
    virtual rectangle GetClientRect (void) const;
    virtual rectangle GetClipRect (void) const;
  private:
    HWND Window;
    PAINTSTRUCT ps;
  };
```

BeginPaint() is invoked by the constructor, while *EndPaint()* is called by the destructor after the device context has been restored to its original condition:

```
paintcontext::paintcontext (HWND aWindow)
  : devicecontext (BeginPaint (aWindow, &ps)),
    Window (aWindow)
  {
  }

paintcontext::~paintcontext ()
  {
  Restore();
```

```
  EndPaint (Window, &ps);
  }
```

The assignment operators must be supplied, because assignment operators are never inherited. However, a couple of **inline** functions (in the header file) do the job with a little casting and *no* runtime overhead:

```
inline paintcontext & paintcontext::operator= (brush & Brush)
  {
  return (paintcontext &) (((devicecontext &) *this) = Brush);
  }

inline paintcontext & paintcontext::operator= (pen & Pen)
  {
  return (paintcontext &) (((devicecontext &) *this) = Pen);
  }
```

The implementation of *GetWindowRect()* simply calls the Windows API function of the same name, adding the necessary code so a *rectangle* object can be returned:

```
rectangle paintcontext::GetWindowRect (void) const
  {
  RECT Rect;
  ::GetWindowRect (Window, &Rect);
  return rectangle (Rect);
  }
```

GetClientRect() also passes the call on to the API function. But *GetClipRect()* queries the *PAINTSTRUCT* structure, *ps*, and returns the appropriate value:

```
rectangle paintcontext::GetClipRect (void) const
  {
  return rectangle (ps.rcPaint);
  }
```

Creating the clientcontext Class

It's less common, but sometimes you want to draw on your client area even when a *WM_PAINT* message has *not* arrived—in response to a mouse click or keystroke, perhaps. To do that, create an object of the *clientcontext* class:

```
class clientcontext : public devicecontext
  {
  public:
    clientcontext (HWND aWindow);
    ~clientcontext ();
    clientcontext & operator= (brush & Brush);
    clientcontext & operator= (pen & Pen);
```

```
    virtual rectangle GetWindowRect (void) const;
    virtual rectangle GetClientRect (void) const;
    virtual rectangle GetClipRect (void) const;
  private:
    HWND Window;
  };
```

Its only difference from *paintcontext* is in its constructor, which must call *GetDC()*, and the destructor, which calls *ReleaseDC()*:

```
clientcontext::clientcontext (HWND aWindow)
  : devicecontext (GetDC (aWindow)),
    Window (aWindow)
  {
  }

clientcontext::~clientcontext ()
  {
  Restore();
  ReleaseDC (Window, Handle);
  }
```

Test Flight

To test the Portable GDI Library with a minimum of fuss, I've written a little test program. The test program can be found on the companion CD-ROM in the GDITEST directory, *beneath* the PORTAGDI directory.

The core of the program is a C windows application skeleton. For details on the skeleton, see *Borland C++ Insider*. It's pretty straightforward, though.

The application creates one window that initializes a timer. In response to each timer tick, the window draws a differently colored and sized rectangle on itself. Only the timer handler is written in C++; and it is this handler that tests the PORTAGDI classes. It is *not* an exhaustive test; but you can certainly add on to this as much as you need to feel the class library is truly robust.

Additional Airlines

Most frequent travelers have signed on with the frequent-flyer programs of all the airlines they ever fly. Still, they know that to actually ever see *benefits* from the programs, they need to concentrate on one or two airlines where possible.

Likewise, the majority of Windows drawing is done using the kinds of device contexts we've just implemented. Still, there are others that would be nice to add: printer device contexts, bitmap contexts, metafile contexts, and so on. But we won't need those extensions for the VBX++ class library.

But, you know what? If you give it a try yourself, I'll bet you won't find it so hard. Just follow the patterns presented here, and you'll see it's really quite easy to build good, solid, C++ classes to deal with Windows—so easy, you'll wonder why anyone ever made such a fuss over MFC or ObjectWindows!

And your classes will have the advantage of fitting into *anyone's* overhead bin.

Creating a Vendor-Free *text* Class

5

I USED TO BE A DIE-HARD COMIC BOOK FAN—hey, what computer programmer wasn't?—paying something like $40 a month on comics before I finally kicked the habit. There's a lot of wisdom in those things, though. One scene stands out particularly in my mind. The Justice League of America had cornered some super-villains who were trying to rob a bank. (It's never been clear to me why someone with super-powers would need to rob banks, but we'll let that slide.) Now, picture this: These people are hurling themselves at each other at express-train speeds, in the lobby of this bank. They are smashing each other into desks (which break), teller stations (which break), and walls (which break). The air is filled with the sounds of super-hero shouts and property destruction, and, when the battle is finally over, thousands and thousands of little deposit slips drifting down like snow.

Wonder Woman discovers the poor folks who were in the bank when the melee started, huddling behind an overturned table, bearing the expressions of terrified mice. "It's all right, now. It's over. You can come out." But the tellers and customers can't move. They can barely breathe. "What's wrong?" she asks. "It's over! The Justice League won!"

Finally one of them, standing in what once was his bank but now has no front wall and has suffered far more damage than the stolen money would ever have amounted to, finds his voice. "When you super types start fighting, all we bystanders can do is hide. It doesn't much matter *who* won, does it?"

Now, I don't know about you, but I sometimes feel that way when Microsoft and Borland start fighting. Their battle extends back to when Borland, out of the blue, offered a Pascal compiler that was ten times better than Microsoft's, for less than one tenth the price. It continues today with Microsoft Visual C++ vs. Borland C++, and shows no signs of abating. And who suffers? We bystanders, who cannot write a Microsoft Foundation Classes application that will compile under Borland C++, or an ObjectWindows application that will compile under Visual C++. Each product claims ANSI standards compliance, but the fact is the ANSI standards are not very powerful—think of the ANSI standards committee as a third-class super-hero with its own agenda, making UNIX viable once more—and both Borland and Microsoft have been forced to improve on them ... in different ways, of course.

Now, we can remain huddled behind that overturned table indefinitely. But I was never the type to remain a victim for long. I've decided to start fighting back, in my own way, to salvage what I can before the super-companies have gotten—or destroyed—it all. One way to fight back is to create your *own* class libraries that *are* independent of any particular vendor. The more of these you have, the less reliance you have to place on over-designed, flimsy code handed you by the self-styled "heroes" of the industry.

Now, this may seem like an impossible task to you. But it's not, if you work on the classes one at a time in true object-oriented fashion. In the previous chapter I showed you how to get started with a vendor-free Windows GDI library. Now we'll free ourselves even more by designing and implementing a really *useful* class for manipulating text.

Creating the text Class

The ANSI C++ standards committee has defined a *String* class that is supposed to be the last word in string classes. Unfortunately, the committee still thinks the sun rises and sets on UNIX and so their *String* class makes no provision for such Windows conveniences as string resources (although it works very well on TTY consoles). Both Borland and Microsoft responded to this by implementing string classes of their own: *CString* from Microsoft and *string* from Borland (note the leading lowercase letter). Of the two, Borland's is closer to the ANSI standard (you can tell because it's over-designed), but not much closer.

> *C programmers may find this odd, but in truth a "string" should be any array of characters—including a NULL. That's the way it's done in other languages. The only reason C is an exception is the dreadfully inefficient string library routines in the standard C library, which use the NULL as a string terminator.*

All three string classes provide methods for handling substrings, deleting portions of strings, searching for individual letters, and so on. We'll want to do these things, too—but in a natural, C++ kind of way. And, since we are interested only in the subset of strings that contain text, we'll call our new class *text* (to avoid adding yet another variation of "string" to the already confusing lexicon) and just build into it the functionality we need for the job at hand. (That's another advantage of using your own classes: You can always enhance them as needed!)

Defining the Header File

As usual when analyzing C++ classes, we start with the class declaration in the header file—in our case, TEXT.H. The file is set off with the usual **#ifndef** structure (described in the previous chapter) to prevent multiple **#include**s. There are a few nested **#include**s, because functions in these library headers are referenced in **inline** functions here. (You should only **#include** headers in your header, that are directly required *by* your header—that's a mouthful!)

```
#ifndef __TEXT_H__
#define __TEXT_H__

#include <windows.h>
#include <stdlib.h>
#include <math.h>
```

Next is a helper class called *range*. This class will be used later to make it easy to pull substrings from a *text* object. It is completely implemented in the header file:

```
class range
  {
  public:
    range (int aFirst, int aLast)
      : First (aFirst), Last (aLast) {}
  private:
    int First, Last;
  friend class text;
  };
```

I'm trying to present this stuff in the order you'll find it in the header file, so bear with me; how and why *range* is used will be clear soon enough.

Likewise, the next item is also a helper class; it allows you to specify, in a single object, both the string table ID *and* the instance of the module containing that string table. (In Windows, remember, strings can be loaded from *any* loaded module, not just the one doing the loading.) Here is the declaration:

```
class stringID
  {
  public:
    stringID (UINT anID, HINSTANCE anInstance = NULL)
      : ID (anID),
        Instance (anInstance) {}
  private:
    UINT ID;
    HINSTANCE Instance;
  friend class text;
  };
```

After that, finally, is the declaration for *text* itself.

Now, usually, I present the entire **class** statement and describe the functions as I come to them in the implementation file. However, so many of the *text* functions are actually implemented **inline** that this isn't practical. So, instead, I'm going to cover each group of functions together, *including* their implementations. If you find this confusing, you might load both the header and implementation files into your favorite editor so you can see the actual code as a piece.

Secret Origins of a text Object

The **class** statement begins, as most do, with the declarations of the constructors and destructor for the class:

```
class text
  {
  public:
```

```
text (const char * Original = 0,
   BOOL aCaseSensitive = FALSE);
text (char Original, short Count = 1,
   BOOL aCaseSensitive = FALSE);
text (const text & Original);
text (long Value);
text (double Value);
text (stringID StringID, BOOL aCaseSensitive = FALSE);
virtual ~text();
   ⇓
   ⇓
```

As you can see, we'll allow construction from a standard C-style string, a single character (allowing for that character to be repeated some number of times), a copy constructor, and constructors that accept a binary **long** or **double**. The destructor is **virtual**, as destructors always should be. (This makes it easy to derive a class from this one later, and use both in a container.)

The implementation for the *text* class constructors is found in TEXT.CPP:

```
#include "text.h"
#include <string.h>
#include <ctype.h>

text::text (const char * Original, BOOL aCaseSensitive)
   : Length (0),
     Storage (NULL),
     CaseSensitive (aCaseSensitive)
   {
   Store (Original);
   }

text::text (char Original, short aCount, BOOL aCaseSensitive)
   : Length (0),
     Storage (NULL),
     CaseSensitive (aCaseSensitive)
   {
   Store (Original, aCount);
   }

text::text (const text & Original)
   : Length (0),
     Storage (NULL),
     CaseSensitive (Original.CaseSensitive)
   {
   Store (Original.Storage);
   }

text::text (long Value)
   : Length (0),
     Storage (NULL),
```

```
    CaseSensitive (FALSE)
  {
  Store (Value);
  }

text::text (double Value)
  : Length (0),
    Storage (NULL),
    CaseSensitive (FALSE)
  {
  Store (Value);
  }

text::text (stringID StringID, BOOL aCaseSensitive)
  : Length (0),
    Storage (NULL),
    CaseSensitive (aCaseSensitive)
  {
  Store (StringID);
  }
```

You can learn two things just by looking at these constructors. First, there
are three properties of the class: *Length, Storage,* and *CaseSensitive* ; these
are declared **private** as class properties almost always should be:

```
class text
  {
      ⇓
      ⇓
  private:
    char * Storage;
    int Length;
    BOOL CaseSensitive;
  };
```

Second, the actual assignment of the value is passed on to a method called
Store(). There are obviously several overloaded versions of *Store()*, almost
one per constructor type. Also, you can see that *Storage* is initialized to
NULL before *Store()* is ever invoked. That makes it easy to write the
destructor:

```
text::~text()
  {
  delete [] Storage;
  }
```

Since **delete** can be invoked safely on a *NULL* pointer, there's no need for
complicated testing to see what, if anything, has been allocated and assigned to *Storage.* The destructor will clean up things nicely.

Safely Stored in the Fortress of Solitude

Like a good secret identity, the *Store()* function is not accessible outside the *text* class or its descendants:

```
class text
    {
        ⇓
        ⇓
    protected:
        void Clear (void);
        void Store (const char * Original);
        void Store (char Original, short Count = 1);
        void Store (long Value);
        void Store (double Value);
        void Store (stringID StringID);
        ⇓
        ⇓
```

The *Clear()* function, also **protected**, is used by each of the *Store()* functions to delete any previous contents of the *text* object—that way, *Store()* can be used for assignments as well as constructors. *That's* why we had to initialize *Storage* to *NULL*:

```
void text::Clear (void)
    {
    Length = 0;
    delete [] Storage;
    Storage = NULL;
    }
```

To store a standard C-style string into a *text* object after clearing the old contents, enough characters must be allocated to store the string *and* the terminating *NULL*. Then a standard C library function can be used to actually copy the string into the stored area:

```
void text::Store (const char * Original)
    {
    Clear ();
    Length = Original ? strlen (Original) : 0;
    Storage = new char [Length + 1];
    if (Length)
        strcpy (Storage, Original);
    else
        Storage[0] = 0;
    }
```

Note that the above code provides for the possibility that the constructor (or, later, the assignment operator) was invoked with a *NULL* pointer. In such a case, *Store()* stores a zero length string—complete with *NULL* terminator so it can be safely used by functions expecting an allocated buffer. This version of *Store()* is invoked by both the C-style string and copy constructors.

Storing a single or repeated character is a slightly different task:

```
void text::Store (char Original, short Count)
   {
   Clear ();
   Length = Count;
   Storage = new char [Length + 1];
   memset (Storage, Original, Count);
   Storage[Length] = 0;
   }
```

Fortunately, there's a C library function *memset()* to do most of the work for us here, too.

Two versions of *Store()* accept a **long** or **double**, respectively; they are intended to provide a *text* version of a binary number. Again, we are able to make use of the C standard library:

```
void text::Store (long Value)
   {
   char Digits[48];
   ltoa (Value, Digits, 10);
   Store (Digits);
   }
```

```
void text::Store (double Value)
   {
   char Digits[48];
   gcvt (Value, 48, Digits);
   Store (Digits);
   }
```

Notice that we *also* make use of our own code—invoking the C-string *Store()* after *ltoa()* or *gcvt()* has converted the binary value into digits for us.

Finally, we have the overloaded *Store()* for *stringID*s:

```
void text::Store (stringID StringID)
   {
   char Buffer[256];
   LoadString (StringID.Instance, StringID.ID,
      Buffer, sizeof Buffer);
   Store (Buffer);
   }
```

LoadString(), of course, is the Windows API call that actually fetches strings from the stringtable. Since stringtable entries can never be more than 255 characters long, a 256-character buffer is adequate to read the requested string into initially before invoking the standard *Store()* to actually place it in the heap.

A Hero's Assignment

Next in the **class** statement are the assignment operators:

```
class text
  {
    ⇓
    ⇓
  public:
    text & operator= (const text & Original);
    text & operator= (const char * Original)
      { Store (Original); return *this; }
    text & operator= (const char Original)
      { Store (Original); return *this; }
    text & operator= (long Value)
      { Store (Value); return *this; }
    text & operator= (double Value)
      { Store (Value); return *this; }
    text & operator= (stringID StringID)
      { Store (StringID); return *this; }

    void SetCaseSensitive (BOOL aCaseSensitive = TRUE)
      { CaseSensitive = aCaseSensitive; }
    BOOL IsCaseSensitive (void) const
      { return CaseSensitive; }
    ⇓
    ⇓
```

I've included the custodial functions for setting and getting the *CaseSensitive* property in this category.

> *It should not surprise you to see that we have six assignment operators—one matching each constructor. This is how it should be done. As a programmer using this class, you should never have to wonder what data types you can safely assign to a* text *object. If you can initialize with it, you can assign from it.*

Only the first operator is not implemented ***inline***. The others just invoke *Store()* and return themselves. Assignment operators *always* return a reference to themselves, to accommodate "stacked" assignments, as in

```
a = b = c;
```

So what does the one remaining assignment do that's special? Easy; it has to check to see if this is an assignment to itself:

```
text & text::operator= (const text & Original)
   {
   if (this != &Original)
     Store (Original.Storage);
   return *this;
   }
```

If you check through *Store()*'s code again, you'll see that it **delete**s the contents of the receiving object before it copies the value from the sending object. If the two objects are one-and-the-same, the result will be an assignment of an empty string.

> *You may wonder who would want to assign an object to itself, and I agree it wouldn't be a useful operation ... sort of like asking Bruce Wayne to keep a secret from Batman. Still, the C++ language allows statements such as this, and we must accommodate it:*
>
> ```
> a = a;
> ```

So, Who's Faster...Flash or Superman?

After assignments, one of the most common operations on text strings is that of comparison. In C, we have to call that icky function *strcmp()* or one of its forty-seven siblings. We'll still need to do that here, of course—there's no point in rewriting the actual algorithm—but at least we can make it invisible to the programmer that we are doing so.

The key is a **protected** function called *Compare()*:

```
class text
   {
     ⇓
     ⇓
   protected:
     int Compare (const text & Test) const;
     ⇓
     ⇓
```

You've seen the *CaseSensitive* property. The idea is that *most* text operations are *not* case sensitive. Still, some are ... and we need to accommodate both. So, when you construct a *text* object, you can optionally specify whether the object is to be case sensitive or not. (The default for each constructor is "not.")

If *either* of the objects in a comparison is case sensitive, a case sensitive comparison is made:

```
int text::Compare (const text & Test) const
   {
   if (CaseSensitive || Test.CaseSensitive)
      return strcmp(Storage, Test.Storage);
   else
      return stricmp(Storage, Test.Storage);
   }
```

That one compiled function is all it takes to supply the horsepower needed for *all* the comparison operators ... and there are many. Not only is every comparison operator represented, but there is an overloaded function for each of the data types whose relationship to *text* we support. (The **long** and **double** data types are omitted, because *text* is supposed to be a text class—*not* a numeric class.) For example, here are the declarations for the equivalence operators alone:

```
class text
   {
      ⇓
      ⇓
public:
      short operator== (const text & Test) const
         { return Compare (Test) == 0; }
      short operator== (const char * Test) const
         { return *this == text (Test); }
      short operator== (char Test) const
         { return *this == text (Test); }
      short operator== (stringID Test) const
         { return (*this) == text (Test); }
      friend short operator== (const char * Test1,
         const text & Test2);
      friend short operator== (char Test1,
         const text & Test2);
      friend short operator== (stringID Test1,
         const text & Test2);
      ⇓
      ⇓
```

Only the first one actually invokes *Compare()*; the others just create temporary *text* objects as needed and then invoke the first. This means only one of the operators could actually have a bug in it; this approach saves a lot of debugging time.

The three **friend** functions handle the case where the comparison is being made to a non-*text* data type on the *left* side of the operator. They, too, are implemented **inline**, but must be coded outside the **class** statement so they are at the bottom of the header file. All they have to do is swap the arguments; for example:

```
inline short operator== (const char * Test1, const text & Test2)
   {
   return (Test2 == Test1);
   }
```

> *I once had a student suggest—seriously!—that a class simply shouldn't allow such a test. Why not leave it to the programmer to write it the way the class supports? Obviously that student was looking at all the tedious code required to fully implement an object class. But the whole idea of object-oriented programming is to build new classes that fit into the language as if they belong there. Besides, no self-respecting super-hero would consider avoiding work at the expense of those ordinary mortals he or she is protecting.*

All six comparison operators are invoked, and I won't bother taking up space here with them because, except for the operator itself, the code is all identical.

I will point out, though, that only equivalence (==) and non-equivalence (!=) are commutative—only they allow *Test1* and *Test2* to be reversed without changing the operator, too. Table 5.1 provides the set of equivalent operations, for your convenience.

The Hero's Sidekick

Just as a super-hero's sidekick is a diminutive version of himself or herself, the subscript operator should return a small portion of the object it operates on. In the case of a *text* object, the programmer would expect to be able to subscript one as if it were a C-style string, retrieving a single character:

Table 5.1   The Set of Equivalent Operations

Test1 == Test2	Test2 == Test1
Test1 < Test2	Test2 >= Test1
Test1 <= Test2	Test2 > Test1
Test1 > Test2	Test2 <= Test1
Test1 >= Test2	Test2 < Test1
Test1 != Test2	Test2 != Test1

```
char & text::operator[] (int i)
  {
  static char X = ' ';
  if ((i >= 0) && (i < Length))
    return Storage[i];
  else
    return X;
  }
```

Of course, we want the *text* subscript to be safe from invalid index values; so, instead of crashing the system as an invalid index will do with a standard C string, *text* returns a handy character stored just for that purpose. Also note that the function returns, not a **char**, but a *reference* to a **char**. This allows the subscripted element to be used on *either side* of an assignment operator, just as can be done with regular C-style strings.

But we don't have to stop there. C++ doesn't limit us to numeric subscripts! So, why not implement a lookup function as a subscript? It could be used like the *instr()* function in Basic:

```
int Position;
text MyText ("Can you find this text?");
Position = MyText["find this"]; // Position == 8
```

Here's the function:

```
int text::operator[] (text SearchFor) const
  {
  char * Test;
  char * Start;
  text Temp;
  if (CaseSensitive || SearchFor.CaseSensitive)
    Start = Test = Storage;
  else
    {
    Temp = UpCase();
    Start = Test = Temp.Storage;
    SearchFor = SearchFor.UpCase();
    }

  Test = strchr (Test, SearchFor.Storage[0]);
  while (Test)
    if (strncmp (Test, SearchFor.Storage,
        SearchFor.Length) ==  0)
      return (int) (Test - Start);
    else
      Test = strchr (++Test, SearchFor.Storage[0]);

  return -1;
  }
```

If neither of the objects demands case sensitivity, a copy is made of the text being searched; both are shifted to upper case (using a method we haven't examined yet). Then the standard C library functions *strchr()* and *strncmp()* are used to attempt to locate the desired text in the source. If found, the offset from the beginning of the text is returned; if not, a -1 is returned.

But we aren't done yet! Remember that *range* class declared and defined at the top of the header file? I said we'd get to it later—and this is later. It's not very likely that anyone would bother to declare a *range* object and let it hang around (though you certainly could). The convenience is in subscripting with a *temporary*:

```
text SubText;
SubText = MyBigText[range (13, 29)];
```

Now that you know how it's to be used, here's the code:

```
text text::operator[] (range Range) const
    {
    register Count = Range.Last - Range.First + 1;
    if ( (Count < 0) || (Count > (Length - Range.First)) )
      Count = (Length - Range.First);
    text Temp;
    Temp.Clear();
    Temp.Storage = new char [Count + 1];
    memcpy (Temp.Storage, &Storage[Range.First], Count);
    Temp.Storage[Temp.Length = Count] = 0;
    return Temp;
    }
```

Elastic Lad to the Rescue!

A common operation on strings, and one botched awfully by the C standard library, is the *append*. You've got one string, and you want to make it longer by appending another string to it. This should be easy and efficient, right? But a series of appends only makes a string longer, and longer...and the *strcat()* function in the C standard library begins *every* operation by searching from the beginning of the string for its end. Besides, it's awkward to type, and sounds like a function that might have written by Catwoman.

In Basic, PL/I, and most other civilized languages, the concatenation operation is signaled by the addition operator; so that's how we'll implement it for the *text* class.

Generally with the operators that allow both an assigned and non-assigned variety, the assignment is the easiest one to implement first. Here are the declarations:

```
class text
   {
      ⇓
      ⇓
   text & operator+= (const text & Append);
   text & operator+= (const char * Append)
      { return *this += text (Append); }
   text & operator+= (const char Append)
      { return *this += text (Append); }
   text & operator+= (stringID Append)
      { return *this += text (Append); }
      ⇓
      ⇓
```

The first overloaded version, the one that appends another *text* object, is again the one that does the work:

```
text & text::operator+= (const text & Append)
   {
   char * Temp = Storage;
   Storage = new char [Length + Append.Length + 1];
   strcpy (Storage, Temp);
   strcpy (&Storage[Length], Append.Storage);
   Length += Append.Length;
   delete [] Temp;
   return *this;
   }
```

The original address for *Storage* is saved in *Temp*, a new buffer is allocated, and the original value is copied into it followed by the characters to be appended. Note that *strcat()* is *not* used; thanks to *Length* we already *know* where to start the append part of the operation so the more efficient *strcpy()* works just fine.

Now that the assigned addition operator is coded, implementing the addition operator is trivial:

```
class text
   {
      ⇓
      ⇓
   text operator+ (text Append) const;
   text operator+ (const char * Append) const
      { return *this + text (Append); }
   text operator+ (const char Append) const
      { return *this + text (Append); }
   text operator+ (stringID Append) const
      { return *this + text (Append); }
   friend text operator+ (const char * Original,
      const text & Append);
   friend text operator+ (const char Original,
```

```
        const text & Append);
    friend text operator+ (stringID Original,
        const text & Append);
    ⇓
    ⇓
```

As with the other operators, the one that does the work is the one that accepts another *text* object as a parameter. Notice, though, that this is *not* a reference to a *text*—it's a copy:

```
text text::operator+ (text Append) const
    {
    text Original (*this);
    return Original += Append;
    }

text operator+ (const char * Original, const text & Append)
    {
    return text (Original) += Append;
    }

text operator+ (const char Original, const text & Append)
    {
    return text (Original) += Append;
    }

text operator+ (stringID Original, const text & Append)
    {
    return text (Original) += Append;
    }
    }
```

For some reason, Borland's compiler declined to make these functions **inline***, and I never fight a compiler on this issue. Some battles are best left unfought.*

Metallo, The Villain without a Heart

The next most common operation is to chop out a chunk from the middle of a *text* string. This might be done to remove a specific substring (removing one of the "veries" from "Metallo is very very dangerous") or to take out a piece based solely on location (whitespace from a machine-readable report being converted into database entries). We already have most of the tools we need to complete this job at super-speed. We'll identify this operation with the minus operator, naturally. Here are the declarations:

```
class text
   {
      ⇓
      ⇓
      text & operator-= (text SearchFor);
      text & operator-= (range Range);

      text operator- (text SearchFor) const;
      text operator- (range Range) const;
      ⇓
      ⇓
```

And here's the implementation:

```
text & text::operator-= (text SearchFor)
   {
   int Start = (*this)[SearchFor];
   if (Start > -1)
      *this = Left(Start) + Mid (Start + SearchFor.Length);
   return *this;
   }

text & text::operator-= (range Range)
   {
   *this = Left (Range.First) +
      Mid (Range.Last + 1, Range.Last - Range.First);
   return *this;
   }

text text::operator- (text SearchFor) const
   {
   return text (*this) -= SearchFor;
   }

text text::operator- (range Range) const
   {
   return text (*this) -= Range;
   }
```

The only tools here you haven't seen are *Left()* and *Mid()*. If you've ever coded in Basic, though, you'll recognize the names and know what they do. (We'll code the C++ versions ourselves in just a moment.)

Triplicate Girl Surrounds the Villains

Triplicate Girl, in case you've forgotten, was born on a planet with three suns and so has the power to become three people. (Good thing she didn't come from a globular cluster!) We often want to take a short *text* object and append one, or three, or many copies of itself. That is obviously a job for the multiplication operator:

```
class text
  {
    ⇓
    ⇓
    text & operator*= (int RepeatCount);
    text operator* (int RepeatCount) const;
    ⇓
    ⇓
```

This one was kind of a fun little challenge—a challenge because I didn't want the overhead of multiple append operations and so had to actually *think* a little; and fun, because I didn't have to think a *lot*:

```
text & text::operator*= (int RepeatCount)
  {
  char * Temp (Storage);
  int TempLength (Length);
  Storage = new char [(Length *= RepeatCount) + 1];
  register i (0);
  for (register c = 0; c < RepeatCount; c++)
    {
    memcpy (&Storage[i], Temp, TempLength);
    i += TempLength;
    }
  Storage[i] = 0;
  delete[] Temp;
  return *this;
  }
```

Revealing That Secret Identity

Casts, which are *also* operators, should be supplied so that anything the object can be constructed as, can be rendered as shown here:

```
class text
  {
    ⇓
    ⇓
    operator long () const { return atol (Storage); }
    operator double () const { return atof (Storage); }
    operator const char * () const  { return Storage; }
    ⇓
    ⇓
```

The casts to **long** and **double** complete the binary/text conversions provided by the constructors. They are implemented ***inline*** so there's no additional machine overhead—and no programmer overhead of trying to remember bizarre function names like *atol()* and *atof()*.

*Another common purpose for casts is to provide safe access to the object's hidden, internal parts; and, in this case, one does just that. However, the cast to **const char ***, which returns the address of Storage, is a bit tricky because the programmer using this class must not be allowed to use a text object in place of a C-style string if the string is to be written to—at least, not without special preparation. That's because text is responsible for allocating memory for the internal buffer in which the text is stored. It is safe, however, to provide a pointer to the buffer in cases where the data that pointer points to, will only be read.*

MFC provides a cast to **const char** *; Borland does not but they *do* have a function that returns a **const char** *. In this case we copy MFC; it's a *lot* more convenient.

Still, we need a way to use *text* objects with existing, C-string functions if they are to be useful. We'll have to pre-allocate the buffer, and then trim it to size. This is accomplished by methods *LockBuffer()* and *UnlockBuffer()*. This might be used, say, in a call to the Windows API function, *GetWindowText()*:

```
text Caption;
GetWindowText (Window, Caption.LockBuffer(128), 128);
Caption.UnlockBuffer ();
```

The methods are declared as follows:

```
class text
    {
        ⇓
        ⇓
    char * LockBuffer (int RequiredSize);
    void UnlockBuffer (int NewSize = -1);
    long GetLength(void) const { return Length; }
        ⇓
        ⇓
```

LockBuffer() only has to allocate the requested number of characters, which it does using the *Store()* method we already know so well:

```
char * text::LockBuffer (int RequiredSize)
    {
    Store (' ', RequiredSize);
    return Storage;
    }
```

For *UnlockBuffer()*, I really wanted to figure out a way to truncate the buffer without having to copy the string, but couldn't. I also considered just letting the extra, unused bytes hang around, but that didn't seem right either. So, we wind up reallocating the text after all:

```
void text::UnlockBuffer (int NewSize)
   {
   if (NewSize == -1)
     NewSize = strlen (Storage);
   if (NewSize < Length)
     {
     char * Temp = Storage;
     Storage = new char [NewSize + 1];
     strcpy (Storage, Temp);
     Length = NewSize;
     delete [] Temp;
     }
   }
```

Divide and Conquer

We already saw the *Left()* and *Mid()* methods used (by the subtraction operator). If there's a *Left()* you'd probably figure there's a *Right()*:

```
text text::Left (int Count) const
   {
   if (Count > Length) Count = Length;
   text Temp;
   Temp.Clear();
   Temp.Storage = new char [Count + 1];
   memcpy (Temp.Storage, Storage, Count);
   Temp.Storage[Temp.Length = Count] = 0;
   return Temp;
   }
```

```
text text::Right (int Count) const
   {
   if (Count > Length) Count = Length;
   text Temp;
   Temp.Clear();
   Temp.Storage = new char [Count + 1];
   memcpy (Temp.Storage, &Storage[Length-Count], Count);
   Temp.Storage[Temp.Length = Count] = 0;
   return Temp;
   }
```

As their counterparts do in Basic, *Left()* returns a substring of *Count* characters, starting from the left; *Right()* returns a substring of *Count* characters, starting from the right.

We all know how I hate abbreviations, but *Mid()* has been used as an abbreviation for "middle" for so long, and in this very context, I won't fight it. Its implementation is abbreviated, too, since it just uses the subscript operator we already wrote:

```
text text::Mid (int Start, int Count) const
    {
    return (*this)[range (Start, Start + Count - 1)];
    }
```

You can also "divide" text into upper and lower case. When people prefer one over the other, they're usually pretty serious about it. The C standard library includes functions (actually, they're macros) that uppercase or lowercase individual characters; so we can make use of those:

```
text text::UpCase (void) const
    {
    text Temp (*this);
    for (register i = 0; i < Temp.Length; i++)
      Temp.Storage[i] = toupper (Temp.Storage[i]);
    return Temp;
    }

text text::DownCase (void) const
    {
    text Temp (*this);
    for (register i = 0; i < Temp.Length; i++)
      Temp.Storage[i] = tolower (Temp.Storage[i]);
    return Temp;
    }
```

We could stop there, but there's an increasing call these days for something called "title case." Here, each letter in a word is set to lowercase except for the first character of each word. In the non-object-oriented world, a programmer would think nothing of coding this operation over and over. We, of course, will have nothing of the sort! So here's the *TitleCase()* method:

```
text text::TitleCase (void) const
    {
    text Temp (*this);
    BOOL AfterSpecial (TRUE);
    Temp.DownCase();
    for (register i = 0; i < Temp.Length; i++)
      if (! isalnum (Temp.Storage[i]))
        AfterSpecial = TRUE;
      else if (AfterSpecial)
        {
        Temp.Storage[i] = toupper (Temp.Storage[i]);
        AfterSpecial = FALSE;
```

```
    }
  return Temp;
  }
```

This code loops through the text buffer, setting a flag when a non-alphanu-meric character is located. (That flag starts out as TRUE, counting the "beginning of the text" as a "special character.") Fortunately, like *UpCase()* and *DownCase()*, *TitleCase()* doesn't need to reallocate the text; the conversion can be done in place.

Testing Your New Powers

One of the wonderful aspects of object-oriented programming is that you can actually *prove* your application. If all of its parts work correctly, the program as a whole works correctly. So time spent testing the methods you've written is time well-spent—certainly more useful than chasing after super-villains!

A proper test program would exercise every single function, making sure that putting data in always gets the expected data out. However, you can still be *reasonably* confident in your class if, as in *text*, most of the methods simply perform conversions and then invoke the worker functions—by testing just the worker functions. To keep our test program to a minimum, that's what I've done. This program should be compiled using the "EasyWin" or "QuickWin" options of your Borland or Microsoft compiler, respectively:

```
#include <windows.h>
#include "text.h"
#include <iostream.h>

void main (void)
  {
  text Test1 ("This is a test string.");
  cout << (const char *) Test1 << endl;

  Test1 = "New text by assignment.";
  cout << (const char *) Test1 << endl;

  Test1 += "..";
  cout << (const char *) Test1 << endl;

  Test1 = Test1.UpCase();
  cout << (const char *) Test1 << endl;
  Test1 = Test1.DownCase();
  cout << (const char *) Test1 << endl;
  Test1 = Test1.TitleCase();
  cout << (const char *) Test1 << endl;
```

```
    Test1 = "Quoting a string";
#ifdef _MSC_VER
    Test1 = (const char *) "\"" + Test1 + (char) '\"';
#else
    Test1 = "\"" + Test1 + (char) '\"';
#endif
    cout << (const char *) Test1 << endl;

    Test1 = 781L;
    Test1 += 'L';
    cout << "As string: " << (const char *) Test1 << endl;
    cout << "As double: " << (double) Test1 << endl;

    Test1 = "Your wretched refuse yearning to breathe free...";
    cout << (const char *) Test1 << endl;

#ifdef _MSC_VER
    cout << "'refuse' at position " << Test1[text("refuse")] << endl;
    cout << "'REFUSE' at position " << Test1[text("REFUSE")] << endl;
    Test1.SetCaseSensitive();
    cout << "'REFUSE' at position " << Test1[text("REFUSE")] << endl;
#else
    cout << "'refuse' at position " << Test1["refuse"] << endl;
    cout << "'REFUSE' at position " << Test1["REFUSE"] << endl;
    Test1.SetCaseSensitive();
    cout << "'REFUSE' at position " << Test1["REFUSE"] << endl;
#endif

    cout << "'" << (const char *) Test1.Left(4) << "'" << endl;
    cout << "'" << (const char *) Test1.Right(7) << "'" << endl;
    cout << "'" << (const char *) Test1.Mid(5, 8) << "'" << endl;

    Test1 -= "refuse ";
    cout << (const char *) Test1 << endl;

    Test1 -= range (33, 37);
    cout << (const char *) Test1 << endl;
    cout << (const char *) Test1[range(5,12)] << endl;

    Test1 = "Ha";
    Test1 *= 10;
    cout << (const char *) Test1 << endl;

    }
```

You'll note there are two places where a **#define** distinguishes between Visual C++ and Borland C++, and slightly different syntax is supplied for each. Visual C++ 1.52 doesn't quite handle ANSI-standard overloaded operators as compatibly as it should and it requires the extra help in figuring out which operator was intended. The wordier code works for Borland C++ as well; but you wouldn't want to type it if you didn't have to.

In the interest of brevity, I have omitted tests for a few of the simpler functions ... the ones I'm certain ... ahem ... can't fail. Of course, I can't recommend that you do that; so feel free to add any permutation you wish.

The Dust Clears

In a battle of giants, it's always the little people who get hurt. Think of the *text* class as one panel of armor in that battle; write similar classes on your own, and who knows: Someday the super-heroes and villains of the software world may just be relegated back to the pages of the comic books where they belong.

Until then, we ordinary mortals will just have to keep on building our vendor-free class libraries ... like the VBX class library we finally have the tools to create ... starting in the next chapter.

Implementing the VBX++ Class Library

6

I
N CHAPTERS 4 AND 5 WE CREATED two class libraries: a vendor-free GDI library and a vendor-free text library. We've now got a reason to code a C++ VBX library, and we have the tools to do it. So ... what is it, exactly, that we intend to build? Perhaps a diagram will help explain it. Figure 6.1 shows the architecture for our system.

VBX++, a C++ class library for the creation of VBXs, will be written vendor-free for compilation with either Visual C++ or Borland C++. It will consist of the following major classes:

- *model*: A base class; you derive a class from this for each custom control to be supported by your VBX. (VBXs can contain more than one control.) The *model* class is a container of properties and events, which are added in *model*'s constructor. You also make one instance of your derived class.

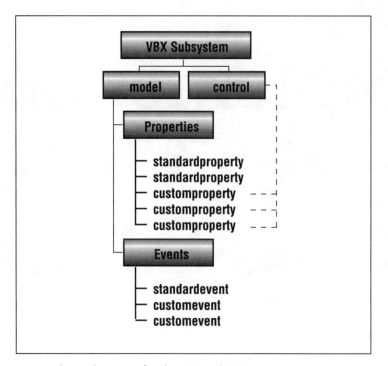

Figure 6.1 The architecture for the VBX subsystem.

- *property* and *event*: Objects of these classes describe control properties and events; they are added to the *model* container. We will also supply pre-defined objects for all the standard properties and events.
- *control*: Objects derived from this class represent each running copy of the control. This is where the message-handling is accomplished. You do not specifically instantiate these objects; they are created dynamically as the underlying controls are created. Custom properties will rely on the *control* to manage their data storage.

Using VBX++: A Preview

Before we see how these classes are implemented, let's look at a quick example of how they might be *used*. Suppose you wanted to make a custom control called "Gradient." This graphical control will support two properties and no events. The class to represent this control might be named *gradient*, and would be derived from *model* thus:

```
class gradient : public model
  {
  public:
    gradient ();
  protected:
    virtual FLONG GetModelFlags (void);
    virtual void
      OnDraw (control & Control,
        devicecontext & dc,
        BOOL Erase,
        rectangle & Rect);
  };
```

The class' constructor has the job of registering, or adding, the control's properties and methods to the object as if it were a simple container:

```
colorproperty
  TopColor ((PSTR) "TopColor"),
  BottomColor ((PSTR) "BottomColor");

gradient::gradient () : model ((PSTR) "Gradient")
  {
  Properties += *Top;
  Properties += *Left;
  Properties += *Height;
  Properties += *Width;
  Properties += TopColor;
  Properties += BottomColor;
  }
```

Note the use of standard properties (which are represented by pointers and must be dereferenced) and custom properties. If there were any events, they'd be added here as well (to an *Events* data member). Also notice that the custom properties are derived, not from a generic *property*, but from a derived class (*colorproperty*) that specifies the property *data type*.

The *GetModelFlags()* method is **virtual**; it overrides the base class method of the same name and its only job is to return the *MODEL* flags you feel pertain to this control:

```
FLONG gradient::GetModelFlags (void)
  {
  return MODEL_fGraphical;
  }
```

The *OnDraw()* method, as shown, uses the portable GDI classes developed in Chapter 4 for the device context and rectangle.

Once the *model*-derived class has been defined, you create one instance of it:

```
gradient Gradient;
```

And that's it! Compile and you've got a VBX custom control. Amazing, isn't it?

Implementing VBX++

Both Microsoft Visual C++ and Borland C++ support precompiled headers, which save a *lot* of compile time—in C++ even more than C. To facilitate this, each of the modules of VBX++ has a **#include** of a single file: VBXXX.H. This file in turn **#include**s all the other header files:

```
#ifndef __VBXXX_H__
#define __VBXXX_H__

#define STRICT
#include <windows.h>

#ifndef VB_VERSION
#include <vbapi.h>
#endif

#include "text.h"
#include "portagdi.h"
#include "control.h"
#include "events.h"
#include "props.h"
#include "model.h"

#endif
```

Out of force-of-habit as much as anything, I put the usual one-time-only trick of processing this file only if a **#define** hasn't yet been defined. That's the purpose of the lines

```
#ifndef __VBXXX_H__
#define __VBXXX_H__
```

and the final **#endif**. Too bad Microsoft didn't include this in VBAPI.H; if you accidentally **#include** this file more than once, you wind up with hundreds of "duplicate declaration" errors.

TEXT.H and PORTAGDI.H are the header files for the two stand-alone classes that VBX++ will use. Of all the modules, they do not **#include** VBXXX.H, because they *are* stand-alone—they only need TEXT.H and PORTAGDI.H, respectively. The other header files are those of the VBX++ components.

VBX++ is packaged as a library with header files. That means our project target is a .LIB file.

While it is commonly recommended that development of a multi-class project use a separate pair of code modules for each class, when classes are as closely related as these—especially considering they will inevitably be used together—it makes sense to package them as a single pair. That doesn't mean PORTAGDI will be crammed into VBXXX.CPP, of course—that's a separate set of related classes. But all the classes we are about to study are declared in VBXXX.H, and defined in VBXXX.CPP.

(I have, however, combined all the GDI classes into PORTAGDI.CPP for convenience, since now that chapter's over, we can treat all those classes as of a piece.)

Microsoft Visual C++ Compiler Options

When creating this project, you must remember two things: First, your target type is "Static Library". Second, do *not* check "Use Microsoft Foundation Classes". The New Project dialog should look more or less like the one shown in Figure 6.2.

After creating the new project, add the components. If you intend to type the code yourself, just add the module names; otherwise, after copying the modules from the code disk to your project directory, add them all to the project.

You also need to change a few compiler options, namely:

1. Make sure you compile for Large Model—even though this is an .LIB project, the library will eventually be used to build VBXs, which are DLLs.

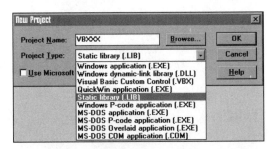

Figure 6.2   Selecting settings with Visual C++'s New Project dialog for VBX++.

2. Consider setting the *Code Generator..CPU* option to compile for 80386 CPUs or better. Windows 3.1, now more or less obsolete, was the last version of Windows to support the 80286 CPUs ... and continuing to support *those* PCs may be carrying this transition period thing a bit too far.

3. Under Precompiled Header options, check "Automatic Use of Precompiled Headers" ... but do *not* type VBXXX.H in the space provided; if you do, MSVC will choke on the TEXT.CPP and PORTAGDI.CPP modules that don't **#include** this file.

4. Under Windows Prolog/Epilog options, select "Protected Mode DLL Functions".

Or, you can take the easy way and copy VBXXX.MAK from the code disk. But at least study the options that have been selected and understand why they were.

Borland C++ Compiler Options

When creating this project, you must remember two things: First, your target type is "Static Library". Second, do *not* check "OWL" or "Class Library". The New Target dialog should look more or less like the one shown in Figure 6.3.

After creating the new project, add the components. If you intend to type the code yourself, just add the module names; otherwise, after copying the modules from the code disk to your project directory, add them all to the project.

Figure 6.3 Selecting settings with Borland C++'s New Target dialog for VBX++.

You also need to change a few compiler options, namely:

1. Under *Precompiled Header* options, type in VBXXX.H under "Stop precompiling after header file:". The TEXT.CPP and PORTAGDI.CPP modules that don't **#include** this file will not be able to use the precompiled headers, but the other modules will.

2. Consider setting the *16-Bit Compiler..Processor* option to compile for 80386 CPUs. Windows 3.1, now obsolete, was the last version of Windows to support the 80286 CPUs.

3. Under *16-Bit Compiler..Entry/Exit Code* options, select "Windows DLL, Explicit Functions Exported".

Or, you can take the easy way and copy VBXXX.IDE from the code disk. But at least study the options that have been selected and understand why they were.

Creating the model Class

VBX++ hooks into the "C" world of the Visual Basic CDK by encapsulating classes from the CDK structures: The *MODEL* structure is a property of the *model* class; the *PROPINFO* structure is managed by the *standardproperty* class, and so on. In this section we'll study the *model* class.

The class declaration for *model* is quite lengthy; I prefer to present it at once, so you can see it in context; but we'll talk about each member as we implement it:

```
#ifndef __MODEL_H__
#define __MODEL_H__

class model
   {
   // Management of static list of instantiated models
   //   including registration
   friend BOOL far pascal _export VBINITCC (USHORT, BOOL);
   friend VOID far pascal _export VBTERMCC (void);
   public:
      enum { MaxModels = 12 };
   private:
      static UINT ModelCount;
      static model * ModelList[MaxModels];
      static USHORT RunVersion;
      static BOOL Runtime;
      MODEL Model;
      static BOOL RegisterModels (USHORT aRunVersion, BOOL aRuntime);
      BOOL RegisterModel ();
      void SetModelData (void);
```

```
protected:
   virtual USHORT GetModelVersion (void);
   virtual FLONG GetModelFlags (void);
   virtual FSHORT GetClassStyles (void);
   virtual FLONG GetWindowStyles (void);
   virtual WORD GetButtonBitmapBaseID (void);
   virtual PSTR GetDefaultControlName (void);
   virtual PSTR GetParentClassName (void);
   virtual BYTE GetDefaultPropertyIndex (void);
   virtual BYTE GetDefaultEventIndex (void);
   virtual BYTE GetValuePropertyIndex (void);
   virtual BYTE GetControlVersion (void);

// Construction of model, including standard properties and events
public:
   model (PSTR aName);
protected:
   propertieslist Properties;
   eventslist Events;
private:
   static standardproperty * Name;
   static standardproperty * Index;
protected:
   static standardproperty * Hwnd;
   static standardproperty * BackColor;
   static standardproperty * ForeColor;
   static standardproperty * Left;
   static standardproperty * Top;
   static standardproperty * Width;
   static standardproperty * Height;
   static standardproperty * Enabled;
   static standardproperty * Visible;
   static standardproperty * MousePointer;
   static standardproperty * Caption;
   static standardproperty * FontName;
   static standardproperty * FontBold;
   static standardproperty * FontItalic;
   static standardproperty * FontStrike;
   static standardproperty * FontUnder;
   static standardproperty * FontSize;
   static standardproperty * TabIndex;
   static standardproperty * Parent;
   static standardproperty * DragMode;
   static standardproperty * DragIcon;
   static standardproperty * BorderStyleOff;
   static standardproperty * TabStop;
   static standardproperty * Tag;
   static standardproperty * Text;
   static standardproperty * BorderStyleOn;
   static standardproperty * ClipControls;
   static standardproperty * None;
   static standardproperty * HelpContextID;
   static standardproperty * LinkMode;
   static standardproperty * LinkItem;
```

```
   static standardproperty * LinkTopic;
   static standardproperty * LinkTimeout;
   static standardproperty * LeftNoRun;
   static standardproperty * TopNoRun;
   static standardproperty * Align;
   static standardproperty * ImeMode;
   static standardproperty * DataSource;
   static standardproperty * DataField;
   static standardproperty * DataChanged;
private:
   static void ConstructStandardProperties (void);
protected:
   static standardevent * Click;
   static standardevent * DblClick;
   static standardevent * DragDrop;
   static standardevent * DragOver;
   static standardevent * GotFocus;
   static standardevent * KeyDown;
   static standardevent * KeyPress;
   static standardevent * KeyUp;
   static standardevent * LostFocus;
   static standardevent * MouseDown;
   static standardevent * MouseMove;
   static standardevent * MouseUp;
   static standardevent * LinkError;
   static standardevent * LinkOpen;
   static standardevent * LinkClose;
   static standardevent * LinkNotify;
   static standardevent * LinkChange;
   static standardevent * ObsoleteEvent;
private:
   void ConstructStandardEvents (void);

// Destructor
public:
   ~model ();
private:
   void DestroyStandardProperties (void);
   void DestroyStandardEvents (void);

// Message dispatching
friend LRESULT CALLBACK _export CtlProc (HCTL, HWND,
     USHORT, USHORT, long);
   controlbag Controls;
   static model * FindModel (HCTL Handle);
   LRESULT Dispatch (control &, USHORT, USHORT, long);
protected:
   virtual LRESULT OnInitialize (control & Control) ;
   virtual void OnActivate (control & Control, UINT active,
     BOOL minimized, HWND hWndOther);
   virtual void OnCancelMode (control & Control) ;
   virtual void OnChar (control & Control, UINT Key,
     UINT RepeatCount, UINT flags);
   virtual int OnCharToItem (control & Control, UINT Key,
```

```
      HWND hWndListBox, UINT caretPos);
  virtual void OnClose (control & Control) ;
  virtual LRESULT OnCompareItem (control & Control,
    UINT ControlID, COMPAREITEMSTRUCT far& compareInfo);
  virtual int OnCreate (control & Control,
    CREATESTRUCT far & Create);
  virtual HBRUSH OnCtlColor (control & Control,
    devicecontext & Dc,
    HWND Child, UINT ControlType);
  virtual void OnDeadChar (control & Control, UINT deadKey,
    UINT RepeatCount, UINT flags);
  virtual void OnDeleteItem (control & Control,
    UINT ControlID,
    DELETEITEMSTRUCT far& deleteInfo);
  virtual void OnDestroy (control & Control) ;
  virtual void OnDrawItem (control & Control, UINT ControlID,
    DRAWITEMSTRUCT far& drawInfo);
  virtual void OnDropFiles (control & Control,
    HANDLE DropInfo);
  virtual void OnEnable (control & Control, BOOL Enabled);
  virtual BOOL OnEraseBkgnd (control & Control,
    devicecontext & Dc);
  virtual HFONT OnGetFont (control & Control) ;
  virtual void OnGetMinMaxInfo (control & Control,
    MINMAXINFO far & Info);
  virtual void OnGetText (control & Control, UINT MaxLength,
    LPSTR Buffer);
  virtual UINT OnGetTextLength (control & Control) ;
  virtual void OnHScroll (control & Control, UINT ScrollCode,
    UINT ThumbPos, HWND hWndCtl);
  virtual void OnKeyDown (control & Control, UINT Key,
    UINT RepeatCount, UINT flags);
  virtual void OnKeyUp (control & Control, UINT Key,
    UINT RepeatCount, UINT flags);
  virtual void OnKillFocus (control & Control,
    HWND hWndGetFocus);
  virtual void OnLButtonDblClk (control & Control, UINT Flags,
    point Point);
  virtual void OnLButtonDown (control & Control, UINT Flags,
    point Point);
  virtual void OnLButtonUp (control & Control, UINT Flags,
    point Point);
  virtual void OnMButtonDblClk (control & Control, UINT Flags,
    point Point);
  virtual void OnMButtonDown (control & Control, UINT Flags,
    point Point);
  virtual void OnMButtonUp (control & Control, UINT Flags,
    point Point);
  virtual void OnMeasureItem (control & Control,
    UINT ControlID,
    MEASUREITEMSTRUCT far& measureInfo);
  virtual void OnMouseMove (control & Control, UINT Flags,
    point Point);
  virtual void OnMove (control & Control, point clientOrigin);
```

```
    virtual UINT OnNCHitTest (control & Control, point  Point);
    void OnPaint (control & Control) ;
    virtual void OnDraw (devicecontext & Dc, BOOL Erase,
      rectangle Rect);
    virtual int OnPower (control & Control, UINT PowerEvent);
    virtual BOOL OnQueryEndSession (control & Control) ;
    virtual void OnRButtonDblClk (control & Control, UINT Flags,
      point Point);
    virtual void OnRButtonDown (control & Control, UINT Flags,
      point Point);
    virtual void OnRButtonUp (control & Control, UINT Flags,
      point Point);
    virtual BOOL OnSetCursor (control & Control,
      HWND hWndCursor,
      UINT hitTest, UINT mouseMsg);
    virtual void OnSetFocus (control & Control,
      HWND hWndLostFocus);
    virtual void OnSetFont (control & Control, HFONT hFont,
      BOOL redraw);
    virtual void OnSetText (control & Control, LPSTR Buffer);
    virtual void OnSize (control & Control, size Size);
    virtual void OnSpoolerStatus (control & Control,
      UINT JobStatus, UINT JobsLeft);
    virtual void OnSysColorChange (control & Control) ;
    virtual void OnTimeChange (control & Control) ;
    virtual void OnTimer (control & Control, UINT TimerID);
    virtual int OnVKeyToItem (control & Control, UINT Key,
      HWND ListBox, UINT caretPos);
    virtual void OnVScroll (control & Control, UINT ScrollCode,
      UINT ThumbPos, HWND hWndCtl);
    virtual void OnWinIniChange (control & Control,
      LPSTR Section);
    virtual void VbCancelMode (control & Control,
      HWND CapturingWindow);
    void VbPaint(HDC dc, LPRECT pRect);
    LRESULT OnMethod (control & Control, WORD MethodID,
      LONG lParam);
    virtual LRESULT OnMethodAddItem (control & Control,
      LPSTR Item, int Index);
    virtual LRESULT OnMethodClear (control & Control);
    virtual LRESULT OnMethodDrag (control & Control,
      int Command);
    virtual LRESULT OnMethodLinkSend (control & Control);
    virtual LRESULT OnMethodMove (control & Control,
      int Count, LONG Left, LONG Top, LONG Width, LONG Height);
    virtual LRESULT OnMethodRemoveItem (control & Control,
      int Index);
    virtual LRESULT OnMethodRefresh (control & Control);
    enum ZOrderCommand { BringToFront, SendToBack };
    virtual LRESULT OnMethodZOrder (control & Control,
      ZOrderCommand Command);
  };

#endif
```

What takes up so much space, of course, are the prototypes for the various message-handling functions.

Now, let's look at MODEL.CPP.

Ironically, after staring at that enormous class declaration, the very first function we find in MODEL.CPP isn't a class member at all! But there are certain "C"-type functions that must be supplied, preferably without any effort on the part of the programmer using VBX++. For example, every DLL (a VBX, remember, is a type of DLL) must have a *LibMain()* function. Now, you know about C++'s *name mangling*, where function names are altered internally to allow for overloaded functions. *LibMain()* must be named *exactly* that, no mangling allowed. The only way to avoid mangling is to declare the function prototype within an **extern "c"** statement. Fortunately, *LibMain()* is pre-declared in WINDOWS.H just that way. Our *LibMain()* obtains and stores the VBX's instance handle:

```
#include "model.h"

HANDLE LibInstance = 0;

int far pascal LibMain (HINSTANCE Instance, WORD, WORD HeapSize, LPSTR)
   {
   if (HeapSize > 0)
      UnlockData (0);
   LibInstance = Instance;
   return TRUE;
   }
```

We'll also need those two CDK-required functions, *VBINITCC()* and *VBTERMCC()*. And, again, those functions must be declared or defined in such a way as to avoid name mangling. We declared them as **friend** functions of the *model* class. Here they are:

```
extern "C" BOOL far pascal _export VBINITCC
   (
   USHORT Version,
   BOOL Runtime
   )
   {
   return model::RegisterModels (Version, Runtime);
   }

extern "C" VOID far pascal _export VBTERMCC (void)
   {
   }
```

VBINITCC() always has the job of registering any *MODEL* structures in the VBX, one per custom control. Here's where we tie in the *model* object, by invoking its **static** *RegisterModels()* member.

You actually cause a *model* object to be used by making one instance of it at the static level. That means that the *model* class must maintain a list of instantiated *model* objects. Such a list is maintained as **static** properties that all *model* objects share:

```
UINT model::ModelCount = 0;
model * model::ModelList[model::MaxModels];
USHORT model::RunVersion;
BOOL model::Runtime;
```

Objects add themselves to this list when they are constructed, as we'll see shortly. The *RegisterModels()* method must enumerate this list, telling each *model* in it to "register thyself:"

```
BOOL model::RegisterModels (USHORT aRunVersion, BOOL aRuntime)
   {
   RunVersion = aRunVersion;
   Runtime = aRuntime;
   for (register UINT i = 0; i < ModelCount; i++)
      if (! ModelList[i]->RegisterModel ())
         return FALSE;
   return TRUE;
   }
```

Each individual *model* registers itself by filling in its *MODEL* structure and then invoking *VBRegisterModel()*, as we recall from the C version VBX skeleton:

```
BOOL model::RegisterModel ()
   {
   SetModelData ();
   return VBRegisterModel (LibInstance, &Model);
   }
```

SetModelData() is a function that makes sure the *MODEL* structure is properly filled in before trying to use it to register. It accomplishes this by invoking a number of **virtual** functions, more or less one per field:

```
struct VBDATA
   {
   model far * Model;
   };
typedef VBDATA far * LPVBDATA;
```

```
void model::SetModelData()
  {
  Model.usVersion = GetModelVersion();
  Model.fl = GetModelFlags() | MODEL_fInitMsg;
  Model.pctlproc = CtlProc;
  Model.fsClassStyle = GetClassStyles();
  Model.flWndStyle = GetWindowStyles();
  Model.cbCtlExtra = sizeof (VBDATA);
  for (register i = 0; i < Properties.GetCount(); i++)
    {
    register UINT Size (Properties[i].GetStorageSize());
    if (Size)
       Properties[i].SetStorageOffset (Model.cbCtlExtra);
    Model.cbCtlExtra += Size;
    }
  Model.idBmpPalette = GetButtonBitmapBaseID();
  Model.npszDefCtlName = GetDefaultControlName();
  Model.npszParentClassName = GetParentClassName();
  Model.npproplist = Properties.GetList();
  Model.npeventlist = Events.GetList();
  Model.nDefProp = GetDefaultPropertyIndex();
  Model.nDefEvent = GetDefaultEventIndex();
  Model.nValueProp = GetValuePropertyIndex();
  switch (Model.usVersion)
    {
    case 100: Model.usCtlVersion = 1; break;
    case 200: Model.usCtlVersion = 2; break;
    default: Model.usCtlVersion = GetControlVersion();
    }
  }
```

Although most of the field assignments are straightforward, there are a few that bear some explanation. For example, to fill in the *Model.fl* field the function calls *GetModelFlags()* but it also *requires* the *MODEL_fInitMsg* flag. (This flag forces a *VBM_INITIALIZE* message to be sent as the control is being created. As you'll see shortly, we *must* receive one of these messages for each control, as it is created.) The *CtlProc()* address is that of the **friend** function declared with the rest of the class; this is the control procedure.

The *Model.cbCtlExtra* field must contain the amount of space used to store the control's custom properties; the **for** loop calculates this number by querying each of the properties in the *model*'s *Properties* collection. Finally, the *Model.usCtlVersion* field is adjusted if the programmer requested a version other than 300; the purpose of this field was different for VB versions 1 and 2.

The **virtual** functions themselves are all straightforward; they exist only to return common default values for the fields. The programmer will override any of these functions as needed, to provide different values:

```
USHORT model::GetModelVersion (void)
    {
    return VB300_VERSION;
    }

FLONG model::GetModelFlags (void)
    {
    return MODEL_fFocusOk | MODEL_fArrows;
    }

FSHORT model::GetClassStyles (void)
    {
    return CS_VREDRAW | CS_HREDRAW;
    }

FLONG model::GetWindowStyles (void)
    {
    return WS_BORDER;
    }

WORD model::GetButtonBitmapBaseID (void)
    {
    return 8000;
    }

PSTR model::GetDefaultControlName (void)
    {
    return Model.npszClassName;
    }

PSTR model::GetParentClassName (void)
    {
    return NULL;
    }

BYTE model::GetDefaultPropertyIndex (void)
    {
    return 0;
    }

BYTE model::GetDefaultEventIndex (void)
    {
    return 0;
    }

BYTE model::GetValuePropertyIndex (void)
    {
    return -1;
    }

BYTE model::GetControlVersion (void)
    {
    return 100;
    }
```

Those are the methods that directly or indirectly support the *model*'s **static** properties. Now we can look at the constructor:

```
model::model (PSTR aClassName)
   {
   if (! ModelCount)
      {
      ConstructStandardProperties ();
      ConstructStandardEvents ();
      }
   if (ModelCount < MaxModels)
      ModelList[ModelCount++] = this;
   Model.npszClassName = aClassName;
   Properties += *Name;
   Properties += *Index;
   }
```

As expected, the *model* adds itself to the **static** *ModelList* property. But before that, it checks to see if this is the *first model* being registered. If it is, it constructs the standard properties and events. These, too, are **static** members of the class. Finally, the "Name" and "Index" properties, which are always required, are added to the *Properties* container.

Next in the implementation file are the **static** instantiations of the standard properties themselves, plus the method that initializes them:

```
standardproperty * model::Name = NULL;
standardproperty * model::Index = NULL;
standardproperty * model::Hwnd = NULL;
standardproperty * model::BackColor = NULL;
standardproperty * model::ForeColor = NULL;
standardproperty * model::Left = NULL;
standardproperty * model::Top = NULL;
     ⇓
     ⇓
standardproperty * model::DataSource = NULL;
standardproperty * model::DataField = NULL;
standardproperty * model::DataChanged = NULL;

void model::ConstructStandardProperties (void)
   {
   Name = new standardproperty (PPROPINFO_STD_NAME);
   Index = new standardproperty (PPROPINFO_STD_INDEX);
   Hwnd = new standardproperty (PPROPINFO_STD_HWND);
   BackColor = new standardproperty (PPROPINFO_STD_BACKCOLOR);
   ForeColor = new standardproperty (PPROPINFO_STD_FORECOLOR);
   Left = new standardproperty (PPROPINFO_STD_LEFT);
   Top = new standardproperty (PPROPINFO_STD_TOP);
   ⇓
   ⇓
   DataField =
      new standardproperty (PPROPINFO_STD_DATAFIELD,
```

```
      VB300_VERSION);
  DataChanged =
    new standardproperty (PPROPINFO_STD_DATACHANGED,
      VB300_VERSION);
  }
```

This was not my first choice. I wanted to simply place the objects themselves in the data segment, letting the system exercise the constructors before execution of the main module. Unfortunately, experimentation proved I couldn't count on the properties' constructors being invoked before the *model*'s constructors; and that was a requirement. This technique works, and is repeated for the standard events:

```
standardevent * model::Click = NULL;
standardevent * model::DblClick = NULL;
standardevent * model::DragDrop = NULL;
  ⇓
  ⇓
standardevent * model::ObsoleteEvent = NULL;

void model::ConstructStandardEvents (void)
  {
  Click = new standardevent (PEVENTINFO_STD_CLICK);
  DblClick = new standardevent (PEVENTINFO_STD_DBLCLICK);
  DragDrop = new standardevent (PEVENTINFO_STD_DRAGDROP);
  ⇓
  ⇓
  ObsoleteEvent =
    new standardevent (PEVENTINFO_STD_NONE, VB200_VERSION);
  }
```

The *model* destructor, then, must **delete** all the standard properties the constructor created—but only when the last model-derived object is destroyed:

```
model::~model ()
  {
  if (! (-ModelCount))
    {
    DestroyStandardProperties ();
    DestroyStandardEvents ();
    }
  }
```

The methods to actually **delete** those objects from the heap are tedious but necessary:

```
void model::DestroyStandardProperties (void)
  {
  delete Name;
  delete Index;
  delete Hwnd;
```

```
    delete BackColor;
    delete ForeColor;
    delete Left;
    delete Top;
        ⇓
        ⇓
    delete DataSource;
    delete DataField;
    delete DataChanged;
    }

void model::DestroyStandardEvents (void)
    {
    delete Click;
    delete DblClick;
    delete DragDrop;
        ⇓
        ⇓
    delete ObsoleteEvent;
    }
```

Now that we've seen how the *model* object gets put into the **static** list of objects, how it gets registered, and how it gets constructed and destroyed (along with the standard properties and events), we're ready to see it in action.

> *As you'll recall, all VBX controls have a* control procedure, *just as all windows have a window procedure. The two are quite similar. In fact, the messages that go to a window procedure go through a control procedure; the difference is that a control procedure receives additional messages. Most of these messages have a* VBM_ *prefix.*

The trick is that when a control procedure receives a message, it gets a *control handle*—not, of course, a pointer to a control object, and *certainly* not a pointer to a *model*! We have to resolve that. Let's look at the control procedure in sections:

```
LRESULT far pascal _export CtlProc
    (
    HCTL Handle,
    HWND Window,
    USHORT Msg,
    USHORT wParam,
    long lParam
    )
    {
```

```
LPVBDATA VbData = (LPVBDATA) VBDerefControl (Handle);
control * Control = NULL;

if (Msg == VBM_INITIALIZE)
   {
   VbData->Model = model::FindModel (Handle);
   Control = new control (Handle);
   VbData->Model->Controls += *Control;
   VbData->Model->OnInitialize (*Control);
   return 0;
   }
else
   Control = VbData->Model->Controls.Find (Handle);
⇓
⇓
```

One of the many times this procedure is invoked, per control instance, will be the *first* time. On those subsequent calls, we'll be able to locate the associated *control* object simply by searching the list of controls for it.

The first time is different, because there is *not yet an associated* control *object!* Fortunately, thanks to the flag we insisted on setting in the *MODEL* structure, we'll get a special first-time message: *VBM_INITIALIZE.* In response to that we figure out what *model* this control is an example of, and create a *control* object to represent it.

Although we want the majority of processing to take place in *control* methods, there are a couple of messages other than *VBM_INITIALIZE* that must be treated specially. One is *WM_NCCREATE*, which arrives for any control represented by a "real" window. Assuming that the default processing succeeds, we use the message to save the window handle—in the case of a graphical control, this "handle" will be NULL—associated with this control:

```
⇓
⇓
if (Msg == WM_NCCREATE)
   if (VBDefControlProc (Handle, Window,
         WM_NCCREATE, 0, lParam))
      {
      Control->Window = Window;
      return TRUE;
      }
   else
      return FALSE;
⇓
⇓
```

Finally, the *WM_NCDESTROY* message signals the death of the physical control, and therefore notifies us to **delete** the object representation of it also:

```
⇓
⇓
if (Msg == WM_NCDESTROY)
   {
   VbData->Model->Controls -= *Control;
   delete Control;
   return VBDefControlProc (Handle,
      Window, WM_NCDESTROY, 0, 0);
   }
⇓
⇓
```

The only task left is to separate the messages directed at standard properties to the default handler, and direct all remaining messages to the *model's Dispatch()* function:

```
⇓
⇓
switch (Msg)
   {
   case VBM_CHECKPROPERTY:
   case VBM_GETPROPERTY:
   case VBM_GETPROPERTYHSZ:
   case VBM_INITPROPPOPUP:
   case VBM_LOADPROPERTY:
   case VBM_LOADTEXTPROPERTY:
   case VBM_SAVEPROPERTY:
   case VBM_SAVETEXTPROPERTY:
   case VBM_SETPROPERTY:
      if (VbData->Model->Properties[wParam].IsStandard())
         return VBDefControlProc (Handle, Window,
            Msg, wParam, lParam);
   }

if (Control)
   return VbData->Model->Dispatch (*Control, Msg,
      wParam, lParam);
else
   return VBDefControlProc (Handle, Window,
      Msg, wParam, lParam);
}
```

FindModel() simply runs through the **static** list of instantiated *models*:

```
model * model::FindModel (HCTL Handle)
   {
   MODEL * SearchModel = VBGetControlModel (Handle);
   for (register i = 0; i < ModelCount; i++)
      if (&(ModelList[i]->Model) == SearchModel)
```

```
         return ModelList[i];
  return NULL;
  }
```

The *Dispatch()* method directs the messages to virtual handlers, first "cracking" the parameters so that the handlers can work with something a little
more meaningful than *wParam* and *lParam*.

Students of MFC or ObjectWindows may wonder why *Dispatch()* is not a
virtual function like its analog in those class libraries. The answer is that I
dislike the use of "message map" type macros in the derived classes. The
justification for not making each handler **virtual** in those libraries, was that
the virtual method tables for a couple dozen window classes would be
excessive. We won't have so many VMTs—one per *model* in the VBX—so I
decided to go the straight and simple route:

```
LRESULT model::Dispatch
    (
    control & Control,
    USHORT Msg,
    USHORT wParam,
    long lParam
    )
  {
  switch (Msg)
    {
    case WM_ACTIVATE:
      OnActivate (Control, wParam,
        HIWORD (lParam), (HWND) LOWORD (lParam));
      return 0;
    case WM_CANCELMODE:
      OnCancelMode (Control);
      return 0;
    case WM_CHAR:
      OnChar (Control, wParam,
        LOWORD (lParam), HIWORD (lParam));
      return 0;
    case VBN_CHARTOITEM:
      return OnCharToItem (Control, wParam,
        (HWND) LOWORD (lParam), HIWORD (lParam));
    case WM_CLOSE:
      OnClose (Control);
      return 0;
//  case VBN_COMMAND:
    case VBN_COMPAREITEM:
      return OnCompareItem (Control,
        wParam, *((LPCOMPAREITEMSTRUCT) lParam));
    case WM_CREATE:
      return OnCreate (Control, *((LPCREATESTRUCT) lParam));
    case VBN_CTLCOLOR:
```

```
      return (LRESULT) OnCtlColor (Control,
         devicecontext ((HDC) wParam),
         (HWND) LOWORD (lParam), HIWORD (lParam));
   case WM_DEADCHAR:
      OnDeadChar(Control, wParam,
         LOWORD (lParam), HIWORD (lParam));
      return 0;
   case VBN_DELETEITEM:
      OnDeleteItem (Control, wParam,
         *((LPDELETEITEMSTRUCT) lParam));
      return 0;
   case WM_DESTROY:
      OnDestroy (Control);
      return 0;
   case VBN_DRAWITEM:
      OnDrawItem (Control, wParam,
         *((LPDRAWITEMSTRUCT) lParam));
      return 0;
   case WM_DROPFILES:
      OnDropFiles (Control, (HANDLE) wParam);
      return 0;
   case WM_ENABLE:
      OnEnable (Control, wParam);
      return 0;
   case WM_ERASEBKGND:
      OnEraseBkgnd (Control, devicecontext ((HDC) wParam));
      return 0;
   case WM_GETFONT:
      return (LRESULT) OnGetFont (Control);
   case WM_GETMINMAXINFO:
      OnGetMinMaxInfo (Control, *((MINMAXINFO far *)lParam));
      return 0;
   case WM_GETTEXT:
      OnGetText (Control, wParam, (LPSTR) lParam);
      return 0;
   case WM_GETTEXTLENGTH:
      return OnGetTextLength (Control);
   case WM_HSCROLL:
   case VBN_HSCROLL:
      OnHScroll (Control, wParam,
         LOWORD (lParam), (HWND) HIWORD (lParam));
      return 0;
   case WM_KEYDOWN:
      OnKeyDown (Control, wParam,
         LOWORD (lParam), HIWORD (lParam));
      return 0;
   case WM_KEYUP:
      OnKeyUp (Control, wParam,
         LOWORD (lParam), HIWORD (lParam));
      return 0;
   case WM_KILLFOCUS:
      OnKillFocus (Control, (HWND) wParam);
      return 0;
   case WM_LBUTTONDBLCLK:
```

```
    OnLButtonDblClk (Control, wParam, point (lParam));
    return 0;
case WM_LBUTTONDOWN:
    OnLButtonDown (Control, wParam, point (lParam));
    return 0;
case WM_LBUTTONUP:
    OnLButtonUp (Control, wParam, point (lParam));
    return 0;
case WM_MBUTTONDBLCLK:
    OnMButtonDblClk (Control, wParam, point (lParam));
    return 0;
case WM_MBUTTONDOWN:
    OnMButtonDown (Control, wParam, point (lParam));
    return 0;
case WM_MBUTTONUP:
    OnMButtonUp (Control, wParam, point (lParam));
    return 0;
case VBN_MEASUREITEM:
    OnMeasureItem (Control, wParam,
      *((LPMEASUREITEMSTRUCT) lParam));
    return 0;
case WM_MOUSEMOVE:
    OnMouseMove (Control, wParam, point (lParam));
    return 0;
case WM_MOVE:
    OnMove (Control, point (lParam));
    return 0;
case WM_NCHITTEST:
    return OnNCHitTest (Control, point (lParam));
case WM_PAINT:
    OnPaint (Control);
    return 0;
case WM_POWER:
    return OnPower (Control, wParam);
case WM_QUERYENDSESSION:
    return OnQueryEndSession (Control);
case WM_RBUTTONDBLCLK:
    OnRButtonDblClk (Control, wParam, point (lParam));
    return 0;
case WM_RBUTTONDOWN:
    OnRButtonDown (Control, wParam, point (lParam));
    return 0;
case WM_RBUTTONUP:
    OnRButtonUp (Control, wParam, point (lParam));
    return 0;
case WM_SETCURSOR:
    return OnSetCursor (Control, (HWND) wParam,
      LOWORD (lParam), HIWORD (lParam));
case WM_SETFOCUS:
    OnSetFocus (Control, (HWND) wParam);
    return 0;
case WM_SETFONT:
    OnSetFont (Control, (HFONT) wParam, lParam != 0);
    return 0;
```

```
        case WM_SETTEXT:
           OnSetText (Control, (LPSTR) lParam);
           return 0;
        case WM_SIZE:
           OnSize (Control, size (lParam));
           return 0;
        case WM_SPOOLERSTATUS:
           OnSpoolerStatus (Control, wParam, (UINT) lParam);
           return 0;
        case WM_SYSCOLORCHANGE:
           OnSysColorChange (Control);
           return 0;
        case WM_TIMECHANGE:
           OnTimeChange (Control);
           return 0;
        case WM_TIMER:
           OnTimer (Control, wParam);
           return 0;
        case VBN_VKEYTOITEM:
           return OnVKeyToItem (Control, wParam,
              (HWND) LOWORD (lParam), HIWORD (lParam));
        case WM_VSCROLL:
        case VBN_VSCROLL:
           OnVScroll (Control, wParam,
              LOWORD (lParam), (HWND) HIWORD (lParam));
           return 0;
        case WM_WININICHANGE:
           OnWinIniChange (Control, (LPSTR) lParam);
           return 0;
//      case VBM_LOADED:
        case VBM_CANCELMODE:
           VbCancelMode (Control, (HWND) wParam);
           return 0;
        case VBM_CHECKPROPERTY:
           return Properties[wParam].TestValue (Control, lParam);
//      case VBM_COPY:
//      case VBM_CREATED:
//      case VBM_DATA_AVAILABLE:
//      case VBM_DATA_GET:
//      case VBM_DATA_INITIATE:
//      case VBM_DATA_METHOD:
//      case VBM_DATA_REQUEST:
//      case VBM_DATA_SET:
//      case VBM_DATA_TERMINATE:
//      case VBM_DRAGDROP:
//      case VBM_DRAGOVER:
//      case VBM_FIREEVENT:
//      case VBM_GETDEFSIZE:
//      case VBM_GETPALETTE:
        case VBM_GETPROPERTY:
           return Properties[wParam].GetValue (Control, lParam);
//      case VBM_GETPROPERTYHSZ:
//      case VBM_HELP:
```

```
//    case VBM_HITTEST:
//    case VBM_INITPROPPOPUP:
//    case VBM_ISMNEMONIC:
//    case VBM_LINKENUMFORMATS:
//    case VBM_LINKGETDATA:
//    case VBM_LINKGETITEMNAME:
//    case VBM_LINKSETDATA:
      case VBM_LOADPROPERTY:
          return Properties[wParam].LoadValue (Control,
            (HFORMFILE) lParam);
//    case VBM_LOADTEXTPROPERTY:
      case VBM_METHOD:
          return OnMethod (Control, wParam, lParam);
//    case VBM_MNEMONIC:
      case VBM_PAINT:
          VbPaint ((HDC) wParam, (LPRECT) lParam);
          return 0;
//    case VBM_PAINTMULTISEL:
//    case VBM_PAINTOUTLINE:
//    case VBM_PALETTECHANGED:
//    case VBM_PASTE:
//    case VBM_QPASTEOK:
      case VBM_SAVEPROPERTY:
          return Properties[wParam].SaveValue (Control,
            (HFORMFILE) lParam);
//    case VBM_SAVETEXTPROPERTY:
//    case VBM_SELECTED:
      case VBM_SETPROPERTY:
          return Properties[wParam].SetValue (Control, lParam);
//    case VBM_WANTSPECIALKEY:
      }
   return VBDefControlProc (Control, Control, Msg, wParam, lParam);
   }
```

You'll notice a number of message identifiers that have been commented out; I have not supplied a handler for them. I simply deferred implementing these more esoteric messages until I need them. So far, I haven't.

The handlers themselves are all so similar that I won't reproduce them all here. Let's look at a sample:

```
LRESULT model::OnInitialize (control & Control)
   {
   return VBDefControlProc (Control, Control,
     VBM_INITIALIZE, 0, 0);
   }
```

The default handlers all simply pass the message on to *VBDefControlProc()*. The *control* class has casts to both *HCTL* and *HWND*, so no explicit casting is required when invoking that function.

The only other thing I'd like to point out regarding these message handlers has to do with *OnPaint(), VbPaint()* and *OnDraw()*.

The first two, the *actual* recipients of their respective messages, are the only handlers that are *not* **virtual**. That's because the programmer shouldn't override them. *OnPaint()* just creates a *paintcontext* object and invokes the **virtual** function *OnDraw()* with it:

```
void model::OnPaint(control & Control)
    {
    paintcontext Dc (Control);
    OnDraw (Dc, Dc.RedrawBackground(), Dc.GetPaintRect());
    }
```

VbPaint() operates similarly, except that it is *given* a device context to work with. In fact, *BeginPaint()* must *not* be invoked; the *VBM_PAINT* message is sent for graphical controls (which do not receive *WM_PAINT* messages) and when a control must be drawn somewhere other than the screen:

```
void model::VbPaint (HDC dc, LPRECT pRect)
    {
    devicecontext Dc (dc);
    OnDraw (Dc, TRUE, rectangle (*pRect));
    }
```

The default *OnDraw()* just draws a rectangle where the control goes; it draws a green rectangle if the control is a graphical control, or blue if it is a window-based control:

```
void model::OnDraw (devicecontext & Dc, BOOL, rectangle Rect)
    {
    BOOL IsGraphical =
        ((Model.fl & MODEL_fGraphical) == MODEL_fGraphical);
    brush Brush (IsGraphical ? color::Green : color::Blue);
    Dc = Brush;
    Dc.DrawRectangle (Rect);
    }
```

Note the use of the assignment operator to select the new *brush* into the *devicecontext*. Isn't that nice-looking?

Handling Methods

All methods are invoked through a single message, *VBM_METHOD*. The message parameters indicate which method is being invoked; the interpretation of other parameters depends on the method.

Our single handler for methods is *OnMethod()*, a *non-***virtual** function:

```
LRESULT model::OnMethod (control & Control, WORD MethodID, LONG Args)
   {
   LRESULT Result = 0;

   switch (MethodID)
      {
      case METH_ADDITEM:
         {
         LPADDITEM AddItem = (LPADDITEM) Args;
         LPSTR Item = VBLockHsz (AddItem->Item);
         int Index = (AddItem->Count > 2) ?
            (int) AddItem->Index : -1;
         Result = OnMethodAddItem (Control, Item, Index);
         VBUnlockHsz (AddItem->Item);
         }
         break;
      case METH_CLEAR:
         Result = OnMethodClear (Control);
         break;
      case METH_DRAG:
         {
         LPDRAG Drag = (LPDRAG) Args;
         int Command = (Drag->Count > 1) ?
            (int) Drag->Command : 1;
         Result = OnMethodDrag (Control, Command);
         }
         break;
      case METH_LINKSEND:
         Result = OnMethodLinkSend (Control);
         break;
      case METH_MOVE:
         {
         LPMOVE Move = (LPMOVE) Args;
         Result = OnMethodMove (Control,
            (int) Move->Count, Move->Left, Move->Top,
            Move->Width, Move->Height);
         }
         break;
      case METH_REMOVEITEM:
         {
         LPREMOVEITEM RemoveItem = (LPREMOVEITEM) Args;
         Result = OnMethodRemoveItem (Control,
            (int) RemoveItem->Index);
         }
         break;
      case METH_REFRESH:
         Result = OnMethodRefresh (Control);
         break;
      case METH_ZORDER:
         {
         LPZORDER ZOrder = (LPZORDER) Args;
```

```
        Result = OnMethodZOrder (Control,
            ZOrder->SendToBack ? SendToBack : BringToFront);
        }
        break;
    default:
        Result = VBDefControlProc (Control, Control,
            VBM_METHOD, MethodID, (long) Args);
    }
    return Result;
    }
```

This message switch identifies the method, appropriately cracks the parameters, and invokes the **virtual** function appropriate to that method.

This, of course, is the function you override when creating a real control that will make use of one of these methods. These base implementations provide appropriate defaults. Now, the *usual* default would be to simply call *VBDefControlProc()*. However, we've already cracked the parameters; we'd have to rebuild the argument struct for each method if we were going to handle each one that way. Besides, the default handling for several of the methods is simply to return error code 444, "Method not applicable in this context":

```
LRESULT model::OnMethodAddItem (control &, LPSTR, int)
    {
    return 444;
    }


LRESULT model::OnMethodClear (control &)
    {
    return 444;
    }


LRESULT model::OnMethodRemoveItem (control &, int)
    {
    return 444;
    }
```

Several other methods are easy to invoke *VBDefControlProc()* for, because, like my ex-wife, they don't *take* any arguments:

```
LRESULT model::OnMethodLinkSend (control & Control)
    {
    return VBDefControlProc (Control, Control,
        VBM_METHOD, METH_LINKSEND, NULL);
    }


LRESULT model::OnMethodRefresh (control & Control)
    {
```

```
  return VBDefControlProc (Control, Control,
    VBM_METHOD, METH_REFRESH, NULL);
  }
```

That leaves us with just two methods for which we must, indeed, recreate the original arguments before invoking *VBDefControlProc()*:

```
LRESULT model::OnMethodMove (control & Control,
      int Count, LONG Left, LONG Top, LONG Width, LONG Height)
  {
  MOVE Args;
  Args.Count = Count;
  Args.Left = Left;
  Args.Top = Top;
  Args.Width = Width;
  Args.Height = Height;
  return VBDefControlProc (Control, Control,
    VBM_METHOD, METH_MOVE, (long) &Args);
  }

LRESULT model::OnMethodZOrder (control & Control,
    ZOrderCommand Command)
  {
  ZORDER Args;
  Args.Count = 2;
  Args.SendToBack = (Command == SendToBack);
  return VBDefControlProc (Control, Control,
    VBM_METHOD, METH_ZORDER, (long) &Args);
  }
```

The control Class

This class encapsulates the control and window handles of the control currently being processed. It obtains pointers to property storage locations for each copy of the control, and includes cast operators for easy use where a control or window handle is expected.

As we saw earlier, the *control* object is created in response to a *VBM_INITIALIZE* message, and its *Window* property was filled in when its *WM_NCCREATE* message arrived. (A graphical control will not receive this, leaving *Window* == NULL.) The *control* object is **delete**d in response to *WM_NCDESTROY*—and even graphical controls receive this message.

The control classes are declared in CONTROL.H and defined in CONTROL.CPP. At the base is *control*, objects of which represent the physical controls as created by Visual Basic:

```
#ifndef __CONTROL_H__
#define __CONTROL_H__
```

```
#include "vbxxx.h"

class control
    {
    public:
        control (HCTL aHandle, model * aModel);
        int operator==(const control & aControl) const;
        void * GetStorageAddress (int Offset) const;
        operator HCTL (void) const { return Handle; }
        operator HWND (void) const { return Window; }
        model & GetModel (void) const { return *Model; }
    private:
        HCTL Handle;
        HWND Window;
        model * Model;
    friend LRESULT CALLBACK _export CtlProc (HCTL, HWND,
        USHORT, USHORT, long);
    };

typedef control * control_ptr;
```

Note that *CtlProc()*, which is already a **friend** function of *model*, is a **friend** also of *control*. Objects of this class can be easily cast to *HWND* or *HCTL* as needed. I won't bother showing the constructor or the equivalence operators since there are no surprises there. Here's the *GetStorageAddress()* function (from CONTROL.CPP):

```
void * control::GetStorageAddress (int Offset) const
    {
    return (void *) ((char *) VBDerefControl (Handle) + Offset);
    }
```

Given an offset, this routine obtains the address of the *VBDATA* structure, adds the offset to it, and returns the result. We'll see this used shortly.

The *controlbag* class exists because we needed an unordered container; ObjectWindows containers are built from templates (which Microsoft Visual C++ 1.52 doesn't support) and MFC 3.0 doesn't come with any bag-type containers at all. Besides, the class itself isn't that big a deal:

```
class controlbag
    {
    public:
        controlbag (UINT aGrowSize = 50);
        virtual ~controlbag ();
        controlbag & operator += (control & Control);
        controlbag & operator -= (control & Control);
        control * Find (HCTL Handle);
```

```
private:
   void Grow (void);
   UINT GrowSize;
   control_ptr * Controls;
   UINT ControlsMax;
   UINT ControlsCount;
};
```

The "bag" is kept in a dynamically managed array of pointers; the array is allocated to an initial size during construction and deallocated during destruction:

```
controlbag::controlbag (UINT aGrowSize)
   : GrowSize (aGrowSize),
     ControlsMax (aGrowSize),
     ControlsCount (0)
   {
   Controls = new control_ptr[GrowSize];
   }

controlbag::~controlbag ()
   {
   for (register UINT i = 0; i < ControlsCount; i++)
      delete Controls[i];
   delete[] Controls;
   }
```

If more *controls* are added to the bag than there is room for, the array is reallocated:

```
void controlbag::Grow (void)
   {
   control_ptr * Temp = Controls;
   ControlsMax += GrowSize;
   Controls = new control_ptr[ControlsMax];
   for (register UINT i = 0; i < ControlsCount; i++)
      Controls[i] = Temp[i];
   delete[] Temp;
   }
```

Rather than using an "add" method to add *controls* to the bag, I've utilized the assigned addition operator:

```
controlbag & controlbag::operator += (control & Control)
   {
   if (ControlsCount == ControlsMax)
      Grow();
   Controls[ControlsCount++] = &Control;
   return *this;
   }
```

What's more, the assigned subtraction operator is perfect for *removing* an element:

```
controlbag & controlbag::operator -= (control & Control)
  {
  for (register UINT i = 0; i < ControlsCount; i++)
    if ((HCTL) *Controls[i] == (HCTL) Control)
      {
      Controls[i] = Controls[-ControlsCount];
      break;
      }
  return *this;
  }
```

(The removed element isn't **delete**d here; since it was passed as a parameter, it is now in the care of another object.)

Finally, the *Find()* method is used by *CtlProc()* to locate a *control* from a control handle:

```
control * controlbag::Find (HCTL Handle)
  {
  for (register UINT i = 0; i < ControlsCount; i++)
    if ((HCTL) *Controls[i] == Handle)
      return Controls[i];
  return NULL;
```

Property Classes

What makes a VBX-style custom control unique? Three things: its appearance, its list of events, and its properties. The property classes support property names and storages, making it easy for you to build whatever standard or custom properties into your control you like.

As you know, certain *VBM_* messages affect property values. These messages *must* receive default processing for standard properties. When the message arrives at the control procedure (part of the *model* class, described previously), *wParam* contains the index of the property. The *property::IsStandard()* function returns *TRUE* for standard properties only; messages for non-standard properties are forwarded to the dispatcher. As we saw earlier, the *model::Dispatch()* function performs "message cracking" and invokes a **virtual** handler for each message. Most handlers are methods of *model*, but the ones that deal with property values are handled by *customproperty* objects.

Declared in PROPS.H, *standardproperty* is the base of the property classes. It stores the *PPROPINFO* value of the standard control and provides virtual functions for querying: *IsStandard()* and *GetStorageSize()*:

```
class standardproperty
   {
   public:
     standardproperty (PPROPINFO aStdProperty,
        USHORT aVersion = VB100_VERSION);
     virtual BOOL IsStandard (void) const;
     virtual UINT GetStorageSize (void) const;
   protected:
     enum errorvalues
        {
        InvalidValue = 380,
        InvalidIndex = 381
        };
   private:
     PPROPINFO PropertyID;
     USHORT Version;
   friend class propertieslist;
   };
```

This class exists *primarily* to be a base class for *customproperty*. However, it is useful in itself because the standard properties, as you will recall, are represented simply by an ID (stored here in the *PropertyID* field).

Also, note the anonymous **enum** of possible error return values.

Because this class has so little to do, the three methods in PROPS.CPP—constructor, *IsStandard()*, and *GetStorageSize()*—are extremely simple:

```
standardproperty::standardproperty
     (PPROPINFO aStdProperty, USHORT aVersion)
   : PropertyID (aStdProperty),
     Version (aVersion)
   {
   }

BOOL standardproperty::IsStandard (void) const
   {
   return TRUE;
   }

UINT standardproperty::GetStorageSize (void) const
   {
   return 0;
   }
```

The derived class, *customproperty*, is much more complex, *even though you will never use it directly*. (We'll look at the derived classes shortly.) Remember the fields of the CDK's *PROPINFO* structure? This class must manage them all, plus deal with the properties when they are "live"—that is, storing and loading them, and so on, for an actual control:

```
class customproperty : public standardproperty
  {
public:
    enum datatypes
      {
      Boolean = DT_BOOL,
      Color = DT_COLOR,
      Enumerated = DT_ENUM,
      CString = DT_HSZ,
      Long = DT_LONG,
      Picture = DT_PICTURE,
      Float = DT_REAL,
      Short = DT_SHORT,
      XPosition = DT_XPOS,
      XSize = DT_XSIZE,
      YPosition = DT_YPOS,
      YSize = DT_YSIZE
      };
    customproperty (PSTR aName, datatypes aDataType);
    virtual BOOL IsStandard (void) const;
    void SetAsArray (UINT anElementCount);
    void SetStorageOffset (int);
    int GetStorageOffset (LONG Index = 0) const;
    virtual UINT GetStorageSize (void) const;
    void SetRefreshOnChange (BOOL Refresh = TRUE)
      { RefreshOnChange = Refresh; }
    LRESULT TestValue (control & Control, LONG Value) const;
    LRESULT SetValue (control & Control, LONG Value);
    LRESULT GetValue (control & Control, LONG Value) const;
    virtual LRESULT TestValue (control & Control,
      LONG Value, LONG Index) const;
    virtual LRESULT TestIndex (LONG Index) const;
    virtual LRESULT SetValue (control & Control,
      LONG Value, LONG Index);
    virtual LRESULT GetValue (control & Control,
      LONG & Value, LONG Index)const;
    virtual LRESULT LoadValue (control & Control,
      HFORMFILE File);
    virtual LRESULT SaveValue (control & Control,
      HFORMFILE File) const;
    BYTE GetElementCount (void) { return ElementCount; }
    virtual void SetInitValue (control &Control, LONG Index);
protected:
    PROPINFO PropertyInfo;
    BYTE ElementCount;
    BYTE ElementSize;
    BOOL RefreshOnChange;
private:
    BOOL IsArray (void) const;
    UINT StorageOffset;
  };
```

The first item, the **enum** *datatypes*, provides a more readable list of the VB data types than the raw CDK does. Note: *This list is slightly abbreviated.* I have omitted from it the VB string data type (*HLSTR*) on the grounds that VB-style strings don't add enough value for us to bother with—if you want a text property, the C string style is adequate. And I omitted the *DT_OBJECT* type, since such types are better implemented as OCXs anyway.

Down near the bottom we store the member data. You'll note *ElementSize*; that will allow derived classes to specify storage requirements. *ElementCount* reveals an odd but useful aspect of this class: *All* properties are treated as array properties! Not as far as VB is concerned, but from the point of view of your derived *customproperty* classes. Believe me, it will make things easier.

Let's look at the constructor:

```
customproperty::customproperty (PSTR aName, datatypes aDataType)
   : standardproperty ((PPROPINFO) &PropertyInfo, 0),
     StorageOffset (0),
     ElementCount (1),
     ElementSize (0),
     RefreshOnChange (TRUE)
   {
   PropertyInfo.npszName = aName;
   PropertyInfo.fl = (FLONG) aDataType |
     PF_fGetMsg | PF_fSetMsg | PF_fSaveMsg;
   PropertyInfo.offsetData = 0;
   PropertyInfo.infoData = 0;
   PropertyInfo.dataDefault = 0;
   PropertyInfo.npszEnumList = NULL;
   }
```

You might recall that the *PPROPINFO* values of the standard properties are not pointers at all—just indexes with bitwise operations performed on them so the underlying VBX mechanism can't mistake them for real pointers. (Ed Yourdon, the father of Structured Design, would turn over in his grave. If he were dead.) Anyway, *that's* the value stored in the *PropertyID* member. Custom controls must place the address of an actual *PROPINFO* structure there, as the constructor does in the member initialization area. Then, in the body of the constructor, the fields of the structure are filled in.

The *standardproperty::IsStandard()* **virtual** function returns *TRUE*. The *customproperty* version must do the opposite:

```
BOOL customproperty::IsStandard (void) const
   {
   return FALSE;
   }
```

Then there are several custodial functions for providing access to the member data. *SetAsArray()*, which is implemented as an **inline** function, refers to the *customproperty*'s appearance *to the VBX manager*. It is invoked to set a number of elements as well as the *PF_fPropArray* flag:

```
inline void customproperty::SetAsArray (UINT anElementCount)
   {
   ElementCount = anElementCount;
   PropertyInfo.fl |= PF_fPropArray;
   }
```

Even if your derived class is managing its own storage for a dynamic array, you may want to invoke this function since the element count you specify is used later to validate indexes.

SetStorageOffset(), also **inline**, is called by *model* when the property storage requirements are being assembled (this is equivalent to placing an entry in the *VBDATA* structure of the VBX skeleton we've worked with, in the original C VBX skeleton described earlier):

```
inline void customproperty::SetStorageOffset (int anOffset)
   {
   StorageOffset = anOffset;
   }
```

GetStorageOffset() takes the requested array index into account:

```
inline int customproperty::GetStorageOffset (LONG Index) const
   {
   return StorageOffset + (ElementSize * (int) Index);
   }
```

Remember, even non-array properties are treated here as one-element arrays, so *Index* in such a case would always be zero.

GetStorageSize() is a **virtual** function that calculates the storage requirement based on *ElementSize* and *ElementCount*:

```
UINT customproperty::GetStorageSize (void) const
   {
   return ElementSize * ElementCount;
   }
```

The *SetRefreshOnChange()* method, an embedded **inline** function, notifies the object that when this property value is altered by the VBX manager, the control should redraw itself.

The next three methods are invoked by *model::Dispatch()* in response to requests that the VBX manager sends the control to test, set or obtain a property value. These methods do a little dispatching of their own, to overloaded methods of the same name (but different calling sequences) of derived classes. The overloaded functions are **virtual**, which is why the derived class actually receives the message. Let's look at the first message handler, *TestMessage()*, which is invoked in response to a *VBM_CHECKPROPERTY* message, along with a **virtual** "helper" method, *TestIndex()*:

```
LRESULT customproperty::TestIndex (LONG Index) const
    {
    return (Index >= 0 && Index < ElementCount) ? 0 : InvalidIndex;
    }

LRESULT customproperty::TestValue (control & Control, LONG Value) const
    {
    LPDATASTRUCT DataStruct ((LPDATASTRUCT) Value);
    LONG Index (0);
    if (IsArray())
        {
        Index = DataStruct->index[0].data;
        Value = DataStruct->data;
        }
    LRESULT Error (TestIndex (Index));
    return Error ? Error : TestValue (Control, Value, Index);
    }
```

You'll recall in our study of the CDK in C, that array properties are treated differently from non-arrays. In an array, *lParam* (called *Value* here) points to a *DATASTRUCT*; the structure's *Data* property is then either the data or a pointer to the data, depending on data type.

To avoid having to deal with arrays and non-arrays separately, all *customproperty* objects are written *as if* they were arrays, even if an array with just one element. (This does not affect the way they appear to the VBX manager.) So the job of this first-level *TestValue()* is to make sure *Value* has the correct value, and to set *Index*, and then call the next level.

Setting the *Index*, though, gives *TestValue()* a chance to verify that the index requested is a reasonable one. In nearly every case, the **virtual** *TestIndex()* supplied with *customproperty* will do the job. In the rare cases where you occasionally *want* an out-of-range index to have a special meaning—for example, the Listbox control uses a -1 to mean "none" of the items in the Listbox—you can override it in the derived class.

The *VBM_SETPROPERTY* message is similar in syntax to the *VBM_CHECKPROPERTY* message; but, of course, the intent is to actually change a property value:

```
LRESULT customproperty::SetValue (control & Control, LONG Value)
   {
   LPDATASTRUCT DataStruct ((LPDATASTRUCT) Value);
   LONG Index (0);
   if (IsArray())
      {
      Index = DataStruct->index[0].data;
      Value = DataStruct->data;
      }
   LRESULT Error (TestIndex (Index));
   if (! Error)
      Error = SetValue (Control, Value, Index);
   if ((! Error) && RefreshOnChange)
      VBInvalidateRect (Control, NULL, FALSE);
   return Error;
   }
```

There is no guarantee that a *VBM_CHECKPROPERTY* message will be sent before the *VBM_SETPROPERTY* message, so the requested index is re-tested. And, if the derived class's *SetValue()* does not return an error and you've said changes to this property should result in a redraw of the control, the call to *VBInvalidateRect()* makes sure this happens.

The *VBM_GETPROPERTY* message is just a little different, in that the *lParam* is always a *pointer* to the data requested ... however, if the property is an array, the *Data* field of the *DATASTRUCT* is usually *not* a pointer, but the recipient of the requested data itself:

```
LRESULT customproperty::GetValue (control & Control, LONG lParam) const
   {
   LPDATASTRUCT DataStruct ((LPDATASTRUCT) lParam);
   LONG far * Data = ((LONG far *) lParam);
   LONG Index (0);
   if (IsArray())
      {
      Index = DataStruct->index[0].data;
      Data = &DataStruct->data;
      }
   LRESULT Error (TestIndex (Index));
   return Error ? Error : GetValue (Control, *Data, Index);
   }
```

The derived *GetValue()* method expects a reference parameter in the second position; *Data* is a pointer always, so it either mimics the pointer value in *lParam* or points to that *Data* field.

The versions of *SetValue()* and *GetValue()* that these functions call are
virtual; however, there are several property data types that *cannot* fail a
value test—**long**, for example. So there is a default *TestValue()* for them. It
is also convenient to supply do-nothing default handlers for *SetValue()* and
GetValue(), as well:

```
LRESULT customproperty::TestValue (control &, LONG, LONG) const
   {
   return 0;
   }

LRESULT customproperty::SetValue (control &, LONG, LONG)
   {
   return 0;
   }

LRESULT customproperty::GetValue (control &, LONG &, LONG) const
   {
   return 0;
   }
```

The next two methods are invoked in response to the *VBM_LOADPROPERTY*
and the *VBM_SAVEPROPERTY* messages, respectively. They are **virtual** "just
in case," but normally should not have to be overridden:

```
LRESULT customproperty::LoadValue (control & Control, HFORMFILE File)
   {
   void * Value = Control.GetStorageAddress (GetStorageOffset());
   return VBReadFormFile (File, Value,
      ElementSize * ElementCount);
   }

LRESULT customproperty::SaveValue (control & Control, HFORMFILE File) const
   {
   void * Value = Control.GetStorageAddress (GetStorageOffset());
   return VBWriteFormFile (File, Value,
      ElementSize * ElementCount);
   }
```

Finally, we deal with the idea of properties with default values. The VBX
CDK allows for the specification of a default property value, by supplying
the *PF_fDefVal* flag to the *PPROPINFO* structure. However, this only tells the
VBX manager what the default property is, and to not bother to store the
property's actual value if it matches the default property. It does *not* actually
set the value!—An odd omission, perhaps; but that's the way it is.

We can overcome that. First, jumping back to the *model* class, we can add
handling to the *OnInitialize()* handler to set any initial values:

```
LRESULT model::OnInitialize (control & Control)
  {
  for (register p = 0; p < Properties.GetCount(); p++)
    for (register i = 0;
        i < Properties[p].GetElementCount();
        i++)
      if (! Properties[p].IsStandard())
        Properties[p].SetInitValue (Control, i);
  return VBDefControlProc (Control, Control,
    VBM_INITIALIZE, 0, 0);
  }
```

As you can see, every element of every property is so initialized. But how? That's the job of the *SetInitValue()* method:

```
void customproperty::SetInitValue (control &Control, LONG Index)
  {
  if ((PropertyInfo.fl & PF_fDefVal) == PF_fDefVal)
    SetValue (Control, PropertyInfo.dataDefault, Index);
  }
```

> *It checks to see if the* PF_fDefVal *flag has been set; usually it is not and nothing happens. However, if it is set, the* PropertyInfo.dataDefault *field contains the desired value...conveniently expressed as a **long**; so a call to the previously described* SetValue() *method completes the job.*

We'll look at a property type that actually uses this mechanism shortly, when we examine the *colorproperty* class.

boolproperty

Although we don't have the space to go over *all* the classes derived from *customproperty*, I'll go through a few to give you a feel for how it's done. The first data type is the *Boolean*, so we'll start with that. Here's the declaration:

```
class boolproperty : public customproperty
  {
  public:
    boolproperty (PSTR aName);
    virtual UINT GetStorageSize (void) const;
    virtual LRESULT TestValue (control & Control,
      LONG Value, LONG Index) const;
    virtual LRESULT SetValue (control & Control,
      LONG Value, LONG Index);
    virtual LRESULT GetValue (control & Control,
      LONG & Value, LONG Index)const;
  };
```

Just one constructor and three methods does it for us, as is true with most of these typed derivatives of *customproperty*. Here's the constructor:

```
boolproperty::boolproperty (PSTR aName)
  : customproperty (aName, Boolean)
  {
  ElementSize = sizeof (BYTE);
  }
```

We intend to store *Boolean* values in a single byte; so the constructor sets the *ElementSize* accordingly. Note also that when specifying the base constructor in the member initialization area, the *datatype* is included.

Although it's pretty unlikely anyone would send a value other than *True* or *False* to a Boolean property, we should check for the possibility:

```
LRESULT boolproperty::TestValue (control &, LONG Value, LONG) const
  {
  if (Value == -1 || Value == 0)
    return 0;
  else
    return InvalidValue;
  }
```

Although this method would not be called directly unless the property were actually created from a further-derived class that set the *PF_fSetCheck* flag, we call it ourselves from *SetValue()*...just to make sure:

```
LRESULT boolproperty::SetValue (control & Control, LONG Value, LONG Index)
  {
  LRESULT Error = TestValue (Control, Value, Index);
  if (! Error)
    {
    BYTE * Storage =
      (BYTE *) Control.GetStorageAddress (GetStorageOffset(Index));
    *Storage = ((BYTE) Value != 0);
    }
  return Error;
  }
```

Now you see why there are two levels of *SetValue()* (and the others): While the *customproperty* level knows about *lParam* and *DATASTRUCT*, this level knows how to convert the result into the correct data type. In this case of *Boolean* data, the conversion is pretty simple; it is more complex, as we'll see shortly, with *Picture, Float,* or *CString* types.

GetValue() is a little simpler, just because *retrieving* a value can't fail (as long as the requested array index is valid):

```
LRESULT boolproperty::GetValue (control & Control, LONG & Value, LONG Index)
const
    {
    BYTE * Storage =
        (BYTE *) Control.GetStorageAddress (GetStorageOffset(Index));
    Value = *Storage ? -1 : 0;
    return 0;
    }
```

colorproperty

The interesting thing about *colorproperty* is that it allows the specification of a default value. This is handled entirely by the constructor:

```
colorproperty::colorproperty (PSTR aName, color DefColor)
    : customproperty (aName, Color)
    {
    ElementSize = sizeof (COLORREF);
    PropertyInfo.dataDefault = (COLORREF) DefColor;
    PropertyInfo.fl |= PF_fDefVal;
    }
```

In addition to setting the *ElementSize*, as all *customproperty*-derived classes must do, *colorproperty* sets the *RefreshOnChange* flag (if the color changes, the control must be redrawn). It also accepts an optional *DefColor* argument (the default color is *color::Black*) and makes sure the needed *PF_fDefVal* flag is set.

enumproperty

The next interesting class is *enumproperty*:

```
class enumproperty : public customproperty
    {
    public:
        enumproperty (PSTR aName, PSTR EnumList);
        virtual LRESULT TestValue (control & Control,
            LONG Value, LONG Index) const;
        virtual LRESULT SetValue (control & Control,
            LONG Value, LONG Index);
        virtual LRESULT GetValue (control & Control,
            LONG & Value, LONG Index)const;
    private:
        BYTE EnumCount;
    };
```

Its constructor must receive a list of *Enumerated* values:

```
enumproperty::enumproperty (PSTR aName, PSTR EnumList)
    : customproperty (aName, Enumerated),
      EnumCount (0)
```

```
{
ElementSize = sizeof (BYTE);
PropertyInfo.npszEnumList = EnumList;
register i (1);
if (EnumList)
   while (EnumList[i-1] || EnumList[i])
      if (EnumList[i++] == 0)
         EnumCount++;
PropertyInfo.enumMax = EnumCount;
}
```

The list, which arrives in the standard CDK format ("Choice 1\0Choice 2\0Choice 3\0", a string terminated with a double NULL—the compiler adds the final one), must be scanned so the object knows how many choices there are. This value is used, not only to set the *PROPERTYINFO.enumMax* field, but to validate assignments made to the property:

```
LRESULT enumproperty::TestValue (control &, LONG Value, LONG) const
   {
   LRESULT Error (0);
   if (Value < 0 || Value >= EnumCount)
      Error = InvalidValue;
   return Error;
   }
```

The *SetValue()* and *GetValue()* methods are similar to their counterparts in *booleanproperty*:

```
LRESULT enumproperty::SetValue (control & Control, LONG Value, LONG Index)
   {
   BYTE * Storage = (BYTE *) Control.GetStorageAddress
(GetStorageOffset(Index));
   *Storage = (BYTE) Value;
   return 0;
   }
```

```
LRESULT enumproperty::GetValue (control & Control, LONG & Value, LONG Index)
const
   {
   BYTE * Storage = (BYTE *) Control.GetStorageAddress
(GetStorageOffset(Index));
   Value = *Storage;
   return 0;
   }
```

textproperty

Actually storing C-style strings would be a hassle, because the property classes require items to occupy a known amount of space. This is where the *text* class comes in, as developed in Chapter 5. As a vendor-non-specific class capable of storing and even doing a little manipulation of text strings, able to manage string storage internally, all we have to store is the object itself. Of course, loading and saving the property to disk becomes a little more work, since we actually have to supply overrides for *LoadValue()* and *SaveValue()*:

```
class textproperty : public customproperty
   {
   public:
      textproperty (PSTR aName);
      virtual LRESULT SetValue (control & Control,
         LONG Value, LONG Index);
      virtual LRESULT GetValue (control & Control,
         LONG & Value, LONG Index)const;
      virtual LRESULT LoadValue (control & Control,
         HFORMFILE File);
      virtual LRESULT SaveValue (control & Control,
         HFORMFILE File) const;
   };
```

Since the constructor has to specify the (linear) storage size of the property, which in this case has nothing to do with the actual size of the string being stored, it does so:

```
textproperty::textproperty (PSTR aName)
   : customproperty (aName, CString)
   {
   ElementSize = sizeof (text);
   }
```

The *text* class already has implemented an assignment operator that accepts a standard C-style string on the right:

```
LRESULT textproperty::SetValue (control & Control, LONG Value, LONG Index)
   {
   text * Storage =
     (text *) Control.GetStorageAddress (GetStorageOffset(Index));
   *Storage = (char far *) Value;
   return 0;
   }
```

C strings aren't so easy to work with, unfortunately; but the *text* class also has a cast to **const char** * so we can use that old standby, *strcpy()*:

```
LRESULT textproperty::GetValue (control & Control, LONG & Value, LONG Index)
const
   {
   text * Storage = (text *) Control.GetStorageAddress
(GetStorageOffset(Index));
   strcpy ((char far *) Value, *Storage);
   return 0;
   }
```

LoadValue() is actually *interesting* because it must read in, not the *text* object, but an actual string of characters of unknown length ... and then *assign* those characters to the *text* object:

```
LRESULT textproperty::LoadValue (control & Control, HFORMFILE File)
    {
    UINT Length;
    char * AsStored;
    LRESULT Error (0);
    text * Storage = (text *) Control.GetStorageAddress (GetStorageOffset());

    Error = VBReadFormFile (File, &Length, sizeof Length);
    if (! Error)
        {
        AsStored = new char[Length];
        Error = VBReadFormFile (File, AsStored, Length);
        AsStored[Length] = 0;
        }
    if (! Error)
        *Storage = AsStored;

    return Error;
    }
```

As you can see, the length is read from disk first, followed by the characters ... and *without* a trailing NULL, which has to be restored. Obviously this must be the inverse operation of that performed by *SaveValue()*:

```
LRESULT textproperty::SaveValue (control & Control, HFORMFILE File) const
    {
    UINT Length;
    LRESULT Error (0);
    text * Storage = (text *) Control.GetStorageAddress (GetStorageOffset());

    Length = *Storage;
    Error = VBWriteFormFile (File, &Length, sizeof Length);
    if (! Error)
        Error = VBWriteFormFile (File,
            (void *) (const char *) *Storage, Length);
    return Error;
    }
```

pictureproperty

The *pictureproperty* class is interesting for the *opposite* reason as the *textproperty* class: We *don't* want to handle storing the property at all! Visual Basic already handles storing the internal data of the *HPIC* format. So, instead of writing a sophisticated set of functions for dealing with this format, all we have to do to override the *PROPINFO* flags in our constructor:

```
pictureproperty::pictureproperty (PSTR aName)
  : customproperty (aName, Picture)
  {
  PropertyInfo.fl = (FLONG) Picture |
    PF_fGetData | PF_fSetData | PF_fSaveData;
  PropertyInfo.offsetData = GetStorageOffset();
  ElementSize = sizeof (HPIC);
  }
```

The flags you see are the ones that tell Visual Basic (or the VBX manager) to perform the data storage for you. That means objects of this class will *never* receive *VBM_SETPROPERTY, VBM_GETPROPERTY, VBM_SAVEPROPERTY* or *VBM_LOADPROPERTY* messages. So we do not even need to provide handlers for them.

floatproperty

The only reason this data type is interesting is that you have to resort to a little trick to get (or put) the **float** value from the *lParam*. The problem is a C one: Although casts in C do not normally perform conversions, in the case of **float** to **long** or **long** to **float**, they do. So we have to trick the C/C++ compiler by first casting the **long** to an address, then casting the address to a **float**:

```
LRESULT floatproperty::SetValue (control & Control, LONG Value, LONG Index)
  {
  float * Storage = (float *) Control.GetStorageAddress
(GetStorageOffset(Index));
  *Storage = *((float *) &Value);
  return 0;
  }
```

A inverse trick allows us to provide our stored value on request:

```
LRESULT floatproperty::GetValue (control & Control, LONG & Value, LONG Index)
const
  {
  float * Storage = (float *) Control.GetStorageAddress
(GetStorageOffset(Index));
  *((float *) &Value) = *Storage;
  return 0;
  }
```

A List of Properties

Before we leave the consideration of properties altogether, there is one more class to examine: *propertieslist*. This is a vendor-free container class, an ordered "array" into which *property* objects may be inserted. We saw this container used in the *model* class; it has a *propertieslist* property. That's how a *model* keeps track of its properties, in fact.

The *propertieslist* class is declared as follows:

```
class propertieslist
   {
   public:
      enum { MaxProperties = 128 };
      propertieslist (USHORT aRunVersion = VB300_VERSION);
      ~propertieslist ();
      propertieslist & operator+= (standardproperty & Property);
      UINT Find (standardproperty & Property);
      customproperty & operator[] (int i);
      NPPROPLIST GetList (void)
         {return (NPPROPLIST) PropertyList; }
      USHORT GetCount (void) { return Count; }
   private:
      USHORT RunVersion;
      USHORT Count;
      standardproperty * Properties[MaxProperties];
      PPROPINFO PropertyList[MaxProperties];
   };
```

In terms of its use, the *propertieslist* class most closely resembles the simple array of *PPROPINFO* pointers pointed to by the *MODEL* structure, passed to *VBRegisterModel()*. In a C language VBX, that array is assembled by the compiler. *propertieslist* works with properties that are not "added" to it until run-time.

To avoid the overhead of dynamically allocating memory slots for each property as it is added to the list, I chose 128 as a reasonable maximum for the number of properties a control may have. More properties than that tend to confuse users, anyway.

The *model* object, when initializing its properties, will pass the actual version of the VBX manager to the *propertieslist* constructor:

```
propertieslist::propertieslist (USHORT aRunVersion)
   : RunVersion (aRunVersion), Count (0)
   {
   PropertyList[0] = NULL;
   }
```

The += operator is used to add properties to the list. Note that a property is added *only* if its *Version* is less than or equal to the actual version of the run-time manager:

```
propertieslist & propertieslist::operator+= (standardproperty & Property)
   {
   if (Property.Version <= RunVersion &&
       (Count < MaxProperties))
     {
     Properties[Count] = &Property;
     PropertyList[Count] = Property.PropertyID;
     PropertyList[++Count] = NULL;
     }
   return *this;
   }
```

This avoids the version mismatch problems experienced when, say, trying to use a VB 3.0 VBX under Microsoft Visual C++ (which only supports VB Version 1.0 VBXs).

Also, notice that we are adding both the property object to the *Properties* array *and* a pointer to the *PropertyList* array. That list is the one that eventually winds up being sent via *VBRegisterModel()*; it must be a contiguous array of pointers and so is managed in this way.

Occasionally, the *propertieslist* object must be queried as to the location within it of a given property. That's the job of the *Find()* method:

```
UINT propertieslist::Find (standardproperty & Property)
   {
   for (register UINT p = 0; p < Count; p++)
     if (&Property == Properties[p])
        return p;
   return Count;
   }
```

The subscript operator returns a reference to the requested property itself:

```
customproperty & propertieslist::operator[] (int i)
   {
   return (customproperty &) *(Properties[i]);
   }
```

That gives us *model*, a nice mechanism for dealing with all the properties associated with the control the *model*-derived class is representing.

Special Events...and Ordinary Ones

One reason for presenting property and event classes together is that, in many ways, they are quite similar. Events are simpler than properties, however, properties are set by messages and therefore involve the *model* and *control* classes; while events only have to be made known to the system—thus involving just the *model* class.

(*Triggering* an event will require an object of the *control* class, but only so the system knows on which control to trigger the event.)

Like properties, events are all based on a standard class, with custom events based on a derived class. The standard class is called *standardevent*:

```
class standardevent
    {
    public:
        standardevent (PEVENTINFO aStdEvent,
            USHORT aVersion = VB100_VERSION);
        virtual BOOL IsStandard (void) const;
        ERR Fire (control & Control, LPVOID Params);
    private:
        PEVENTINFO EventID;
        USHORT Version;
    friend class eventslist;
    };
```

As with the *standardproperty* class, the *standardevent* constructor just stores the event ID and version supplied, making this one class suitable for all standard events:

```
standardevent::standardevent (PEVENTINFO aStdEvent,
    USHORT aVersion)
    : EventID (aStdEvent), Version (aVersion)
    {
    }
```

Also like *standardproperty* objects, *standardevent* objects identify themselves as *being* standard, using the **virtual** function *IsStandard()*:

```
BOOL standardevent::IsStandard (void) const
    {
    return TRUE;
    }
```

The *Fire()* method merely encapsulates the *VBFireEvent()* function:

```
ERR standardevent::Fire (control & Control, LPVOID Params)
    {
    UINT EventID = Control.GetModel().Events.Find (*this);
    return VBFireEvent (Control, EventID, Params);
    }
```

Fire() is implemented as a method of *standardevent* even though standard events are rarely fired explicitly—the system does it for you, in response to defined events such as a mouse click or keystroke. However, you can fire them yourself if you have reason to.

The encapsulation of custom events is much more interesting, because I've taken the time to build into the *customevent* class some tools to make using it *much* easier than the equivalent work in C. Here's the declaration:

```
class customevent : public standardevent
   {
   public:
      customevent
         (
         PSTR aName,
         PSTR aParamList,
         BOOL UnloadOk = TRUE
         );
      virtual BOOL IsStandard (void) const;
   private:
      void ParseParamList (void);
      EVENTINFO EventInfo;
      WORD ParamTypes [12];
   };
```

The *customevent* class encapsulates the *EVENTINFO* structure, just as the *customproperty* class encapsulated the *PROPINFO* structure. So, it should come as no surprise that the *customevent* constructor initializes that structure:

```
customevent::customevent
      (
      PSTR aName,
      PSTR aParamList,
      BOOL UnloadOk
      )
   : standardevent ((PEVENTINFO) &EventInfo, 0)
   {
   EventInfo.npszName = aName;
   EventInfo.npParmTypes = (PWORD) &ParamTypes;
   EventInfo.npszParmProf = aParamList;
   ParseParamList ();
   EventInfo.fl = UnloadOk ? 0 : EF_fNoUnload;
   }
```

You can see, in the constructor's argument list, a pointer to a string, *aParamList*. And while that pointer is stored in the *EventInfo* structure, another field—*EventInfo.npParmTypes*—is also initialized. Where did that address come from? Or, rather, how did it gain a valid content?

Strictly speaking, at the time of that assignment, it doesn't have a valid value. But it will before it is referenced by the VBX manager, thanks to the member function *ParseParamList()*:

```
void customevent::ParseParamList (void)
   {
   EventInfo.cParms = 0;
   register ParamListLength = strlen (EventInfo.npszParmProf);
   for (register i = 5; i < ParamListLength; i++)
      if (toupper (EventInfo.npszParmProf[i-4]) == ' ' &&
            toupper (EventInfo.npszParmProf[i-3]) == 'A' &&
            toupper (EventInfo.npszParmProf[i-2]) == 'S' &&
            toupper (EventInfo.npszParmProf[i-1]) == ' ')
         switch (toupper (EventInfo.npszParmProf[i]))
            {
            case 'I':
               ParamTypes[EventInfo.cParms++] = ET_I2;
               break;
            case 'L':
               ParamTypes[EventInfo.cParms++] = ET_I4;
               break;
            case 'S':
               if (toupper (EventInfo.npszParmProf[i+1]) == 'I')
                  ParamTypes[EventInfo.cParms++] = ET_R4;
               else
                  ParamTypes[EventInfo.cParms++] = ET_HLSTR;
               break;
            case 'D':
               ParamTypes[EventInfo.cParms++] = ET_R8;
               break;
            case 'C':
               ParamTypes[EventInfo.cParms++] = ET_CY;
               break;
            }
   EventInfo.cwParms = EventInfo.cParms * 2;
   }
```

You may recall that the *EVENTINFO* structure contains two pieces of parallel data: a list of parameters (a string) and a list of data types *of* those parameters (an array of **int**s). It is entirely possible for the programmer to inadvertently make those two lists mutually inconsistent. What *ParseParamList()* does is to read the parameter description string, and from it, *derive* the data type list.

The *eventslist* class is precisely analogous to the *propertieslist* class:

```
class eventslist
   {
   public:
      enum { MaxEvents = 32 };
      eventslist (USHORT aRunVersion = VB300_VERSION);
      eventslist & operator+= (standardevent & Event);
      UINT Find (standardevent & Event);
      standardevent & operator[] (int i);
      NPEVENTLIST GetList (void)
```

```
      { return (NPEVENTLIST) EventList; }
  private:
    USHORT RunVersion;
    USHORT Count;
    standardevent * Events[MaxEvents];
    PEVENTINFO EventList[MaxEvents];
  };
```

We define a generous maximum of 32 events. The constructor does the usual job of preparing the object, in this case an empty container:

```
eventslist::eventslist (USHORT aRunVersion)
  : RunVersion (aRunVersion), Count (0)
  {
  EventList[0] = NULL;
  }
```

And the += operator again signifies the appending of another *event* object being added to the container:

```
eventslist & eventslist::operator+= (standardevent & anEvent)
  {
  if (anEvent.Version <= RunVersion &&
      (Count < MaxEvents))
    {
    Events[Count] = &anEvent;
    EventList[Count] = Events[Count]->EventID;
    EventList[++Count] = NULL;
    }
  return *this;
  }
```

The *Find()* and subscript operator functions are also similar to their *propertieslist* counterparts.

Just Do It

I opened this chapter with a simplified example of *using* VBX++ to create a control called "Gradient." To demonstrate the use of what we've since developed, let's create a *real* control by that name.

The *gradient* control is intended to be used for visual enhancement. It paints itself as a gradually darkening series of lines, one pixel wide, so that the top of the control is a full rendition of the color the user selects, and the bottom is full black, with the area in between a smooth gradation of shades from top to bottom. You've seen the effect in a number of places, including the backdrop of the screen generated by the Setup

Wizard. It's a hassle to write; by encapsulating the behavior in a control, the job is done once and for all.

The first step is, of course, creating a project for the new control. You'll want to make copies of VBXXX.RC plus the .BMP and .ICO files to put in your project directory; add those to the project. You'll also need a module definition (.DEF) file, and one .CPP module—for example, GRADIENT.CPP. Finally, be sure to add two libraries to the project: VB\CDK\VBAPI.LIB, of course; but also VBXXX.LIB, which contains the classes we've worked on for the last three chapters.

The module definition file should look something like this:

```
LIBRARY          GRADIENT
DESCRIPTION      'Gradient VBX Custom Control'
EXETYPE          WINDOWS
CODE             PRELOAD MOVEABLE DISCARDABLE
DATA             PRELOAD MOVEABLE SINGLE
HEAPSIZE         4096
```

You'll want to modify the copied resources to provide reasonable bitmaps for the VB toolbox; I suggest something like the bitmaps shown in Figure 6.4. And don't forget to update the *VERSIONINFO* resource!

Those tasks done, we can turn to the GRADIENT.CPP module. It begins with a **#include** and the declaration of the *gradient* class:

```
#include <vbxxx.h>

class gradient : public model
  {
  public:
    gradient ();
  protected:
    virtual FLONG GetModelFlags (void);
    virtual void OnDraw (control & Control,
      devicecontext & Dc, BOOL Erase, rectangle Rect);
  private:
    colorproperty TopColorProp;
  };
```

To accommodate the **#include**, don't forget to add the VBXXX directory (folder) to the directory search list for both **#include**s and libraries.

Figure 6.4 Gradient's toolbox bitmaps.

Three methods and one property are all it takes to implement *gradient*. So far, so good; we have managed to achieve our goal of making it simple to declare a new control. How about the implementation?

Well, the first task is constructing the control:

```
gradient::gradient ()
  : model ((PSTR) "Gradient"),
    TopColorProp ((PSTR) "TopColor", RGB (255, 255, 255))
  {
  Properties += *Top;
  Properties += *Left;
  Properties += *Height;
  Properties += *Width;
  Properties += TopColorProp;
  }
```

The name of the control is passed on to the base constructor; the custom property is also constructed, and all the properties, standard and custom, that we want this control to support are added to the inherited *Properties* collection. (There are no events triggered by this control; if there were, we would similarly add them to the *Events* collection.)

Because we want *gradient* to be a "graphical" control for reduced overhead, the *GetModelFlags()* function is overridden:

```
FLONG gradient::GetModelFlags (void)
  {
  return MODEL_fGraphical;
  }
```

The *OnDraw()* function turns out to be more of a demonstration of the portable GDI classes than of VBX++. Its job is to draw lines from top to bottom of the control, with each line a tad darker than the one above it, until the bottom line comes out solid black:

```
void gradient::OnDraw (control & Control,
    devicecontext & Dc, BOOL, rectangle Rect)
  {
  color TopColor (TopColorProp.GetValue(Control));
  color LineColor;
  register Percent;

  register Offset (Rect.top);
  Rect.top = 0;
  Rect.bottom -= Offset;

  for (register i = 0; i < Rect.bottom; i++)
    {
```

```
    Percent = 100 - ((i * 100) / Rect.bottom);
    LineColor =
        red ((BYTE) ((red) TopColor) * (BYTE) Percent / 100);
    LineColor =
        green ((BYTE) ((green) TopColor) * (BYTE) Percent / 100);
    LineColor =
        blue ((BYTE) ((blue) TopColor) * (BYTE) Percent / 100);

    pen Pen (LineColor, 2, pen::InsideFrame);
    Dc = Pen;
    Dc.MoveTo (Rect.left, Offset + i);
    Dc.LineTo (Rect.right, Offset + i);
    }
}
```

The use of the *Offset* local variable becomes clear when you realize that a graphical control uses its *parent's* client coordinates; so *Rect.top* is not likely to be zero. To make the subsequent math easier, we modify *Rect* so that it is.

We then draw each line. Each of the color elements—red, green and blue—is calculated from the value of the *TopColorProp* property and the percentage from the top this line happens to be. Once we have that color, a *pen* of that color can be constructed. A little-known facet of pens is that if the *pen::InsideFrame* style is supplied and the width of the pen is greater than 1, a dithered pen will be used. *LineTo()* is more efficient than *DrawRectangle()* so that's the approach used here.

The *pen* is selected into the *devicecontext* using the += operator; the line is drawn. At that point the *pen* goes out of scope; remember that the pen's destructor automatically removes it from a device context if it has been selected into one, before the pen is destroyed. (The new pen is replaced by the one originally supplied by the DC.)

Finally, we fulfill our obligation to instantiate exactly one instance of our new control:

```
gradient Gradient;
```

That gives us all we need. We build and *voila!* GRADIENT.VBX is born. We can add it to the list of Visual Basic controls in a project; we can place it on a form; we can set a *TopColor* as well as location on the form. Figure 6.5 shows an example.

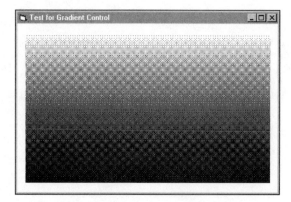

Figure 6.5 The Gradient Control in action.

Did we meet our goal of making VBXs a snap to create? I'd say so ... more or less. But we still had to copy a couple of files. Not so many as with the C-style skeleton, but still ... can't *anything* be done about that?

As a matter of fact, we *can* make the creation of VBXs easier still ... as you'll see in the next section.

PART 3

A VBX Generator

Introducing the VBX Genie   169

Creating the User Interface   177

Generating Code   223

Self-Installing IDE Tools   235

Creating a Setup Program for
   VBX Genie   261

The VBX for the Find and
   Replace Dialogs   297

Adding Tool Tips to Standard
   Controls   317

Introducing the VBX Genie

7

UNTIL THE LIKES OF VISUAL C++ and Borland C++ came along, I was never a big fan of CASE (Computer-Aided Software Engineering) tools. For one thing, I don't really believe in "Software Engineering" at all; I believe in Software Artistry. Sure, we have to know how to make our artists' tools work, just as a painter must know the qualities of his or her paints, brushes, and media. But the actual assembly job is more than an assembly job. The original promise of CASE was to enforce "simple" engineering rules and thus suck top-quality applications from mediocre programmers. In the end, those tools did indeed suck; but they didn't actually help anyone generate a top-quality application. Mediocre programmers still turned out mediocre programs, and artists found themselves stifled by some mediocre academic's notion of how an application should be laid out.

The Visual C++ and Borland C++ IDEs (Integrated Development Environments) qualify as CASE tools, but they take a different approach: They generate skeleton code according to your specifications, and then get out of the way. They are thus collections of tools, not pretenders to the lead programmer's throne—something that I not only approve of, but emulate whenever possible.

For example, the work of building up the basic structure for a software component like a VBX is not very complex, as we've seen; but it's boring. There's the MODEL structure, the construction of the properties and events lists, and the headers for all the various message handlers. Why should you have to type them, or even cut and paste them, when the computer could *generate* them for you according to specifications *you* provide?

Of course a full-blown VBX generator is not a trivial task. But it is worth having, and it is *certainly* worth learning how to build! So, in each chapter in this part of the book, we'll tackle another aspect of the design and implementation of a code generator, the *VBX Genie*. And, when we're done, you'll not only have a VBX code generator—you'll know how to write your own code generator, and even have some reusable tools to help you do just that!

The Design of a Code Generator

Any code generator consists of the same three basic components:

- A code template. This is the code you want generated, but it also includes some method of replacing certain portions with generated code.
- A module to generate the code that is blended with the rest of the code template.
- A module that obtains the information required to actually generate the desired code.

It is sometimes possible to leave one or more of these features out of a *very* simple code generator. For example, if all you are going to generate are small snippets of code such as C++ **class** headers, you may not need a template at all. Or, if the replaceable information does not require user input—the date and time, for example, which can be obtained from the system—it may be possible to omit the user interface.

However, in the case of the VBX Genie we'll create in this book, all three components will be needed. Before we jump in and code the Genie, let's discuss each of its three components in a little more detail.

The Code Template

The basic code VBX Genie will generate is just what we've already seen: the VBX Skeleton and/or the VBX++ Class Library, as requested by the user. But we'll have to allow for programmatic modification of that code. Such modifications would include the property and event definitions, and the optional functions for handling *VBM_METHOD* messages. In the case of VBX Skeleton, those modifications must be made in the middle of the code; in the case of VBX++, the generator instead must produce one file in addition to the Class Library components: the derived class of the new control.

It turns out that all code modifications (for this project, at least!) are one of two types. In the first type, simple substitutions of text must be made. This is similar to a global search-and-replace operation. For example, you might have a set of files you use as the basis for all projects of a certain type. Within those files you might make reference to a project name; but that name is different for each project. So, in your original files, you might include a string like "$PROJECTNAME" wherever you want the project name to appear. Then, after you've made your copy, you could use your IDE's search-and-replace mechanism to change any occurrence of "$PROJECTNAME" to the correct name for that particular project.

This is exactly the way we'll handle it in VBX Genie (except we'll automate the process, of course).

The second type of modification is the inclusion (or exclusion) of chunks of *optional code*. These are blocks you only need to include in the finished files under certain circumstances. In C and C++, you can manage this with **#define**s and **#ifdef** and **#ifndef** macros. We'll need to implement a similar mechanism somehow.

> *By the way, in my experiences writing code generators, I've only come upon one other type of template modification: the repeating code. This is the kind of thing where you include in the template a "loop"; and based on the value of a variable supplied by the code generator, code within this "loop" is duplicated, with the current value of the loop's index variable inserted where needed into the emitted code. However, we won't need this for the code generated by VBX Genie.*

The Code Generator

Given that you've somehow come up with values for controlling modifications to the code from the template, you need a code generator to actually emit the code and make the changes. If the code template resides in an external file, that file must be located and read into memory (or, if it can't be found, the error must be dealt with). It is preferable to attach the template files to your .EXE as programmer-defined resources, so they can't be lost. In either case, once in memory, the template "variables"—I call them *substitutions*—must be replaced by the desired values; and the unselected optional code must be removed. Then the files can be created.

Because this aspect of the job is so generic, the modules that implement the code generator can be reused in any code-generator project—not just VBX Genie.

The User Interface

A "genie" is an application of the type known as a "tool." Such an application is run infrequently and for short periods (as opposed to, say, a word processor) and consequently its user interface must be optimized for occasional use. That means, we can't expect the user to be a VBX Genie expert! The interface should be designed for clarity, not speed of access.

There are two common ways to design tool-type applications in Windows. One is to use a sequence of panels or dialog boxes, each of which contains a "Next" and a "Previous" button. There are usually also "Finish" and "Exit" buttons. This design is best for a tool in which a fixed, step-by-step approach is desirable. The user can always go back to an earlier step if necessary, but doing so is a bit clunky.

The second technique is to allow equal access of all components at once. The Windows 95 user interface has blessed this technique in its "property pages" concept. The idea is that there's really just one step to what you want to do; but there are too many options to place on a single dialog. None of the options comes "first" or "last," so a series of panels is inappropriate. In property boxes, the various aspects or properties of the thing you are trying to modify or create are grouped logically and ordered across a set of tabbed sub-dialogs called *pages*.

That fits the creation of VBXs perfectly, so that's the technique we'll use in designing VBX Genie. Figure 7.1 shows a snapshot of VBX Genie, as seen with its Project property page visible.

Figure 7.1   Our first look at VBX Genie.

Like other Windows 95 dialogs, VBX Genie looks clean and simple, offering easy, uncluttered access to each of the major groupings of properties. As a tool-type application, it is not document-centric. Although it generates files, it does not "edit" a "document." Therefore, there is no *File* menu—indeed, there's no menu at all. Even though VBX Genie is implemented as a .EXE file, it *appears to the user* as a dialog.

After the user has selected the desired options, he or she will click the OK button and the real fun begins. VBX Genie will find or create a specified directory (or "folder," as they're called in Windows 95) and generate several files in that directory. Then, since VBX Genie is best used as a tool attached to your programming environment's *Tools* menu, it will interact with the IDE to actually create and open an appropriate project for the new VBX.

Choosing an Implementation Language

VBX Genie *could* be written in MFC or ObjectWindows. However, while either of those languages can certainly do the job, the fact is that VBX Genie is going to be a user-interface-intensive project. And it's going to have to control Visual C++ or Borland C++ to get them to create new projects. These are things that, shall we say, do not play to the strengths of either C++ class library.

Visual Basic, on the other hand, is a perfect match for applications where the emphasis is on the user interface. And, fortunately, Visual Basic 4.0 has recently been released, complete with new features that make this project, in particular, an easy one to do.

In addition to the ability to attach resources to a .EXE file, VB4 supports programmer-defined objects, just like C++. Well, *almost* like C++: Inheritance is *not* supported. But 85 percent of the value of C++ lies in simple encapsulation; and VB objects handle that just fine.

Figure 7.2 shows the top-level objects that we'll need.

Keep in mind that Figure 7.2 presents a functional layout; it shows the major objects but not any inheritance-style hierarchy they might have. The important things to note are as follows:

• Everything happens under control of Prime, the main form.
• The code generator, which is invoked from Prime, actually does much of its work by letting the objects write code for themselves. That is, the *Properties* class writes property code, the *Events* class writes events code, and so on.

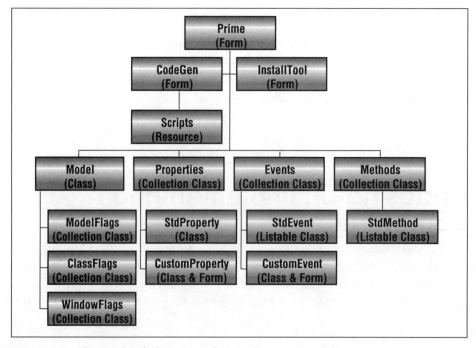

Figure 7.2 The top-level objects used to implement VBX Genie.

- The code generator keeps its script in the application resource pool, using the new VB4 feature to allow this.

- The *Listable* class is used by six different classes. That's code re-use in action!

- The map of objects corresponds directly to the user interface map. Form follows function!

In the next few chapters, we're going to implement VBX Genie line-by-line. Keep the chart shown in Figure 7.2 handy as we do. VXB Genie is *not* a trivial program—but I maintain that even the most complex application can *seem* simple, and wind up being as robust as a simple program, if you've employed appropriate object-oriented methods. Let's see if I'm right!

Creating the User Interface 8

N OW THAT WE'VE LAID THE GROUNDWORK for VBX Genie, we should be ready to start designing and coding it. We have a lot of territory to cover; in fact we'll need this chapter and the next two chapters to develop all of the needed code.

Since the user interface is what you see first when VBX Genie runs, it makes sense for us to start by designing and coding the interface. The other reason for coding the interface first is that it is the easiest component to build. Because of the highly visual and interactive nature of VBX Genie, we'll shift gears and use Visual Basic instead of C++. This will provide us with an unexpected bonus—we'll create a powerful tool whose interface we can easily modify and expand to add additional features.

We'll start by examining the main form and the programmer-defined classes that make VBX work. Then, we'll add the code for each of the tabbed pages of the interface. The advantage of this approach is that we'll build the interface in the same order that the user would interact with it when creating a VBX software component.

Creating the Main Form—the Prime Directive

If you recall from Chapter 7, VBX Genie was designed around a dialog window that contained six selectable tabs:

- Project
- Version
- Model
- Properties
- Events
- Methods

Each tab can be chosen by the user to select different VBX Genie options. To create this type of interface, we'll need to start with a main form, which we'll call Prime.

Early on in my experience with Visual Basic, I started naming my startup form "Prime." Well, I *originally* called it "Main," but I had to quit when I discovered an odd interaction between a form named "Main" and a **Sub Main**, if there was one. In any case, "Form1" was never really an option, as far as I was concerned!

This particular Prime has a dialog border and no menu, because it is of the type of program that doesn't stay on screen very long. Microsoft calls them "wizards," Borland calls them "experts," I call them "genies." They are designed to do a specific, focused job, and then get out of your face. VBX Genie will actually run as a tool from the *Tools* menu of either Microsoft Visual C++ 1.5x (the 16-bit version) or Borland C++ 4.52 (the version that emits correct machine code).

Since VBXs *must* be 16-bit DLLs, there's no point in writing VBX Genie to run under 32-bit Windows. It is therefore assembled in the 16-bit version of Visual Basic 4.0 (which comes with the Professional Edition), and can use VBXs in its construction (such as my IniData control from my book *Windows Programming Power with Custom Controls*).

There is, frankly, too much information to be gathered to do so on one flat panel. My choices were the multi-page style Microsoft uses for most of their wizards or the tabbed style used for property pages and most of their other dialogs these days. I chose the latter, for the relative ease to the user in flitting back and forth between various types of options.

Coding Prime

As the functional chart presented in Chapter 7 shows, Prime will need to manage (or at least, own) objects of several types. These objects represent the model flags, class flags, window flags, properties, events, and methods of the target VBX, respectively. These objects are declared in Prime's **(General) (Declarations)** section:

```
Option Explicit

Dim ModelFlags As New ModelFlagsClass
Dim ClassFlags As New ClassFlagsClass
Dim WindowFlags As New WindowFlagsClass
Dim Properties As New PropertiesClass
Dim Events As New EventsClass
Dim Methods As New MethodsClass
```

The keyword **New** in each of these statements tells you that, as the Prime form is being initialized, these objects will also be initialized. Like C++ objects, they are responsible for constructing themselves, so that as soon as Prime is ready to execute code, these objects will be ready to help.

There is a new event, *Initialize*, that is triggered when the form is being initialized, before it is "loaded." That event exists to make the form seem more like the class object it is. (Class objects also have an *Initialize* event, but of course not a *Load* event.) However, in the case of a form, *Initialize* is of limited use, because the form has *not* yet been loaded and, therefore, its controls do not exist.

For that reason, Prime has its initial executable code in its *Load* event:

```
Private Sub Form_Load()
IniDatal.FileName = MakePath("", App.Path, App.EXEName, ".ini")
If Not AlreadyInstalled Then
   Unload Me
   Exit Sub
End If

Dim C As WaitCursor
Set C = New WaitCursor
```

```
LoadVersionDefaults

ModelFlags.SetListbox lst_ModelFlags
ModelFlags.SetProperties Properties
ClassFlags.SetListbox lst_ClassFlags
WindowFlags.SetListbox lst_WindowFlags
Properties.SetListbox lst_Properties
Properties.SetModelFlags ModelFlags
Properties.SetEvents Events
Events.SetListbox lst_Events
Events.SetProperties Properties
Events.SetMethods Methods
Methods.SetListbox lst_Methods
Methods.SetEvents Events

cmb_VBVersion.ListIndex = 2
End Sub
```

The first statement readies the IniData control with the fully qualified path for VBX Genie's .INI file. That way VBXGEN.INI will *not* add to the clutter of the \WINDOWS directory.

The *AlreadyInstalled* function checks to see if VBX Genie has yet been installed into your compiler's *Tools* menu. If not, it installs itself and returns **False**, on the assumption that the *reason* you just ran it, was to install it. Otherwise it returns **True** and processing continues.

The two lines with the *WaitCursor* class are there because VB doesn't automatically put up an hourglass cursor while waiting for a form to show itself.

> *The* WaitCursor *class is a reusable component that switches the cursor to an hourglass when it is created, and switches back when it goes out of scope.*

For some bizarre reason, *WaitCursor* doesn't work properly when simply **Dim**med, even as **New**, and not referenced. Apparently there is some degree of optimization at work; too bad the engineers of VB spent time on that instead of implementing short-circuit expression evaluation. But I digress.

Once the defaults for the Version page are set, the remainder of the procedure attaches each of the objects declared in the **(General) (Declarations)** section to its own listbox, and sets up the inter-object linkages required to support the interactions between *MODEL* flags, properties, events, and methods. (Obviously, we'll have to inspect these functions more closely when we get to the coding of the various objects. For now, just accept that the function does what its name implies it should.)

The very last executable line sets a combo box choice to entry index 2. That combo box, located on the Model page, contains a list of the three VBX manager versions that have been released—1.0, 2.0, and 3.0. There is no code to *place* those values in the combo box, because VB4 allows us to do that at design time.

Now, you might have noticed that nowhere have we actually *loaded* any of those list boxes. Were these magic classes doing it somehow? Not at all. It's the *version combo box* that triggers it. After all, if the user selects a different version of VBX manager, the list boxes will have to be reloaded, anyway. Since the combo box's *Click* event is triggered when a change is made, either manually or programmatically, we can take advantage of that to initially load, *and* to reload, the list boxes as needed:

```
Private Sub cmb_VBVersion_Click()
ModelFlags.TargetVersion = Val(cmb_VBVersion)
ModelFlags.LoadListbox
ClassFlags.TargetVersion = Val(cmb_VBVersion)
ClassFlags.LoadListbox
WindowFlags.TargetVersion = Val(cmb_VBVersion)
WindowFlags.LoadListbox
Properties.TargetVersion = Val(cmb_VBVersion)
Properties.LoadListbox
Events.TargetVersion = Val(cmb_VBVersion)
Events.LoadListbox
Methods.TargetVersion = Val(cmb_VBVersion)
Methods.LoadListbox
End Sub
```

You now see that each of these user-defined classes has a property, *TargetVersion*, that it uses (apparently!) to decide which items to place in the list box.

Wiring in the Tab Control

There's one more general occurrence to describe before moving on to a page-by-page description of the application, regarding the tab control. This is an SSTab control, bundled with Visual Basic 4.0 and written by Sheridan Software. It's a great tab control, easily the best one I've used. (It certainly beats Microsoft's "property page" tabs, which are just the tabs—not control containers—and not much help. Besides, they won't run in a 16-bit application.)

The SSTab control experiences a *GotFocus* event whenever the user changes from one page to another, even if the control already *had* the focus. So a little code in the handler for that event suffices to re-set the focus to the first control on the newly active page:

```
Private Sub SSTab1_GotFocus()
On Error Resume Next
Select Case Index
Case 0:
   Select Case SSTab1(Index).Tab
   Case 0:
      txt_Name.SetFocus
   Case 1:
      txt_FileVersion(0).SetFocus
   Case 2:
      cmb_VBVersion.SetFocus
   Case 3:
      lst_Properties.SetFocus
   Case 4:
      lst_Events.SetFocus
   Case 5:
      lst_Methods.SetFocus
   End Select
End Select
End Sub
```

The reason for the **On Error** statement at the start is that the *GotFocus* event is *also* triggered when the form first becomes active and the controls it contains are not yet in any condition to have the focus shifted to them. This is a benign error we can safely ignore.

One other problem regarding the tab pages requires handling the form's **KeyDown** event. The SSTab control is designed to "turn" pages in response to **Control+Tab** or **Shift-Control+Tab**, just like the views in an MDI application. Unfortunately, when the tab control has items on it—and what good would it be, otherwise?—it never gets those keystrokes because the currently active *item* does. To the rescue comes another new Visual Basic 4.0 feature: If you ask (by setting the form's *KeyPreview* property to **True**), the form gets first crack at all keystroke events:

```
Private Sub Form_KeyDown(KeyCode As Integer, Shift As Integer)
If (Shift And vbCtrlMask) = vbCtrlMask Then
   If KeyCode = Asc(vbTab) Then
      ActivateTab SSTab1(0), Shift And vbShiftMask
      KeyCode = 0
   End If
End If
If KeyCode = vbKeyF1 Then
   About.Show vbModal
   KeyCode = 0
End If
End Sub
```

To prevent the keystroke from going on any farther, set the *KeyCode* argument to zero.

While at it, I'm intercepting the F1 key and using it to display an About box.

Supporting the Project Page

Recall that the first of the tabbed pages is labeled "Project." You might have noticed there was nothing on our object map marked "project." That's because the amount of project information to be stored is minor enough to store it in the Prime form, itself. (Remember, in VB4, forms *are* objects, the equal of programmer-defined classes.)

The major interaction of the various controls on Prime comes from the very first field, labeled "Name." As the user types a value into this field, the value is copied into the "Directory" field on this page, and several other fields on the Version and Model pages. Now, we want this to happen *only* if those other fields haven't been expressly altered by the user. We accomplish that using the *Tag* property that nearly every VB control possesses. While it is empty, changes to the Name field (the control's name is actually *txt_Name*) are reflected into these other controls. However, if the *user* makes a change to one of these controls, the new value is written into the *Tag* property as well, so *Name* knows not to alter it:

```
Private Sub txt_Name_Change()
Dim aDrive As String
Dim aDir As String
Dim aRoot As String
Dim aExt As String

If txt_Directory.Tag = "" Then
    SplitPath txt_Directory.Text, aDrive, aDir, aRoot, aExt
    txt_Directory.Text = LCase$(MakePath(aDrive, aDir, txt_Name, ""))
End If

If txt_ProductName.Tag = "" Then
    txt_ProductName.Text = txt_Name.Text
End If

If txt_ClassName.Tag = "" Then
    txt_ClassName.Text = txt_Name.Text
End If

cmd_OK.Enabled = VerifyOK
End Sub
```

(The *SplitPath* and *MakePath* functions work like their namesakes in the C standard library; the code resides in a module called FILES.BAS.)

The *VerifyOK* function tests any fields that could possibly have invalid values, on all the pages, to make sure the OK button is disabled unless all the values are appropriate. There are only three fields this could happen to; and each one of them, in its *Change* event, calls *VerifyOK*:

```
Private Function VerifyOK() As Boolean
VerifyOK = True
If Len(txt_Name.Text) = 0 Then
   VerifyOK = False
   Exit Function
End If
If Len(txt_ClassName.Text) = 0 Then
   VerifyOK = False
   Exit Function
End If
If Len(txt_DefControlName.Text) = 0 Then
   VerifyOK = False
   Exit Function
End If
End Function
```

VerifyOK is *a function. So why doesn't it require an open/close parenthesis pair appended to it? Simple—because, finally, the Visual Basic language has been enhanced to not require these vestiges of a non-C-programmer's nightmares. The enhancement is backward-compatible; you can still append the parentheses if you feel you must.*

Supporting the Version Page

Well, one page down; five to go. The Version page, which accepts information used by the VERSIONINFO resource of the control, looks like the dialog shown in Figure 8.1.

There is interaction between the "Year," "Company Name," "Author," and "Copyright Notice" fields. The starting value of *txt_Copyright.Tag* property is "©YYYY by OWNER All Rights Reserved." Whenever *txt_Year, txt_CompanyName,* or *txt_Author* is altered, a **Sub** called *SetCopyright* is invoked:

```
Private Sub SetCopyright()
Dim Notice As String
Notice = txt_Copyright.Tag
```

```
Dim i As Integer
i = InStr(Notice, "YYYY")
If i > 0 Then
    Notice = Left$(Notice, i - 1) + txt_ReleaseYear.Text + Mid$(Notice, i + 4)
End If

i = InStr(Notice, "OWNER")
If i > 0 Then
    Dim Owner As String
    If opt_CopyrightOwnerIsCompany Then
        Owner = txt_CompanyName.Text
    Else
        Owner = txt_Author.Text
    End If
    Notice = Left$(Notice, i - 1) + Owner + Mid$(Notice, i + 5)
End If

txt_Copyright.Text = Notice
End Sub
```

This does not prevent the user from manually putting anything he or she pleases into the "Copyright" field:

```
Private Sub txt_Copyright_Change()
If txt_Copyright Is ActiveControl Then
    txt_Copyright.Tag = txt_Copyright.Text
End If
End Sub
```

In fact, if what the user puts there includes the magic strings "YYYY" or "OWNER," the automatic updating will continue if the user modifies those other fields!

Figure 8.1 The Version Page used with VBX Genie.

Please notice, also, that the copyright owner may be either the author or the company. Both fields are stored in the VERSIONINFO resource, but only the "owner" appears automatically in the copyright notice.

It would, of course, be annoying to have to re-enter the company and author names every time a VBX was generated. You can't see it at run-time, but VBX Genie has an IniData control resting on its surface. That control (presented in my book, *Windows Programming Power with Custom Controls* and included on the companion CD-ROM with this book) allows easy, VB-style access to a .INI file. When the Prime form is being unloaded (as it is when the application shuts down), it detects if a change has been made to either of these values; if one has, the user is prompted to save the information for the next time:

```
Private Sub Form_QueryUnload(Cancel As Integer, UnloadMode As Integer)
Dim Msg As String
Dim Result As Integer
If txt_CompanyName.Text <> txt_CompanyName.Tag Then
        Msg = "You've changed the Company Name on the Versions page to '" + _
            txt_CompanyName.Text + _
            "'. Do you want to make the new value your default?"
        Result = MsgBox(Msg, vbYesNoCancel + vbQuestion)
        If Result = vbCancel Then
            Cancel = True
            Exit Sub
        ElseIf Result = vbYes Then
            IniData1.KeyName = "Company Name"
            IniData1.Text = txt_CompanyName.Text
        End If
End If
If txt_Author.Text <> txt_Author.Tag Then
        Msg = "You've changed the Author on the Versions page to '" + _
            txt_Author.Text + _
            "'. Do you want to make the new value your default?"
        Result = MsgBox(Msg, vbYesNoCancel + vbQuestion)
        If Result = vbCancel Then
            Cancel = True
            Exit Sub
        ElseIf Result = vbYes Then
            IniData1.KeyName = "Author"
            IniData1.Text = txt_Author.Text
        End If
End If
End Sub
```

This function illustrates two new features of VB4. First, there is (finally!) a line continuation character. It's the one we've been using in books and magazine articles all along, a space followed by an underscore. Second, we no longer have to include **Const**ants from CONSTANT.TXT to make the *MsgBox* function work. All constants are managed by the new Browser, and are available with no additional effort. They do have new names, though, requiring a global search-and-replace of old names such as *MB_ICONINFORMATION* with *vbInformation.*

If the contents of the "Author" and "Company Name" fields are saved when the form is unloaded, then you'd expect any previously-saved values are retrieved when the form is loaded; and indeed, this is the case. The *LoadVersionDefaults* **Sub** is invoked from the *Load* event:

```
Sub LoadVersionDefaults()
IniData1.Section = "Version"
IniData1.KeyName = "Company Name"
txt_CompanyName.Text = IniData1.Text
txt_CompanyName.Tag = IniData1.Text

IniData1.KeyName = "Author"
txt_Author.Text = IniData1.Text
txt_Author.Tag = IniData1.Text
txt_ReleaseYear.Text = Format$(Year(Now))
End Sub
```

Remember that programmatic alterations of a Textbox trigger *Change* events, just as manual alterations do. So the "Copyright Notice" is appropriately updated, automatically.

Introducing the Listable Classes

Before we move on to the Model page, let's take a moment to consider how we are going to implement the rest of this project. We have MODEL flags to manage—that is, we must be able to display them, the user must be able to select some, and we must be able to derive compilable code from the ones that have been selected. We also have window class flags and window flags, and the same is true of them. All these flags have identifiers and descriptions; all can be selected. Moreover, all will appear in list boxes.

Now, if we take the word "description" to include "name," it turns out that the *exact* same set of requirements applies to standard properties ... and standard events ... and methods! Sure, they each have a few "extra" requirements ... but it sure sounds like a job for class inheritance to me.

However, Visual Basic classes do not support inheritance in the C++ sense. For some reason the designers of OLE don't like that kind of inheritance. They prefer something called "aggregation," which implements inheritance through properties—sort of like inheriting money from your grandmother, on condition that you keep her corpse seated at the dining room table. It's not as convenient as true inheritance; we'll have to code a few "passthrough" **Sub***s. But it still saves code and makes for a more robust application than not using any kind of inheritance at all.*

There are actually two parallel lines of inheritance, here. One is the set of collection classes we'll need; the other is the set of things they'll contain. Figure 8.2 shows a simplified hierarchy chart to help make things clearer.

The base collection class is called *ListablesClass*; the base class for items it will contain is called the *ListableClass*. Since this is our first use of VB classes, it makes a good introduction to VB classes in general.

All files (except graphics components) in VB4 are stored in text format (VB3's binary option no longer exists). That means that Notepad or any

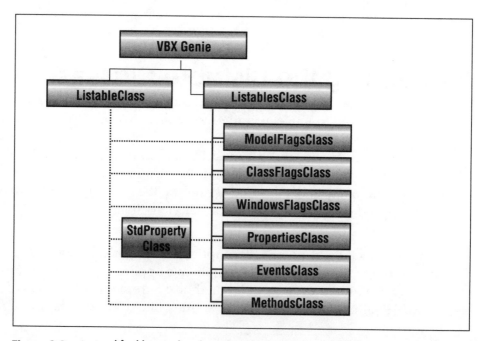

Figure 8.2 A simplified hierarchy chart that shows the two parallel lines of inheritance.

similar ASCII or ANSI text editor can be used to read them. Forms and controls are no longer the only VB objects with properties; even code modules have them. The properties are set in VB from the usual Properties window; in ASCII, the properties for a class look like something like this:

```
VERSION 1.0 CLASS
BEGIN
  MultiUse = -1  'True
END
Attribute VB_Name = "ListablesClass"
Attribute VB_Creatable = False
Attribute VB_Exposed = False
Attribute VB_Description = "Base collection class for Model, Class and Window
flags, and properties, events and methods."
```

VB4 can be used to create OLE servers; most of this information is used to manage that. However, the *VB_Description* can be viewed from the new Browser and thus serves as a form of documentation. (The description, in fact, is *set* in the Browser.) Figure 8.3 shows a sample of the Browser window, as it examines the *ListablesClass* module.

Please don't confuse the properties of the *module* with those of the *class*. VB classes define properties just like controls (another form of VB object) do.

Supporting Collections

ListablesClass is what's called a "user-defined collection class." Visual Basic supplies a **Collection** object, a very good one in fact, that can often be used as-is. But when you have special needs, you wind up deriving a new class from it using aggregation, the only tool for inheritance VB provides. That

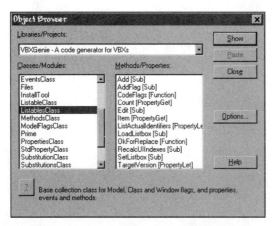

Figure 8.3 The Object Browser window for VBX Genie.

means that, to make *ListablesClass* a "user-defined collection," we simply give it at least one property that *is* a **Collection**:

```
Option Explicit

Private List As New Collection
Private UI As ListBox
```

As you look at these properties, you'll see they are marked **Private**—they cannot be referenced outside this class. The other possibility is **Public**.

> *The keyword **Dim** is still allowed, but it means "private" in a class or form and "public" in a code module. I suggest you say what you mean rather than rely on a default that is different depending on where it's used.*

The way you decide between the two access scopes isn't quite the same as C++, where all properties are generally best made **private**. Basically, if a property needs to be protected—if you want control over what values are assigned to it—you make it **Private**. You would also make it **Private** if you want actions to take place when a value is assigned to it or when its value is read. If neither of those conditions holds, you can safely mark it **Public**.

The VB **Collection** class has an *Add* method, so the *ListablesClass* should have one, too. Ours has built-in recovery for an attempt to add an item with a duplicate key:

```
Public Sub Add(Listable As Object)
On Error Resume Next
List.Add Listable, Listable.Description
If Err <> 0 Then
    Err = OkForReplace(Listable)
End If
If Err = 0 Then
    Listable.SetListbox UI
    Listable.LoadListbox Index(Listable.Description)
    RecalcUIIndexes
End If
End Sub
```

This procedure is not limited to adding objects of the *ListableClass*—VB collections can hold *any* object or, indeed, anything at all.

It's the *OkForReplace* function that recovers from duplicate entries:

```
Private Function OkForReplace(Listable As Object)
OkForReplace = False
Dim Response As Integer
Response = MsgBox("You already have a " + _
    Listable.KindOf + _
    " by the name '" + _
    Listable.Description + _
    "'. Do you want to replace it?", _
    vbYesNo + vbQuestion, _
    "Duplicate " + Listable.KindOf)
If Response = vbYes Then
    If Not List(Listable.Description).Standard Then
        Unload List(Listable.Description)
    End If
    List.Remove Listable.Description
    List.Add Listable, Listable.Description
    OkForReplace = True
End If
End Function
```

Once the object has been added, its connection to the user interface element, the list box, is set and its *LoadListbox* procedure is invoked. All the items in a *ListablesClass* collection area are expected to set up a two-way linkage with the list box in which they are displayed. The items themselves will always know what position they occupy in the list box—that's the *UIIndex* property. Meanwhile, in the list box, the *ItemData* array contains index pointers back into the *ListablesClass* collection.

Introducing the Property Functions

As a user-defined collection, we must provide methods that will make *ListablesClass* look as much as possible like a regular VB **Collection**, albeit one with extra abilities. That means supplying "passthrough" procedures. However, these won't look quite like any VB procedures you've seen before:

```
Public Property Get Count() As Integer
Count = List.Count
End Property

Public Property Get Item(ID As Variant) As Object
Set Item = List.Item(ID)
End Property
```

They represent a totally new approach that is similar to overloading the assignment and cast operators in C++. VB4 provides what are called *property functions* for setting and retrieving values. Outside the class, these functions look like regular properties, and can participate in operations on either side of an equal sign. Within the function, as much or as little as you need can be accomplished. Property functions are available in **Let**, **Get** and **Set** flavors. **Let** is used with regular variables; **Set** is required for object variables. **Get** may be used with either.

The *Item* method, defined above, brings up one sore point about creating user-defined collections. In the built-in VB **Collection** class, *Item* is a *default* method. That means the two following statements are equivalent:

```
a = List(6)
a = List.Item(6)
```

Of course we'd like to do the very same thing with our user-defined collections ... but we can't. Visual Basic provides no means to identify any one of an object's methods as being a default method, so you have to spell it out all the time.

When building a user-defined collection, some methods may be supplied that allow the programmer to treat all the items in a collection as if they were one thing. For example, suppose you wanted to set a certain flag in all the items in the collection or a property. You can create a property procedure in the collection class to do the enumerating of the contained elements for you:

```
Public Property Let ListActualIdentifiers(ByVal Value As Boolean)
Dim i As Integer
For i = 1 To List.Count
   List(i).ListActualIdentifiers = Value
Next i
End Property

Public Sub SetListbox(L As ListBox)
Set UI = L
Dim i As Integer
For i = 1 To List.Count
    List(i).SetListbox L
Next i
End Sub

Public Property Let TargetVersion(ByVal Value As Integer)
Dim i As Integer
For i = 1 To List.Count
    List(i).TargetVersion = Value
Next i
End Property
```

It is customary to repeat the same method name as long as the job the method does is accurately reflected in the name, within the context of the object type. So *ListablesClass* has a *LoadListbox* method that does the aggregate portion of the job of loading a list box, while still allowing the items it contains to actually put themselves in it:

```
Public Sub LoadListbox()
Dim PreviousSelection As Integer
If UI.ListCount > 0 And UI.ListIndex > -1 Then
   PreviousSelection = UI.ItemData(UI.ListIndex)
Else
   PreviousSelection = -1
End If
UI.Clear
Dim i As Integer
For i = 1 To List.Count
   List(i).LoadListbox i
Next i
RecalcUIIndexes PreviousSelection
End Sub

Private Sub RecalcUIIndexes(Optional PreviousSelection As Variant)
Dim i As Integer
If IsMissing(PreviousSelection) Then
    PreviousSelection = -1
End IfFor i = 0 To UI.ListCount - 1
    List(UI.ItemData(i)).UIIndex = i
    If UI.ItemData(i) = Val(PreviousSelection) Then
        UI.ListIndex = i
        UI.TopIndex = i
    End If
Next i
End Sub
```

The code for *RecalcUIIndexes* is broken into its own procedure so it can be called independently of *LoadListbox* ... for example, when items are added to the collection. (Look back at the *Add* method.)

> *By the way, don't miss another of VB4's new features:* **Optional** *parameters. Any or all of a procedure's parameters may be* **Optional**, *as long as they are* **variant** *and no required parameters follow them in the argument list. The built-in* IsMissing *function tells if an optional parameter was supplied or not.*

Finishing the Initialization

The *ListablesClass* contains a few other methods, but I'm going to hold off explaining them until I can put them into the context in which they're used. For now, let's look at the kind of items the *ListablesClass* will contain: the *ListableClass*.

Since objects of the *ListableClass* are intended to have identifiers, descriptions, and be selectable, it should not surprise you to see properties that support these things in its **(General) (Declarations)** section:

```
Option Explicit

Public Identifier As String
Public Description As String
Private Selected_ As Boolean
Private Version As Integer

Public ListActualIdentifiers As Boolean
Public TargetVersion As Integer

Private UI As Control
Public UIIndex As Integer
```

Although other parts of the application could create *ListableClass* objects and set their properties manually, it's easier to accomplish all the initialization through one call to a simple procedure, like *Init*:

```
Public Sub Init(aIdentifier As String, _
   aDescription As String, _
   ByVal aVersion As Integer)
Identifier = aIdentifier
Description = aDescription
Version = aVersion
End Sub
```

This helps support data hiding, too—some of those properties are **Private**. The *SetListbox* function of the *ListablesClass* calls the method of the same name of each object it contains:

```
Public Sub SetListbox(L As ListBox)
Set UI = L
End Sub
```

Not all property procedures reference variables in memory at all. For example, when *ListableClass* objects are used as standard properties, events, or methods, their *Standard* property must return **True**; custom properties and events will return **False**. What's that, you say? That you didn't *see* a "Standard" property? Well, that's the point! The property is implemented in code, not storage:

```
Public Property Get Standard() As Boolean
Standard = True
End Property
```

By not supplying a **Property Let** function, we make *Standard* a "read-only" property. Slick, huh?

In the case of the *Selected* property, we do need to store a value—in the **Private** variable *Selected_*—so the **Get** function, as trivial as *Standard*'s, does just that:

```
Public Property Get Selected() As Boolean
Selected = Selected_
End Property
```

Why implement *Selected* with property functions? Because the **Let** function has more to do:

```
Public Property Let Selected(ByVal Value As Boolean)
Selected_ = Value
If Not (UI Is Nothing) Then
   UI.Selected(UIIndex) = Value
End If
End Property
```

See, we want these things to be tied in to their respective list boxes. So when a flag, property, event, or method is selected, we want the corresponding listbox entry to *show* that it is selected. And we want the object to do it itself, so we don't have to worry about it from "outside."

Two of the remaining properties, *ListActualIdentifiers* and *TargetVersion*, are both **Public** and are set by *ListablesClass* property procedures that you've already seen. The former is a variable of the new **Boolean** data type that tells the object whether the list box is to display the *Identifier* or the *Description* field. The second allows the object to filter itself from the list box entirely, if the target VBX version is earlier than the version of the flag, property, event, or method itself.

This all takes place in the remaining method of this class, *LoadListbox*:

```
Public Sub LoadListbox(ByVal Index As Integer)
If Version <= TargetVersion Then
   If ListActualIdentifiers Then
     UI.AddItem Identifier
   Else
     UI.AddItem Description
   End If
   UI.ItemData(UI.NewIndex) = Index
   UI.Selected(UI.NewIndex) = Selected_
End If
End Sub
```

As you can see, the listbox entry's *ItemData* property is set to the index (passed by the caller) of this item. That way each listbox entry can easily access the *ListableClass* object associated with it. The final property, *UIIndex*, provides a link from the *ListableClass* object back to the listbox entry. (*UIIndex* is set by the caller of *LoadListbox* after all items have been loaded.)

Notice that elements in the multi-selection list box will be pre-selected, based on whether the item itself is selected—that is, if its *Selected* property is **True**.

As you look at this collection of methods, you may wonder why we have to bother with specialized classes for model, class, and window flags at all. What more could they possibly do? Well, just one thing—but it's a really helpful thing. They can actually define the appropriate flags for each collection. So let's see how that works.

Supporting the Model Page

In VBXs, the *MODEL* structure is the one that ties together all the code and data for a given control. As such, it should come as no surprise that the Model page is the most complex in VBX Genie. It contains tabbed pages of its own! Figure 8.4 shows how it looks when displaying the *MODEL* flags.

Besides the *MODEL* flags, this page also provides access to the window class flags and the window flags. All three of these sub-pages are laid out similarly, and all three are managed by the *ListablesClass* we just examined.

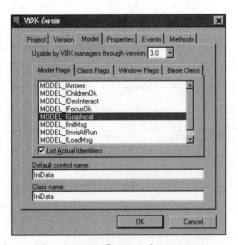

Figure 8.4 Displaying the MODEL flags with VBX Genie.

The *MODEL* flags are directly managed by the *ModelFlagsClass*, which is derived from—excuse me, "aggregated" from—*ListablesClass*. This collection is the most complex of the three flag collections, because it is the only one with complex interactions between certain flags and some standard properties. That complexity is hinted at in the **(General) (Declarations)** section:

```
Option Explicit

Private Flags As New ListablesClass
Private Properties As PropertiesClass
```

Since the *MODEL* flags interact with the standard properties, we have a pointer to a *PropertiesClass* object. (It's a pointer rather than an object in its own right, because the **Private** statement is lacking the keyword **New**.)

The *Flags* member is obvious enough; I warned you this class would be "derived" (using aggregation) from *ListablesClass*. But where are the flags themselves defined? In a procedure called Initialize—but if you drop down the "Proc" combo box on the code window while the "object" combo box reads "(General)", you won't see it. You see, in addition to properties, VB's user-defined classes have constructors and destructors. Okay, they are called "initializers" and "terminators"—but that's just terminology.

> *Initializers and terminators are easy to miss because they are not part of the* **(General)** *object; they belong to the module's* **Class** *object.*

The initializer is the perfect place to populate a collection property such as *Listables*:

```
Private Sub Class_Initialize()
Flags.AddFlag "MODEL_fArrows", _
    "Require arrow keys at run-time", 1
Flags.AddFlag "MODEL_fChildrenOk", _
    "Child control container", 1
Flags.AddFlag "MODEL_fDesInteract", _
    "Receive right mouse-button messages at design-time", 1
Flags.AddFlag "MODEL_fFocusOk", _
    "Can receive focus at run-time", 1
Flags.AddFlag "MODEL_fGraphical", _
    "Graphical control", 2
Flags.AddFlag "MODEL_fInitMsg", _
    "Receive VBM_INITIALIZE messages", 1
Flags.AddFlag "MODEL_fInvisAtRun", _
    "Invisible at run-time", 2
```

```
Flags.AddFlag "MODEL_fLoadMsg", _
    "Receive VBM_CREATED and VBM_LOADED messages", 1
Flags.AddFlag "MODEL_fMnemonic", _
    "Respond to hot keys", 1
End Sub
```

If you look at the procedures that *are* listed as belonging to **(General)**, you'll see a lot of familiar names. *Selected*, for example, is on the list. You might expect that this version of *Selected* has to invoke the base class version and you're right, of course—but it also has to manage those interactions I was talking about:

```
Public Property Let Selected(ByVal Index As Integer, ByVal Value As Boolean)
Static Busy As Boolean
If Busy Then Exit Property
Busy = True
Flags.Item(Index).Selected = Value
Select Case Flags.Item(Index).Identifier
    Case "MODEL_fInvisAtRun"
        If Value Then
            Properties.Selected("Visible") = False
        End If
    Case "MODEL_fGraphical"
        If Value Then
            Properties.Selected("hWnd") = False
        End If
End Select
Busy = False
End Property
```

But the bulk of procedures in this class are mere "passthroughs" to the matching procedures of the *ListablesClass*:

```
Public Property Let ListActualIdentifiers(ByVal aValue As Boolean)
Flags.ListActualIdentifiers = aValue
End Property

Public Sub LoadListbox()
Flags.LoadListbox
End Sub

Public Property Let TargetVersion(ByVal Value As Integer)
Flags.TargetVersion = Value
End Property
```

This kind of tedious coding may be why many programmers pronounce "aggregation," *ag-gra-va-tion*.

The other two flag classes in VBX Genie are all similarly designed. You'll always find a *Flags* property, for example, that is an object of *ListablesClass* type. *ClassFlagsClass* and *WindowFlagsClass* are even simpler than *ModelFlagsClass*, because they have no interactions to worry about. So, why do we have them? Simple: So they can populate their own collections with the appropriate set of flags. Here's the initializer for *ClassFlagsClass*:

```
Private Sub Class_Initialize()
Flags.AddFlag "CS_BYTEALIGNCLIENT", _
   "Align x-axis on byte boundary", 0
Flags.AddFlag "CS_CLASSDC", _
   "Share device context with other controls of this class", 0
Flags.AddFlag "CS_DBLCLKS", _
   "Receive double-click messages", 0
Flags.AddFlag "CS_HREDRAW", _
   "Redraw if horizontal size changes", 0
Flags.AddFlag "CS_OWNDC", _
   "Private device context", 0
Flags.AddFlag "CS_VREDRAW", _
   "Redraw if vertical size changes", 0
Flags.AddFlag "CS_SAVEBITS", _
   "Minimize redraws when possible", 0
End Sub
```

The third parameter to *Add* is supposed to be the version of the VBX manager in which this flag was introduced. That applies to *MODEL* flags only, of course; window class flags were introduced with Windows itself and long predate even the first version of Visual Basic; so these flags are given "versions" of zero. The same goes for the flags of the *WindowFlagsClass*:

```
Private Sub Class_Initialize()
Flags.AddFlag "WS_CLIPCHILDREN", _
   "Don't erase contained child controls", 0
Flags.AddFlag "WS_CLIPSIBLINGS", _
   "Don't erase overlapping controls", 0
Flags.AddFlag "WS_GROUP", _
   "First control of group navigable via arrow keys", 0
Flags.AddFlag "WS_HSCROLL", _
   "Has horizontal scroll bar", 0
Flags.AddFlag "WS_TABSTOP", _
   "Can tab to this control", 0
Flags.AddFlag "WS_VSCROLL", _
   "Has vertical scroll bar", 0
End Sub
```

Some window flags truly don't apply to VBX controls, such as WS_OVERLAPPED. These have been omitted from the list.

At the form level, the user can interact with the *MODEL* flags classes in three ways. First, the version combo box (from the Version page) can be clicked. We've already seen the code that uses that to trigger a reloading of all the list boxes. Second, the user could check or uncheck the "List Actual Identi-fiers" checkbox:

```
Private Sub chk_ListModelIdentifiers_Click()
ModelFlags.ListActualIdentifiers = _
   (chk_ListModelIdentifiers = vbChecked)
ModelFlags.LoadListbox
End Sub

Private Sub chk_ListClassIdentifiers_Click()
ClassFlags.ListActualIdentifiers = _
   (chk_ListClassIdentifiers = vbChecked)
ClassFlags.LoadListbox
End Sub

Private Sub chk_ListWindowIdentifiers_Click()
WindowFlags.ListActualIdentifiers = _
   (chk_ListWindowIdentifiers = vbChecked)
WindowFlags.LoadListbox
End Sub
```

Finally, the user might actually click one of the flag entries:

```
Private Sub lst_ModelFlags_Click()
If Screen.ActiveControl Is lst_ModelFlags Then
   Dim i As Integer
   i = lst_ModelFlags.ListIndex
   ModelFlags.Selected(lst_ModelFlags.ItemData(i)) = _
      lst_ModelFlags.Selected(i)
End If
End Sub

Private Sub lst_ClassFlags_Click()
If Screen.ActiveControl Is lst_ClassFlags Then
   Dim i As Integer
   i = lst_ClassFlags.ListIndex
   ClassFlags.Selected(lst_ClassFlags.ItemData(i)) = _
      lst_ClassFlags.Selected(i)
End If
End Sub

Private Sub lst_WindowFlags_Click()
If Screen.ActiveControl Is lst_WindowFlags Then
   Dim i As Integer
   i = lst_WindowFlags.ListIndex
   WindowFlags.Selected(lst_WindowFlags.ItemData(i)) = _
      lst_WindowFlags.Selected(i)
End If
End Sub
```

Now, suppose the user *does* click, say, the *MODEL_fGraphical* flag. The list box's *Click* event will be triggered, causing the *ModelFlags* object's *Selected* property function to mark not only that particular flag as being selected, but to make sure the *hWnd* standard property is *not* selected.

Wrapping Up the Model Page

Let's recap. We've got the *ListablesClass*, which is the basis for the *ModelFlagsClass*, *ClassFlagsClass*, and *WindowFlagsClass* objects that are actually used by the Prime form to work with its model, class, and window flags, respectively, and is filled with *ListableClass* objects.

> *If you are new to object-oriented programming, this may seem like an awfully roundabout way to get anything done! But think about it: In each of these functions there is hardly any code—and, therefore, hardly any chance to get it wrong. Even if you do inadvertently insert a bug, it'll be easy to find and fix because, function by function, all the code is so simple. It is the relationships that are complex, and relationships are easy to get right ... at, least when you are talking about programming, and not people!*

There is one more tab on the Model page, labeled "Base Class." Remember, VBXs controls can be based on an existing Windows class, or even a custom control you've written. This tab consists of a simple combo box with the standard Windows controls pre-entered with VB4—that can be done at design-time!—and the user's selection is not read until the OK button is pressed, which we'll consider later on.

Supporting the Properties Page

The next tab on Prime represents all the properties, standard and custom, that are used in this control. The page looks like the window shown in Figure 8.5.

The three required properties, *Name, Index,* and *Parent*, have been pre-selected, as have a small number of commonly-included standard properties such as *Enabled*. As you can see, this is a multi-select list box; the user simply clicks on an item to select it, and again to de-select it.

Some properties are "group" properties. For example, if you select one of the font-related properties, you *must* select all of them. The same goes for link-related and drag-related properties. That should happen automatically,

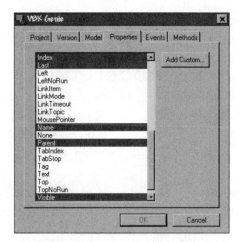

Figure 8.5 Viewing VBX Genie's Properties Page.

so we'll have to take that into account while implementing this page. Also, a few of the properties either require, or are mutually exclusive with, certain *MODEL* flags and that should work automatically, as well.

The items you see in the list box are all standard properties. Although custom properties are certainly something we'll have to support, *most* of the items in this listbox, selected or not, will mostly be standard properties.

We can't quite use *ListableClass* objects as standard properties, because of the interactions between them and *MODEL* class flags. That means we'll have to define a *StdPropertyClass*. Here's its **(General) (Declarations)** section:

```
Option Explicit

Private Base As New ListableClass
Public ModelFlags As ModelFlagsClass
Public Required As Boolean
```

Well—what do you know!—this class aggregates *ListableClass*, too. And we know how that works. So what does *StdPropertyClass* add to the party?

Well, there's the *ModelFlags* pointer—that's for the interactions between standard properties and *MODEL* flags, obviously. There is also a *Required* flag. None of the VBX flags, nor events nor methods, is ever *required*; so that's the reason it is a feature of this class, alone. It is also possible for a standard property to be pre-selected when it is placed into the properties list box; this would happen, for example, in the case of a required standard property like *Name* or *Index*. These things are handled in the *Init* method, after invoking the base class' version of *Init*:

```
Public Sub Init(aIdentifier As String, _
   aDescription As String, _
   ByVal aVersion As Integer, _
   ByVal aRequired As Boolean, _
   ByVal aSelected As Boolean)
Base.Init aIdentifier, aDescription, aVersion
Required = aRequired
Selected = aSelected Or aRequired
End Sub
```

Because it is possible for the user to try to de-select a required standard property—and because we mustn't allow that—the *Selected* **Property Let** function has a special task:

```
Public Property Let Selected(ByVal Value As Boolean)
If Required And Value = False Then
   Base.Selected = True
   MsgBox Base.Description + " is a required property.", _
      vbExclamation, _
      "Properties"
Else
   Base.Selected = Value
End If
End Property
```

Note that, if the user has de-selected a required item, this function *re*-selects it, even before displaying the message box. (Re-selecting it *after* the message box has cleared looks disconcerting to the user.)

The rest of the methods in *StdPropertyClass* are all passthroughs to the base class, so we won't bother to examine them here.

The *PropertiesClass*, another user-defined collection, is designed to hold all these standard property objects. Here's its **(General) (Declarations)** section:

```
Option Explicit

Private List As New ListablesClass
Private ModelFlags As ModelFlagsClass
Private Events As EventsClass
```

As with the specialized flags classes, it creates a set of standard property items when it is initialized:

```
Private Sub Class_Initialize()
' "Name" and "Index" MUST be the first two items in this list
AddStdProperty "PPROPINFO_STD_NAME", _
   "Name", 1, True, True
AddStdProperty "PPROPINFO_STD_INDEX", _
   "Index", 1, True, True
```

```
AddStdProperty "PPROPINFO_STD_ALIGN", _
   "Align", 2, False, False
AddStdProperty "PPROPINFO_STD_BACKCOLOR", _
   "BackColor", 1, False, False
AddStdProperty "PPROPINFO_STD_BORDERSTYLEOFF", _
   "BorderStyle", 1, False, False
AddStdProperty "PPROPINFO_STD_CAPTION", _
   "Caption", 1, False, False
AddStdProperty "PPROPINFO_STD_CLIPCONTROLS", _
   "ClipControls", 2, False, False
AddStdProperty "PPROPINFO_STD_DATACHANGED", _
   "DataChanged", 3, False, False
AddStdProperty "PPROPINFO_STD_DATACHANGED", _
   "DataField", 3, False, False
AddStdProperty "PPROPINFO_STD_DATACHANGED", _
   "DataSource", 3, False, False
AddStdProperty "PPROPINFO_STD_DRAGICON", _
   "DragIcon", 1, False, False
AddStdProperty "PPROPINFO_STD_DRAGMODE", _
   "DragMode", 1, False, False
AddStdProperty "PPROPINFO_STD_ENABLED", _
   "Enabled", 1, False, True
AddStdProperty "PPROPINFO_STD_FONTBOLD", _
   "FontBold", 1, False, False
AddStdProperty "PPROPINFO_STD_FONTITALIC", _
   "FontItalic", 1, False, False
AddStdProperty "PPROPINFO_STD_FONTNAME", _
   "FontName", 1, False, False
AddStdProperty "PPROPINFO_STD_FONTSIZE", _
   "FontSize", 1, False, False
AddStdProperty "PPROPINFO_STD_FONTSTRIKE", _
   "FontStrike", 1, False, False
AddStdProperty "PPROPINFO_STD_FONTUNDER", _
   "FontUnder", 1, False, False
AddStdProperty "PPROPINFO_STD_FORECOLOR", _
   "ForeColor", 1, False, False
AddStdProperty "PPROPINFO_STD_HELPCONTEXTID", _
   "HelpContextID", 2, False, False
AddStdProperty "PPROPINFO_STD_HWND", _
   "hWnd", 1, False, False
AddStdProperty "PPROPINFO_STD_IMEMODE", _
   "ImeMode", 2, False, False
AddStdProperty "PPROPINFO_STD_TOPNORUN", _
   "TopNoRun", 2, False, False
AddStdProperty "PPROPINFO_STD_LEFTNORUN", _
   "LeftNoRun", 2, False, False
AddStdProperty "PPROPINFO_STD_TOP", _
   "Top", 1, False, False
AddStdProperty "PPROPINFO_STD_LEFT", _
   "Left", 1, False, False
AddStdProperty "PPROPINFO_STD_HEIGHT", _
   "Height", 1, False, False
AddStdProperty "PPROPINFO_STD_WIDTH", _
   "Width", 1, False, False
```

```
AddStdProperty "PPROPINFO_STD_LINKITEM", _
   "LinkItem", 2, False, False
AddStdProperty "PPROPINFO_STD_LINKMODE", _
   "LinkMode", 2, False, False
AddStdProperty "PPROPINFO_STD_LINKTIMEOUT", _
   "LinkTimeout", 2, False, False
AddStdProperty "PPROPINFO_STD_LINKTOPIC", _
   "LinkTopic", 2, False, False
AddStdProperty "PPROPINFO_STD_MOUSEPOINTER", _
   "MousePointer", 1, False, False
AddStdProperty "PPROPINFO_STD_NONE", _
   "None", 2, False, False
AddStdProperty "PPROPINFO_STD_PARENT", _
   "Parent", 1, True, True
AddStdProperty "PPROPINFO_STD_TABINDEX", _
   "TabIndex", 1, False, False
AddStdProperty "PPROPINFO_STD_TABSTOP", _
   "TabStop", 1, False, False
AddStdProperty "PPROPINFO_STD_TAG", _
   "Tag", 1, False, False
AddStdProperty "PPROPINFO_STD_TEXT", _
   "Text", 1, False, False
AddStdProperty "PPROPINFO_STD_VISIBLE", _
   "Visible", 1, False, True
' "Last" MUST be the final item in this list
AddStdProperty "PPROPINFO_STD_LAST", _
   "Last", 2, False, True
End Sub
```

Each of the standard properties is an object of the *StdPropertyClass*, which is instantiated and made part of the collection in the *AddStdProperty* method:

```
Private Sub AddStdProperty(Identifier As String, _
   Description As String, _
   ByVal Version As Integer, _
   ByVal Required As Integer, _
   ByVal Selected As Integer)
Dim Item As New StdPropertyClass
Item.Init Identifier, Description, Version, _
   Required, Selected
List.Add Item
End Sub
```

The interactions of properties with each other and with flags and events, comes to the fore when a property is selected (or de-selected):

```
Public Property Let Selected(ByVal ID As String, ByVal Value As Boolean)
Static Busy As Boolean
If Busy Then Exit Property

Busy = True
If Left$(ID, 4) = "Data" Then
   List.Item("DataChanged").Selected = Value
```

```
      List.Item("DataField").Selected = Value
      List.Item("DataSource").Selected = Value
   ElseIf Left$(ID, 4) = "Drag" Then
      List.Item("DragIcon").Selected = Value
      List.Item("DragMode").Selected = Value
      Events.Selected("Drag") = Value
   ElseIf Left$(ID, 4) = "Font" Then
      List.Item("FontBold").Selected = Value
      List.Item("FontItalic").Selected = Value
      List.Item("FontName").Selected = Value
      List.Item("FontSize").Selected = Value
      List.Item("FontStrike").Selected = Value
      List.Item("FontUnder").Selected = Value
   ElseIf Left$(ID, 4) = "Link" Then
      List.Item("LinkItem").Selected = Value
      List.Item("LinkMode").Selected = Value
      List.Item("LinkTimeout").Selected = Value
      List.Item("LinkTopic").Selected = Value
      Events.Selected("Link") = Value
   Else
      List.Item(ID).Selected = Value
      If Value Then
         Select Case ID
         Case "Caption"
            List.Item("Text").Selected = False
         Case "ClipControls"
            ModelFlags.Item("MODEL_fChildrenOk").Selected = True
         Case "hWnd"
            ModelFlags.Item("MODEL_fGraphical").Selected = False
         Case "TopNoRun", "LeftNoRun"
            ModelFlags.Item("MODEL_fInvisAtRun").Selected = True
            List.Item("Top").Selected = False
            List.Item("Left").Selected = False
            List.Item("Height").Selected = False
            List.Item("Width").Selected = False
            List.Item("TopNoRun").Selected = True
            List.Item("LeftNoRun").Selected = True
         Case "LinkItem", "LinkMode", "LinkTimeout", "LinkTopic"
            ModelFlags.Item("MODEL_fLoadMsg").Selected = True
         Case "Text"
            List.Item("Caption").Selected = False
         Case "Top", "Left", "Height", "Width", "Visible"
            ModelFlags.Item("MODEL_fInvisAtRun").Selected = False
            List.Item("Top").Selected = True
            List.Item("Left").Selected = True
            List.Item("Height").Selected = True
            List.Item("Width").Selected = True
            List.Item("TopNoRun").Selected = False
            List.Item("LeftNoRun").Selected = False
         End Select
      End If
   End If
End If
Busy = False
End Property
```

Here, each of the interactions is clearly spelled out, as long as you can read Visual Basic syntax.

Notice the use of the **Static** *Busy* variable. With all these interactions, it would be inevitable that an endless recursion would begin, without some sort of mechanism for preventing it. The *Busy* flag provides that mechanism.

You may recall that the *ListableClass* provides a property called *Standard* that is always set to **True**. (And, in fact, the *StdPropertyClass* does the same because it's more efficient than implementing such a trivial task as a passthrough.) Obviously the *PropertiesClass* will need to store custom properties as well as standard ones. That topic deserves a section all of its own.

Supporting Custom Properties

Custom properties are the main reason VBX controls are as useful as they are. But, they sure have a lot of variety to manage! They come in different data types, including interesting ones like "enumerated," which include a value list, and have more storage options than you'll find at a Tupperware party. The "Add Custom..." button on the Property page of the Prime form brings up a dialog box designed to organize this complexity as shown in Figure 8.6.

Although there are five tabbed pages on this form, most of the action is on the first. This is where the user specifies the custom property's data type. If it is an enumerated property, the choices can be specified. And if there is

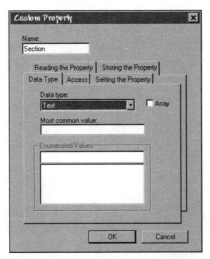

Figure 8.6 The Custom Property dialog box used to organize custom properties.

one value this property will usually have, it can be specified so the VBX manager won't bother to store it.

Visual Basic has always had forms, and since VB2, forms have been considered objects—user-defined objects, at that, although it didn't matter much since they couldn't have public "properties" or even functions. However, in VB4 a form is just a class with a pretty face. So we can implement a custom property class *as a form*, and thus avoid the hassles of trying to match a data object with a bunch of user-interface elements. They'll just all *be* there.

I was tempted to name the new class "CustomPropertyClass" but at the last minute gave into some nameless dread that I might not be able to tell my forms from my classes (in spite of the different icons that represent them in the Project Window), and went for *CustomPropertyForm*. Its **(General) (Declarations)** section has these properties:

```
Option Explicit

Public OK As Boolean

Public Description As String
Private Selected_ As Integer

Private DataType As String
Private DefaultValue As String
Private Enumerations As New Collection
Public Listables As New ListablesClass

Public UI As ListBox
Public UIIndex As Integer
```

The *OK* property is used by the owner of this object to determine whether or not the user hit the OK button. *Description* and *Selected_* you already know. *DataType, DefaultValue, Enumerations,* and *Listables* serve obvious purposes; we'll look into them more closely in a moment. *UI* and *UIIndex* are also familiar to you from the *ListableClass*.

I mentioned earlier that forms have an *Initialize* event, just as classes do. The event takes place prior to the *Load* event; when it executes, the form has not yet been built up in memory and none of the form's controls is present. It is therefore useful only for initializing non-control properties, such as *Flags*:

```
Private Sub Form_Initialize()
Flags.AddFlag "PF_fGetHszMsg", "", 0
Flags.AddFlag "PF_fPropArray", "", 0
```

```
Flags.AddFlag "PF_fEditable", "", 0
Flags.Item("PF_fEditable").Selected = True
Flags.AddFlag "PF_fNoMultiSelect", "", 0
Flags.AddFlag "PF_fNoShow", "", 0
Flags.AddFlag "PF_fUpdateOnEdit", "", 0
Flags.AddFlag "PF_fNoRuntimeW", "", 0
Flags.AddFlag "PF_fNoRuntimeR", "", 0
Flags.AddFlag "PF_fSetData", "", 0
Flags.Item("PF_fSetData").Selected = True
Flags.AddFlag "PF_fSetMsg", "", 0
Flags.AddFlag "PF_fSetCheck", "", 0
Flags.AddFlag "PF_fGetData", "", 0
Flags.Item("PF_fGetData").Selected = True
Flags.AddFlag "PF_fGetMsg", "", 0
Flags.AddFlag "PF_fSaveData", "", 0
Flags.Item("PF_fSaveData").Selected = True
Flags.AddFlag "PF_fSaveMsg", "", 0
Flags.AddFlag "PF_fLoadMsgOnly", "", 0
End Sub
```

You should recognize the names of these flags from our work with the VBX skeleton; they are all the property flags that are used to define custom properties. Here, a few of them are pre-selected. They will eventually supply values to checkboxes on the form.

It's important to understand that if the user defines five custom properties, there will be five occurrences of this form in memory, even though only one, or none, will be visible at any given time. Each is absolutely attached to its data. Therefore, the user interface elements must be populated from the object's properties during the form's *Activate* event:

```
Private Sub Form_Activate()
cmd_OK.Enabled = VerifyOK
OK = False
txt_Description.Text = Description
cmb_DataType.ListIndex = _
   ConvertDataType(DataType)
chk_PropArray = _
   Checked(Flags.Item("PF_fPropArray").Selected)
txt_CommonValue = DefaultValue
SetEnumerations cmb_Enumerations
chk_PropertyHSZ = _
   Checked(Flags.Item("PF_fGetHszMsg").Selected)
chk_MultiSelect = _
   Checked(Not Flags.Item("PF_fNoMultiSelect").Selected)
chk_Show = _
   Checked(Not Flags.Item("PF_fNoShow").Selected)
chk_UpdateOnEdit = _
   Checked(Flags.Item("PF_fUpdateOnEdit").Selected)
chk_RunTimeWrite = _
```

```
     Checked(Not Flags.Item("PF_fNoRuntimeW").Selected)
   chk_RunTimeRead = _
     Checked(Not Flags.Item("PF_fNoRuntimeR").Selected)
   opt_SetData = _
     Checked(Flags.Item("PF_fSetData").Selected)
   opt_SetMsg = _
     Checked(Flags.Item("PF_fSetMsg").Selected)
   opt_SetMsgData = _
     Checked(Flags.Item("PF_fSetData").Selected And _
     Flags.Item("PF_fSetMsg").Selected)
   chk_SetCheck = _
     Checked(Flags.Item("PF_fSetCheck").Selected)
   opt_GetData = _
     Checked(Flags.Item("PF_fGetData").Selected)
   opt_GetMsg = _
     Checked(Flags.Item("PF_fGetMsg").Selected)
   opt_SaveData = _
     Checked(Flags.Item("PF_fSaveData").Selected)
   opt_SaveMsg = _
     Checked(Flags.Item("PF_fSaveMsg").Selected)
   End Sub
```

This is done during the *Activate* event because a form is loaded only once, but may be activated many times if the user decides to change some of his or her original settings.

You might ask, "Why not just fill the fields once, and leave them then, if the form stays loaded?" That would be all right if there was no Cancel button. But there is, and repopulating the fields during activation is a way of letting the user start off fresh. Nothing much happens if the user hits the Cancel button:

```
Private Sub cmd_Cancel_Click()
Hide
End Sub
```

The data elements are updated only if the user clicks the OK button:

```
Private Sub cmd_OK_Click()
Description = txt_Description.Text
DataType = ConvertDataType(cmb_DataType.ListIndex)
Flags.Item("PF_fPropArray").Selected = chk_PropArray
DefaultValue = txt_CommonValue
GetEnumerations cmb_Enumerations
Flags.Item("PF_fGetHszMsg").Selected = chk_PropertyHSZ
Flags.Item("PF_fNoMultiSelect").Selected = _
   Not chk_MultiSelect
Flags.Item("PF_fNoShow").Selected = Not chk_Show
Flags.Item("PF_fUpdateOnEdit").Selected = _
   chk_UpdateOnEdit
Flags.Item("PF_fNoRuntimeW").Selected = _
```

```
    Not chk_RunTimeWrite
Flags.Item("PF_fNoRuntimeR").Selected = _
    Not chk_RunTimeRead
Flags.Item("PF_fSetData").Selected = _
    opt_SetData Or opt_SetMsgData
Flags.Item("PF_fSetMsg").Selected = _
    opt_SetMsg Or opt_SetMsgData
Flags.Item("PF_fSetCheck").Selected = chk_SetCheck
Flags.Item("PF_fGetData").Selected = opt_GetData
Flags.Item("PF_fGetMsg").Selected = opt_GetMsg
Flags.Item("PF_fSaveData").Selected = opt_SaveData
Flags.Item("PF_fSaveMsg").Selected = opt_SaveMsg
OK = True
Hide
End Sub
```

I won't bore you with the simple VB things that make the form work. However, I do have an innovation I'd like to share. In the past, I've always designed combo box forms with a command button associated with the combobox, for adding new items or deleting existing ones. Such a scheme is certainly clear enough for the user to figure out, but it's annoying to have to click the button when you are adding several items in a row. So I've tried it a little differently this time, in a way I hope users will be able to figure out.

The combo box on the custom property form is only enabled, anyway, if the data type is "enumeration." If it is, the user can enter any number of possible values; these are stored with the property and appear in the VBX manager's Properties window for the control, as you know. On the custom property form, when you enter a value in the edit portion of the combo box, it will be added to the list for you automatically if you move to any other field. That's accomplished in the combo box's *LostFocus* event:

```
Private Sub cmb_Enumerations_LostFocus()
Dim i As Integer
i = cmb_Enumerations.ListIndex
If cmb_Enumerations.Text > "" And _
      cmb_Enumerations.Text <> _
        cmb_Enumerations.List(i) Then
   cmb_Enumerations.AddItem cmb_Enumerations.Text
   cmb_Enumerations.Text = ""
   cmd_OK.Enabled = VerifyOK
End If
End Sub
```

Alternatively, the user can press the Insert key to get the same effect. And, if the text in the edit portion matches the currently selected item—as it would if the user had just clicked on one of the list items with the mouse—the user can *delete* the item by pressing the Delete key:

```
Private Sub cmb_Enumerations_KeyDown(KeyCode As Integer, _
   Shift As Integer)
Dim Temp As String, i As Integer
i = cmb_Enumerations.ListIndex

If KeyCode = vbKeyDelete Then
   If cmb_Enumerations.Text = _
         cmb_Enumerations.List(i) Then
      cmb_Enumerations.RemoveItem i
      cmd_OK.Enabled = VerifyOK
   End If

ElseIf KeyCode = vbKeyInsert Then
   cmb_Enumerations.AddItem cmb_Enumerations.Text
   cmb_Enumerations.Text = ""
   cmd_OK.Enabled = VerifyOK

ElseIf KeyCode = vbKeyUp And _
      ((Shift And vbShiftMask) > 0) Then
   If i > 0 Then
      Temp = cmb_Enumerations.List(i)
      cmb_Enumerations.RemoveItem i
      cmb_Enumerations.AddItem Temp, i - 1
      cmb_Enumerations.ListIndex = i - 1
      KeyCode = 0
   Else
      Beep
   End If

ElseIf KeyCode = vbKeyDown And _
      ((Shift And vbShiftMask) > 0) Then
   If i < cmb_Enumerations.ListCount - 1 Then
      Temp = cmb_Enumerations.List(i)
      cmb_Enumerations.RemoveItem i
      cmb_Enumerations.AddItem Temp, i + 1
      cmb_Enumerations.ListIndex = i + 1
      KeyCode = 0
   Else
      Beep
   End If

End If
End Sub
```

The same event handler also allows the user to reposition items in the list
by holding down the Shift key while using the up and down arrows.

As an example of the kinds of interactions this form supports, look at the
Common Value field. If the data type is Enumerated, then either the Common Value must appear in the enumerations list, or the Editable check box
must be checked so that the user can type the Common Value in for him or
herself. The Common Value field's *LostFocus* event ensures this:

```
Private Sub txt_CommonValue_LostFocus()
If cmb_DataType.Text = "Enumerated" Then
   If InEnumerations(txt_CommonValue.Text) Then
      Exit Sub
   End If
   If MsgBox("The common value '" + _
         txt_CommonValue.Text + _
         "' does not appear in your choice " + _
         "of enumerations. Would you like to add it?", _
         vbYesNo + vbQuestion, _
         "Custom Property") = vbYes Then
      cmb_Enumerations.AddItem txt_CommonValue.Text
      cmd_OK.Enabled = VerifyOK
   Else
      If chk_Editable <> vbChecked Then
         MsgBox "The 'User can type data directly' box on the Access page has
been checked.", vbInformation, "Custum Property"
         chk_Editable = vbChecked
      End If
   End If
End If
End Sub
```

Returning, then, to the *PropertiesClass*, we can inspect the *AddCustomProperty* method:

```
Public Sub AddCustomProperty()
Dim Property As New CustomPropertyForm
Property.Show vbModal
If Property.OK Then
   Property.Selected = True
   List.Add Property
Else
   Unload Property
End If
End Sub
```

An instance of the form/class is created and called *Property*. It is displayed as a modal form; when execution returns to this procedure, it is because the user has either hit the OK or the Cancel button; the *OK* property reveals which. If it was the Cancel button, we have no further use for this object. However, letting it go out of scope is not enough; we must actually unload the form first.

If the OK button *was* clicked, we can add the new object to the *List* collection, using the same method built-in to *ListablesClass* that we've already used, with support for handling duplicate entries and so on.

Editing an *existing* custom property is even simpler from the point of view of the custom property:

```
Public Sub EditCustomProperty(Description As String)
List.Edit Description
End Sub
```

We didn't inspect the *Edit* method of the *ListablesClass* before because I was afraid it would be too confusing out of context. Now that you realize it will only be invoked when trying to edit a custom property form (or a custom event form, which we'll see shortly), its code should be clear enough:

```
Public Sub Edit(ByVal Description As String)
List(Description).Show vbModal
If Description <> List(Description).Description Then
   Dim Listable As Object
   Listable = List(Description)
   List.Remove Description
   Add Listable
   Description = Listable.Description
End If
List(Description).Selected = True
End Sub
```

When VBX Genie is finally done and unloading, the application must specifically unload any of the custom property forms (or, for that matter, custom event forms) that may have been added to any *List*. That's a job for the Prime form's *Unload* event:

```
Private Sub Form_Unload(Cancel As Integer)
Set Properties = Nothing
Set Events = Nothing
Dim i As Integer
For i = 1 To Forms.Count - 1
   Unload Forms(i)
Next i
End Sub
```

In this handler, we explicitly clear the *Properties* and *Events* collections—the only ones that even *might* contain any forms. When that's done, we can run through the *Forms* collection to pick off any strays.

Unlike other collections, the built-in *Forms* collection starts from an index of zero. The Prime form, currently *being* unloaded as the event is processed, is guaranteed to be element zero, so we can start our search at element one.

Supporting the Events Page

In keeping with the established fact that people are more productive with things that look familiar, the Events page is practically identical to the Properties page. Figure 8.7 shows the Events page.

Figure 8.7 VBX Genie's Events page.

The *EventsClass* is also similar to the *PropertiesClass*, where it differs is in the fact that events are somewhat simpler than properties—there are no interactions with *MODEL* flags. That doesn't mean to say there are no interactions at all; a few exist with properties and methods, but these are easier to manage than the awkward *MODEL* interactions. So there is no "StdEventClass;" the *EventsClass* object will be populated (mostly) with plain old *ListableClass* objects. Here's the **(General) (Declarations)** section:

```
Option Explicit

Private List As New ListablesClass
Private Properties As PropertiesClass
Private Methods As MethodsClass
```

As a collection of events, it must populate itself with all the standard events. This is done in the class' *Initialize* event:

```
Private Sub Class_Initialize()
AddStdEvent "PEVENTINFO_STD_CLICK", _
   "Click", 1
AddStdEvent "PEVENTINFO_STD_DBLCLICK", _
   "DblClick", 1
AddStdEvent "PEVENTINFO_STD_DRAGDROP", _
   "DragDrop", 1
AddStdEvent "PEVENTINFO_STD_DRAGOVER", _
   "DragOver", 1
AddStdEvent "PEVENTINFO_STD_GOTFOCUS", _
   "GotFocus", 1
AddStdEvent "PEVENTINFO_STD_KEYDOWN", _
   "KeyDown", 1
```

```
AddStdEvent "PEVENTINFO_STD_KEYPRESS", _
    "KeyPress", 1
AddStdEvent "PEVENTINFO_STD_KEYUP", _
    "KeyUp", 1
AddStdEvent "PEVENTINFO_STD_LAST", _
    "Last", 2
AddStdEvent "PEVENTINFO_STD_LINKCLOSE", _
    "LinkClose", 2
AddStdEvent "PEVENTINFO_STD_LINKERROR", _
    "LinkError", 2
AddStdEvent "PEVENTINFO_STD_LINKNOTIFY", _
    "LinkNotify", 2
AddStdEvent "PEVENTINFO_STD_LINKOPEN", _
    "LinkOpen", 2
AddStdEvent "PEVENTINFO_STD_LOSTFOCUS", _
    "LostFocus", 1
AddStdEvent "PEVENTINFO_STD_MOUSEDOWN", _
    "MouseDown", 1
AddStdEvent "PEVENTINFO_STD_MOUSEMOVE", _
    "MouseMove", 1
AddStdEvent "PEVENTINFO_STD_MOUSEUP", _
    "MouseUp", 1
AddStdEvent "PEVENTINFO_STD_NONE", _
    "None", 2
End Sub
```

As mentioned, standard events can be actual *ListableClass* objects, as seen in the *AddStdEvent* method:

```
Private Sub AddStdEvent(Identifier As String, _
    Description As String, _
    ByVal Version As Integer)
Dim Item As New ListableClass
Item.Init Identifier, Description, Version
List.Add Item, Description
End Sub
```

Most of the other methods of this class (disregarding the coding methods, which we haven't examined yet anyway) are identical to those of the *PropertiesClass*—including the class *Terminate* method, which also must unload any custom event forms the user has created.

Supporting Custom Events

Just as custom properties were implemented by a class masquerading as a form, so are custom events. The form is simpler than the one for custom properties, since custom events have fewer options, as shown in Figure 8.8.

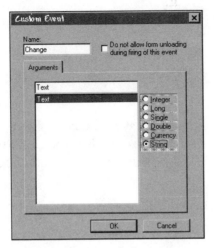

Figure 8.8 VBX Genie's Custom Event dialog.

However, looks can be deceiving. The arguments a custom event may have are much more complex than the event itself, and that's where the bulk of code is spent.

Here's the *CustomEventForm*'s **(General) (Declarations)** section:

```
Option Explicit

Public OK As Boolean

Public Description As String
Public Selected_ As Integer

Private EF_fNoUnload As Boolean
Private Arguments As New Collection

Public UI As ListBox
Public UIIndex As Integer

Private DataTypes As New Collection
```

Looking at the things that distinguish this from *CustomPropertyForm*, we see just one flag (*EF_fNoUnload*) instead of a collection of them; a collection of *Arguments* that may optionally be associated with a custom event, and a collection of data types for those arguments.

Again, as with custom properties, the form's *Activate* event transfers data from the properties to the form's controls:

```
Private Sub Form_Activate()
cmd_OK.Enabled = VerifyOK
OK = False
txt_Description.Text = Description
chk_NoUnload = EF_fNoUnload
SetArguments cmb_Arguments
End Sub
```

Event arguments are kept two ways. One is as objects of the *EventArgClass*, which we'll examine shortly. The other is in the combo box and its *ItemData* array property, which ties in with the set of data type option buttons you saw on the form.

The *SetArguments* procedure unravels the data from the *EventArgClass* objects:

```
Private Sub SetArguments(C As ComboBox)
Dim i As Integer
For i = 1 To Arguments.Count
   C.AddItem Arguments(i).Description
   C.ItemData(C.NewIndex) = _
      Arguments(i).DataType.VB_Code
Next i
End Sub
```

In this procedure, we loop through the *Arguments* collection, adding each *Description*—that would be the argument name—to the combo box, then copying the argument's data type into that item's *ItemData* field.

The inverse of this occurs when the user clicks the OK button:

```
Private Sub GetArguments(C As ComboBox)
Set Arguments = New Collection
Dim i As Integer
Dim Arg As EventArgClass
For i = 1 To C.ListCount
   Set Arg = New EventArgClass
   Arg.Name = C.List(i - 1)
   Set Arg.DataType = _
      DataTypes(ItemData(i - 1))
   Arguments.Add Arg
Next i
End Sub
```

The first statement in this procedure not only creates a new collection—it also, automatically, disposes of the old one! This turns out to be the easiest way to repopulate it with (possibly) altered values. (Remember, this form will be used to edit a custom event as well as add it.) So, you can see where a new object of the *EventArgClass* is created.

Event arguments each have an associated data type. The problem is that we have to interpret these data types in different ways in different places. At the moment, they must present themselves in the form of a checked option button. Later, when we are generating the VBX code, we'll have to use them to produce the correct VBX CDK constants and flags—and there are two types of those. In a traditional application, all that code would be scattered throughout. In an object-oriented program, it's still required—but at least it's packaged in one place, so we can write it and then forget about it.

The *EventArgDataTypeClass* is a simple one, designed to hold together the information for a single data type:

```
Option Explicit

Public Name As String
Public VB_Identifier As String
Public VB_Code As Integer

Public VBX_Identifier As String
```

Its only code is the function that fills in these fields:

```
Public Sub Init(aName As String, _
    aVB_Identifier As String, _
    ByVal aVB_Code As Integer, _
    aVBX_Identifier As String)
Name = aName
VB_Identifier = aVB_Identifier
VB_Code = aVB_Code
VBX_Identifier = aVBX_Identifier
End Sub
```

These objects are created when the *CustomeEventForm* is created; the *DataTypes* collection is initialized—where else?—in the form's *Initialize* event handler:

```
Private Sub Form_Initialize()
Dim dtNull As New EventArgDataTypeClass
dtNull.Init "Null", "vbNull", vbNull, "-Unused-"
DataTypes.Add dtNull, "Null"

Dim dtInteger As New EventArgDataTypeClass
dtInteger.Init "Integer", "vbInteger", vbInteger, "ET_I2"
DataTypes.Add dtInteger, "Integer"

Dim dtLong As New EventArgDataTypeClass
dtLong.Init "Long", "vbLong", vbLong, "ET_I4"
DataTypes.Add dtLong, "Long"
```

```
Dim dtSingle As New EventArgDataTypeClass
dtSingle.Init "Single", "vbSingle", vbSingle, "ET_R4"
DataTypes.Add dtSingle, "Single"

Dim dtDouble As New EventArgDataTypeClass
dtDouble.Init "Double", "vbDouble", vbDouble, "ET_R8"
DataTypes.Add dtDouble, "Double"

Dim dtCurrency As New EventArgDataTypeClass
dtCurrency.Init "Currency", "vbCurrency", vbCurrency, "ET_CY"
DataTypes.Add dtCurrency, "Currency"

Dim dtDate As New EventArgDataTypeClass
dtDate.Init "Date", "vbDate", vbDate, "-Unused-"
DataTypes.Add dtDate, "Date"

Dim dtString As New EventArgDataTypeClass
dtString.Init "String", "vbString", vbString, "ET_HLSTR"
DataTypes.Add dtString, "String"
End Sub
```

The collection is very cleverly arranged so that the elements' collection index *is* the Visual Basic constant that represents that data type. In other words, the data type represented by *vbNull* is kept as *DataTypes(1)*—and *vbNull* is equal to one. Likewise for *vbInteger* and the others.

The advantage to representing a data type as one of these objects will become clear in the next chapter when we start generating code.

By the way, even though we are passing around references to some of these data types—for example, the selected data type object is copied from the *DataTypes* collection into the *EventArgClass* object—you don't have to worry that these items won't be deleted when they should, or that they'll be deleted before they should.

> *Every Visual Basic object includes a built-in reference count, and isn't released until there are no more references to it.*

Adding the Methods Page

After properties and events, methods are going to seem to be somewhat of a letdown. Figure 8.9 shows the Methods page in action.

As you know, there are no "custom methods" for VBXs; so it follows that there is no "Add Custom..." button on this page. Other than that, the Prime

Figure 8.9   VBX Genie's Methods page.

form's control of this page is similar to that which we've already seen. There is a *MethodsClass* that is even simpler than the *EventsClass*. Its **(General) (Declarations)** section is similar:

```
Option Explicit

Private List As New ListablesClass
Private Events As EventsClass
Public UI As ListBox
```

Like *EventsClass*, *MethodsClass* is able to use *ListableClass* objects directly. It allocates them in its *Initialize* procedure:

```
Private Sub Class_Initialize()
AddStdMethod "METH_ADDITEM", "AddItem", 1
AddStdMethod "METH_CLEAR", "Clear", 2
AddStdMethod "METH_DRAG", "Drag", 1
AddStdMethod "METH_LINKSEND", "LinkSend", 2
AddStdMethod "METH_MOVE", "Move", 1
AddStdMethod "METH_REMOVEITEM", "RemoveItem", 1
AddStdMethod "METH_REFRESH", "Refresh", 1
AddStdMethod "METH_ZORDER", "ZOrder", 2
End Sub
```

AddStdMethod looks too much like *AddStdEvent* to bother showing it here. Most of the other methods for this class are also identical to their already-examined counterparts in other classes. The *Selected* property function is similar in philosophy but not execution; it reflects the interdependencies between methods and events:

```
Public Property Let Selected(ID As Variant, Value As Boolean)
Static Busy As Boolean
If Busy Then Exit Property
Busy = True
If ID = "Drag" Then
   Events.Selected("Drag") = Value
   List.Item("Drag").Selected = Value
ElseIf Left$(ID, 4) = "Link" Then
   If Value Then Events.Selected("Link") = Value
   List.Item("LinkSend").Selected = Value
ElseIf ID = "AddItem" Or ID = "RemoveItem" Then
   List.Item("AddItem").Selected = Value
   List.Item("RemoveItem").Selected = Value
   If Value Then
      List.Item("Clear").Selected = True
   End If
Else
   List.Item(ID).Selected = Value
End If
Busy = False
End Property
```

If you want to be picky, you could ask, "What about the interdependencies between methods and properties?" Well, it turns out that hooking up to events is enough because there's a ripple effect. For example, let's say the user selects the **LinkSend** method. As shown above, that action will cause all the link events to be selected, too ... and, if you refer back to the *EventsClass.Selected* method, you'll see that it makes sure the link-related properties are selected or not, as the link-related events are.

And, if the user selects link-related properties, will **LinkSend** be selected, too? No, because processing **LinkSend** method messages is completely optional; *VBDefControlProc()* will handle them implicitly if the VBX doesn't handle them explicitly.

Generating 9 Code

THE WHOLE PURPOSE OF VBX GENIE, of course, is to generate code. Yet, that winds up being the simpler part of the job; as is usual with Windows applications, the user interface takes up most of the actual lines of code.

Still, the generation of code itself is exciting in its own right. And the technique I've employed in VBX Genie is one I haven't seen elsewhere, although it seems pretty obvious to me.

But first, we get to examine a new feature of Visual Basic 4.0: resources!

Attaching the Code Script

As a C or C++ Windows programmer, you know about the *resource pool:* a collection of things the end user might see, such as icons, message strings, menus, and dialogs. Partly to aid in internationalization, but also because it turned out to be a good idea, all these things are kept *away* from an application's code. They can actually be modified without touching the application itself; in fact, with modern editing tools, they can even be altered without *recompiling* the application at all!

But as a Visual Basic programmer, you had to live without this convenience up through VB3. VBX Genie has to have access to code scripts, from which it generates the finished VBX code; and the first version of VBX Genie had to keep these scripts in a standalone file. That meant error handling had to deal with the possibility that the file was missing. Besides, scripts weren't the only outboard resource: We had the toolbox bitmaps and the icon to worry about; these had to be copied into the destination directory and *any one* of them *could* be missing. End users are so careless.

Well, *that* problem can be disposed of. VB4 *does* support resources, although it doesn't supply a tool for working with them. But that's okay; if you are intending to write VBXs, you have Microsoft's App Studio (packaged with Microsoft Visual C++) or Borland's Resource Workshop (packaged with Borland C++). Either of these is capable of compiling what's known as a *resource script* into the binary .RES file that Visual Basic will accept and incorporate into the finished .EXE file.

These days, using App Studio or Resource Workshop, it's easy to forget that we used to have to create resources *entirely* in script form, using a text editor. However, the new tools only directly support standard resources, such as menus, dialogs, and so on. Resource scripts also support *user-defined* resources. That's right, you can make up your own resource type name! If you want a "Flashlight" resource or a "Sandbar" resource, you can have 'em. In the present case, I decided on a couple new types like "Module" and "Toolbox." Once my scripts were prepared, all I had to do was reference them in the script (VBXGEN.RC):

```
8000 TOOLBOX 8000.bmp
8001 TOOLBOX 8001.bmp
8003 TOOLBOX 8003.bmp
8006 TOOLBOX 8006.bmp

MAIN TOOLICON main.ico
```

```
DEF   MODULE main.def

HEADER     MODULE internal.h

MAIN MODULE main.c
HELP MODULE help.c
RC MODULE main.rc
VISUAL     MODULE visual.c
MAK  MODULE main.mak

PORTAGDI_H MODULE portagdi.h
PORTAGDI_CPP MODULE portagdi.cpp
VBXXX_H    MODULE vbxxx.h
VBXXX_CPP  MODULE vbxxx.cpp
MAIN_CPP   MODULE main.cpp
```

As with some standard resources, user-defined resources begin with a name, followed by a resource type—which you can make up—followed by the name of the file that contains the resource.

If you start up App Studio or Resource Workshop and open this .RC file, and then use the *File..Save As* command to save it as a .RES file, the files you specified will be copied, byte-by-byte, into an organized form from which they can be retrieved. And that gives you VBXGEN.RES, which can be added to the VBX Genie project.

If you are using App Studio, be sure you use the 16-bit version that comes with Visual C++ 1.5x. The 32-bit version produces 32-bit resources, which are incompatible with 16-bit modules such as VBXs.

The easiest way to add files to a project is to drag them there from File Manager or Windows Explorer (depending on your version of Windows). Figure 9.1 shows how the Project Window looks with the addition of the resource pool.

Creating the Code Scripts

The code scripts are basically the same as the VBX Skeleton and VBX++ files described earlier in this book. We can't reprint the whole thing here; it would take pages and pages! But you are welcome to open the files on the accompanying CD-ROM and study them any time you like.

The scripts are basically C or C++ code modules, with the addition of special commands called *substitutions*. These commands begin with a "$"

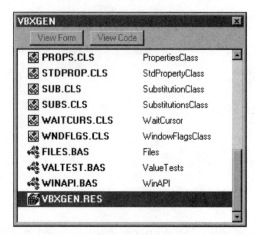

Figure 9.1 The Project Window with the added resource pool.

and are typed in all caps, which makes them stand out. Wherever a substitution is found, VBX Genie will supply some generated code. The rest of the script is copied verbatim.

Generating Code

Actually generating the code is a job split into two parts. One seems simpler than it is: creating the substitution values. The other, you'd expect to be harder than it is: actually churning out the files.

All this happens, of course, when the user clicks the OK button on the Prime form:

```
Private Sub cmd_OK_Click()
Dim WC As WaitCursor
Set WC = New WaitCursor
Dim CodeGen As New CodeGenerator
If DirExists(txt_Directory.Text) Then
   CodeGen.Directory = txt_Directory.Text
   CodeGen.Substitute("$PROJECT") = _
      txt_Name.Text
   CodeGen.Substitute("$DIRECTORY") = _
      txt_Directory.Text
   DefineVersion CodeGen
   DefineModel CodeGen
   DefineProperties CodeGen
   DefineEvents CodeGen
   DefineMethods CodeGen
   If opt_C.Value Then
```

```
         CodeGen.TargetLanguage = "C"
      Else
         CodeGen.TargetLanguage = "C++"
      End If
      CodeGen.Show vbModal
      Unload Me
   End If
End Sub
```

The *WaitCursor* I've described; *DirExists* is a utility function in the FILES.BAS code module. *CodeGenerator*, yes, is another class ... one that, like custom properties, is packaged as a form. As a class, it includes an array property called *Substitute*. You assign values to this array specifying a keyword; wherever that keyword is found in the code scripts, the value will be *substituted* for it.

The *DefineVersion*, *DefineModel*, and similar calls are provided merely to break up what would otherwise be a monolithic procedure.

DefineVersion simply reads the values of the various controls on the form pertaining to the VBX version and creates substitutions for them:

```
Private Sub DefineVersion(CodeGen As CodeGenerator)
CodeGen.Substitute("$FILEVERSIONTEXT") = _
   txt_FileVersion(0).Text + "." + _
   txt_FileVersion(1).Text + "." + _
   txt_FileVersion(2).Text + "." + _
   txt_FileVersion(3).Text
CodeGen.Substitute("$FILEVERSION") = _
   txt_FileVersion(0).Text + "," + _
   txt_FileVersion(1).Text + "," + _
   txt_FileVersion(2).Text + "," + _
   txt_FileVersion(3).Text
CodeGen.Substitute("$PRODUCTVERSIONTEXT") = _
   txt_ProductVersion(0).Text + "." + _
   txt_ProductVersion(1).Text + "." + _
   txt_ProductVersion(2).Text + "." + _
   txt_ProductVersion(3).Text
CodeGen.Substitute("$PRODUCTVERSION") = _
   txt_ProductVersion(0).Text + "," + _
   txt_ProductVersion(1).Text + "," + _
   txt_ProductVersion(2).Text + "," + _
   txt_ProductVersion(3).Text
CodeGen.Substitute("$COMPANYNAME") = txt_CompanyName.Text
CodeGen.Substitute("$PRODUCT") = txt_ProductName.Text
CodeGen.Substitute("$AUTHOR") = txt_Author.Text
CodeGen.Substitute("$RELEASEYEAR") = txt_ReleaseYear.Text
CodeGen.Substitute("$COPYRIGHT") = txt_Copyright.Text
End Sub
```

DefineModel, on the other hand, is a little sneakier:

```
Private Sub DefineModel(CodeGen As CodeGenerator)
Select Case Val(cmb_VBVersion.Text)
  Case 1
     CodeGen.Substitute("$VBVERSION") = "VB100_VERSION"
  Case 2
     CodeGen.Substitute("$VBVERSION") = "VB200_VERSION"
  Case 3
     CodeGen.Substitute("$VBVERSION") = "VB200_VERSION"
End Select
CodeGen.Substitute("$MODELFLAGS") = ModelFlags.Code
CodeGen.Substitute("$CLASSFLAGS") = ClassFlags.Code
CodeGen.Substitute("$WINDOWFLAGS") = WindowFlags.Code
CodeGen.Substitute("$DEFCONTROLNAME") = txt_DefControlName.Text
CodeGen.Substitute("$CLASSNAME_CPP") = LCase$(txt_ClassName.Text)
CodeGen.Substitute("$CLASSNAME") = txt_ClassName.Text
If cmb_ParentClass.Text = "(None)" Then
   CodeGen.Substitute("$PARENTCLASS") = "NULL"
Else
   CodeGen.Substitute("$PARENTCLASS") = Quote(cmb_ParentClass.Text)
End If
End Sub
```

ModelFlags.Code? ClassFlags.Code? Where did these come from?

I didn't show them to you in the previous chapter because I wanted to cover all the coding components at once. The idea is, each object in VBX Genie "knows" how to *code itself*. That way, at the Prime form, we can concentrate on the substitution names; in the data classes, we can concentrate on the code generation.

The *Code* methods of *ModelFlagsClass*, *ClassFlagsClass*, and *Window FlagsClass* are identical:

```
Public Function Code() As String
Code = Flags.CodeFlags
End Function
```

That's right; it's just a passthrough to the underlying *ListablesClass.CodeFlags* method:

```
Public Function CodeFlags() As String
Dim Result  As String
Dim i As Integer
For i = 1 To List.Count
  If List(i).Selected Then
     If Result > "" Then Result = Result + " | "
     Result = Result + List(i).Identifier
  End If
```

```
Next i
If Result = "" Then Result = "0"
CodeFlags = Result
End Function
```

The idea is to take each flag and logically OR it with the other selected items in the collection. If no flags were selected, a simple "0" is returned. The *Result* string can therefore be used *anywhere* a typical set of C-style flags is required.

My first stab at writing a code generator was more complex than I like. I was letting the script do more of the work, by breaking it into smaller segments. With that experience behind me, I decided to code *DefineProperties* more simply. You'll note it is generating code for both the C and C++ language output; since some of the substitutions are shared, and the time it takes to generate one is minimal, there seemed to be no reason not to:

```
Private Sub DefineProperties(CodeGen As CodeGenerator)
CodeGen.Substitute("$VBDATALIST") = _
   Properties.CodeVbDataList
CodeGen.Substitute("$PROPERTYLIST_CPP") = _
   Properties.CodePropertyListCPP
CodeGen.Substitute("$PROPERTY_INITIALIZATIONS_CPP") = _
   Properties.CodePropertyInitsCPP
CodeGen.Substitute("$PROPERTYAPPENDS_CPP") = _
   Properties.CodePropertyAppendsCPP
CodeGen.Substitute("$PROPERTYLIST") = _
   Properties.CodePropertyList
CodeGen.Substitute("$ONSETPROPERTY") = _
   Properties.CodePropertySet
CodeGen.Substitute("$ONGETPROPERTY") = _
   Properties.CodePropertyGet
CodeGen.Substitute("$ONLOADPROPERTY") = _
   Properties.CodePropertyLoad
CodeGen.Substitute("$ONSAVEPROPERTY") = _
   Properties.CodePropertySave
CodeGen.Substitute("$ONCHECKPROPERTY") = _
   Properties.CodePropertyCheck
CodeGen.Substitute("$ONGETSTRINGPROPERTY") = _
   Properties.CodePropertyGetstring
End Sub
```

Rather than examine each one of these coding methods, let's just take one and examine it as an example of its fellows. Here's *CodeVbDataList*, which generates the elements of the *VbData* structure in VISUAL.C:

```
Public Function CodeVbDataList() As String
Dim i As Integer
Dim Result As String
For i = 1 To List.Count
```

```
    If List.Item(i).Selected And _
        Not List.Item(i).Standard Then
      If List.Item(i).DirectStore Then
        If Result > "" Then
          Result = Result + vbCrLf
        End If
        Result = Result + vbTab + _
          List.Item(i).CodeDataType + " " + _
          List.Item(i).Description + ";"
      End If
    End If
Next i
If Result = "" Then Result = vbTab + "UINT : 16;"
CodeVbDataList = Result
End Function
```

As you see, the *PropertiesClass* object examines each property in its collection, picking out only the ones that are both non-standard (in other words, custom) and selected. It then checks to see if they are being stored directly by the VBX manager:

```
Public Function DirectStore() As Boolean
DirectStore = Flags.Item("PF_fGetData").Selected Or _
  Flags.Item("PF_fLoadMsgOnly").Selected Or _
  Flags.Item("PF_fSaveData").Selected Or _
  Flags.Item("PF_fSetData").Selected
End Function
```

If they are, then the property's data type and name are emitted in a way, complete with tabs and new line characters, to make them look right and compile correctly in the target structure.

All the code methods look about the same. Each generates code for a specific location in the target script; each is associated with a particular substitution name. These things all come together when the *CodeGenerator* form as shown in Figure 9.2.

The form, as a class, includes properties that will enable it to do its job:

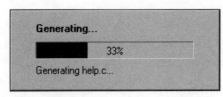

Figure 9.2 The CodeGenerator form.

```
Option Explicit

Private Substitutions As New SubstitutionsClass

Private Steps As Integer
Private CurrentStep As Integer

Private TargetIDE As String
Private Language As String

Private VBAPI_Path As String
```

The *SubstitutionsClass* is a collection of *SubstitutionClass* objects; *CodeGenerator's Substitute* method allowed it to populate itself:

```
Public Property Let Substitute(aGeneric As String, _
   aValue As Variant)
Substitutions.Substitute(aGeneric) = aValue
End Property
```

The form's *Activate* event handler actually causes the output files to be generated:

```
Private Sub Form_Activate()
Dim W As WaitCursor
Set W = New WaitCursor
Select Case Language
Case "C"
   GenerateC
Case "C++"
   GenerateCPP
End Select
Dim Message As String
Message = "Your VBX project has been generated"
Select Case TargetIDE
Case "MSVC150"
   If AddToProject_MSVC150 Then
      Message = Message + " and loaded"
   End If
Case "BC45"
   If AddToProject_BC45 Then
      Message = Message + " and loaded"
   End If
End Select
MsgBox Message + ".", vbInformation
Unload Me
End Sub
```

The *GenerateC* and *GenerateCPP* methods, obviously, do the real work. Let's look at *GenerateC*:

```
Private Sub GenerateC()
If TargetIDE = "MSVC150" Then
    Steps = 13
    GenerateTextFile "MAK", "MODULE", Prime.txt_Name + ".mak", True
Else
    Steps = 12
End If
GenerateTextFile "DEF", "MODULE", "main.def", True
GenerateTextFile "HEADER", "MODULE", "internal.h", False
GenerateTextFile "MAIN", "MODULE", "main.c", True
GenerateTextFile "HELP", "MODULE", "help.c", False
GenerateTextFile "RC", "MODULE", "main.rc", True
GenerateTextFile "VISUAL", "MODULE", "visual.c", True
GenerateBinaryFile 8000, "TOOLBOX", "8000.bmp"
GenerateBinaryFile 8001, "TOOLBOX", "8001.bmp"
GenerateBinaryFile 8003, "TOOLBOX", "8003.bmp"
GenerateBinaryFile 8006, "TOOLBOX", "8006.bmp"
GenerateBinaryFile 8006, "TOOLBOX", "8006.bmp"
GenerateBinaryFile "MAIN", "TOOLICON", "main.ico"
End Sub
```

Steps is a module variable that is used to calculate the amount of fill in the form's progress bar. Our granularity is one file, regardless of its size.

The files are written by *GenerateBinaryFile* and *GenerateTextFile*. Of the two, the first is simpler:

```
Private Sub GenerateBinaryFile(Index As Variant, _
    Format As String, FileName As String)
UpdateUI FileName
Dim Buffer As String
Buffer = LoadResData(Index, Format)
On Error Resume Next
Kill FileName
Open FileName For Binary Access Write As #1
Put #1, 1, Buffer
Close #1
DoEvents
End Sub
```

LoadResData is a new Visual Basic function; you give it a resource name ("index") and type ("MODULE" for example) and it fills your buffer for you. One caution: Resources are padded when loaded, so you might possibly wind up with a few more bytes than you thought. This isn't a problem with binary resources, because their structures are usually also padded to the same boundaries; but we'll have to deal with it when we get to text resources, by breaking the text into individual lines and then writing them out a line at a time:

```
Private Sub GenerateTextFile(Index As Variant, _
    Format As String, FileName As String, _
```

```
    ByVal Template As Boolean)
UpdateUI FileName
Dim Lines As New Collection
LoadResText Index, Format, Lines
If Template Then Transform Lines
On Error Resume Next
Kill FileName
Open FileName For Output As #1
Dim i As Integer
For i = 1 To Lines.Count
   Print #1, Lines(i)
Next i
Close #1
DoEvents
End Sub
```

Most text files can be copied as is; some contain substitutions and so must be "transformed." Such files are called *templates,* and the *Template* argument to this function tells it whether the current file is one. If it is, the *Transform* procedure is invoked:

```
Private Sub Transform(Lines As Collection)
Dim i As Integer
Dim Command As String, Arg As String
i = 1
While i <= Lines.Count
   Command = GetCommand(Lines(i), Arg)
   If Left$(Command, 3) = "$IF" Then
      If (Command = "$IFDEF" And Len(Arg) = 0) Or _
            (Command = "$IFNDEF" And Len(Arg) > 0) Then
         Do
            Lines.Remove i
            Command = GetCommand(Lines(i), Arg)
         Loop Until Command = "$ENDIF"
      Else
         Lines.Remove i
      End If
   ElseIf Command = "$ENDIF" Then
      Lines.Remove i
   ElseIf InStr(Lines(i), "$") > 0 Then
      Dim Temp As String
      Temp = Substitutions.Transform(Lines(i))
      If Temp <> Lines(i) Then
         Lines.Remove i
         Lines.Add Temp, , i
      End If
      i = i + 1
   Else
      i = i + 1
   End If
Wend
End Sub
```

This is just regular string-manipulating stuff; if you look at the input scripts and this code, you should be able to figure it out. This is where the *Substitutions* collection is invoked; it runs through each of the *SubtitutionClass* objects it contains and allows it to perform an actual substitution if appropriate:

```
Public Function Transform(ByVal Text As String) As String
Dim i As Integer
For i = 1 To List.Count
   If InStr(Text, "$") = 0 Then Exit For
   Text = List(i).Transform(Text)
Next i
Transform = Text
End Function
```

The lower level *Transform* does the actual string manipulation:

```
Public Function Transform(Text As String) As String
Dim i As Integer
i = InStr(Text, Generic)
While i > 0
   Text = Left$(Text, i - 1) + _
     Value + _
     Mid$(Text, i + Len(Generic))
   i = InStr(Text, Generic)
Wend
Transform = Text
End Function
```

The end result of all these fairly small, not terribly complex pieces of code is the generation of some dozen or so files—the user's new VBX project.

That project actually will be opened automatically by Microsoft Visual C++ or Borland C++, whichever the user ran VBX Genie from. The code to communicate with those IDEs—and it's plenty and tedious!—is described in the next chapter.

Self-Installing IDE Tools

10

THE VBX GENIE, DEVELOPED IN the previous chapters, generates C or C++ language code from which a VBX can be compiled. This, of course, requires the use of a compiler. So, although VBX Genie *could* be used as a stand-alone program, it is more useful as a tool that ties in with your C/C++ integrated development environment, like Microsoft's App Wizard or Borland's App Expert, does.

As such a tool, it would have access to information possessed by the IDE, such as the current working directory. And it would be able to generate not just the code for the VBX, but the VBX project as well.

In this chapter we'll learn how to attach VBX Genie to the *Tools* menu of the two most popular development environments, and, by extension, how to attach *any* tool you write.

Bottling the Genie

Now, there's nothing stopping you from adding VBX Genie *manually* to, say, the Microsoft Visual C++ 1.52 *Tools* menu. That isn't hard to do; just use the *Options..Tools* command and fill in a few fields in a dialog box. But if you do, after running VBX Genie, you'll still have to create a MSVC project and add the VBX Genie-generated files to it. You'll have to specify the appropriate project type, remember to turn off "Use Microsoft Foundation Classes," and add VBAPI.LIB to the project components.

How annoying! Because VBX Genie should do all this *for* you. Microsoft's Control Wizard (for making OCXs) does. And *anything* Microsoft does, we can do better ... or, at least, for less money.

What IDEs should we support? Well, we can eliminate Microsoft Visual C++ 2.x and 4.0 right off the bat; you *cannot* write 32-bit VBXs, and MSVC 2.x and 4.0 *only* produce 32-bit machine code. We will want MSVC 1.5x, though; and Borland C++ 4.x. You may well want to support one of the few other IDEs out there; but I can't help you ... I don't own copies of 'em.

There are three aspects to this job:

1. We'll need to add code to automatically install VBX Genie the first time it is run. (We can glean some additional benefit from this. If we're careful about isolating the code, we should be able to reuse the "Install Tool" form in other genies/wizards/experts/fairies/whatevers we choose to write.)

2. We'll need to generate an appropriate .MAK or .IDE file for the project.

3. We'll need to add code to send keystrokes to MSVC or BCW to open the newly created project.

Hand Me That Hammer

It won't surprise you to learn that VBX Genie will need to know whether it is creating a project for MSVC 1.5x or BCW 4.x. But how can it find out?

Simply: We'll demand that the IDE identify itself on the command line. For example,

```
VBXGEN /IDE=MSVC150
```

There's a nice side benefit to this technique; by the *absence* of this flag on the command line, we know VBX Genie is *not* being run from an IDE—and, therefore, that it is being run to install itself.

To check this, we'll add a bit of code to the Prime form's *Load* event handler:

```
Sub Form_Load ()
IniData1.FileName = MakePath("", App.Path, App.EXEName, ".ini")
If Not CheckInstallation Then
   Unload Me
   Exit Sub
End If
   <awr>
   <awr>
```

CheckInstallation will have the job of looking to see if VBX Genie is running stand-alone; if so, it will load and initialize a new, tool-installing form; let the form handle the install; and then return:

```
Private Function CheckInstallation() As Boolean
If InStr(UCase$(Command$), "/IDE=") = 0 Then
    Load InstallTool
    InstallTool.Image1.Picture = Icon
    InstallTool.MSVC200.Enabled = False
    InstallTool.Show vbModal
    CheckInstallation = False
    End
Else
    CheckInstallation = True
End If
End Function
```

Now, how does the InstallTool form work? And why do we start out by disabling one of its controls? Well, first, let's see how it *looks*. Figure 10.1 shows the Installing VBX Genie dialog.

You'll notice that the "Microsoft Visual C++ 2.x" checkbox is disabled. I mentioned earlier that MSVC 2.x can't be used to build VBXs anyway. We

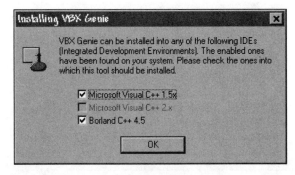

Figure 10.1   Selecting options with the Installing VBX Genie dialog.

only include it on this form because I wanted the form to be *reusable* and familiar to users, like the Open File dialog. And even though the caption and text include references to "VBX Genie," the form can be used in other projects with only small changes to accommodate the needs of different tools in the actual installation itself.

The InstallTool form looks a little different at design-time (see Figure 10.2), because of its ready-for-customizing text and image control, and its invisible-at-run-time control.

In addition to the IniData control (InstallTool has its own), you can see that the caption, text, and icon are all different.

When the InstallTool form is first loaded, it modifies its own caption and text:

```
Sub Form_Load ()
Caption = Caption + App.Title
Label1 = App.Title + Label1
End Sub
```

The Captions of the form and Label1 (the text block) are modified by the addition of the application title, as obtained from the *App.Title* property. (This value comes from the Make EXE File dialog box.) So, with no further work on your part, the form's appearance, at least, is reusable across applications.

After loading the form, we disabled the MSVC 2.x checkbox:

```
InstallTool.MSVC200.Enabled = False
```

The InstallTool form itself carries this idea further. On the form, all three check boxes are initially enabled; but InstallTool knows you may want to specifically exclude one. So it waits until *after* the *Load* event, until the

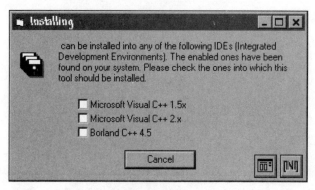

Figure 10.2 Selecting options with the Installing dialog.

Activate event (when the caller actually *Shows* the form), to check for the presence of the three tools. The location routine will disable the checkbox for any tool that is missing from the user's system, so any checkboxes still enabled are checked:

```
Private Sub Form_Activate ()
LocateAvailableTools
MSVC150.Value = -MSVC150.Enabled
MSVC200.Value = -MSVC200.Enabled
BC45.Value = -BC45.Enabled
End Sub
```

LocateAvailableTools does the dirty work, but it only looks for tools if their checkbox is still enabled:

```
Private Sub LocateAvailableTools ()
MSVC150.Enabled = IsMSVC150_Available(MSVC150.Enabled)
MSVC200.Enabled = IsMSVC200_Available(MSVC200.Enabled)
BC45.Enabled = IsBC45_Available(BC45.Enabled)
End Sub
```

This is like going on a scavenger hunt, isn't it? But there's an advantage to coding short, focused procedures in any language: There's less that can go wrong. And, in this case, with potentially three IDEs to locate, it'll make it a *lot* easier to follow the logic for each if we keep them separate.

So ... how do we find out if the user has installed Microsoft Visual C++ 1.5x on his or her system? Fortunately, this is pretty easy. MSVC 1.5x keeps its options in a .INI file, MSVC.INI. So did version 1.0; so we're lucky that there's an entry *saying* what version's been installed. The entry looks something like this:

```
[Microsoft Visual C++]
Version=1.50 .0000.0000
   <awr>
   <awr>
```

The entry says "1.50" even with version 1.52, by the way; but we won't worry about that. All we have to do is read the first three characters and we'll know what we want to know:

```
Private Function IsMSVC150_Available _
   (ByVal ShouldTest As Boolean) As Boolean
IsMSVC150_Available = False
If ShouldTest Then
   IniData1.FileName = "msvc.ini"
   IniData1.Section = "Microsoft Visual C++"
   IniData1.KeyName = "Version"
```

```
      IsMSVC150_Available = _
         (Left$(IniData1.Text, 3) = "1.5")
   End If
   End Function
```

Notice we only actually test if the *ShouldTest* parameter—which is actually the *Enabled* property of the checkbox—is *True*.

To check for Borland C++ is a similar chore. BCW keeps some information in a .INI file, as well. True, version information isn't there; but tools are installed the same way for version 4.0 through 4.5x; so I just picked any item I knew I wouldn't find in even older versions (like 3.1) to search for:

```
Private Function IsBC45_Available _
   (ByVal ShouldTest As Boolean) As Boolean
IsBC45_Available = False
If ShouldTest Then
   IniData1.FileName = "bcw.ini"
   IniData1.Section = "IDE"
   IniData1.KeyName = "DefaultDesktopDir"
   IsBC45_Available = (IniData1.Text > "")
End If
End Function
```

(If you still have version 4.0, by the way, get rid of it *quick!* There are some *serious* bugs in that puppy. And 4.02 isn't really any better. You need at least 4.5.)

That leaves the search routine for MSVC 2.x unexamined. And, since we don't need it for this project, it will remain uncompleted, for now. (A hook remains if you ever want to use the InstallTool form for another project.)

At one point Microsoft stated an intention to do away with .INI files and keep that kind of information in the Registration Database, along with all the OLE stuff. The idea was that *GetPrivateProfileString()* and its siblings would suddenly just start working with the registration database instead of files.

Well, for whatever reason, that day has *not* come to pass, at least not in the current version of Windows NT or in Windows 95, as far as 16-bit applications are concerned. Apparently working with the Registration Database is too complex for that series of functions.

There is no Cancel button on the InstallTool form because unchecking the checkboxes and then clicking the OK button would have the same effect. The OK button inspects each of the checkboxes to see which IDEs, if any, the user wants to install to; it then installs to those:

```
Private Sub cmd_OK_Click()
If MSVC150.Value Or BC45.Value Then
   Locate_VBAPI
End If
If MSVC150.Value Then
   Install_MSVC150
End If
If MSVC200.Value Then
   Install_MSVC200
End If
If BC45.Value Then
   Install_BC45
End If
Hide
End Sub
```

(Even though the *Value* property of a checkbox will never *be* "True"—minus one—it will *test* True with a value of one.)

The initial function invocation, *Locate_VBAPI*, will allow the user to specify the location of the Visual Basic CDK components. As part of the installation, we'll have to add this directory to the IDE search paths for **#INCLUDE** files and libraries. The routine itself is simple, making use of the Common Dialog control cunningly stashed away on the form:

```
Private Sub Locate_VBAPI()
CmDialog1.DefaultExt = "lib"
CmDialog1.DialogTitle = "Locate VBAPI.LIB"
CmDialog1.FileName = "vbapi.lib"
CmDialog1.Filter = "VBAPI.LIB|vbapi.lib|All files|*.*"
CmDialog1.FilterIndex = 1
CmDialog1.Flags = cdlOFNHideReadOnly Or cdlOFNFileMustExist

On Error Resume Next
CmDialog1.ShowOpen
If Err = 0 Then
   VBAPI_Path = Left$(CmDialog1.FileName, _
      Len(CmDialog1.FileName) - 10)
   If Len(VBAPI_Path) = 2 Then
      VBAPI_Path = VBAPI_Path + "\"
   End If
   IniData1.FileName = _
      MakePath("", App.Path, App.EXEName, ".ini")
   IniData1.Section = "VBAPI"
   IniData1.KeyName = "Path"
   IniData1.Text = VBAPI_Path
End If
End Sub
```

Although the Common Dialog box that appears will request the location of VBAPI.LIB, Visual Basic stores the header file VBAPI.H in the same directory; so finding one finds both. We then strip the file name (and terminating backslash) from the name and store it in a static string variable, *VBAPI_Path*— it is also stored in VBX Genie's .INI file.

Installing to MSVC 1.5x

MSVC 1.5x stores tool configurations, as mentioned, in its .INI file. There's a key name, "ToolNumber", whose value is the number of tools currently configured. For each of those tools, there are several key names, each of which end in a ToolNumber. For example, if you had three tools defined, there would be key names of "ToolMenuText1", "ToolMenuText2", and "ToolMenuText3". It's sort of an array in an environment that doesn't support arrays.

This information is significant because you wouldn't want to install the same tool twice. So the first step in installing to this IDE is to check for pre-existing installations:

```
Private Function GetToolNumber_MSVC150 _
   (ByVal ToolName As String) As String
Dim ToolCount As Integer, t As Integer
IniData1.KeyName = "ToolNumber"
ToolCount = Val(IniData1.Text)

For t = 1 To ToolCount
   IniData1.KeyName = "ToolMenuText" + Format$(t)
   If IniData1.Text = ToolName Then
      GetToolNumber_MSVC150 = Format$(t)
      Exit Function
   End If
Next t

Dim Digits As String
Digits = Format$(ToolCount + 1)
IniData1.KeyName = "ToolNumber"
IniData1.Text = Digits
GetToolNumber_MSVC150 = Digits
End Function
```

This function will either return the number—as an *available* string—of the tool if it is already installed or the number of the *next* tool. It also updates the ToolNumber in the MSVC.INI file.

Now that we have the ToolNumber, the key names can be constructed and the proper values set. Remember, in a .INI file, if the key names already exist, they will just be updated; if not, they'll be added. MSVC wants five pieces of description for a tool: the name as it will appear on the menu (ToolMenuText*n*), the path name of the .EXE file (ToolPathName*n*), any runtime arguments that might be required (ToolArguments$n$), the startup directory if one is required (ToolInitialDir$n$), and whether or not the user should be queried for arguments each time the tool is run (ToolAskArguments$n$). That makes the procedure that updates or sets these items look like this:

```
Private Sub Install_MSVC150 ()
IniData1.FileName = "msvc.ini"
IniData1.Section = "Microsoft Visual C++"

Dim N As String
N = GetToolNumber_MSVC150("&" + App.Title)

IniData1.KeyName = "ToolPathName" + N
IniData1.Text = MakePath("", App.Path, App.EXEName, ".exe")
IniData1.KeyName = "ToolMenuText" + N
IniData1.Text = "&" + App.Title
IniData1.KeyName = "ToolArguments" + N
IniData1.Text = "/IDE=MSVC150"
IniData1.KeyName = "ToolInitialDir" + N
IniData1.Text = "$Dir"
IniData1.KeyName = "ToolAskArguments" + N
IniData1.Text = "0"

IniData1.KeyName = "Include1"
If InStr(IniData1.Text, VBAPI_Path) = 0 Then
    IniData1.Text = IniData1.Text + ";" + VBAPI_Path
End If
IniData1.KeyName = "Lib1"
If InStr(IniData1.Text, VBAPI_Path) = 0 Then
    IniData1.Text = IniData1.Text + ";" + VBAPI_Path
End If

MsgBox App.Title + " has been installed. Please restart Visual C++ for it to
become available as part of the Tools menu.", vbInformation
End Sub
```

The ToolInitialDir$n$ entry, "$Dir", is a macro supplied by MSVC, which is expanded when the tool is run. MSVC supplies many such macros.

Our final touch with MSVC is to add the Visual Basic CDK directory to the directory paths MSVC will search. MSVC saves one current and three previous entries. We don't concern ourselves with previous entries, modifying just the current ones: Include1 and Lib1.

Creating a Brand-New MSVC Project

What's the cleanest way to urge an IDE to create a new project?

It *should* be DDE ... except that neither Microsoft nor Borland has published a DDE interface to their C++ IDEs.

Okay, how about sending keystrokes to the IDE itself?

That'll work with Borland's IDE. And it *should* work with Microsoft's. After all, Visual Basic and the **SendKeys** statement are *their* invention, as is Windows. However, there's some sort of kink in the hose; you can't close the Edit Project dialog with the "%O" keystroke as you'd think you could. You *can* tab over to the Close button and send an {ENTER}; but there's another, more serious problem.

In MSVC, when you create a new project, the "Use Microsoft Foundation Classes" checkbox retains its value from the previous project. By sending keys, you can *toggle* it—but there's no easy way to find out what its current value *is*. And there are several other project options that work the same way.

So, for MSVC at least, the easiest way to generate a project is to actually generate one—the .MAK file for one, that is.

Fortunately, that's easy for us to do. We already have the mechanism; we can just add a couple of substitutions and we're on our way. The reason the job is so simple is that the potentially hardest part, creating the skeleton .MAK file itself, is something that MSVC is willing to do for us.

A .MAK file, as emitted by MSVC, specifies the project name, target type, memory model, and components. I've made one of these files, and replaced the hard-coded elements with VBXGEN-style substitutions. After doing so, I get the following file, called MAIN.MAK and kept in the resource directory with the other skeleton code files:

```
# Microsoft Visual C++ generated build script - Do not modify

PROJ = $PROJECT
DEBUG = 1
PROGTYPE = 2
CALLER =
ARGS =
DLLS =
D_RCDEFINES = -d_DEBUG
R_RCDEFINES = -dNDEBUG
ORIGIN = MSVC
ORIGIN_VER = 1.00
PROJPATH = $DIRECTORY\
USEMFC = 0
CC = cl
CPP = cl
CXX = cl
CCREATEPCHFLAG =
CPPCREATEPCHFLAG =
```

```
CUSEPCHFLAG =
CPPUSEPCHFLAG =
FIRSTC =
FIRSTCPP =
RC = rc
CFLAGS_D_VEXE = /nologo /W3 /FR /G2 /Zi /D_DEBUG /Zp /Od /GD /ALw /Gc /
Fd"TEST16.PDB"
CFLAGS_R_VEXE = /nologo /W3 /FR /G2 /DNDEBUG /Gs /Zp /Ox /GD /ALw /Gc
LFLAGS_D_VEXE = /NOLOGO /ONERROR:NOEXE /NOD /PACKC:61440 /CO /ALIGN:16
LFLAGS_R_VEXE = /NOLOGO /ONERROR:NOEXE /NOD /PACKC:61440 /ALIGN:16
LIBS_D_VEXE = oldnames libw commdlg shell olecli olesvr ldllcew
LIBS_R_VEXE = oldnames libw commdlg shell olecli olesvr ldllcew
RCFLAGS = /nologo
RESFLAGS = /nologo
RUNFLAGS =
DEFFILE = MAIN.DEF
OBJS_EXT =
LIBS_EXT = vbapi.lib
!if "$(DEBUG)" == "1"
CFLAGS = $(CFLAGS_D_VEXE)
LFLAGS = $(LFLAGS_D_VEXE)
LIBS = $(LIBS_D_VEXE)
MAPFILE = nul
RCDEFINES = $(D_RCDEFINES)
!else
CFLAGS = $(CFLAGS_R_VEXE)
LFLAGS = $(LFLAGS_R_VEXE)
LIBS = $(LIBS_R_VEXE)
MAPFILE = nul
RCDEFINES = $(R_RCDEFINES)
!endif
!if [if exist MSVC.BND del MSVC.BND]
!endif
$IFDEF $LANGUAGE_C
SBRS = HELP.SBR \
      MAIN.SBR \
      VISUAL.SBR
#ENDIF
$IFDEF $LANGUAGE_CPP
SBRS = VBXXX.SBR \
      MAIN.SBR \
      PORTAGDI.SBR
#ENDIF

$IFDEF $LANGUAGE_C
HELP_DEP = internal.h
MAIN_DEP = internal.h
VISUAL_DEP = internal.h
$ENDIF
$IFDEF $LANGUAGE_CPP
VBXXX_DEP = vbxxx.h portagdi.h
PORTAGDI_DEP = portagdi.h
MAIN_DEP = vbxxx.h
$ENDIF
```

```
MAIN_RCDEP = main.ico

all: $(PROJ).VBX $(PROJ).BSC

$IFDEF $LANGUAGE_C
HELP.OBJ: HELP.C $(HELP_DEP)
  $(CC) $(CFLAGS) $(CUSEPCHFLAG) /c HELP.C

MAIN.OBJ: MAIN.C $(MAIN_DEP)
  $(CC) $(CFLAGS) $(CUSEPCHFLAG) /c MAIN.C

VISUAL.OBJ:  VISUAL.C $(VISUAL_DEP)
  $(CC) $(CFLAGS) $(CUSEPCHFLAG) /c VISUAL.C

MAIN.RES: MAIN.RC $(MAIN_RCDEP)
  $(RC) $(RCFLAGS) $(RCDEFINES) -r MAIN.RC
$ENDIF
```

```
$IFDEF $LANGUAGE_CPP
VBXXX.OBJ: VBXXX.CPP $(VBXXX_DEP)
  $(CC) $(CFLAGS) $(CUSEPCHFLAG) /c VBXXX.CPP

MAIN.OBJ: MAIN.CPP $(MAIN_DEP)
  $(CC) $(CFLAGS) $(CUSEPCHFLAG) /c MAIN.CPP

PORTAGDI.OBJ: PORTAGDI.CPP $(PORTAGDI_DEP)
  $(CC) $(CFLAGS) $(CUSEPCHFLAG) /c PORTAGDI.CPP

MAIN.RES: MAIN.RC $(MAIN_RCDEP)
  $(RC) $(RCFLAGS) $(RCDEFINES) -r MAIN.RC
$ENDIF
```

```
$(PROJ).VBX:: MAIN.RES
```

```
$IFDEF $LANGUAGE_C
$(PROJ).VBX:: HELP.OBJ MAIN.OBJ VISUAL.OBJ $(OBJS_EXT) $(DEFFILE)
  echo >NUL @<<$(PROJ).CRF
HELP.OBJ +
MAIN.OBJ +
VISUAL.OBJ +
$(OBJS_EXT)
$(PROJ).VBX
$(MAPFILE)
d:\msvc\lib\+
d:\msvc\mfc\lib\+
$(LIBS)
$(DEFFILE);
<<
  link $(LFLAGS) @$(PROJ).CRF
  $(RC) $(RESFLAGS) MAIN.RES $@
  @copy $(PROJ).CRF MSVC.BND
```

```
$ENDIF
$IFDEF $LANGUAGE_CPP
$(PROJ).VBX:: VBXXX.OBJ MAIN.OBJ PORTAGDI.OBJ $(OBJS_EXT) $(DEFFILE)
    echo >NUL @<<$(PROJ).CRF
VBXXX.OBJ +
MAIN.OBJ +
PORTAGDI.OBJ +
$(OBJS_EXT)
$(PROJ).VBX
$(MAPFILE)
d:\msvc\lib\+
d:\msvc\mfc\lib\+
$(LIBS)
$(DEFFILE);
<<
    link $(LFLAGS) @$(PROJ).CRF
    $(RC) $(RESFLAGS) MAIN.RES $@
    @copy $(PROJ).CRF MSVC.BND
$ENDIF

$(PROJ).VBX:: MAIN.RES
    if not exist MSVC.BND $(RC) $(RESFLAGS) MAIN.RES $@

run: $(PROJ).VBX
    $(PROJ) $(RUNFLAGS)


$(PROJ).BSC: $(SBRS)
    bscmake @<<
/o$@ $(SBRS)
<<
```

I've highlighted the additions or alterations I made.

There is an addition of four substitutions: $MSVC150, $LANGUAGE_C, $LANGUAGE_CPP, and $DIRECTORY. The first is set by calling *SetTargetIDE*, a procedure defined in the CodeGenerator form, when Prime is loaded:

```
Public Sub SetTargetIDE()
Dim Buffer As String, i As Integer
i = InStr(UCase$(Command$), "/IDE=")
If i > 0 Then
    Buffer = Mid$(Command$, i + 5)
    i = InStr(Buffer, " ")
    If i > 0 Then Buffer = Left$(Buffer, i - 1)
    TargetIDE = UCase$(Buffer)
End If
End Sub
```

TargetIDE is just a static variable in CodeGenerator that will be referenced later when the decision has to be made for which IDE to generate the project.

The remaining substitutions are set, along with the others, in Prime's handler for the OK button's *Click* event.

With this information, generating an MSVC project is really simple. The user selects *Tools..VB Genie*, which runs VBX Genie. He or she then customizes the various pages, and clicks the OK button. The project .MAK file gets generated with all the others. The last step is for VBX Genie to close the previous project, if one was opened, and to open the new one. This function is part of the CodeGenerator module:

```
Private Function AddToProject_MSVC150() As Boolean
Dim Window As Integer
Window = FindApplication("Microsoft Visual C++")
If Window <> 0 Then
   SetActiveWindow Window
   'File..Save All
   SendKeys "%FV", True
   'Window..Close All
   SendKeys "%WA", True
   ' Project..Close
   SendKeys "%PC", True
   ' Project..Open <project name> <Enter>
   SendKeys "%PO" + _
      Brace(MakePath("", Prime.txt_Directory, Prime.txt_Name, "")) + _
      "{Enter}", True
End If
AddToProject_MSVC150 = (Window <> 0)
End Function
```

The *Brace* function accommodates the use of the various new characters in long file names. The problem is that these characters have special meanings to the **SendKeys** statement, so they must be delimited with braces:

```
Public Function Brace(ByVal Text As String)
Dim Braced As String, i As Integer, C As String
For i = 1 To Len(Text)
   Select Case Mid$(Text, i, 1)
   Case "+", "^", "%", "~", "(", ")", "[", "]"
      Braced = Braced + "{" + Mid$(Text, i, 1) + "}"
   Case Else
      Braced = Braced + Mid$(Text, i, 1)
   End Select
Next i
Brace = Braced
End Function
```

If the user chooses to build the project at this point, it should happen without error.

Installing VBX Genie as a Borland C++ Tool

If only we could add tools to the Borland IDE as simply as we can in Visual C++! But Borland, heady with the success of serialized objects, stores its environment in a file full of C++ objects, which no one else can read or write. (So, why do they have a .INI file, too? Beats me!)

Fortunately, the dialogs Borland uses to describe new tools respond properly to Visual Basic **SendKeys** transmissions ... once we've located the Borland C++ IDE, started it, and locked onto its main window.

The InstallTool form can let the user locate the BCW.EXE file with the common dialog control's Open File dialog:

```
Private Function StartBCW() As Integer
StartBCW = 0

CmDialog1.CancelError = True
CmDialog1.DefaultExt = "exe"
CmDialog1.DialogTitle = "Locate Borland C++ IDE"
CmDialog1.FileName = "bcw.exe"
CmDialog1.Filter = "Borland C++|bcw.exe|Programs|*.exe"
CmDialog1.FilterIndex = 1
CmDialog1.Flags = cdlOFNHideReadOnly Or cdlOFNFileMustExist

On Error Resume Next
CmDialog1.ShowOpen
If Err = 0 Then
   Dim x As Integer, Window As Integer
   x = Shell(CmDialog1.FileName, vbMaximizedFocus)
   For x = 1 To 100
      Window = FindApplication("Borland C++")
      If Window <> 0 Then Exit For
   Next x
   StartBCW = Window
End If
End Function
```

The function *StartBCW* returns zero if it failed, or the handle of Borland C++'s main window. The routine for *locating* that window is *FindApplication*, which encapsulates the Windows API calls for locating a window, given a portion of its caption. This function is located in WinAPI.BAS, a module devoted to dealing with the native Windows API:

```
Public Function FindApplication(ByVal Text As String) As Integer
Dim Window As Integer, Buffer As String
```

```
Window = GetWindow(Prime.hWnd, GW_HWNDFIRST)
While Window <> 0
   Buffer = Space$(GetWindowTextLength(Window) + 1)
   GetWindowText Window, Buffer, Len(Buffer)
   If Left$(Buffer, Len(Text)) = Text Then
      FindApplication = Window
      Exit Function
   End If
   Window = GetWindow(Window, GW_HWNDNEXT)
Wend
FindApplication = 0
End Function
```

GetWindow is a Windows API function. Given a window handle—for example, the one to our own main window, Prime—you can use this function to iterate through the list of all windows at that level. *GetWindowTextLength* and *GetWindowText* make it possible to retrieve the text from each window we retrieve.

The **Declare** statements for these API calls (and others we'll use shortly) have been copied into the Declarations section of WINAPI.BAS:

```
Option Explicit

Declare Function GetWindow Lib "User" _
   (ByVal hWnd As Integer, ByVal wCmd As Integer) As Integer
Global Const GW_HWNDFIRST = 0
Global Const GW_HWNDNEXT = 2

Declare Function GetWindowTextLength Lib "User" (ByVal hWnd As Integer) As
Integer
Declare Sub GetWindowText Lib "User" (ByVal hWnd As Integer, ByVal lpString As
String, ByVal aint As Integer)

Declare Sub SetActiveWindow Lib "User" (ByVal hWnd As Integer)
```

So, now we have a function (*StartBCW*) that will locate and load Borland C++, and return the handle to its main window. That's a good deal of the job done right there!

The next task is to send the appropriate keystrokes to the IDE to add the new tool. The sequence "<alt>OT" will activate the *Options..Tools* command and cause the Tools dialog to appear. This dialog contains a list of all installed tools. It looks like the dialog shown in Figure 10.3.

That's the good news. The bad news is, there's no easy way to determine programmatically if VBX Genie is *already in* that list.

However, that doesn't mean there's *no* way. And we *have* to know whether to add a *new* tool or edit an existing one. So it's back to the Windows API.

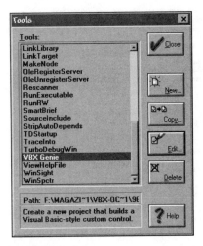

Figure 10.3 Using the Tools dialog.

Fortunately, Borland C++ comes with a pretty slick tool called WinSight. It lists all windows on screen (including hidden ones), arranges them in an outline, displays some helpful information, and allows you to query them further.

With the Tools dialog displayed as above, WinSight reveals the information shown in Figure 10.4.

Now, this is good stuff! We can see that the Tools dialog is a popup (no surprise there) and that the list box is, indeed, an ordinary list box. What's more, by highlighting it (as shown in Figure 10.4) and pressing the ENTER key, we can find out even more, as shown in Figure 10.5.

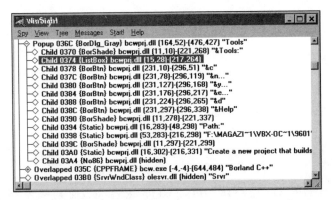

Figure 10.4 Using WinSight to display information on windows.

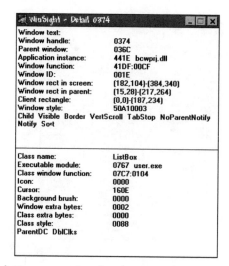

Figure 10.5 Displaying more detail with WinSight.

Now, window handles come and go. But a window ID lasts forever, or at least until the next major rewrite. So "all" we have to do is:

1. Get a handle to the "Tools" dialog, locating it by caption as we did the Borland C++ main window.

2. Use the *GetDlgItem* API call to get a handle to the list box using its ID.

3. Query the listbox items using *SendMessage* and the standard listbox messages, looking for the desired entry. If we find it, programmatically press the <u>E</u>dit button; if not, press the <u>N</u>ew button.

Here's that code:

```
Private Sub OpenBCWToolEdit(ByVal Window As Integer)
SetActiveWindow Window
DoEvents
' Options..Tools
SendKeys "%OT", True
DoEvents

Window = FindWindow("BorDlg_Gray", "Tools")
If Window = 0 Then Error 31024
Window = GetDlgItem(Window, &H1E)
If Window = 0 Then Error 31024

Dim i As Long
i = SendMessage(Window, LB_FINDSTRINGEXACT, -1, (App.Title))
If i > -1 Then
    i = SendMessage(Window, LB_SETCURSEL, i, "")
    SendKeys "%E", True
```

```
Else
    SendKeys "%N", True
End If
DoEvents
End Sub
```

There are three new Windows API calls made in this procedure: *FindWindow,*
GetDlgItem, and *SendMessage.* I took the declarations from the Visual Basic
API Declares help file, but I had to tweak them a bit, before adding them to
the WINAPI.BAS declaration section:

```
Declare Function FindWindow Lib "User" (ByVal ClassName As String, ByVal
WindowCaption As String) As Integer
Declare Function GetDlgItem Lib "User" (ByVal Dialog As Integer, ByVal ItemID
As Integer) As Integer
Declare Function IsChecked Lib "User" Alias "IsDlgButtonChecked" (ByVal hDlg As
Integer, ByVal nIDButton As Integer) As Integer

Declare Function SendMessage Lib "User" (ByVal Window As Integer, ByVal MsgID
As Integer, ByVal wParam As Integer, ByVal lParam As String) As Long
Const WM_USER = &H400
Global Const LB_FINDSTRINGEXACT = (WM_USER + 35)
Global Const LB_SETCURSEL = (WM_USER + 7)
```

The prepackaged VB4 **Declare** statements are better than they were in VB3,
but they still aren't perfect. *FindWindow* will hunt for a match of window
class and caption (and the caption has to match exactly, from beginning to
end). In the API Text Viewer applet, both parameters are listed as "Any" to
accommodate the fact that a NULL (zero) can be passed in either position.
However, "Any" doesn't accommodate the conversion of a Visual Basic
String to a C-style string.

SendMessage presents a similar problem; in various messages the fourth
parameter, *lParam,* can be of a wide variety of data types. Fortunately, here
we are using it for just one data type (**String**, again).

The two messages we intend to send, *LB_FINDEXACTSTRING* and
LB_SETCURSEL, are both based on *WM_USER,* so the constants for all three
must be included.

The **Error** number that's triggered if either of the window-locating functions
fails, is one borrowed from the list of pre-defined errors. This particular one,
31024, comes from the OLE set and translates to the message, "Unable to
create link." Hopefully the user would understand that the link referred to was
the one to Borland C++. I don't know what could cause this problem, but
whatever it is, we certainly can't do anything about it in the program to recover!

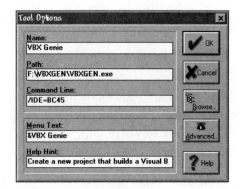

Figure 10.6 Using the Tool Options dialog.

Now that the Tool Options dialog has appeared, we get to fill it in. Figure 10.6 how it should look after the appropriate data has been added.

Here's the procedure to send the appropriate keystrokes to the dialog:

```
Private Sub FillInBCWToolOptions()
SendKeys "%N" + Brace(App.Title), True
DoEvents
SendKeys "%P" + Brace(MakePath("", App.Path, App.EXEName, ".exe")), True
DoEvents
SendKeys "%C/IDE=BC45", True
DoEvents
SendKeys "%M&" + Brace(App.Title), True
DoEvents
SendKeys "%HCreate a new project that builds a Visual Basic-style custom _ ,
  control.", True
DoEvents
'Close the Tool Options dialog
SendKeys "{ENTER}", True
DoEvents
'Close the Tools dialog
SendKeys "%C", True
DoEvents
End Sub
```

Now we have enough pieces to build *Install_BC45:*

```
Private Sub Install_BC45()
Dim Window As Integer
Window = StartBCW()
OpenBCWToolEdit Window
FillInBCWToolOptions
SendKeys "%FX", True 'Close BCW
MsgBox "VBX Genie has been installed into Borland C++' Tools menu.", _ ,
  vbInformation
End Sub
```

Creating a Brand-New Borland C++ Project

As with installing VBX Genie, creating a new project in Borland C++ is more complex than with Microsoft Visual C++, because it has to be done entirely with **SendKeys**. At least, BCW responds properly to them! Well, *most* of them. There was one spot where ... but I'll tell you about that when we get to it.

Once VBX Genie has created the project directory and files, as with Visual C++, you'll need to issue a *Project..New* command and fill in the fields of the resulting dialog box. In this case, the dialog is titled "New Target" and requires *more* than just the list of files that make up the project; this is also where the desired class libraries (such as OWL) are requested. Figure 10.7 shows how we want the dialog box to look.

A problem is evident almost immediately: We have to uncheck a couple of checkboxes (OWL and Class Library). But Microsoft never provided a keyboard method of specifying you want a checkbox unchecked, regardless of its previous state. This can be done programmatically, using the *CheckDlgButton* Windows API function ... except, when I tried it here, I couldn't make it work! Strictly speaking, these are not standard checkboxes; they are BorCheck controls, part of the BWCC collection of custom controls. They're *supposed* to *work* identically to standard checkboxes, however; so it's all the more annoying when they don't.

Figure 10.7 Using the New Target dialog.

Fortunately, my last stab was successful: Using the *IsDlgButtonChecked* function to see if the button was checked, and *then* sending the keystroke to uncheck it if it was. (Even then there was a snag: It didn't work at first ... not until I rearranged the order in which I set the various fields! Sheesh!)

Before closing this dialog, the Advanced button must be pressed and *that* dialog filled in. I don't know why they called it "Advanced" when "Initial nodes" would have been more accurate, as shown in Figure 10.8.

We'll want to turn *off* the initial node ("No Source Node") and also uncheck .rc and .def. That's because VBX Genie has already generated those files and we want to add them to the project manually.

Finally, we need to modify the project options. This dialog is activated with the *Options..Project* menu command. We'll have to modify the search paths for the include and library directories; we'll also have to turn off the two Case Sensitive link options as shown in Figure 10.9.

Figure 10.8 Selecting options with the Advanced Options dialog.

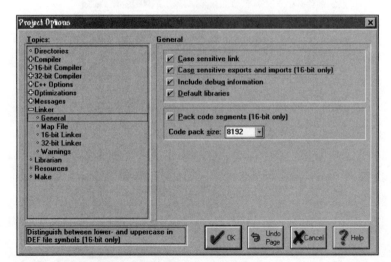

Figure 10.9 Using the Project Options dialog.

You'll note that, once again, these are checkboxes.

Here's the code that does this massive job. It makes heavy use of **SendKeys**, as well as *FindWindow* and *IsChecked*, an alias for *IsDlgButtonChecked*:

```
Function AddToProject_BC45() As Boolean
Dim Window As Integer
Window = FindApplication("Borland C++")
If Window <> 0 Then
   SetActiveWindow Window
   'Window..Close All..Windows
   SendKeys "%WAW", True
   'File..Save All
   SendKeys "%FL", True
   ' Project..Close
   SendKeys "%PL", True
   ' Project..New <project name> <Enter>
   SendKeys "%PN", True
   ' Turn off OWL, Class Library, choose static library
   Window = FindWindow("BorDlg_Gray", "New Target")
   If IsChecked(Window, &H2775) Then SendKeys "%O", True
   If IsChecked(Window, &H2776) Then SendKeys "%C", True
   SendKeys "%S", True
   ' Project path and name
   SendKeys "%P" + Brace(MakePath("", Prime.txt_Directory, _ ,
      Prime.txt_Name, "") + ".ide"), True
   ' Target name
   SendKeys "%T" + Brace(Prime.txt_Name + ".vbx"), True
   ' Target type: DLL
   SendKeys "%YD", True
   ' Platform: Win16
   SendKeys "%L{Home}", True
   ' Target model: Large
   SendKeys "%ML", True
   ' Open Advanced dialog
   SendKeys "%A", True
   Do
      DoEvents
      Window = FindWindow("BorDlg_Gray", "Advanced Options")
   Loop Until Window <> 0
   ' Don't produce initial nodes
   SendKeys "%N", True
   If IsChecked(Window, &H68) Then SendKeys "%R", True
   If IsChecked(Window, &H69) Then SendKeys "%D", True
   SendKeys "{Enter}", True
   ' Close New Target dialog
   SendKeys "{Enter}", True
   ' Add nodes to the project
   SendKeys "{Insert}", True
   SendKeys "vbapi.lib{Enter}", True
   SendKeys "{Up}{Insert}", True
   SendKeys "main.def{Enter}", True
   SendKeys "{Up}{Insert}", True
```

```
   SendKeys "main.rc{Enter}", True
   Select Case Language
   Case "C"
      SendKeys "{Up}{Insert}", True
      SendKeys "help.c{Enter}", True
      SendKeys "{Up}{Insert}", True
      SendKeys "visual.c{Enter}", True
      SendKeys "{Up}{Insert}", True
      SendKeys "main.c{Enter}", True
   Case "C++"
      SendKeys "{Up}{Insert}", True
      SendKeys "portagdi.cpp{Enter}", True
      SendKeys "{Up}{Insert}", True
      SendKeys "vbxxx.cpp{Enter}", True
      SendKeys "{Up}{Insert}", True
      SendKeys "main.cpp{Enter}", True
   End Select
   ' Display Project Options Dialog
   SendKeys "%OP", True
   DoEvents
   ' go to top of list
   SendKeys "%T^{Home}", True
   ' copy the include path
   SendKeys "%I^{Insert}", True
   Dim Buffer As String
   Buffer = Clipboard.GetText()
   If InStr(Buffer, VBAPI_Path) = 0 Then
      Buffer = Brace(Buffer + ";" + VBAPI_Path)
      SendKeys Buffer, True
   End If
   SendKeys "%B^{Insert}", True
   Buffer = Clipboard.GetText()
   If InStr(Buffer, VBAPI_Path) = 0 Then
      Buffer = Brace(Buffer + ";" + VBAPI_Path)
      SendKeys Buffer, True
   End If
   Clipboard.Clear
   ' Display Linker general options page
   SendKeys "%T^{Home}{Down 7}{+}{Down}"
   ' Get dialog's window handle,
   ' General Linker Options page
   Window = FindWindow("BorDlg_Gray", "Project Options")
   Do
      DoEvents
      Window = GetDlgItem(Window, &H7D3)
   Loop Until Window <> 0
   ' Set "Case Sensitive" options to unchecked
   If IsChecked(Window, &H20) Then SendKeys "%C", True
   If IsChecked(Window, &H21) Then SendKeys "%E", True
   ' Close the Project Options dialog
   SendKeys "{Enter}", True
End If
AddToProject_BC45 = (Window <> 0)
End Function
```

Quite a task, eh? But with that code in place, VBX Genie works equally well as a tool for Microsoft Visual C++ *and* Borland C++. What a headache! But what a triumph as well.

And, with that, VBX Genie is *done!*

11

Creating a Setup Program for VBX Genie

O
N OUR 17th DAY IN THE GRAND CANYON, even the hardiest of us whitewater rafters were ready for a shower. Over two weeks earlier, a van had dropped us off at Lee's Ferry and we had walked a few dozen yards to the rafts. So those rafters who hadn't done the Canyon before undoubtedly expected a similarly effortless egress from the river.

We knew we would be picked up in the morning at our last campsite by a "jet boat." None of us was certain quite what that was, but it sounded fast. Sure enough, just after breakfast the loudest noise we'd heard in 17 days heralded the jet boat's arrival. We loaded our gear and ourselves and were soon on our way, speeding at fifty MPH into Lake Meade...until we crashed against a hidden sandbar. When we had un-tangled ourselves, we jumped over the side of the boat to survey the damage.

We were still miles from our pickup point. Robby, the lead boatman, could radio for help—but not until a plane flew overhead to relay his calls. We had enough leftover food for snacks, and we had plenty of coffee. There were the inevitable whiners. But it was a pleasant day, and some of us sunbathed while others swam, or explored a nearby island.

When another jet boat approached from the other side of the sandbar, we figured we'd been rescued. But, not yet! First we had to unload the first boat, transferring our gear onto the second. The second boat was too small to hold our gear and ourselves, so we had to wait until it returned empty before we could board. Meanwhile, the first boat was much lighter without our gear; so, with the second boat pulling it, we all stood on the sandbar and *lifted* the entrapped boat, freeing it.

Then we got to go home.

The VBX Genie Setup Chronicles

I bring all this up because it parallels what happened when I tried to run the Visual Basic 4 16-bit Setup Wizard, to generate distribution disks for the VBX Genie. When I tried testing the disks by installing onto a variety of machines, I found—to my dismay!—that the installs worked on *some* machines, but not others. Worse, when the installations failed, they often left the target computer in a corrupted state. Just like that last day of the rafting trip, the adventure was not over.

Thanks to the MSBASIC forum on CompuServe, I was able to garner some clues for other programmers had discovered the same thing. The Microsoft techies who frequent that forum weren't able to help, because Setup Wizard always worked perfectly for *them!*

But that, actually, was a clue. I began paying attention to the details of the other programmers' problems and a pattern emerged, which I will share with you.

Platforms or Sandbars?

At the time of this writing there are four Windows platforms in use, although only two are in current release. They are Windows 95 and Windows NT, both blessed by Microsoft; and the recently-orphaned Windows 3.1 and Windows for Workgroups 3.11. OLE was introduced while Windows 3.1 and Windows for Workgroups were still being sold; there were a number of bugs in its initial and patched releases, and the DLLs that implemented it proliferated like crazy. Windows 3.1/3.11 didn't actually come *with* OLE, but all of Microsoft's more recent applications (like Microsoft Office) did; so most—but not all!—Win31 machines had OLE DLLs on them.

> *Windows 95 actually comes* with *most of the OLE DLLs...but not all of them. (The rest are installed with Visual Basic 4.) Now, here's the problem:* The Windows 95 OLE DLLs are not backward compatible with Windows 3.1/3.11!

If you've installed Visual Basic 4 on a Win31 platform, Setup Wizard will use your Win31 DLLs to create application distribution disks. You can safely install onto another Win31 machine. If you attempt to install on the average Win95 machine, where Microsoft Office is already installed, that will succeed, too; because your older DLLs will not be copied to the target machine. However, if the Win95 computer has not yet installed a new OLE application (like Visual Basic 4 or Microsoft Office 95), it will be missing *one* of the OLE DLLs—which will be supplied from your distribution disk. *But it will conflict with the other, newer OLE DLLs because they* **must** *be used as a set!*

If you installed Visual Basic 4 on a Win95 machine, your applications' installations will always corrupt the target machine, because the Win95 OLE DLLs are a later version than the ones on the target machine and so will overwrite them.

This sounds like a Catch-22, right? But I was determined to find an answer. I had installed VB4 on my Win95 machine, so I checked all the files in \VB\SETUPKIT\KITFILES\SYS16 (where the VB installation copied them from \WINDOWS\SYSTEM—an interesting approach, since if you subsequently update your DLLs the set in SYS16 will become outdated).

I then cross-checked these files against the ones that came on my Windows 95 distribution disks. (Yes, I got Win95 on floppies.) All but four of the files are installed with Windows 95, so including Windows 95 versions is redundant anyway. So, by replacing the Windows 95 files with Windows 3.1 files in \VB\SETUPKIT\KITFILES\SYS16 we should *just about* solve the problem...*except* for those four files. For the others, Setup will install them on a Win 3.1 system if they are missing or outdated, but will find "later versions" present on a Windows 95 system, and so will *not* overwrite them.

That leaves the remaining four files, which are:

- OLE2.REG
- OLE2PROX.DLL
- SCP.DLL
- STDOLE.TLB

These are the crux of the problem. Files with these names do *not* come with Windows 95 itself or (of course) with Win31.

The solution is to keep both versions of these four files (with different names) on the distribution disk; to have two versions of SETUP.LST (which Setup reads to decide what to copy onto the target machine); and to add a pre-step to SETUP.EXE to detect whether the install is to Win31 or Win95, and then rename the .LST file appropriately so the regular Setup can then proceed normally.

Sound confusing? You bet! And any task that confusing is bound to be done wrong more often than not. So, we'd better automate it.

What Does Setup Wizard Actually Do?

Before we write our Setup Wizard Workaround and Workaround Installer, we should look at what Setup Wizard does when the workaround *isn't* there.

The Setup Wizard does its job in seven steps. In step one, you simply specify the VB project file of the project you wish to distribute. Step two allows you to specify where you want the distribution files to be placed. You are given a choice of floppy drive (including a disk density specification) or a directory on your hard drive. Unfortunately, you cannot "break up" a directory into logical "floppy"-sized chunks; if your eventual distribution medium is going to be floppy disk, you must say so now.

Step four lists any OLE servers your application might have referenced, such as Microsoft Word or Excel. This list does *not* include OLE controls, and it is usually empty. Step five is where the OLE controls are listed.

Step six is significant if your application is an OLE server. If it is, you might want to install it into a common directory with other such servers. Otherwise, the default value of "Application Directory" is normally appropriate.

Step seven identifies all the file components required by your application. Don't be surprised to find a bunch of OLE DLLs in there, even if your application is not an OLE server or client! Visual Basic *itself* is an OLE server, even just the runtime DLL; so the OLE DLLs are required. This means that 16-bit VB apps that, in version 3.0 could be distributed on a single floppy, now require a minimum of two. (The same app compiled for 32-bits can be distributed on one, because all the 32-bit Windows platforms are guaranteed to already have the required 32-bit OLE DLLs installed.) This is the step that causes the biggest setup problem, so let's examine it a little more closely.

A Closer Look at the Setup Problem

When you install Visual Basic, a file called SWDEPEND.INI is created in your Windows directory. (The VB documentation makes an erroneous reference to "SWDEPEND.TXT"—there's no such file.) SWDEPEND.INI contains a list of files associated with each of the usual VB components. For example, the Crystal Reports OCX requires a whole gaggle of DLLs; these associations are indicated:

```
[CRYSTL16.OCX]
Dest=$(WinSysPath)
Register=$(DLLSelfRegister)
Uses1=CRPE.DLL
Uses2=CRXLATE.DLL
Uses3=uxddisk.dll
Uses4=uxfdif.dll
Uses5=uxfrec.dll
Uses6=uxfsepv.dll
Uses7=uxftext.dll
Uses8=pdbdao.dll
Uses9=pdctdao.dll
Uses10=pdirdao.dll
Uses11=pdsodbc.dll
Uses12=PDBBND.DLL
```

The above list, by the way, is *incorrect* (although it's the one VB Setup creates). That's another one of the things our Workaround Installer can fix.

The good part of this is that you can easily add more entries to the .INI file. You would likely do this as part of your installation of a new VBX or OCX. By doing so, Setup Wizard would then automatically make sure the required components were distributed with any applications using your newly installed control.

Setup Wizard also uses a file called SETUPWIZ.INI. If you installed VB4 over a 3.0 installation, you'll find what appears to be entries duplicating the DLL associations of SWDEPEND.INI, though if you look more closely you'll see these are limited to VBXs. SWDEPEND.INI replaces SETUPWIZ.INI for this function, although other sections of SETUPWIZ.INI are still in use.

Anyway, back to Step seven; you manually add any files you like to your distribution—a help file is the most likely; but other commonly added components might be a license file or a README.TXT file.

You might have noticed in the snippet for SWDEPEND.INI above, that the usual target for that tool is specified. This can be overridden by clicking the File Details button and making the change you desire.

By far the longest operation occurs when you hit the Finish button. It is at this point that Setup Wizard performs a compression of the required files. Now, why doesn't Setup Wizard compress the OLE DLLs once, and store the compressed versions in KITFILES\SYS16 instead of the apt-to-get-outdated originals? I don't know...they didn't ask me for advice when they were designing this thing. But the result is that *every* use of Setup Wizard can easily take five or ten minutes compression time, depending on your hardware.

When it's done, in addition to the compressed files, you'll find on your distribution floppy or directory, several uncompressed files. One is SETUP.EXE, a small program that reads another file, SETUP.LST, to determine what files must be copied in order for SETUP1.EXE to execute. Since SETUP1.EXE is a Visual Basic application, this is *most* of them! SETUP.EXE displays a small dialog while it does its job. When those files, including SETUP1.EXE, have been copied to the target hard disk, SETUP1.EXE takes over. That's when the pretty, shaded background shows up. This program also reads SETUP.LST to figure out what remaining files need to be copied, and where to put them. It then expands the remaining files, adds the program group icons, and quits.

The SETUP.LST file is worth examining, because we'll be making heavy use of its quirks to implement the workaround. First, in spite of its name, it is a .INI file. That means the usual Windows "profile" functions—or my IniData control—can be used to read or modify it. It is divided into three sections. The first, the Bootstrap section, is the one read by the first SETUP.EXE program:

```
[BootStrap]
File1=1,,SETUP1.EX_,SETUP1.EXE,$(WinPath),$(EXESelfRegister),,8/15/ _
1995,138144,4.0.0.2422
File2=1,,VSHARE.38_,VSHARE.386,$(WinSysPath),,,11/8/1994,14933,3.11.0.401
File3=1,,STKIT416.DL_,STKIT416.DLL,$(WinSysPath),,,8/15/1995,5120,4.0.2422.0
```

Each file is described by as many as ten parameters that specify such things as the file size, date, and version in addition to the file's name and whether or not it had to span more than one floppy disk. This information helps to protect the distribution disk from tampering.

The Files section is formatted identically; it contains the list of files to be expanded by SETUP1.EXE. The remaining section, Setup, contains miscellaneous information used by SETUP1.EXE to customize the installation:

```
[Setup]
Title=Setup Wizard Workaround
DefaultDir=$(ProgramFiles)\SWWRKRND
Setup=SETUP1.EXE
AppExe=SWWRKRND.EXE
Btrieve=0
```

There's one other, interesting little item...well, *big* item—in SETUP.LST. It starts:

```
; The following lines may be deleted in order to obtain extra
; space for customizing this file on a full installation diskette.
;
; XXXXXXXXXXXXXXXXXXXXXXXXXXXXXXXXXXXXXXXXXXXXXXXXXXXXXXXXXXX
; XXXXXXXXXXXXXXXXXXXXXXXXXXXXXXXXXXXXXXXXXXXXXXXXXXXXXXXXXXX
; XXXXXXXXXXXXXXXXXXXXXXXXXXXXXXXXXXXXXXXXXXXXXXXXXXXXXXXXXXX
; XXXXXXXXXXXXXXXXXXXXXXXXXXXXXXXXXXXXXXXXXXXXXXXXXXXXXXXXXXX
; XXXXXXXXXXXXXXXXXXXXXXXXXXXXXXXXXXXXXXXXXXXXXXXXXXXXXXXXXXX
```

and goes on for freaking *ever*. In fact, it takes up so much space that SETUP.LST winds up taking up at least 6K disk space. Remember that Setup Wizard is using the sizes of files to determine disk layout. Microsoft expected, that if you needed to add a little something to the SETUP.LST file, you could do so by deleting these filler lines to make room. This turns out to be beneficial to our project, because we'll be *deleting* SETUP.LST and replacing it with *two* files—without the filler lines, so they'll both fit.

Creating Our Plan of Attack

When we were on that jet boat, mired on a sand bar and going nowhere fast, most of us did *not* complain. The fact is, we had enjoyed ourselves in the Canyon so much that we didn't *really* want the vacation to end. So we made the most of our temporary sojourn; and we enthusiastically helped transfer our bags, and free the boat, because we knew it would be more fun than flying home.

When I see a programming chore coming up like this, I don't complain. Well, okay, I complain a *little*. But then I take a breath, look at the chore as a new project, and determine to complete it as I would any other project. Sure, it'll take me longer than some short-sighted fix; but then I won't have solved the large-scale problem at all—my bags may be in the bus, but the boat is still on the sandbar. And the benefits of treating this problem as a project are the same as from any properly-designed and implemented project: Lots of reusable software components that will save me time later on, on *other* projects.

To create the Setup Wizard Workaround, we need two main components:

- A "genie" to copy the files and correct other Setup Wizard glitches, that will be run once per machine.
- Another "genie" to modify the corrected Setup Wizard output and add the new "pre-setup" .EXE file, that will be run once per use of the Setup Wizard.

A closer look reveals a couple of lower level components that might be useful in a general sense. For example, both these "genies" are apt to be multi-page applications similar to many of Microsoft's Wizards (including Setup Wizard, itself). So why not create a generic "Genie" skeleton first, then use it as a basis for both genies? Also, the first genie will have to expand a bunch of compressed files. That suggests a reusable "file expanding" module, as well as a module implementing a "progress bar." Yep, time to pour a new cup of coffee: We're going to be busy.

Creating the Pre-Setup Program

Although it's not likely to be reusable in another project, one piece we may as well get out of the way is the "pre-setup" program. This will be a small Windows executable whose job is simply to identify the executing system as Win31 or Win95, rename either SETUP.31 or SETUP.95 to SETUP.LST, and kick off the *original* SETUP.EXE (which will have to be renamed).

Although we'll call the project PRESETUP, the actual executable will have to be named SETUP.EXE, because that's what people expect; and this file *must* be run before the original setup—which we'll rename SETUPA.EXE.

Don't confuse the file name with the module name. The file name is the name by which you identify the executable on disk; but the module name is the name Windows will use to reference this application once it's been loaded into memory. You can have lots of different files with the same names (in different folders, of course); but Windows only allows one code segment of a given module name in memory at a time. (You can run several copies of the application, but the code is loaded just once. In 16-bit Windows, anyway.)

PRESETUP must be as compact and as simple as possible. That means it must be written in C. (Assembler wouldn't be smaller *enough* to warrant the hassle.) Its segments must be pre-loaded, since the program will be run from a floppy disk. Here's the module definition file for the program:

```
NAME       PRESETUP
CODE       PRELOAD MOVEABLE DISCARDABLE
DATA       PRELOAD MOVEABLE MULTIPLE
HEAPSIZE   1024
```

This project contains just one code module and no header files of its own. The code module is called MAIN.C and, for all its simplicity, I've divided it into several functions to make it even simpler. Let's look at *WinMain()* first:

```
int PASCAL WinMain
    (
    HINSTANCE Instance,
    HINSTANCE PrevInstance,
    LPSTR CmdLine,
    int CmdShow
    )
    {
    ResetDiskFromPreviousUse();
    if (IsWindows95())
       Rename ("SETUP.95", "SETUP.LST");
    else
       Rename ("SETUP.31", "SETUP.LST");
    WinExec ("SETUPA.EXE", SW_SHOWNORMAL);
    return 0;
    }
```

We'll look at *ResetDiskFromPreviousUse()* in a bit, after I've shown you what might need to be reset. The purpose of the *IsWindows95()* function is obvious; it decides which of the two SETUP.* files to rename. *WinExec()* then kicks off the original Setup (now called SETUPA.EXE). And that's it!

To use *ResetDiskFromPreviousUse()*, the program will have to rename SETUP.LST to either SETUP.31 or SETUP.95, whichever is missing. That will allow your distribution disks to be reused after your end user has upgraded an older platform to the newer one:

```
static void near pascal ResetDiskFromPreviousUse (void)
   {
   OFSTRUCT of;
   if (OpenFile ("SETUP.31", &of, OF_EXIST) == HFILE_ERROR)
      Rename ("SETUP.LST", "SETUP.31");
   if (OpenFile ("SETUP.95", &of, OF_EXIST) == HFILE_ERROR)
      Rename ("SETUP.LST", "SETUP.95");
   }
```

OpenFile(), of course, is the Windows function that, among other things, allows us to easily test for the existence of a file. *Rename()*, which you also saw invoked from *WinMain()*, is my own concoction:

```
static void near pascal Rename (char * OldName, char * NewName)
    {
    if (rename (OldName, NewName) != 0)
        {
        int Result = MessageBox (NULL, "Unable to write to setup disk. Please
release the write-protect tab and retry.",
            "Setup",
            MB_RETRYCANCEL | MB_ICONEXCLAMATION);
        if (Result == IDRETRY)
            Rename (OldName, NewName);
        }
    }
```

The *rename()* function—notice the subtle difference in name—comes from the standard C library. Since *Rename()* is only called if *OldName* does, in fact, exist, the only reason *rename()* can fail is if *OldName* is marked Read Only or is on a write-protected disk. The Setup Wizard Workaround will be placing the SETUP.31 and SETUP.95 files on the floppy, so we *know* they aren't marked Read Only; that leaves a write-protect tab as the only possibility. The user is given a chance to remove the disk and retry—in which case *Rename()* is called recursively. (That's why we had to make sure the segments were marked PRELOAD in the module definition file: So Windows wouldn't mind having the disk on which SETUP.EXE is located, being removed and replaced.)

That leaves us with one more function:

```
static BOOL near pascal IsWindows95 (void)
    {
    return (HIBYTE (LOWORD (GetVersion ()))) == 95);
    }
```

The old, reliable *GetVersion()* function from the Windows API returns either 31 (for Windows 3.1 or Windows for Workgroups 3.11) or 95 (for Windows 95).

To minimize the disk space taken up by the PRESETUP, be sure to compile for release, and with optimization specified for size. Now, although space is precious, we *do* want to include an icon so the SETUP program will look inviting when seen in a Windows 95 folder (which includes icons for each file listed). I borrowed the original SETUP.EXE icon, but altered the colors of the box to make the icon unique.

PRESETUP must be compiled to 16-bits so it can be run from either Win31 or Win95. That means either using Borland C++ or Microsoft Visual C++ 1.5x. I used the latter, and got a size of 4.45KB, which I think is acceptable.

The next big job will be getting the PRESETUP executable, SETUP.EXE, copied to a place from which it can be used. We'll get to that presently, after we take on the preliminary task of solving the creation of "genies" once and for all.

Building the Generic Genie

If you call yourself a Windows programmer, you've seen genies before...except that they are more often called Wizards, Experts, or some other catch phrase. (One piece of shareware I've run across is called a "lizard"! How I wish *I'd* thought of that one!)

We've already written one genie, the VBX Genie. It uses the property page style to offer its users access to the various options that can be set. More often, however, this type of application presents a series of pages to the user. The user can navigate from page to page, but the information presented and obtained has a linear sequence that this technique makes clear.

Such a genie is not hard to write, and the housekeeping is minimal. We'll need a main form and an About form. The main form will have at least two frames on it, and a series of buttons. Figure 11.1 shows the main form in design mode.

Although you can't see much of the frame underneath the one marked "Finish," it too is plain. These frames (and possibly more) will be filled in when you create a *real* genie from this skeleton.

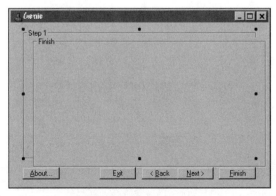

Figure 11.1 The main form for the Generic Genie (in design mode).

Each frame is an element of an array of frames, and each element corresponds to a "page." I would prefer for the frame indexes to be 1, 2, 3 ... to exactly match the page number. However, the easiest way to add additional frames is by copying one into the Clipboard and then pasting it in; but if there is no index zero, that's the index the new frame will automatically take—*not* the number of the last frame plus one. This is such a hassle to remember to correct, that I decided to just number the pages from zero to— well, I almost said "the total number of pages minus one." But, there's pages and then there's *pages*. The very last frame is not considered a "page" exactly; it shows up only when the Finish button has been clicked. So the frames will actually be numbers from zero to *PageCount*, whatever that is.

The form itself is named Prime, as my startup forms always are. Here are Prime's **(General) (Declarations)**:

```
Option Explicit

Const PageCount = 1
Dim CurrentPage As Integer
```

Obviously, the *PageCount* constant is intended to be modified when you derive a real genie from the generic one. Of course, you *might* leave it at one—a genie with one data entry page and one "Finish" page is not unheard of.

CurrentPage will have an initial value of zero, of course. That is taken care of, indirectly, when the form loads:

```
Private Sub Form_Load()
If PageCount = 1 Then
    cmd_Next.Visible = False
    cmd_Back.Visible = False
    cmd_Exit.Left = cmd_Next.Left
End If
TurnPage 1
End Sub
```

Before doing anything else, the **Sub** checks to see if this is a one-page wonder. If so, the Next and Back buttons are made invisible and the Exit button is moved over for best appearance. Then, the current page is set to the first page, by the *TurnPage* subroutine:

```
Private Sub TurnPage(ByVal NextPage As Integer)
If CurrentPage > 0 Then
   Frame1(CurrentPage - 1).Visible = False
End If
```

```
CurrentPage = NextPage
Frame1(CurrentPage - 1).Top = 150
Frame1(CurrentPage - 1).Left = 300
Frame1(CurrentPage - 1).Visible = True
cmd_Back.Enabled = (CurrentPage > 1)
cmd_Next.Enabled = (CurrentPage < PageCount)
cmd_Finish.Enabled = (CurrentPage = PageCount)
cmd_Exit.Enabled = (CurrentPage <= PageCount)
On Error Resume Next
If cmd_Finish.Enabled Then cmd_Finish.SetFocus
Refresh
End Sub
```

Notice that *CurrentPage* is always a real page number, starting at one, while the frames are indexed from zero. So every place *CurrentPage* is used to index a frame, one is subtracted from it.

TurnPage begins by making the previously shown frame, if there was one, invisible. It then sets the *CurrentPage* to the desired number, and makes the frame for that page visible in its place. It also *positions* that frame, which frees you from having to place all the frames on top of each other in design mode. This way, you can easily slide all the frames out of the way, except for the one you're working on.

The Back, Next, and Finish buttons are enabled based on the page. If there are any pages left—that is, *CurrentPage* is less than *PageCount*—the Next button is enabled. If *CurrentPage* is greater than one, the Back button is enabled. If *CurrentPage* is *greater* than *PageCount*, that can only mean the Finish button has been clicked. And if this is the last page, the Finish button is enabled and the focus set to it. (If the form hasn't yet been displayed, which is the case the very first time this subroutine is invoked, trying to set the focus will cause an error. It's an error we can safely ignore, however; hence, the *On Error* statement.) Finally, the form's *Refresh* method is invoked—this will guarantee a repaint of the whole thing, including buttons.

Since *TurnPage* does most of the work, the Next button has little to do but invoke it:

```
Private Sub cmd_Next_Click()
TurnPage CurrentPage + 1
End Sub
```

TurnPage disables the Next button when *CurrentPage* is equal to the *PageCount*, so there's no danger of pushing *CurrentPage* out of range.

As you'd expect, the Back button is the Next button's mirror image:

```
Private Sub cmd_Back_Click()
TurnPage CurrentPage - 1
End Sub
```

The Finish button will eventually be enhanced to do some work; for now it just displays that final frame and displays an appropriately generic message box:

```
Private Sub cmd_Finish_Click()
Dim W As WaitCursor
Set W = New WaitCursor
TurnPage PageCount + 1

' To do: Put your code here

MsgBox "What you wanted to do has been completed.", vbInformation
Unload Me
End Sub
```

The two remaining buttons are About and Exit. The Exit button simply unloads the main form:

```
Private Sub cmd_Exit_Click()
Unload Me
End Sub
```

And the About button almost as simply loads the About form:

```
Private Sub cmd_About_Click()
About.Image1.Picture = Icon
About.Show vbModal
End Sub
```

Why do we place our icon on the About form here? After all, About boxes are traditionally hard-coded. However, we aren't traditional here! And that brings us to another reusable component...

Adding the Reusable About Box

In VB3, the App object made accessible a small amount of information to the application. In VB4 that amount has grown by enough that an automatic About box is now feasible.

At design time, the form looks like the one shown in Figure 11.2.

The dotted square shows the location of the Image control where the icon will sit. If the caller doesn't set the icon here, the Image control is transparent, which isn't unattractive. "App Title," "Version," and "Copyright" show the

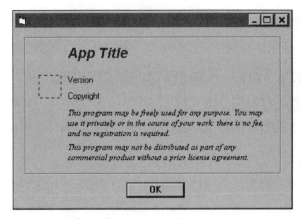

Figure 11.2 Creating the form for the About box.

locations of the Label controls that will display this information. The disclaimer text is appropriate for giveaways (such as the applications in this book); if you are a commercial programmer, you may wish to alter this text to something more threatening.

The three labels have their values set in the form's *Load* event handler:

```
Private Sub Form_Load()
lbl_AppName = App.Title
lbl_Version = "Version " + _
    Format$(App.Major) + "." + _
    Format$(App.Minor) + "." + _
    Format$(App.Revision)
lbl_Copyright = App.LegalCopyright
End Sub
```

When run from the Generic Genie, the About box looks like the one shown in Figure 11.3.

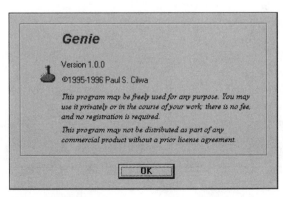

Figure 11.3 Displaying the About box at runtime.

But, remember, this About box will have appropriate values for any application that shows it. That makes it a useful, reusable component.

Creating the Setup Wizard Workaround Installer

Here's the part where we fix the Setup Wizard...a step at a time...automating the process. Now that we have our Generic Genie, we have a framework we can use to actually build the Setup Wizard Workaround Installer.

The basic program *is* the Generic Genie. To the Prime form, we add an additional frame, for a total of three, and two controls: an IniData control to provide access to SETUPWIZ.INI and an invisible Label control to provide DDE communications with the Windows 95 Task Bar.

The first two pages are simply text; the first states the problem, and the second outlines the steps the Workaround Installer will take to solve the problem. This is the same information described above, so there's no point in repeating it here.

The final page is displayed as the corrections are made; since they are extensive, a progress bar is included. The final page looks like the one shown in Figure 11.4 while running.

As you can see, the five major steps are detailed. These steps are reflected in the *cmd_Finish_Click* handler:

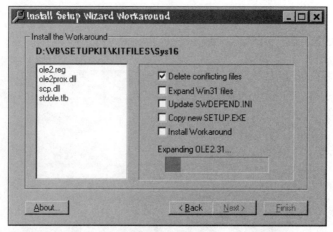

Figure 11.4   The final form for the Setup Wizard Workaround.

```
Private Sub cmd_Finish_Click()
Dim W As WaitCursor
Set W = New WaitCursor
TurnPage PageCount + 1
DeleteConflictingFiles
ExpandWin31Files
UpdateSWDepend
ReplaceSetupApp
InstallWorkaroundGenie
MsgBox "The Setup Wizard Workaround has been installed.", _
   vbInformation
Unload Me
End Sub
```

So, all we have to do to understand how the Setup Wizard Workaround Install works, is to study the procedures that execute each of those five steps.

The first step deletes the files from the SETUPKIT\SYS16 folder that would conflict with Windows 3.1 files of the same name. But where is that folder? Not everyone installs to C:\VB—I, for example, keep all my development tools on a drive D:. That bit of information is garnered and saved in the Prime form's *Load* event handler:

```
Private Sub Form_Load()
cmd_Next.Visible = (PageCount > 1)
cmd_Back.Visible = (PageCount > 1)
If Not cmd_Next.Visible Then
   cmd_Exit.Left = cmd_Next.Left
End If
TurnPage 1

IniData1.FileName = "SetupWiz.Ini"
IniData1.Section = "SetupWiz"
IniData1.KeyName = "Bootstrap"
Dim Drive As String, Path As String, Root As String, Ext As String
SplitPath IniData1.Text, Drive, Path, Root, Ext
WizardPath = Drive + Path
lbl_KitFiles = WizardPath + "\Sys16"
lst_KitFiles.Path = lbl_KitFiles

PB.Init ProgressBar, lbl_Progress
End Sub
```

You'll recognize the first block of code from the Generic Genie. The second block is where the IniData control queries SETUPWIZ.INI for the location of the setup kit files. This path is stored under the Bootstrap key. The DLLs are kept in a subdirectory below that called SYS16. (The last line, regarding the progress bar, is something I'll talk about shortly.)

Once we know where the DLLs are located, it's a fairly simple job to delete the ones we don't want:

```
Private Sub DeleteConflictingFiles()
ChDrive lst_KitFiles.Path
ChDir lst_KitFiles.Path
Dim i As Integer
For i = lst_KitFiles.ListCount To 1 Step -1
   Select Case UCase$(lst_KitFiles.List(i - 1))
   Case "OLE2.REG", "OLE2PROX.DLL", "SCP.DLL", "STDOLE.TLB"
   Case Else
      SetAttr lst_KitFiles.List(i - 1), 0
      Kill lst_KitFiles.List(i - 1)
   End Select
Next i
lst_KitFiles.Refresh
Step(1).Value = vbChecked
End Sub
```

The **Select Case** statement makes sure that all files *except* the four that are not included with Windows 95 itself, are deleted.

In the next step, the replacement Windows 3.11 files are moved into that directory in place of the files that were deleted. This is also a simple job, but it takes long enough that a progress bar is a good idea–and that leads us to another reusable component.

Coding the Reusable ProgressBarClass

VB4 comes with the Sheridan 3D Controls OCX, an OLE control version of the VBX that came with VB3. One of these controls is the SSPanel. This control makes a great progress bar, thanks to its "flood fill" capability. However, you (the programmer) have to put values into its *FloodPercent* property, which means you also have to do the math to determine what percentage of the bar should be filled with color. That aspect of the job is repetitious enough to try and encapsulate it somehow.

The answer is a VB user-defined object. I call it the *ProgressBarClass*. Here are its properties:

```
Option Explicit

Private UI As SSPanel
Private LabelUI As Control
Private Steps_ As Long
Public StepsType As String

Private CurrentStep As Long
```

As in the VBX Genie, *UI* is the control associated with this object. *LabelUI* is an extra control, used to display explanatory text—as you'll see, this is an optional feature. The **Private** property *Steps_* is the storage for a **Public** property *Steps* that is implemented using a **Property Let** function. *StepsType* is text that will be sent to the *LabelUI*, if one is supplied; and *CurrentStep* will be managed internally.

The *Init* function provides values for two of those properties:

```
Public Sub Init(aUI As SSPanel, aLabelUI As Control)
Set UI = aUI
Set LabelUI = aLabelUI
End Sub
```

The *Steps* property is used to tell the object how many steps there are whose progress is to be tracked. In addition to assigning that number to the *Steps_* property, the other properties are reset, including the progress bar itself:

```
Public Property Let Steps(ByVal NewValue As Integer)
UI.FloodPercent = 0
UI.Refresh
LabelUI.Caption = ""
LabelUI.Refresh
Steps_ = NewValue
StepsType = ""
End Property
```

Now, it is *possible* for an application to directly set the current step to anything (within the range, that is, of 1 and the number of total steps):

```
Public Property Let Step(ByVal NewValue As Integer)
if NewValue < 1 then NewValue = 1
If NewValue > Steps_ Then NewValue = Steps_
UI.FloodPercent = ((NewValue - 1) * 100) / Steps_
UI.Refresh
CurrentStep = NewValue
End Property
```

The SSPanel is updated to show one *less* than *NewValue* as completed; the *CurrentStep* is then set to the new value.

This *can* be done, but it is not the most common way of using this object. Remember, *CurrentStep* is initialized to zero when the number of *Steps* is set. Normally, processing would begin with step one and continue from there; so at the beginning of each step the *StepStarted* method is invoked:

```
Public Sub StepStarted(Optional StepName)
UI.FloodPercent = (CurrentStep * 100) / Steps_
```

```
UI.Refresh
CurrentStep = CurrentStep + 1
If CurrentStep > Steps_ Then CurrentStep = Steps_
If Not LabelUI Is Nothing Then
   If IsMissing(StepName) Then StepName = ""
   Dim Caption As String
   Caption = Trim$(StepsType + " " + StepName)
   If Caption > "" Then Caption = Caption + "..."
   LabelUI.Caption = Caption
   LabelUI.Refresh
End If
End Sub
```

The optional parameter is used to provide a caption for the step if *LabelUI* was supplied when the object was initialized. It is used in combination with the *StepsType* parameter. A common combination would be to set *StepsType* to "Copying" and to call *StepStarted* with the name of the file currently being copied.

When the step has been completed, another method is called:

```
Public Sub StepCompleted()
UI.FloodPercent = (CurrentStep * 100) / Steps_
UI.Refresh
If Not LabelUI Is Nothing Then
   LabelUI.Caption = ""
   LabelUI.Refresh
End If
End Sub
```

Sometimes an operation might complete in fewer steps than expected. In such a case, the *StepsCompleted* method can be called to wrap things up:

```
Public Sub StepsCompleted()
UI.FloodPercent = 100
UI.Refresh
CurrentStep = Steps_
If Not LabelUI Is Nothing Then
   LabelUI.Caption = ""
   LabelUI.Refresh
End If
End Sub
```

Just to be sure, though, when the *ProgressBarClass* object is deleted, its *Terminate* function is triggered:

```
Private Sub Class_Terminate()
If Not UI Is Nothing Then
   UI.FloodPercent = 0
End If
End Sub
```

By setting the progress bar's *FloodPercent* to zero, it returns to a neutral appearance.

So, now you know what that last line was in the Prime form's *Load* event handler: A *ProgressBarClass* object called *PB* was being initialized to point to the progress bar and the label just above it.

Expanding the Win31 Files

We didn't bother using the progress bar in step one, because deleting those files took too little time to worry about. But there are thirteen files to be expanded, and that will take long enough to justify a progress display.

The expanding function calls the *Expand* function thirteen times, once for each file to be expanded:

```
Private Sub ExpandWin31Files()
PB.Steps = 13
PB.StepsType = "Expanding"

Expand MakePath("", App.Path, "Compobj", ".DL_"), lbl_KitFiles + "\COMPOBJ.DLL"
Expand MakePath("", App.Path, "Ctl3Dv2", ".DL_"), lbl_KitFiles + "\CTL3DV2.DLL"
Expand MakePath("", App.Path, "Ole2", ".31_"), lbl_KitFiles + "\OLE2.31"
Expand MakePath("", App.Path, "Ole2", ".DL_"), lbl_KitFiles + "\Ole2.DLL"
Expand MakePath("", App.Path, "Ole2Conv", ".DL_"), lbl_KitFiles + _
    "\OLE2CONV.DLL"
Expand MakePath("", App.Path, "Ole2Disp", ".DL_"), lbl_KitFiles + _
    "\OLE2DISP.DLL"
Expand MakePath("", App.Path, "Ole2Nls", ".DL_"), lbl_KitFiles + "\OLE2NLS.DLL"
Expand MakePath("", App.Path, "Ole2Prox", ".31_"), lbl_KitFiles + _
    "\OLE2PROX.31"
Expand MakePath("", App.Path, "Scp", ".31_"), lbl_KitFiles + "\SCP.31"
Expand MakePath("", App.Path, "StdOle", ".31_"), lbl_KitFiles + "\STDOLE.31"
Expand MakePath("", App.Path, "Storage", ".DL_"), lbl_KitFiles + "\STORAGE.DLL"
Expand MakePath("", App.Path, "TypeLib", ".DL_"), lbl_KitFiles + "\TYPELIB.DLL"
Expand MakePath("", App.Path, "VShare", ".38_"), lbl_KitFiles + "\VSHARE.386"
PB.StepsCompleted
lst_KitFiles.Refresh

Step(2).Value = vbChecked
End Sub
```

The *Expand* function arranges for the actual expansion:

```
Private Sub Expand(ByVal SourceFile As String, DestFile As String)
Dim Drive As String, Dir As String, Root As String, Ext As String
SplitPath DestFile, Drive, Dir, Root, Ext
PB.StepStarted Root + Ext
CopyCompressedFile SourceFile, DestFile
End Sub
```

Note that it isn't necessary to call the *ProgressBarClass* object's *StepCompleted* method unless some time will pass between the completion of one step and the beginning of the next. That's not the case here.

The *CopyCompressedFile* function, which does the actual copying, is in the FILES.BAS module—you may remember it from VBX Genie. To refresh your memory, here's the code:

```
Public Sub CopyCompressedFile( _
   ByVal SourceFilename As String, _
   ByVal DestFilename As String)
Dim Source As OFSTRUCT, SourceFile As Integer
Dim Dest As OFSTRUCT, DestFile As Integer
SourceFile = LZOpenFile(SourceFilename, _
   Source, OF_READ)
DestFile = LZOpenFile(DestFilename, _
   Dest, OF_CREATE)
LZCopy SourceFile, DestFile
LZClose SourceFile
LZClose DestFile
End Sub
```

LZOpenFile(), LZCopy(), and *LZClose()* are, of course, from the Windows API. They copy a file compressed with—what else?—the COMPRESS.EXE program, and expand it to the desired location.

Now, where did these files come from? The ones on the CD-ROM accompanying this book are the latest Win31-compatible set authorized by Microsoft. Each one was compressed using a command line similar to this:

```
compress -r OLE2.DLL
```

The "-r" flag tells compress to include in the compressed file its uncompressed name. We do this but *LZCopyFile()* doesn't make use of this information, because it's the right thing to do. (There are other functions that *do* make use of it.)

Most of the files are compressed and restored to their own names. The ones you may have noticed with .31 extensions are the files with conflicting Win95 counterparts that we must provide because they don't come with Windows 95. By altering the extension to .31, we avoid what would otherwise be a naming conflict.

Updating SWDEPEND.INI

As you'll recall, SWDEPEND.INI is used by Setup Wizard to keep track of what files require other files. We have to modify several things there, so a separate "step" is allocated for that. Let's look at the code a section at a time.

In step two, we used the Progress Bar for monitoring the expansion of the OLE DLLs. Now that that's over, we can start using it to track these individual steps:

```
Private Sub UpdateSWDepend()
PB.Steps = 5
PB.Step = 2
PB.StepStarted
```

Now we're ready to correct the .INI file. Our first task is to tell it to use SETUPA.EXE as the bootstrap file, instead of SETUP.EXE:

```
IniData1.FileName = "SWDEPEND.INI"
IniData1.Section = "SetupWiz"
IniData1.KeyName = "Bootstrap"
IniData1.Text = lbl_KitFiles + "\..\SETUPA.EXE"
```

Remember, the original SETUP.EXE is soon to be *renamed* SETUPA.EXE, so we really aren't changing anything here. However, we're also going to want to require that the PRESETUP program (*called* SETUP.EXE) be included. We can do that by adding a Uses*n* key. However, "n" must be a new number, exactly one higher than the highest already present. The following code figures out what this is, and adds the new entry:

```
Dim i As Integer
Do
    i = i + 1
    IniData1.KeyName = "Uses" + Format$(i)
Loop Until IniData1.Text = ""
IniData1.Text = lbl_KitFiles + "\SETUP.EXE:0"
```

It's essential that PRESETUP not be compressed by Setup Wizard—otherwise, how could it run? *It* is the program that uncompresses the others! The ":0" appended to the file name is the signal to Setup Wizard to not compress this file.

Our next task is to correct a misspelling present in the SWDEPEND.INI file as installed by Visual Basic Setup:

```
IniData1.Section = "CRYSTL16.OCX"
IniData1.KeyName = "Uses2"
IniData1.Text = "CRXLATE.DLL"
```

Finally, we must add references to the additional four files:

```
IniData1.Section = "OLE2.DLL"
i = 0
Do
    i = i + 1
```

```
    IniData1.KeyName = "Uses" + Format$(i)
Loop Until IniData1.Text = ""
IniData1.Text = "OLE2PROX.31"
IniData1.KeyName = "Uses" + Format$(i + 1)
IniData1.Text = "OLE2.31"
IniData1.KeyName = "Uses" + Format$(i + 2)
IniData1.Text = "SCP.31"
IniData1.KeyName = "Uses" + Format$(i + 3)
IniData1.Text = "STDOLE.31"

Step(3).Value = vbChecked
End Sub
```

Installing PRESETUP

PRESETUP, you'll recall, has been named SETUP.EXE. To avoid confusion, and since this is such a small file, I've decided to make it a *resource* of the Setup Wizard Workaround Installer. That means an INSTALL.RC file must be written that identifies the file and names the resource:

```
SETUP   EXE   PRESETUP\SETUP.EXE
```

As with the VBX Genie resources, you'll have to use a 16-bit resource editor (like Microsoft's App Studio or Borland's Resource Workshop) to produce the required INSTALL.RES file.

With that done, the actual code to rename the original SETUP.EXE and put the new one in its place is straightforward:

```
Private Sub ReplaceSetupApp()
PB.StepStarted
ChDrive lbl_KitFiles
ChDir lbl_KitFiles
GenerateBinaryFile "SETUP", "EXE", "Setup.exe"
ChDir ".."
On Error Resume Next
Name "setup.exe" As "SetupA.exe"
Step(4).Value = vbChecked
End Sub
```

Installing the Workaround

Finally we get to the last step: Installing the Workaround itself—the program that the user will run each time he or she runs Setup Wizard.

Now, the problem is that we haven't actually *written* the Setup Wizard Workaround. Or, rather, *you* haven't. I did; I did it first, before writing the installation. But I knew it would to confusing to try to explain in that order.

So, let's just assume that, somehow, we have a file called SWWRKRND.EXE. This executable has just sort of dropped into our laps through a time warp and we can install it now, even though we won't actually "write" it until the next section.

Given that, here's the procedure that installs it:

```
Private Sub InstallWorkaroundGenie()
PB.StepStarted
Expand MakePath("", App.Path, "SWWrkrnd", ".EX_"), WizardPath + "\SWWRKRND.EXE"

Dim Try As Integer
On Error Resume Next
For Try = 1 To 20
   lbl_Progman.LinkTopic = "PROGMAN|PROGMAN"
   If Err = 0 Then
      Exit For
   End If
   DoEvents
Next Try
lbl_Progman.LinkMode = 2
For Try = 1 To 10
   DoEvents
Next Try
lbl_Progman.LinkTimeout = 100

lbl_Progman.LinkExecute "[CreateGroup(""Visual Basic 4.0 (16-bit)"",1)]"
lbl_Progman.LinkExecute "[ReplaceItem(Application Setup Wizard)]"
Err = 0
lbl_Progman.LinkExecute "[AddItem(" + WizardPath + "\SWWRKRND.EXE,Application
Setup Wizard,,,)]"
PB.StepCompleted
Step(5).Value = vbChecked
End Sub
```

In the brief first section, the compressed file is actually expanded and put in place. The remaining code uses DDE to convince the Task Bar—which still calls itself "Progman"—to replace the existing Application Setup Wizard icon with one pointing to the Setup Wizard Workaround.

The Setup Wizard Workaround

Finally, let's look at the little program that will modify the output from the Setup Wizard, right on the distribution disks, making them safe for use with Win31 *and* Win95.

It's intended that the Workaround always be used in conjunction with the Setup Wizard—so why not let the Workaround *start* the Setup Wizard? It can replace Setup Wizard's icon in the Start Menu; and when you click it, Setup Wizard will start automatically—but then, when Setup Wizard's job is complete, the Workaround will take over.

To see how this happens, let's look at the Workaround's code, which is of course centered in its Prime form. Here's the handler for the *Load* event:

```
Private Sub Form_Load()
IniData1.FileName = "SetupWiz.INI"
IniData1.Section = "SetupWiz"
IniData1.KeyName = "Bootstrap"
Dim Drive As String, Path As String, Root As String, Ext As String
SplitPath IniData1.Text, Drive, Path, Root, Ext
KitFilesPath = Drive + Path + "\Sys16"

ChDrive Drive
ChDir Path

Dim TaskID As Integer, Dummy As Integer
TaskID = Shell("SetupWiz.exe", vbNormalFocus)
Do While GetModuleUsage(TaskID) > 0
    Dummy = DoEvents()
Loop

cmd_Next.Visible = (PageCount > 1)
cmd_Back.Visible = (PageCount > 1)
If Not cmd_Next.Visible Then
    cmd_Exit.Left = cmd_Next.Left
End If
TurnPage 1
End Sub
```

The first block of code is familiar; it came direct from the Generic Genie. But we've added onto the form one of my IniData controls, which provides access to the Setup Wizard's .INI file. By checking the value of the Bootstrap key of the SetupWiz section, we can find the path in which the Setup Wizard is located. By adding "\SYS16" to that, we've got the location of the OLE DLLs (which we store for future reference). We then change the current drive and directory to that location.

Finally, we run Setup Wizard. VB's *Shell* function returns a "task ID;" this value can be sent to the Windows API function *GetModuleUsage()*, which returns the number of copies of a task that are running. We hang in the *DoEvents()* loop until that number drops down to zero—that is, Setup Wizard has been shut down. At that point the Workaround can take over, so the *Load* handling is complete.

By the way, one of the few ways in which VB4 is *more* restrictive than VB3, is that API *Declare* statements can't be placed in the **(General) (Declarations)** section of forms. They can't go in class modules, either—they are only permitted in code modules. So I've gotten into the habit of including a WINAPI.BAS module in most projects, each containing the *Declare* statements needed by that project. The Workaround, for example, needs only the one *Declare*:

```
Option Explicit

Declare Function GetModuleUsage _
   Lib "Kernel" _
   (ByVal hModule As Integer) As Integer
```

So, unless the user made the effort to see its icon while Setup Wizard was running, the first he or she will see of the Workaround is Page 1, as shown in Figure 11.5.

This page is a pretty basic use of the Directory, Drive, and File controls. The Drive control begins by looking at the current drive; the Directory control looks at the current directory on that drive. If the user changes the active drive using the Drive control, the new drive is sent to the Directory:

```
Private Sub Drive1_Change()
On Error Resume Next
Dir1.Path = Drive1.Drive
ChDrive Drive1.Drive
End Sub
```

The *On Error* statement is there to prevent crashes in the event of an apparent Windows 95 bug I encountered while working on the project;

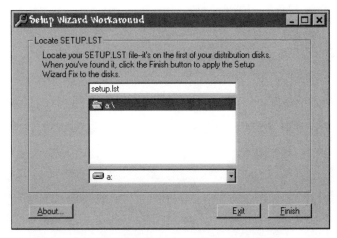

Figure 11.5 Page 1 of the Setup Wizard Workaround dialog.

sometimes, for no apparent reason, a perfectly good hard drive will become inaccessible until the computer is rebooted. (It doesn't happen often.)

If the Directory is changed—either directly by the user or indirectly by changing the active drive—the File control is updated:

```
Private Sub Dir1_Change()
File1.Path = Dir1.Path
ChDir Dir1.Path
End Sub
```

The File control was previously (at design time) given a "wildcard" of SETUP.LST, so it will appear empty until it is set to a drive and directory that contains a file by that name. Since there can only *be* one file of a given name in a single directory, the File control—which is actually a list box—has been shortened so it looks more like an edit control or label.

We won't want the Finish button to be enabled, unless this file is present:

```
Private Sub File1_PathChange()
cmd_Finish.Enabled = (File1.ListCount > 0)
End Sub
```

You may recall that, in the Generic Genie, the Finish button is enabled whenever the last regular page is displayed. We have to alter that behavior here:

```
Private Sub TurnPage(ByVal NextPage As Integer)
If CurrentPage > 0 Then
   Frame1(CurrentPage - 1).Visible = False
End If
CurrentPage = NextPage
Frame1(CurrentPage - 1).Top = 150
Frame1(CurrentPage - 1).Left = 300
Frame1(CurrentPage - 1).Visible = True
cmd_Back.Enabled = (CurrentPage > 1)
cmd_Next.Enabled = (CurrentPage < PageCount)
cmd_Exit.Enabled = (CurrentPage <= PageCount)
cmd_Finish.Enabled = _
   (CurrentPage = PageCount) And _
   (File1.ListCount > 0)
On Error Resume Next
If cmd_Finish.Enabled Then cmd_Finish.SetFocus
Refresh
End Sub
```

Even though in its present incarnation, the Workaround's *PageCount* is one, I've left that part of the test in, in case it ever becomes necessary to add another page.

After the user has found the SETUP.LST file, he or she may click the Finish button:

```
Private Sub cmd_Finish_Click()
Dim W As WaitCursor
Set W = New WaitCursor
TurnPage PageCount + 1
Finish
MsgBox "Your distribution disks have been modifed " + _
   "for safe use on Win31 and Win95 systems.", _
   vbInformation
Unload Me
End Sub
```

There was too much work to be done to pack it all in here; I broke it out into a subroutine called *Finish*. But in order to understand the code you'll see there, we need to look at a few other components first.

The first is a set of collections. These are declared in the **(General) (Declarations)** section of Prime:

```
Dim BootStrap As New Collection
Dim Files As New Collection
Dim Setup As New Collection
```

Each of these collections represents one section of a SETUP.LST file. The entries in *BootStrap* and *Files* are going to be objects of a user-defined class, *FileEntry*. Let's look at the properties of that class, defined in FILE.CLS's **(General) (Declarations)** section:

```
Option Explicit

Private DiskNo As Integer
Private Split As Boolean
Public FileName As String
Public TargetName As String
Private TargetPath As String
Private Register As String
Private Remote As String
Private FileDate As Date
Private FileSize As Long
Private Version As String

Public Enabled As Boolean

Private SplitText(True To False) As String
```

According to the Visual Basic documentation, the entries in SETUP.LST have all these fields. Not all are used for every entry; but we have to allow for them. The *Enabled* property is the main exception; I've added that so we can turn individual items on or off when creating the new SETUP.31 and SETUP.95 files.

The *SplitText* array is an internal variable used for dealing with the constant Microsoft uses in the SETUP.LST files. It is initialized when an object of this class is created:

```
Private Sub Class_Initialize()
SplitText(True) = "SPLIT"
End Sub
```

The *Init* function will be used once per item when it is created, to set all those properties:

```
Public Sub Init(ByVal aDiskNo As String, _
   ByVal aSplit As String, _
   ByVal aFilename As String, _
   ByVal aTargetname As String, _
   ByVal aPathname As String, _
   ByVal aRegister As String, _
   ByVal aRemote As String, _
   ByVal aDate As String, _
   ByVal aSize As String, _
   ByVal aVersion As String)
DiskNo = Val(aDiskNo)
Split = (aSplit = "SPLIT")
FileName = aFilename
TargetName = aTargetname
TargetPath = aPathname
Register = aRegister
Remote = aRemote
If aDate > "" Then FileDate = CDate(aDate)
FileSize = Val(aSize)
Version = aVersion
Enabled = True
End Sub
```

That takes care of *making* one these things. It needs to be able to recreate the original text, as well. This is done with a **Property Get** function:

```
Public Property Get Text()
Dim Result As String
Result = Format$(DiskNo) + "," + SplitText(Split) + "," + _
   FileName + "," + TargetName + "," + TargetPath + "," + _
   Register + "," + Remote + "," + _
   Display(FileDate) + "," + _
   Display(FileSize) + "," + Version + ","
While Right$(Result, 1) = ","
   Result = Left$(Result, Len(Result) - 1)
Wend
```

```
Text = Result
End Property
```

The various fields are simply concatenated together, delimited by commas. Some of the fields are stored internally in binary form; the *Display* function cleverly handles formatting all of them, thanks to its one parameter of the **Variant** data type:

```
Private Function Display(Data As Variant) As String
If TypeName(Data) = "Date" Then
   If Data < CDate("1/1/1980") Then
      Display = ""
   Else
      Display = Format$(Data, "m/d/yyyy")
   End If
Else
   If Data = 0 Then
      Display = ""
   Else
      Display = Format$(Data)
   End If
End If
End Function
```

Now that you've seen how the *FileEntry* class is implemented, it's time to see it in action. The *LoadSection* subroutine reads all the entries in a given SETUP.LST section, creates a *FileEntry* object for each one, and adds it to a specified collection:

```
Private Sub LoadSection(Section As String, List As Collection)
IniData1.Section = Section
Dim File As FileEntry
Dim i As Integer
For i = 1 To IniData1.KeyCount
   IniData1.KeyName = IniData1.KeyList(i - 1)
   If IniData1.Text > "" Then
      Set File = New FileEntry
      File.Init IniData1.List(0), _
         IniData1.List(1), _
         IniData1.List(2), _
         IniData1.List(3), _
         IniData1.List(4), _
         IniData1.List(5), _
         IniData1.List(6), _
         IniData1.List(7), _
         IniData1.List(8), _
         IniData1.List(9)
      List.Add File, IniData1.List(2)
   End If
Next i
End Sub
```

Remember, those ten potential items are separated by commas; so the IniData control's *ListDelimiter* property is set to "," so it can do the tokenizing for us. The third component of the list is the actual file name, so that is used as the key into the collection to retrieve this particular item. (That's the second parameter to the collection's *Add* method.)

There are three sections in a SETUP.LST file, and two of them consist entirely of file entries; so the above subroutine can be used for both. The third section consists of several, simple text items that must be stored. The *SetupEntry* class, defined in SETUP.CLS, was designed for them. Objects of this class have two simple properties:

```
Option Explicit

Public Key As String
Public Value As String
```

Both are **Public**, but an *Init* procedure is supplied to make it easier to initialize both at once:

```
Public Sub Init(ByVal aKey As String, ByVal aValue As String)
Key = aKey
Value = aValue
End Sub
```

This class, by the way, is reusable—objects of this class, plus a standard collection, make a "dictionary," a collection of keyed items. But we're going to use it now in the *LoadSetupSection* subroutine, back in PRIME.FRM:

```
Private Sub LoadSetupSection()
IniData1.Section = "Setup"
Dim i As Integer
Dim Item As SetupEntry
For i = 1 To IniData1.KeyCount
   IniData1.KeyName = IniData1.KeyList(i - 1)
   Set Item = New SetupEntry
   Item.Init IniData1.KeyName, IniData1.Text
   Setup.Add Item, IniData1.KeyName
Next i
End Sub
```

Now that you've seen some of the preliminary stuff, let's look at the *Finish* procedure. It's still kinda long, though; so let's look at it in segments. First, we reset the IniData control to look at the SETUP.LST file the user just located:

```
Private Sub Finish()
Dim i As Integer
IniData1.FileName = MakePath("", File1.Path, File1.FileName, "")
```

Next, we invoke *LoadSection*, which we just saw, to enumerate the files in the "Bootstrap" section of the SETUP.LST file, and add them to the *BootStrap* collection:

```
Label1(1) = "Loading " + IniData1.FileName + "..."
Refresh
LoadSection "BootStrap", BootStrap
CorrectBootStrap
LoadSection "Files", Files
LoadSetupSection
Kill IniData1.FileName
```

These entries are then corrected *in* the collection, by the *CorrectBootstrap* procedure:

```
Private Sub CorrectBootStrap()
BootStrap("OLE2.3_").TargetName = "OLE2.REG"
BootStrap("OLE2PROX.3_").TargetName = "OLE2PROX.DLL"
BootStrap("SCP.3_").TargetName = "SCP.DLL"
BootStrap("STDOLE.3_").TargetName = "STDOLE.TLB"
BootStrap.Remove "SETUP.EXE"
End Sub
```

We just have to correct the expanded names for the Win31 OLE files. We also remove the entry for SETUP.EXE, which was there simply as a place-holder, placed (again) by the Workaround Installation. We can then load the Files and Setup sections. With all the information from SETUP.LST stored safely in memory, we can delete the file to make room for the replacements.

One replacement is SETUP.31, the version of SETUP.LST that will be used on Win31 machines. The IniData control is reset to create the new file (which it will do when the first key value is set):

```
Label1(1) = "Creating SETUP.31..."
Refresh
Dim Drive As String, Path As String, Root As String, Ext As String
SplitPath IniData1.FileName, Drive, Path, Root, Ext
IniData1.FileName = MakePath(Drive, Path, Root, ".31")
BootStrap("OLE2.RE_").Enabled = False
BootStrap("OLE2PROX.DL_").Enabled = False
BootStrap("SCP.DL_").Enabled = False
BootStrap("STDOLE.TL_").Enabled = False
DumpSection "BootStrap", BootStrap
DumpSection "Files", Files
DumpSetupSection
```

The files in the *BootStrap* collection that should *not* be copied to a Win31 installation are disabled. Then all three sections are "dumped," that is, written to SETUP.31. (We'll look at the dumping code shortly. It's simple.)

Creating SETUP.95 is a similar proposition...and then the job is done:

```
Label1(1) = "Creating SETUP.95..."
Refresh
IniData1.FileName = MakePath(Drive, Path, Root, ".95")
BootStrap("OLE2.RE_").Enabled = True
BootStrap("OLE2PROX.DL_").Enabled = True
BootStrap("SCP.DL_").Enabled = True
BootStrap("STDOLE.TL_").Enabled = True
BootStrap("OLE2.3_").Enabled = False
BootStrap("OLE2PROX.3_").Enabled = False
BootStrap("SCP.3_").Enabled = False
BootStrap("STDOLE.3_").Enabled = False
DumpSection "BootStrap", BootStrap
DumpSection "Files", Files
DumpSetupSection
End Sub
```

Dumping the Bootstrap or Files section means running through the appropriate collection, obtaining each entry in turn, and using the *Text* property to rebuild the correct string for the key value:

```
Private Function DumpSection(Section As String, List As Collection)
IniData1.Section = Section
Dim i As Integer
For i = 1 To List.Count
   If List(i).Enabled Then
      IniData1.KeyName = "File" + Format$(i)
      IniData1.Text = List(i).Text
   End If
Next i
End Function
```

This code is deceptively simple; remember, it is the *FileEntry* objects that are doing most of the work.

Writing out the Setup section is a similar task:

```
Private Function DumpSetupSection()
IniData1.Section = "Setup"
Dim i As Integer
For i = 1 To Setup.Count
   IniData1.KeyName = Setup(i).Key
   IniData1.Text = Setup(i).Value
Next i
End Function
```

Loading the Bus and Heading on Home

Looking back at that seventeen-day trip through the Grand Canyon, many of the days and adventures kind of blend together. The time I fell asleep sunning myself and was awakened by a flash flood—was that in Deer Creek or Havasu Creek? But the jet boat adventure stands apart, partly because it was at the very end of the trip, but mostly because it was an unexpected adventure.

Here I thought I was all ready to knock out a quick installation program for VBX Genie, and instead would up spending a couple of extra weeks figuring out why Setup Wizard didn't work properly, and why, and how to work around it manually, and how to ease the workaround for others, and how to package that workaround in terms of reusable components. Some people complain because Microsoft apparently doesn't test their stuff on end-user type equipment, with different pre-installed software and hardware. Not me! If it wasn't for them and the way they do things, I'd have missed out on this unexpected adventure…and so would you…and you'd have just thumbed past 20 blank pages.

The best adventures are usually the ones you didn't plan for.

A VBX for the Find and Replace Dialogs

12

A

S MUCH AS I'D RATHER BE RAFTING the Grand Canyon, I sometimes actually have to work. Recently I spent two weeks in Manhattan. I don't spend much time there, and I've never really built up an internal map of the city. But it was never necessary, because I could always take a cab.

Manhattan cabs are inexpensive and, at least at the hours I travel, plentiful. I could always say, "Take me to the Downtown Athletic Club," for example, and in a few minutes I'd be there.

However, something had happened between my previous trip to Manhattan and this one. Apparently there's quite a turnaround in cab drivers, because the new crop doesn't know where anything is. Conversations run on the order of:

"Take me to the Downtown Athletic Center."

"Eh?"

"Um, 18 West Street?"

"Eh?"

"Near Battery Park?"

"Ah! Ze Battery Factory, no?"

"No, no! Battery Park! You know, near the Statten Island Ferry!"

"Saturn berry? I do not know...."

Believe me, things are getting pretty sad when I know Manhattan better than a Manhattan cab driver.

That was the same way I felt when Microsoft included a Common Dialog control with Visual Basic—and left out two of the common dialogs! Didn't they know they were there?

The Dialog Dilemma

When Windows was first released, all the Windows applications—Notepad, Write, PIF Edit, Terminal, and so on—used identical File Open and File Save dialog boxes. This added a needed level of constancy but while writing our own Windows apps, we discovered that we had to duplicate those dialog boxes ourselves if we wanted them. Charles Petzold, in his book *Programming Windows*, explained how to do so but the process still seemed a little annoying because we to had to repeat work that had already been done.

Borland took advantage of this situation when they released Turbo Pascal for Windows and, later, Turbo C++ for Windows: They *included* file open and save dialogs and encouraged us to use them. Granted, there was a small bug in the Turbo Pascal open dialog procedure code, but, still....

Now, it's an interesting note that, while most corporations seem to buy Microsoft compilers, most individuals buy Borland compilers...and a lot of innovative software comes from garages, not corporate skyscrapers. So, many shrink-wrapped applications—and virtually all shareware apps—used Borland's file open and save dialogs. You can easily tell because these applications had a green check mark for "OK" and a universal no symbol for "Cancel." Microsoft's dialogs, on the other hand, use more traditional buttons for OK and Cancel. Check out the differences between the two approaches as shown in Figures 12.1 and 12.2.

This coincided with Microsoft's dealing with rumors that the company withheld all the "good stuff" from application developers. This way, they could enjoy an "unfair advantage" in the applications marketplace. Obviously the presence of the Borland dialogs proved that this wasn't so. In any case, Microsoft solved both problems by releasing the Common Dialog DLL.

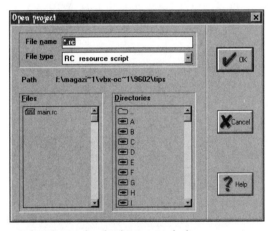

Figure 12.1 The Borland standard File Open dialog.

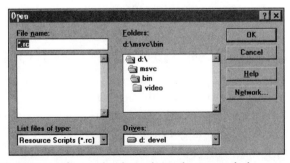

Figure 12.2 The Microsoft standard (16-bit) File Open dialog.

This DLL, used for several years now by C and C++ programmers, provides not only file open and save dialogs, but color, font, and printing dialogs. It also includes find and replace dialogs.

It was possible to access all but the Find and Replace dialogs from Visual Basic all along, because the common dialogs are kept in a DLL and the routines that make them work are published parts of the Windows API (ever since Windows 3.1). However, Find and Replace both require the owning window to process custom messages. After all, the Find dialog can ask users what they want to find; but it can't actually *find* anything, because it doesn't know anything about how your document is stored internally (or externally, for that matter). So the custom messages are sent at appropriate times; that's where you call the code that actually does the finding.

Unfortunately, you can't process custom Window messages in Visual Basic, so Find and Replace common dialogs were out of the VB programmer's reach.

When the Common Dialog VBX was introduced, I expected it to include the Find and Replace dialogs. Open and Save were there. So were Color, Font, and Print...but no Find or Replace! It seemed preposterous that the two dialogs that had been truly out of our reach before, should remain so...but there it was. As if to make amends, the Common Dialog VBX added easy access to the Windows Help engine, which is *not* a part of the Common Dialog DLL. But that was small consolation.

Well, now that we have completed the VBX Genie, we can easily get out of the Microsoft cab and build our *own* taxi: one that will provide the needed callback functions for the Find and Replace dialogs. Our project will serve as an excellent example of how we can use powerful software components to solve a critical programming problem.

The Find and Replace Dialogs

Since we want to encapsulate the Find and Replace dialogs, we'd best understand how they work. Like all the Common Dialogs, Find and Replace require the programmer to fill in a structure and then pass it to a function that makes the dialog actually appear. When the user closes the dialog, the structure is updated and can be queried.

Since Find and Replace are meant to work together, they use the same structure and, in fact, you can use one instance of this structure if you like.

If you do, the string a user tries to "find" will be presented in a subsequent Replace dialog as a seed value. Users like this, perceiving it as a feature rather than a bug.

The C **struct** is defined as follows:

```
typedef struct tagFINDREPLACE
   {
   DWORD lStructSize;
   HWND hwndOwner;
   HINSTANCE hInstance;
   DWORD Flags;
   LPSTR lpstrFindWhat;
   LPSTR lpstrReplaceWith;
   UINT wFindWhatLen;
   UINT wReplaceWithLen;
   LPARAM lCustData;
   UINT   (CALLBACK* lpfnHook)(HWND, UINT, WPARAM, LPARAM);
   LPCSTR  lpTemplateName;
   } FINDREPLACE;
```

The *lStructSize* field is filled in with the size of the structure; this is used in lieu of a "version" field to support future enhancement. *hwndOwner* will be the handle of the window that is to receive any messages from the dialogs; that means that, even though the FindReplace control will be invisible at run-time, it cannot have the *MODEL_fGraphical* style; it will have to be based on an underlying Windows window.

hInstance would be used if we wanted to supply our own template for the Find and Replace dialog; but if we wanted to do that, we'd just create the dialogs in Visual Basic, wouldn't we? So we just set *hInstance* to NULL.

Flags is where we would request to do that; but *Flags* is also used for half a dozen other things. There are flags to set search direction ("up" or "down"), replacement scope ("replace all"), whether letter case is significant, and whether the search should be restricted to whole words.

The string pointers *lpstrFindWhat* and *lpstrReplaceWith* are just that: pointers. You have to supply the memory for each of these; you indicate how much you've supplied with the *wFindWhatLen* and *wReplaceWithLen* field values. The callback function, *lpfnHook()*, is used with *lpTemplatename* and several *Flags* bits, to completely replace the default Find/Replace mechanism. This is sort of like bringing your own car to Manhattan and hiring a cabby to drive it; we won't be doing this.

Once filled in, the *FINDREPLACE* structure is passed to either the *FindText()* or *ReplaceText()* function. These functions may alter the *Flags* and *lpstrFindWhat* and *lpstrReplaceWith* fields; but, as mentioned, it is usually a good idea to preserve the user settings anyway.

The *FindText()* and *ReplaceText()* functions display the appropriate dialog (in modeless fashion), but nothing happens yet. The dialogs appear as they do in Figures 12.3 and 12.4, respectively, but it's not until the user clicks the "Find Next," "Replace," or the "Replace All" button, that the custom-defined message will be sent to the window that owns the dialog.

That window had better be prepared to acknowledge that message if it intends to do anything about it. To recognize the message, the window must first have registered it. The SDK's *RegisterWindowMessage()* function does that. The string to register is already defined in WINDOWS.H as *FINDMSGSTRING*, so registration is easy:

```
FRMsg = RegisterWindowMessage (FINDMSGSTRING);
```

RegisterWindowMessage() takes a string and returns a number guaranteed to be unique *for that Windows session*. So it allows apps running at the same time to cooperate, but does not guarantee that same numeric value will represent that string every time the program runs over multiple Windows sessions. That means you can't hard-code the message

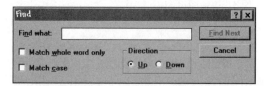

Figure 12.3 The common Find dialog.

Figure 12.4 The common Replace dialog.

ID, and *that* means you can't catch it in a **switch** statement; **switch** requires constants. However, a simple **if** statement prior to the **switch** will work nicely.

Generating the FindReplace Control Skeleton

You now know enough to use the VBX Skeleton Genie to generate the base code for a control that will bring the Find and Replace dialogs within the reach of VB programmers...including you! There're a number of options to specify; let's look at them page by page.

To start, of course, you choose VBX Genie from the *Tools* menu of your C/C++ development environment. The first page that appears is the Project page; you'll want to adjust the options so it looks like the ones shown in Figure 12.5.

Of course, you'll probably place your project on a different disk drive than I did!

The page shown in Figure 12.6 deals with the control's version information.

Since *I* wrote this VBX, the copyright information should appear just as it does here. I trust you understand that, when you create your *own* VBXs, you put your own name on this page!

Figure 12.5 Selecting project setup options with VBX Genie.

Figure 12.6 Setting up the FindReplace control's Version information.

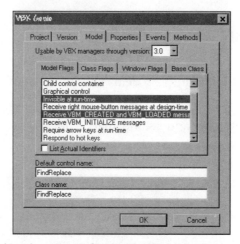

Figure 12.7 Including the settings for the Model page.

The Model page comes next, as shown in Figure 12.7.

Although you can't see the Class or Window flags panels, or the Base Class panel in the above illustration, that's okay—you don't need to make any changes to them, anyway.

The next page allows you to select the standard properties this control will support. Here's the list:

- Name, Index, Parent (required)
- HelpContextID

- LeftNoRun, TopNoRun
- Tag

In addition, the FindReplace control needs the following custom properties:

Action   Data Type: **Enum**
                    Flags: No runtime read, omit from properties, Set
                    via Message
                    Allowed Values: "Find", "FindAgain", "Replace"

Direction   Data Type: **Enum**
                    Flags: Default Value, Set Direct to Data
                    Allowed Values: "Up", "Down"
                    Common Value: "Up"

EnableMatchCase Data Type: **Boolean**
                    Flags: Default Value, Set via Message
                    Common Value: "True"

EnableWholeWord Data Type: **Boolean**
                    Flags: Default Value, Set via Message
                    Common Value: "True"

EnableDirection Data Type: **Boolean**
                    Flags: Default Value, Set via Message
                    Common Value: "True"

MatchCase   Data Type: **Boolean**
                    Flags: Default Value, Set Direct to Data
                    Common Value: "False"

WholeWord   Data Type: **Boolean**
                    Flags: Default Value, Set Direct to Data
                    Common Value: "False"

The FindReplace control does not use any of the standard events, but it does implement a few custom ones; they are listed here with their arguments:

Find   Direction as Integer
                    MatchCase as Integer
                    WholeWord as Integer
                    FindWhat as String

Replace	Direction as Integer
	MatchCase as Integer
	WholeWord as Integer
	FindWhat as String
	ReplaceWith as String
ReplaceAll	Direction as Integer
	MatchCase as Integer
	WholeWord as Integer
	FindWhat as String
	ReplaceWith as String

The control does not respond to any of the standard methods, so when all this information is supplied, you are ready to click the OK button and generate that skeleton!

Storing and Accessing the FINDREPLACE Structure

VBX Genie generates an entry in the *VBData* structure for each property you stated you want VB to set directly. That's nice, but we need to replace those automatic entries with one for a *FINDREPLACE* **struct**:

```
typedef struct
  {
  FINDREPLACE Data;
  } VBDATA, far * LPVBDATA;
```

The next related job is to modify the property definitions of those properties so that VB will place the data in the appropriate location. Specifically, there are three properties whose values are stored in the *Flags* property:

```
PROPINFO Property_Direction =
  {
  "Direction",
  DT_ENUM | PF_fDefVal | PF_fGetData | PF_fSaveData | PF_fSetData,
  _offsetin (FINDREPLACE, Flags), 0x10,
  (long) 1,
  "Up\0Down\0", 2
  };

PROPINFO Property_MatchCase =
  {
  "MatchCase",
  DT_BOOL | PF_fDefVal | PF_fGetData | PF_fSaveData | PF_fSetData,
  _offsetin (FINDREPLACE, Flags), 0x12,
```

```
(long) FALSE,
NULL, 0
};

PROPINFO Property_WholeWord =
  {
  "WholeWord",
  DT_BOOL | PF_fDefVal | PF_fGetData | PF_fSaveData | PF_fSetData,
  _offsetin (FINDREPLACE, Flags), 0x11,
  (long) FALSE,
  NULL, 0
  };
```

We are taking advantage here of one of the few features of Visual Basic
custom controls that VBX Genie *doesn't* directly support: automatic bit-
storage. It's specified in the fourth field of the *PROPINFO* structure, a
hexadecimal number whose two nybbles describe how the storage is to be
accomplished. The high-order nybble tells VB in how many bits the item is
to be stored, and the low-order nybble states the number of bits the data bit
must be shifted left within the offset specified by the third parameter.

Our next task is to initialize the *VbData* structure and to register those Find/
Replace messages described previously. Both those things are handled in
the *OnCreate()* function:

```
#define FINDREPWHATSIZE 256

UINT FindReplaceMessage;
UINT FindReplaceHelpMessage;

static void near pascal OnCreate
    (
    HCTL Control,
    HWND Window
    )
  {
  LPVBDATA VbData = (LPVBDATA) VBDerefControl (Control);
  VbData->Data.lStructSize = sizeof VbData->Data;
  VbData->Data.hwndOwner = Window;
  VbData->Data.hInstance = NULL;
  VbData->Data.Flags = 0;
  VbData->Data.lpstrFindWhat = malloc (FINDREPWHATSIZE);
  VbData->Data.lpstrFindWhat[0] = 0;
  VbData->Data.lpstrReplaceWith = malloc (FINDREPWHATSIZE);
  VbData->Data.lpstrReplaceWith[0] = 0;
  VbData->Data.wFindWhatLen = FINDREPWHATSIZE;
  VbData->Data.wReplaceWithLen = FINDREPWHATSIZE;
  VbData->Data.lCustData = 0;
  VbData->Data.lpfnHook = NULL;
  VbData->Data.lpTemplateName = NULL;
```

```
FindReplaceMessage = RegisterWindowMessage (FINDMSGSTRING);
FindReplaceHelpMessage = RegisterWindowMessage (HELPMSGSTRING);
}
```

The buffers for the *lpstrFindWhat* and *lpstrReplaceWith* fields are allocated by good ol' *malloc()*, so we have to free those buffers in *OnDestroy()*:

```
static void near pascal OnDestroy
    (
    HCTL Control
    )
{
LPVBDATA VbData = (LPVBDATA) VBDerefControl (Control);
free (VbData->Data.lpstrFindWhat);
free (VbData->Data.lpstrReplaceWith);
}
```

Those messages that we registered must be caught and dispatched by the control procedure; the best place to do this is at the beginning of the procedure:

```
long far pascal _export CtlProc
    (
    HCTL Control,
    HWND Window,
    USHORT Msg,
    USHORT wParam,
    long lParam
    )
{
long Error = 0;

if (Msg == FindReplaceMessage)
    {
    OnFindReplace (Control, (FINDREPLACE far *) lParam);
    return 0;
    }
```

OnFindReplace(), the handler for the first message, is where the cool stuff happens. This is the place where the custom events are fired.

To fire the events, the arguments to the event handlers must first be prepared. Some of these arguments are actually stored as bits in the *Flags* field of the *FINDREPLACE* structure; but Visual Basic doesn't understand bits. Others are stored as C-style strings, but Visual Basic doesn't understand those, either. So all these parameters must be converted into VB data types prior to firing the events. Then, after the event has been handled, the VB string argument handles must be released.

Here's the code that accomplishes this:

```
static void near pascal OnFindReplace
    (
    HCTL Control,
    FINDREPLACE far * Data
    )
{
int Direction;
int MatchCase;
int WholeWord;
struct
    {
    HLSTR ReplaceWith;
    struct
        {
        HLSTR FindWhat;
        LPINT WholeWord;
        LPINT MatchCase;
        LPINT Direction;
        LPVOID Index;
        } Find;
    } Replace;

Replace.ReplaceWith =
    VBCreateHlstr (Data->lpstrReplaceWith, lstrlen (Data->lpstrReplaceWith));
Replace.Find.FindWhat =
    VBCreateHlstr (Data->lpstrFindWhat, lstrlen (Data->lpstrFindWhat));
Replace.Find.WholeWord = &WholeWord;
Replace.Find.MatchCase = &MatchCase;
Replace.Find.Direction = &Direction;

WholeWord = Boolean[((Data->Flags & FR_WHOLEWORD) != 0)];
MatchCase = Boolean[((Data->Flags & FR_MATCHCASE) != 0)];
Direction = ((Data->Flags & FR_DOWN) != 0);

if (Data->Flags & FR_FINDNEXT)
    VBFireEvent (Control, IEVENTINFO_Find, &(Replace.Find));
else if (Data->Flags & FR_REPLACE)
    VBFireEvent (Control, IEVENTINFO_Replace, &Replace);
else if (Data->Flags & FR_REPLACEALL)
    VBFireEvent (Control, IEVENTINFO_ReplaceAll, &Replace);

VBDestroyHlstr (Replace.ReplaceWith);
VBDestroyHlstr (Replace.Find.FindWhat);
}
```

Note the use of the *Boolean* array to provide inexpensive conversion from C-style BOOL values to Visual Basic's.

Most of the properties are set by *VBM_SETPROPERTY* messages, which are handled by the *OnSetProperty()* function. The function skeleton was generated by VBX Genie; we have to fill it in. The Action property will be processed by a helper function; the others are bits that must be set or cleared depending on the incoming value:

```
static BOOL near pascal OnSetProperty
    (
    HCTL Control,
    HWND Window,
    USHORT PropertyIX,
    long Value,
    long far * Error
    )
{
LPVBDATA VbData = (LPVBDATA) VBDerefControl (Control);
switch (PropertyIX)
    {
    case IPROPINFO_Action:
        OnAction (Control, (int) Value);
        break;
    case IPROPINFO_EnableMatchCase:
        if (Value)
            VbData->Data.Flags &= (~FR_NOMATCHCASE);
        else
            VbData->Data.Flags |= FR_NOMATCHCASE;
        break;
    case IPROPINFO_EnableDirection:
        if (Value)
            VbData->Data.Flags &= (~FR_NOUPDOWN);
        else
            VbData->Data.Flags |= FR_NOUPDOWN;
        break;
    case IPROPINFO_EnableWholeWord:
        if (Value)
            VbData->Data.Flags &= (~FR_NOWHOLEWORD);
        else
            VbData->Data.Flags |= FR_NOWHOLEWORD;
        break;
    default:
        return FALSE;
    }
}
```

As in the Common Dialog, OLE2, and other controls, the Action property is an enumerated property that causes certain actions to take place. There wouldn't have to *be* an "Action" property, if the original designers of VBXs hadn't inexplicably withheld the ability to create custom methods, as we can create custom properties and events. But, since they did, "Action" it is.

The handler for setting this property (and therefore making something happen, like the appearance of a Find or Replace dialog) is *OnAction()*. The three possible values for this property are *Action_Find, Action_FindAgain,* and *Action_Replace*.

```
static void near pascal OnAction (HCTL Control, int Action)
    {
    LPVBDATA VbData = (LPVBDATA) VBDerefControl (Control);
```

```
switch (Action)
   {
   case Action_Find:
      FindText (&(VbData->Data));
      break;
   case Action_FindAgain:
      if (! VbData->Data.lpstrFindWhat[0])
         FindText (&(VbData->Data));
      else
         {
         VbData->Data.Flags &= (~FR_DIALOGTERM);
         VbData->Data.Flags |= FR_FINDNEXT;
         OnFindReplace (Control, &(VbData->Data));
         }
      break;
   case Action_Replace:
      ReplaceText (&(VbData->Data));
      break;
   };
}
```

Action_Find has the simple job of invoking the *FindText()* function from the
Common Dialog DLL. *Action_Replace* likewise invokes *ReplaceText()*. The
interesting member of the trio is *Action_FindAgain*, which traditionally
behaves identically to *Action_Find* if no search text has yet been specified.
On the other hand, if there *is* search text in the *FINDREPLACE* structure, we
want the same thing to happen *as if* the Find dialog were visible and the
user had just clicked the "Find Next" button.

So, in the code, we check the first byte of the *lpstrFindWhat* buffer. If it is
NULL, we know no text has yet been specified, and we call *FindText()*. If
not, there's text there; and we directly invoke the same routine that would
have been invoked by a message from the Find or Replace dialog:
OnFindReplace().

OnGetProperty(), invoked in response to a VBM_GETPROPERTY message,
is similar to its sibling—except, of course, that the Action property is not
represented, since it is a write-only property:

```
static BOOL near pascal OnGetProperty
    (
    HCTL Control,
    HWND Window,
    USHORT PropertyIX,
    LPVOID Value,
    long far * Error
    )
{
LPVBDATA VbData = (LPVBDATA) VBDerefControl (Control);
switch (PropertyIX)
```

```
    {
    case IPROPINFO_EnableMatchCase:
      (*(long *) Value) = (! (VbData->Data.Flags & FR_NOMATCHCASE));
      break;
    case IPROPINFO_EnableDirection:
      (*(long *) Value) = (! (VbData->Data.Flags & FR_NOUPDOWN));
      break;
    case IPROPINFO_EnableWholeWord:
      (*(long *) Value) = (! (VbData->Data.Flags & FR_NOWHOLEWORD));
      break;
    default:
      return FALSE;
    }
  }
```

Loading a property in from disk is simplified, because we only receive
messages for three properties, and all three are Boolean values. We can,
therefore, save them in single bytes. We can also make use of the
OnSetProperty() function to actually apply the loaded values, further saving
code:

```
static BOOL near pascal OnSaveProperty
    (
    HCTL Control,
    HWND Window,
    USHORT PropertyIX,
    HFORMFILE FormFile,
    long far * Error
    )
{
LPVBDATA VbData = (LPVBDATA) VBDerefControl (Control);
long Value;
char Byte;
switch (PropertyIX)
    {
    case IPROPINFO_EnableMatchCase:
    case IPROPINFO_EnableDirection:
    case IPROPINFO_EnableWholeWord:
      OnGetProperty (Control, Window,
        PropertyIX, &Value, Error);
      Byte = (char) Value;
      *Error = VBWriteFormFile (FormFile, &Byte, sizeof Byte);
      break;
    default:
      return FALSE;
    }
}
```

Likewise, loading a property from disk can make use of the *OnSetProperty()*
function to do all the work except the actual reading from the form file:

```
static BOOL near pascal OnLoadProperty
    (
    HCTL Control,
    HWND Window,
    USHORT PropertyIX,
    HFORMFILE FormFile,
    long far * Error
    )
{
LPVBDATA VbData = (LPVBDATA) VBDerefControl (Control);
char Value;
switch (PropertyIX)
    {
    case IPROPINFO_EnableMatchCase:
    case IPROPINFO_EnableDirection:
    case IPROPINFO_EnableWholeWord:
        *Error = VBReadFormFile (FormFile, &Value, sizeof Value);
        OnSetProperty (Control, Window, PropertyIX, Value, Error);
        break;
    default:
        return FALSE;
    }
}
```

Note how we saved the Boolean values as single bytes, even though they are treated as **long**s in most of the code. Although we didn't make use of it in this control, consider yet another technique for saving storage space: storing bits for up to eight properties in a *single* byte. You do this by actually writing or reading all eight properties in response to a message for just one. You "handle" the load and store messages for the other seven by simply returning *TRUE*. Visual Basic itself stores the standard Top, Left, Bottom, and Right properties as a unit in this way.

Supporting Context-Sensitive, Online Help

That leaves us with just one stone unturned: the implementation of on-line user help. If the programmer supplies a HelpContextID property value (other than zero), the Find and Replace dialogs should display a Help button; pressing it should bring up the online help file associated with the application, selecting the topic whose number matches the HelpContextID. On the *other* hand, if the HelpContextID has *not* been given, the Help button shouldn't show up at all.

We can do this, thanks to our specifying the *MODEL_fLoadMsg* flag. This flag causes a *VBM_LOADED* message to arrive *after* the control properties have all been set; so we can use that message to check and see what value the HelpContextID property has. We capture the message, of course, in the control procedure **switch** statement:

```
switch (Msg)
   {
    /
    /
   case VBM_LOADED:
      OnLoaded (Control);
      break;
```

The *OnLoaded()* function checks the value of the HelpContextID property as described, using it to decide whether to OR the proper flag into the *Flags* field of the *FINDREPLACE* structure:

```
static void near pascal OnLoaded (HCTL Control)
   {
   long Value;
   VBGetControlProperty (Control,
      IPROPINFO_STD_HELPCONTEXTID, &Value);
   if (Value != 0)
      {
      LPVBDATA VbData = (LPVBDATA) VBDerefControl (Control);
      VbData->Data.Flags |= FR_SHOWHELP;
      }
   }
```

Now, when the dialog box sends the help message to the control procedure, it only has to convert it into the WM_KEYDOWN message for the F1 key that Visual Basic will respond to:

```
long far pascal _export CtlProc
      (
      HCTL Control,
      HWND Window,
      USHORT Msg,
      USHORT wParam,
      long lParam
      )
   {
   long Error = 0;

   if (Msg == FindReplaceMessage)
      {
      OnFindReplace (Control, (FINDREPLACE far *) lParam);
      return 0;
      }

   if (Msg == FindReplaceHelpMessage)
      {
      SendMessage (Window, WM_KEYDOWN, VK_F1, 0);
```

```
    return 0;
    }

switch (Msg)
    /
    /
```

That's all there is to it!

Distributing the Control

As I always say, the control isn't finished until the online help is ready. Since preparing online help is not the focus of this book, I can't tell you here how to create such a document. However, here's one hint: Be sure to include a page of constants that the programmer can copy to the Clipboard. In the case of the FindReplace control, there are just five constants:

```
' Action property
Const FR_FindFirst = 1
Const FR_FindNext = 2
Const FR_Replace = 3

' Direction property
Const FR_Up = 0
Const FR_Down = 1
```

Testing the FindReplace Control

To test the FindReplace control, prepare a small project in which the FindReplace control is the only VBX. Place one of the new controls on the form, and add the menu shown in Figure 12.8.

The menu commands should be implemented as follows:

```
Sub mnu_SearchFind_Click ()
FindReplace1.Action = FR_FindFirst
End Sub
```

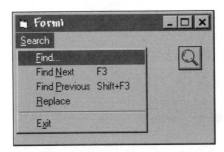

Figure 12.8 Adding the Search menu.

```
Sub mnu_SearchFindNext_Click ()
FindReplace1.Direction = FR_Down
FindReplace1.Action = FR_FindNext
End Sub

Sub mnu_SearchFindPrevious_Click ()
FindReplace1.Direction = FR_Up
FindReplace1.Action = FR_FindNext
End Sub

Sub mnu_SearchReplace_Click ()
FindReplace1.Action = FR_Replace
End Sub

Sub mnu_SearchExit_Click ()
Unload Me
End Sub
```

Since the statements for the command handlers are so typical, they should be (and are) also included in the control's help file, so when implementing these features you just copy and paste to your application code.

You can also provide event handlers for the control events, such as:

```
Sub FindReplace1_Find (Direction As Integer, MatchCase As Integer, WholeWord As
Integer, FindWhat As String)
MsgBox "Asked to find '" + FindWhat + "'."
End Sub

Sub FindReplace1_Replace (Direction As Integer, MatchCase As Integer, WholeWord
As Integer, FindWhat As String, ReplaceWith As String)
MsgBox "Asked to replace '" + FindWhat + "' with '" + ReplaceWith + "'."
End Sub

Sub FindReplace1_ReplaceAll (Direction As Integer, MatchCase As Integer,
WholeWord As Integer, FindWhat As String, ReplaceWith As String)
MsgBox "Asked to replace all '" + FindWhat + "' with '" + ReplaceWith + "'."
End Sub
```

Now try running the application. Try the commands. See the difference in the appearance of the Find and Replace dialogs when you do, or do not, supply a HelpContextID. (VB will not be able to actually *display* a help topic, of course, unless the HelpContextID you supply is a valid one for the help file associated with an application.)

With the addition of the FindReplace VBX to your toolbox, you'll find it much easier to write a Visual Basic application that includes *all* the features Windows users have come to expect.

And using such an application is much like riding in a cab where the driver *does* know where he or she is going—it's a pleasure instead of a chore.

Adding Tool Tips to Standard Controls

13

SEVEN HUNDRED YEARS before I got there, the Anasazi people lived along the side canyons of the Colorado River. Recently, I was standing in the ruins of one of their homes with a group of other people rafting the Grand Canyon.

Judging by its foundation, one home I saw had probably been a pleasant one, probably for a family of four. And they certainly had one fantastic view! But the rafters were puzzling over the doghouse-sized rock just outside the foundations, near where the door had been. It was adorned with whorls and symbols which, of course, none of us could read—the Anasazi written language has never been translated. Since by now I had obtained a reputation as the trip know-it-all, a couple of the other rafters asked me what I thought it meant.

I studied the symbols critically and made my pronouncement: "12002 Canyon Way," I said.

We humans love to label things. And we are most uncomfortable when things are *not* labeled, which probably explains "tool tips," those little tags that identify the otherwise unidentifiable buttons and other controls in our Windows applications. One of many annoying aspects of Microsoft's bullying us into their 32-bit world is that they have refused to provide tool tip support for 16-bit Visual Basic applications. So, this chapter, we'll provide it ourselves.

A Sign of the Times

Tool tips, as you must know, are those little labels that pop up when the mouse cursor rests momentarily over a bitmap button whose purpose might otherwise be obscure.

The most straightforward way to implement tool tips, of course, is to simply design the ability *into* your buttons. That is, instead of using the buttons that come with Visual Basic, create your *own* owner-draw buttons that have the tool-tip capability built in. This would still be done in a VBX, of course. But it would *not* supply tool-tip capability to any other control types, and sometimes that would be a nice feature.

Another approach is to write the code in VB. It's easy enough; each control has a *GetFocus* and *KillFocus* event. Between those, you would add a Timer control and a floating Label control. This would give you the makings of a tool tip you could display anywhere...but wouldn't it be nicer to implement this in a more object-oriented way?

My VBX solution will work with *any* custom control, even an OCX control—as long as it has an *hWnd* property (which only leaves out graphical controls such as Image and Label). It will appear to be a container object to which you add captions (using the *AddItem* method). And, since it's a VBX, you can use it with Visual Basic 3.0 as well as the 16-bit version of 4.0.

A Signpost Up Ahead...

The Tips control is an interesting project because of the oddball things it entails. We'll have to create a new window class, subclass existing window classes (including OLE server windows!), even fake Visual Basic into treating window handles as if they were array indexes.

From the programmer/user's standpoint, one Tips control is placed on any form that includes buttons, or other controls, that need tool tips. When the end user's mouse "flies by" the control, the tip window is displayed.

The idea behind the Tips control is that you'll "add" a number of control/ captions to it using the *AddItem* method. Controls must be identified by their *hWnd* properties, which happen to be numeric values; so we can use them as indexes. That is, the syntax for adding a tip to the Tips control will look like this:

```
Tips1.AddItem "Print the current document", btn_Print.hWnd
```

This means that the one Tips control must maintain a list of other controls that have been "added" to it.

As a control is added to this collection, the Tips control will *subclass* it— that means that all messages to the original control's window procedure will *first* be intercepted by a window procedure supplied by the Tips control for this purpose. The additional behavior this window will supply is twofold: First, the control will note when the mouse cursor is positioned over itself, and start a timer. (If the cursor is moved away from the control, the timer is canceled.) Second, if the timer's elapsed time passes and the mouse cursor is still positioned over the control, a popup tip window is created and displayed.

The tip window itself is of a class that must be written for the occasion. We need a window class that is resizable according to its textual contents, a feature the Static class does not offer. That's okay, though; a resizable text class is a trivial portion of the project—and it is reusable, to boot.

Sign Language

We'll use VBX Genie to give us a head start on this project. The name of the project is "Tips." The next step is harder: We need to decide in what language we want to write this VBX. I recommend C, because we'll have to subclass the other control windows and we'll want the finer control C can give us.

The only Model flag we need is "Invisible at runtime." For standard properties, we'll use BackColor, ForeColor, Enabled, the font properties, TopNoRun, LeftNoRun, and, of course, the required Name, Index, and Parent properties.

The custom properties are as follows:

• *Delay:* A **short** that holds the number of milliseconds the mouse must be positioned over a control before the tool tip appears.

- *Captions:* A property array of strings that allows captions to be changed at runtime.

- *AutoColor:* A Boolean property that indicates whether the user wants the tool tip window colors to be taken from the predefined system colors, or from the standard ForeColor and BackColor properties.

The Tips control supports no events—not even standard events—but you need to request support for the AddItem, RemoveItem, and Clear methods.

After generating the project, we'll have to modify just one file in it: VISUAL.C. This file begins as follows:

```
#include "internal.h"
#include <string.h>

#define segment(p) \
  ((HANDLE) (((unsigned long) (void far *) (p)) >> 16L))
#define _offsetin(struc, fld) ((USHORT)&(((struc *)0)->fld))
#define VBERR_BADINDEX 381

static long Boolean[2] = { 0, -1 };
```

The next block of code in VISUAL.C is the *VbData* structure:

```
#define MAXTOOLS 64
typedef struct
  {
  HWND TipParent;
  HWND TipWindow;
  HFONT TipFont;
  UINT Delay;
  BOOL AutoColor;
  HBRUSH AutoBrush;
  BOOL Enabled;
  BOOL MouseCaptured;
  int ToolsCount;
  struct
    {
    HSZ Caption;
    HWND Window;
    WNDPROC WndProc;
    } Tools[MAXTOOLS];
  } VBDATA, far * LPVBDATA;
```

As always, this structure provides space for both public and internal properties of the control. Of special interest is the **#define** *MAXTOOLS*. I personally think support for 64 buttons on a form is adequate. If you disagree, feel free to make the number larger.

The generated list of property structures is as follows:

```
PROPINFO Property_About =
   {
   "(About)",
   DT_HSZ | PF_fGetMsg | PF_fNoRuntimeW | PF_fGetHszMsg,
   0, 0, 0, NULL, 0
   };

PROPINFO Property_Delay =
   {
   "Delay",
   DT_SHORT | PF_fSetData | PF_fGetData | PF_fSaveData,
   _offsetin (VBDATA, Delay), 0,
   OL,
   NULL, 0
   };

PROPINFO Property_Captions =
   {
   "Captions",
   DT_HSZ | PF_fPropArray | PF_fSetMsg | PF_fGetMsg,
   0, 0,
   OL,
   NULL, 0
   };

PROPINFO Property_AutoColor =
   {
   "AutoColor",
   DT_BOOL | PF_fSetData | PF_fGetData | PF_fSaveData,
   _offsetin (VBDATA, AutoColor), 0,
   OL,
   NULL, 0
   };

PPROPINFO Properties [] =
   {
   PPROPINFO_STD_NAME,
   PPROPINFO_STD_INDEX,
   PPROPINFO_STD_BACKCOLOR,
   PPROPINFO_STD_ENABLED,
   PPROPINFO_STD_FONTBOLD,
   PPROPINFO_STD_FONTITALIC,
   PPROPINFO_STD_FONTNAME,
   PPROPINFO_STD_FONTSIZE,
   PPROPINFO_STD_FONTSTRIKE,
   PPROPINFO_STD_FONTUNDER,
   PPROPINFO_STD_FORECOLOR,
   PPROPINFO_STD_TOPNORUN,
   PPROPINFO_STD_LEFTNORUN,
   PPROPINFO_STD_PARENT,
   PPROPINFO_STD_LAST,
```

```
&Property_About,
&Property_Delay,
&Property_AutoColor,
&Property_Captions,
NULL
};
```

```
enum
  {
  Index_Property_Name,
  Index_Property_Index,
  Index_Property_BackColor,
  Index_Property_Enabled,
  Index_Property_FontBold,
  Index_Property_FontItalic,
  Index_Property_FontName,
  Index_Property_FontSize,
  Index_Property_FontStrike,
  Index_Property_FontUnder,
  Index_Property_ForeColor,
  Index_Property_TopNoRun,
  Index_Property_LeftNoRun,
  Index_Property_Parent,
  Index_Property_Last,
  Index_Property_About,
  Index_Property_Delay,
  Index_Property_Captions,
  Index_Property_AutoColor,
  Index_Property_End
  };
```

The Tips control triggers no events, so the *Events* array is sparse, to say the least:

```
PEVENTINFO Events [] =
  {
  NULL
  };
```

```
enum
  {
  Index_Event_End
  };
```

Coding the Methods

Even though we'll be using the window handles of various controls as if they were indexes to the *Captions* array of the Tips control, they are *not* truly indexes. We can make them seem that way to the user of this control, but we'll have to translate the window handle into a *real* array index if we want to make any use of it. That's the job of the *FindIndex()* function:

```
static int near pascal FindIndex (HWND Window, LPVBDATA VbData)
   {
   register i;
   for (i = 0; i < VbData->ToolsCount; i++)
     if (VbData->Tools[i].Window == Window)
        return i;
   return -1;
   }
```

VBX Genie always precedes a method-handling function with the structure used later (by *OnMethod()*) to interpret the parameters sent to it:

```
typedef struct
   {
   long Count;
   HSZ Item;
   long Index;
   } ADDITEM;
typedef ADDITEM far * LPADDITEM;
```

Before the actual code for *OnMethodAddItem()*, we need to provide a forward declaration for a tool window procedure—I'll explain why, shortly:

```
LRESULT _export FAR PASCAL ToolWndProc
    (
    HWND Window,
    UINT Msg,
    WPARAM wParam,
    LPARAM lParam
    );
```

Now we can look at the code for this method:

```
LRESULT near pascal OnMethodAddItem
    (
    HCTL Control,
    HWND Window,
    LPSTR Buffer,
    HWND Tool
    )
   {
   LPVBDATA VbData = (LPVBDATA) VBDerefControl (Control);
   register i = FindIndex (Tool, VbData);

   if ((i > -1) || (VbData->ToolsCount == MAXTOOLS))
     return VBERR_BADINDEX;

   i = (VbData->ToolsCount)++;
   VbData->Tools[i].Caption =
     VBCreateHsz (segment (Control), Buffer);
   VbData->Tools[i].Window = Tool;
```

```
VbData->Tools[i].WndProc =
   (WNDPROC) GetWindowLong (Tool, GWL_WNDPROC);
SetWindowLong (Tool, GWL_WNDPROC, (long) ToolWndProc);
SetProp (Tool, "TipControlH",
   (HANDLE) HIWORD ((long) Control));
SetProp (Tool, "TipControlL",
   (HANDLE) LOWORD ((long) Control));
SetProp (Tool, "TipIndex", (HANDLE) i);
return 0;
}
```

After dereferencing the control handle to get the pointer to *VbData*, the function checks to see if this window has already been added to the list. If it has, or if there is no more room in the list, it returns an error. Otherwise, we store the caption that will appear in the Tip window for this tool; that requires creating a new HSZ-style handle by invoking *VBCreateHsz()*. Then we add the handle of the tool window itself, so *FindIndex()* will be able to locate it later.

Finally, we can proceed to subclass the tool being added to the list.

Going to the Head of the Subclass

Subclassing is the SDK technique where you insert a window procedure *between* the message dispatching mechanism and a window's original window procedure. That way, you get first crack at the messages going through, and you can add, suppress, or modify behavior.

I'll defer an explanation of the subclassing window procedure itself until we get to that code; for now, just accept that it is there and will do the job. That leaves us with the actual job of making the subclass happen.

The first task is to obtain the address of the window's *original* window procedure. This is done using *GetWindowLong()* with the *GWL_WNDPROC* index. You've got to save that address because your subclassing window procedure will need it to complete the link back for messages whose behavior you don't want to change.

Once you have that address, you are free to replace it with the address of your subclass procedure by calling *SetWindowLong()*. You *don't* want to call *GetClassLong()*; that would subclass *every window of this class*, not just the one you are interested in. However, now you have the problem of communicating with the subclassed window—or, rather, of its communicating with you. You need to set some additional properties of the window, but of course you mustn't use any of the window's extra bytes—you don't know how many there are, and they are almost certainly being used anyway. Fortunately, Windows provides us with an alternative method of attaching properties to a window: *SetProp()*. This function takes a window handle and a case-insensitive string, and a 16-bit value of the *HANDLE* data type. The value is attached to the window, associated with the string, and can be retrieved by calling *GetProp()*.

It is a bit of a hassle that one of these "props" is limited to 16-bits, because an *HCTL* is 32-bits. That's why I had to split it and save it as two properties in the above code.

When the user invokes the *RemoveItem* method, we must *un*-subclass the window:

```
typedef struct
   {
   long Count;
   long Index;
   } REMOVEITEM;
typedef REMOVEITEM far * LPREMOVEITEM;

LRESULT near pascal OnMethodRemoveItem
     (
     HCTL Control,
     HWND Window,
     HWND Tool
     )
   {
   LPVBDATA VbData = (LPVBDATA) VBDerefControl (Control);
   register i = FindIndex (Tool, VbData);

   if (i > -1)
      {
      if (IsWindow (VbData->TipWindow))
         DestroyWindow (VbData->TipWindow);
      VBDestroyHsz (VbData->Tools[i].Caption);
      SetWindowLong (VbData->Tools[i].Window, GWL_WNDPROC,
         (long) VbData->Tools[i].WndProc);
      RemoveProp (Tool, "TipControlH");
      RemoveProp (Tool, "TipControlL");
      RemoveProp (Tool, "TipIndex");
      if (i < -(VbData->ToolsCount))
         {
         VbData->Tools[i] = VbData->Tools[VbData->ToolsCount];
         SetProp (VbData->Tools[i].Window, "Index", (HANDLE) i);
         }
      return 0;
      }
   else
      return VBERR_BADINDEX;
   }
```

Just in case this code was executed while a tip window was actually being displayed, we destroy it. We then restore the original window procedure address to the window (via *SetWindowLong()*) and remove the properties we had previously assigned to it. We then perform the simple housekeeping task of removing the element from the *Tips* array, by moving the last element of the array into its place, and reducing *TipsCount* by one. While at it, the "Index" property of that last item is changed to reflect the new value. *SetProp()* can be called as often as needed to alter any existing values, as well as to add a new property.

The *Clear* method is implemented similarly:

```
LRESULT near pascal OnMethodClear
    (
    HCTL Control,
    HWND Window
    )
    {
    LPVBDATA VbData = (LPVBDATA) VBDerefControl (Control);
    register i;
    for (i = 0; i < VbData->ToolsCount; i++)
        {
        if (IsWindow (VbData->TipWindow))
            DestroyWindow (VbData->TipWindow);
        if (IsWindow (VbData->Tools[i].Window))
            {
            SetWindowLong (VbData->Tools[i].Window, GWL_WNDPROC,
                (long) VbData->Tools[i].WndProc);
            RemoveProp (VbData->Tools[i].Window, "TipControlH");
            RemoveProp (VbData->Tools[i].Window, "TipControlL");
            RemoveProp (VbData->Tools[i].Window, "TipIndex");
            }
        VBDestroyHsz (VbData->Tools[i].Caption);
        }
    VbData->ToolsCount = 0;
    return 0;
    }
```

The *OnMethod()* function is the dispatcher, generated by VBX Genie, of various method invocations to the correct handler:

```
static long near pascal OnMethod
    (
    HCTL Control,
    HWND Window,
    USHORT Method,
    void far * Args
    )
    {
    LRESULT Result = 0;
```

```
switch (Method)
   {
   case METH_ADDITEM:
      {
      LPADDITEM AddItem = Args;
      LPSTR Item = VBLockHsz (AddItem->Item);
      int Index = (AddItem->Count > 2) ?
         (int) AddItem->Index : -1;
      Result = OnMethodAddItem (Control,
         Window, Item, (HWND) Index);
      VBUnlockHsz (AddItem->Item);
      }
      break;
   case METH_CLEAR:
      Result = OnMethodClear (Control, Window);
      break;
   case METH_REMOVEITEM:
      {
      LPREMOVEITEM RemoveItem = Args;
      Result = OnMethodRemoveItem (Control, Window,
         (HWND) RemoveItem->Index);
      }
      break;
   default:
      Result = VBDefControlProc (Control,
         Window, VBM_METHOD, Method, (long) Args);
   }
return Result;
}
```

Setting Properties

Most of the properties supported by the Tips control are either standard properties or custom properties that are written directly to the *VbData* structure by the VBX manager. However, one is not: the *Captions* property, which is a property array and allows the user to programmatically change the text to be displayed in the tip window after a given caption and window have been set using the *AddItem* method. The property can be set programmatically:

```
static BOOL near pascal OnSetProperty
    (
    HCTL Control,
    HWND Window,
    USHORT PropertyIX,
    long Value,
    long far * Error
    )
{
LPVBDATA VbData = (LPVBDATA) VBDerefControl (Control);
LPDATASTRUCT Data = (LPDATASTRUCT) Value;
switch (PropertyIX)
```

```
            {
        case Index_Property_Captions:
            {
            register i =
                FindIndex ((HWND) Data->index[0].data, VbData);
            if (i > -1)
                {
                VBDestroyHsz (VbData->Tools[i].Caption);
                VbData->Tools[i].Caption =
                    VBCreateHsz (segment (Control),
                        (LPSTR) Data->data);
                if (VbData->TipWindow)
                    InvalidateRect (VbData->TipWindow, NULL, TRUE);
                }
            else
                *Error = VBERR_BADINDEX;
            }
            break;
        default:
            return FALSE;
        }
    return TRUE;
    }
```

Since *Captions* is an array property, *Value* is a pointer to a *DATASTRUCT* instead of being the desired value, itself. The previous caption, which was stored as a VBX-managed HSZ-type string, must be destroyed (actually, released) before a new HSZ string can be created in its place.

Retrieving a caption is also supported:

```
static BOOL near pascal OnGetProperty
    (
    HCTL Control,
    HWND Window,
    USHORT PropertyIX,
    LPVOID Value,
    long far * Error
    )
    {
    LPVBDATA VbData = (LPVBDATA) VBDerefControl (Control);
    LPDATASTRUCT Data = (LPDATASTRUCT) Value;
    switch (PropertyIX)
        {
        case Index_Property_Captions:
            {
            register i =
                FindIndex ((HWND) Data->index[0].data, VbData);
            if (i > -1)
                *((HSZ far *) Data->data) =
                    VBCreateHsz (segment (Control),
                        VBDerefHsz (VbData->Tools[i].Caption));
```

```
      else
         *Error = VBERR_BADINDEX;
      }
      break;
   default:
      return FALSE;
   }
  return TRUE;
  }
```

Even though we've been storing the caption as an HSZ, and that's what's wanted, we cannot just copy the HSZ handle. Instead, we have to create a new string; the VBX manager will destroy the duplicate when it is no longer needed.

Since we make no change to the *OnGetStringProperty()* function, I won't bother describing it here. That brings us to the event handlers called by the control procedure, and *their* helper functions—starting with the ones that deal with the colors displayed by the tip window.

System Colors in VB

We all know that the standard properties ForeColor and BackColor provide little color maps to assist the user's setting a specific background or foreground color. And we know that the color is actually represented as a hexadecimal **Long** in the property bar. You might even know that colors are represented as three consecutive bytes, with a byte dedicated to the red value, the green value, and the blue value, and one byte unused.

But if that high-order byte is unused, why is it not always 0x00 unless you explicitly change it? For example, the ForeColor property for a label control begins life with the value:

&H80000012&

This works because the meaning of a color in VB has been enhanced over that of a simple *COLORREF* in the Windows SDK. The unused, high-order byte has been *given* a use: If its value is 0x80, the meaning is: "This is a system color, and the low-order byte is the index to *GetSysColor()* of the desired color." The index in the above case is that of *COLOR_WINDOWTEXT*, the normal color for text in a control or on a form. The color palette provides no way to return or specify a system color, but you can always just type in the value.

Windows 95 provides more system colors than its predecessors, including a pair of colors for tool tip boxes and tool tip text. They are system colors 23 and 24 (decimal), respectively. *GetSysColor()* works with them, too. So you'd figure, we could just set the ForeColor property to &H80000018& and get the color we want automatically, right? Wrong! VB4, 16-bit version, refuses to accept such a number as a value in this field, changing it (for some inadequately explored reason) to &H80000005&. And even though VB accepts &H80000017&, this value always returns a solid black. So we are stuck with moving the setting of colors to the control itself...and the *AutoColor* property will turn that feature on—or off, if the VB programmer prefers to specify the desired colors for the user.

That defers the problem to the Tips control. It's true that if we simply invoke *GetSysColor()* under Windows 95, with indexes of 23 and 24, we'll get the user-defined colors for tool tip windows. However, what if the application is being run under Windows 3.1, where these colors are not defined? *GetSysColor()* will return black for undefined colors. We can use this as a cue to drop back to the *COLOR_WINDOWTEXT* and *COLOR_WINDOW* indexes—but only if *both* values are black; because it is certainly possible that the user will have *chosen* black for either the text or the tool tip window background...but not both.

This logic is encapsulated in the *GetInfoTextColor()* and *GetInfoBkColor()* functions:

```
static COLORREF near pascal GetInfoTextColor (void)
   {
   COLORREF Result = GetSysColor (23);
   if ((Result == 0) && (GetSysColor (24) == 0))
      Result = GetSysColor (COLOR_WINDOWTEXT);
   return Result;
   }

static COLORREF near pascal GetInfoBkColor (void)
   {
   COLORREF Result = GetSysColor (24);
   if ((Result == 0) && (GetSysColor (23) == 0))
      Result = GetSysColor (COLOR_WINDOW);
   return Result;
   }
```

In any control in which you have requested the ForeColor and BackColor standard properties, you are required to send a *WM_CTLCOLOR* message to your parent window. That message alters the text color of the device context handle (passed as *wParam*) and returns a brush of the selected background color.

If the user has selected the AutoColor property, it will be the Tips control that has to supply that brush. Now, we can't just make it on the fly and hand it over, because we retain ownership of it and must eventually delete it. That means we'll have to create the brush when the Tips control itself is created:

```
static void OnCreate (HCTL Control, HWND Window)
  {
  LPVBDATA VbData = (LPVBDATA) VBDerefControl (Control);
  VbData->TipParent = Window;
  VbData->Enabled = TRUE;
  VBSetControlProperty (Control, Index_Property_ForeColor,
    GetInfoTextColor ());
  VBSetControlProperty (Control, Index_Property_BackColor,
    GetInfoBkColor ());
  VbData->AutoBrush = CreateSolidBrush (GetInfoBkColor ());
  }
```

While we're at it, we also seed the initial values of the foreground and background colors from the user's palette. Those colors won't necessarily match the *end* user's palette, but we have to have *some* initial value.

The brush we've created must be deleted when the Tips control is destroyed:

```
static void OnDestroy (HCTL Control, HWND Window)
  {
  LPVBDATA VbData = (LPVBDATA) VBDerefControl (Control);
  DeleteObject (VbData->AutoBrush);
  OnMethodClear (Control, Window);
  }
```

We also have to dispose of any caption HSZs we're still storing; the call to *OnMethodClear()* takes care of that.

If the user has selected the AutoColor property, we'll have to respond to the *WM_SYSCOLORCHANGE* message by recreating that brush:

```
static void OnSysColorChange (HCTL Control)
  {
  LPVBDATA VbData = (LPVBDATA) VBDerefControl (Control);
  if (IsWindow (VbData->TipWindow))
    DestroyWindow (VbData->TipWindow);
  DeleteObject (VbData->AutoBrush);
  VbData->AutoBrush = CreateSolidBrush (GetInfoBkColor ());
  }
```

Our tip window will send a *WM_CTLCOLOR* message to the Tips control; it is up to the Tips control to figure out what to do with it:

```
static HBRUSH near pascal OnCtlColor (HCTL Control,
    HWND Window, HDC dc)
  {
  LPVBDATA VbData = (LPVBDATA) VBDerefControl (Control);
  HBRUSH Result;
  if (VbData->AutoColor)
     {
     SetTextColor (dc, GetInfoTextColor ());
     Result = VbData->AutoBrush);
     }
  else
     Result = (HBRUSH) SendMessage (GetParent (Window),
        WM_CTLCOLOR, (WPARAM) dc,
        MAKELONG (Window, CTLCOLOR_STATIC));
  return Result;
  }
```

In this handler, the current value of the AutoColor property is checked first. If TRUE, the function responds to the *WM_CTLCOLOR* message itself, by setting the text color and returning a brush handle. Otherwise, the parent of this window is queried for the brush, which is how you get stock color properties in a VBX.

That leads us to the control procedure itself. All of it is either the obvious, default code supplied by VBX Genie, or calls to the functions we've just seen...*except*: There is added code for handling the *WM_SETFONT* and *WM_GETFONT* messages:

```
case WM_SETFONT:
   ((LPVBDATA) VBDerefControl (Control))->TipFont =
      (HFONT) wParam;
   break;
case WM_GETFONT:
    return (LRESULT) (int)
   ((LPVBDATA) VBDerefControl (Control))->TipFont;
```

Support for these messages is required if your control uses any of the standard Font properties. The usual handling is just what you see here: The font is stored (for *WM_SETFONT*) or returned (in *WM_GETFONT*). We do not *own* the font—it still belongs to our parent, or whatever window sent the message to us—so we don't have to delete the fonts later.

With that understood, the entire control procedure is as follows:

```
long far pascal _export CtlProc
    (
    HCTL Control,
    HWND Window,
    USHORT Msg,
    USHORT wParam,
    long lParam
    )
```

```
{
switch (Msg)
   {
   case WM_CREATE:
      OnCreate (Control, Window);
      break;
   case WM_SYSCOLORCHANGE:
      OnSysColorChange (Control);
      break;
   case WM_CTLCOLOR:
      return (LRESULT) (int) (HBRUSH)
         OnCtlColor (Control, Window, (HDC) wParam);
   case WM_SETFONT:
      ((LPVBDATA) VBDerefControl (Control))->TipFont =
         (HFONT) wParam;
      break;
   case WM_GETFONT:
       return (LRESULT) (int)
      ((LPVBDATA) VBDerefControl (Control))->TipFont;
   case WM_ENABLE:
      ((LPVBDATA) VBDerefControl (Control))->Enabled = wParam;
      break;
   case VBM_METHOD:
      return OnMethod (Control,
         Window, wParam, (void far *) lParam);
   case VBM_SETPROPERTY:
      {
      LRESULT Result = 0;
      if (OnSetProperty (Control,
          Window, wParam, lParam, &Result))
         return Result;
      }
      break;
   case VBM_GETPROPERTY:
      {
      LRESULT Result = 0;
      if (OnGetProperty (Control,
          Window, wParam, (LPVOID) lParam, &Result))
         return Result;
      }
      break;
   case VBM_GETPROPERTYHSZ:
      if (OnGetStringProperty (Control,
          Window, wParam, (HSZ far *) lParam))
         return 0;
      else
         break;
   case VBM_INITPROPPOPUP:
      switch (wParam)
         {
         case Index_Property_About:
            return (LRESULT) (int) PopupAbout ();
         }
      break;
```

```
      case VBM_HELP:
        if (OnHelp (Window,
              LOBYTE (wParam),
              HIBYTE (wParam),
              Properties, Events))
           return 0;
        break;
      case WM_DESTROY:
        WinHelp (Window, HelpFileName (), HELP_QUIT, 0);
        OnDestroy (Control, Window);
        break;
      }
   return VBDefControlProc (Control, Window, Msg, wParam, lParam);
   }
```

The actual *MODEL* structure, and the *VBINITCC()* and *VBTERMCC()* functions, are generated by VBX Genie and need not be modified:

```
MODEL Model =
   {
   VB300_VERSION,
   MODEL_fInvisAtRun,
   (PCTLPROC) CtlProc,
   0,
   0,
   sizeof (VBDATA),
   8000,
   "Tips",
   "Tips",
   NULL,
   Properties,
   Events,
   0,
   0,
   (BYTE) -1,
   100
   };

BOOL far pascal _export VBINITCC
     (
     USHORT Version,
     BOOL Runtime
     )
   {
   if (! Runtime)
      RegisterVbPopups ();
   RegisterTipClass (LibInstance);
   return VBRegisterModel (LibInstance, &Model);
   }

VOID FAR PASCAL _export VBTERMCC (void)
   {
   UnregisterVbPopups ();
   }
```

The *RegisterTipClass()* function is implemented in TIP.C and prototyped in INTERNAL.H; we'll see it shortly.

Signs and Portents

Don't confuse the Tips control, of which you'll probably place one on a given form, with the tip windows that show up as the mouse cursor is passed over various buttons. The Tips control *subclasses* each of the tool windows—you saw how that was accomplished in the code for the *OnMethodAddItem()* function—and then they take over the job of monitoring themselves for mouse fly-bys. This is handled in an *OnMouseMove()* event handler:

```
static void near pascal ReleaseTip (HWND Window, LPVBDATA VbData);

#define PROBABLY_UNIQUE_TIMER_ID 10021

static void OnMouseMove (LPVBDATA VbData,
    HWND Window, POINT Point)
  {
  if (! VbData->MouseCaptured)
    {
    SetCapture (Window);
    SetTimer (Window, PROBABLY_UNIQUE_TIMER_ID,
      VbData->Delay, NULL);
    VbData->MouseCaptured = TRUE;
    }
  else
    {
    RECT Rect;
    GetClientRect (Window, &Rect);
    if (! PtInRect (&Rect, Point))
      ReleaseTip (Window, VbData);
    }
  }
```

When this event occurs, things may be in one of two states: Either the mouse has already *been* captured, or it has not. If not, a timer is set. It's important that this timer not conflict with any timer the subclassed control might have going for it. So I took a number at random and defined it as *PROBABLY_UNIQUE_TIMER_ID*; that's the number used to identify our timer. If you suspect a conflict with some control, just try a different number.

Capturing the mouse means we'll continue to receive messages from it even after it moves out from over the subclassed control. So, if the mouse has already been captured, we check to see if its coordinates are still within our own rectangle. If not, *ReleaseTip()* is called, which either kills the timer or, alternatively, an existing tip window.

If the user lets the mouse cursor rest over the subclassed control for *VbData->Delay* number of milliseconds, the timer will send a message to it. That message is handled by the *OnTimer()* function:

```
static void near pascal OnTimer (LPVBDATA VbData,
    HWND Window, int i)
  {
  static BOOL Busy = FALSE;
  RECT Rect;
  if (! Busy)
    {
    Busy = TRUE;
    KillTimer (Window, PROBABLY_UNIQUE_TIMER_ID);
    if (IsWindow (VbData->TipWindow))
      DestroyWindow (VbData->TipWindow);
    if (VbData->Enabled)
      {
      GetWindowRect (Window, &Rect);
      VbData->TipWindow = CreateWindow ("Tip",
        VBDerefHsz (VbData->Tools[i].Caption),
        WS_POPUP | SS_SIMPLE,
        Rect.right - 10,
        Rect.bottom - 10,
        50, 50,
        VbData->TipParent,
        0,
        LibInstance,
        (LPVOID) VbData->TipParent);
      SendMessage (VbData->TipWindow,
        WM_SETFONT, (WPARAM) VbData->TipFont, FALSE);
      ShowWindow (VbData->TipWindow, SW_SHOWNOACTIVATE);
      }
    Busy = FALSE;
    }
  }
```

Our very first concern, in this function, is that another *WM_TIMER* message not trigger it while we're still processing the previous one. Preventing that is the job of the **static** *Busy* variable. And we immediately kill the timer.

Then, if there happens to *be* a tip window showing, we destroy it. There shouldn't be; but I'd rather be on the safe side.

We then create the tip window for the current tool, as long as the control is currently enabled. Note that the *WS_VISIBLE* flag is *not* supplied—we'll have to invoke *ShowWindow()* eventually. Note also that we send, as the last parameter, the handle of the tip control itself. That's to accommodate an odd behavior in Windows I had never before noticed.

See, the eighth parameter to *CreateWindow()* is supposed to be the handle to a control's parent. This normally works just as one would expect. However, the Tips control is a child window, and the tip window itself is a popup. Apparently Windows (or, at least, Windows 95) automatically makes the parent of a popup window, the first popup or overlapped window it finds by starting with the actual parent and repeatedly calling *GetParent()*. Since we need to have the tip window send a *WM_CTLCOLOR* message to the Tips control (something normally sent to a parent window), we have to supply the Tips control's window handle in some other way—and as a parameter to *CreateWindow()* is the way I chose.

After creating the window, we send it a *WM_SETFONT* message, passing on the font that the Tips control received using the same sort of message from the VBX manager.

Finally, we call *ShowWindow()* to present the new tip window, supplying the *SW_SHOWNOACTIVATE* style so that the focus does not leave whatever window previously had it.

We've already seen that a *WM_MOUSEMOVE* message might result in the tip window being destroyed, or the timer killed. That's handled in the *ReleaseTip()* function:

```
static void near pascal ReleaseTip (LPVBDATA VbData, HWND Window)
    {
    ReleaseCapture ();
    KillTimer (Window, PROBABLY_UNIQUE_TIMER_ID);
    VbData->MouseCaptured = FALSE;
    if (VbData->TipWindow)
        {
        DestroyWindow (VbData->TipWindow);
        VbData->TipWindow = NULL;
        }
    }
```

If the timer has already been killed (as it would have been when the tip window was created), the *KillTimer()* function will fail; but it will do so quietly and with no repercussions, so there's no harm in making this a general cleanup function.

All that's left to examine here, then, is the subclass window procedure that ties this all together:

```
LRESULT _export FAR PASCAL ToolWndProc
    (
    HWND Window,
```

```
    UINT Msg,
    WPARAM wParam,
    LPARAM lParam
    )
{

HCTL Control =
   (HCTL) MAKELONG (GetProp (Window, "TipControlL"),
      GetProp (Window, "TipControlH"));
LPVBDATA VbData = VBDerefControl (Control);
register i = (int) GetProp (Window, "TipIndex");
switch (Msg)
   {
   case WM_MOUSEMOVE:
      OnMouseMove (VbData, Window, MAKEPOINT (lParam));
      break;
   case WM_KILLFOCUS:
   case WM_DESTROY:
      if ((HWND) lParam != VbData->TipWindow)
         ReleaseTip (VbData, Window);
      break;
   case WM_TIMER:
      OnTimer (VbData, Window, i);
      break;
   }
return CallWindowProc (VbData->Tools[i].WndProc,
   Window, Msg, wParam, lParam);
}
```

You can see how the two halves of the *Control* handle are reassembled, and how the tool's original window procedure is invoked (from *CallWindowProc()*) at the end, instead of *DefWindowProc()*. The original procedure is *always* called, even for messages we've handled, so the original tool's behavior should not be altered in any way.

The Tip Window

I've implemented the tip window itself in a separate code module, on the off-chance I might want to reuse it someday. It's a fairly simple window, and in fact I began my development of the Tips control by creating a simple STATIC popup. But I wanted an automatic-sizing window, which is not a feature of the STATIC class; so I was on my own. The "Tip" class is implemented in TIP.C.

As with practically any window, the tip window must maintain some local information. I store this in a local **struct** called *MyData*, analogous to *VbData* in the control procedure:

```
typedef struct
   {
   HFONT Font;
   HWND Tool;
   } MYDATA, far * LPMYDATA;
```

As is normal, this structure is allocated during processing of the *WM_NCCREATE* message:

```
static BOOL near pascal OnNcCreate (HWND Window,
     LPCREATESTRUCT cs)
   {
   BOOL Result = (BOOL) DefWindowProc (Window,
     WM_NCCREATE, 0, (LPARAM) cs);
   LPMYDATA MyData;
   if (! Result)
     return Result;
   MyData = malloc (sizeof MyData);
   if (MyData)
      {
      memset (MyData, 0, sizeof MyData);
      MyData->Tool = (HWND) (long) cs->lpCreateParams;
      if (! MyData->Tool)
         MyData->Tool = cs->hwndParent;
      SetWindowLong (Window, 0, (long) MyData);
      return TRUE;
      }
   else
      return FALSE;
   }
```

It is *absolutely essential* that you call the default handler for *WM_NCCREATE* before you do anything else. And this message might fail, if not enough memory is available to create the window. Likewise, if there isn't enough additional memory for your local **struct**, you must fail the message, which you do by returning *FALSE* instead of *TRUE.*

We expect to receive a *WM_SETFONT* message shortly after being created. In addition to storing the font handle, we must actually measure the amount of room that will be required by the new font to display the window's caption:

```
static void near pascal OnSetFont (LPMYDATA MyData,
     HWND Window, HFONT Font)
   {
   RECT Rect;
   HDC dc = GetDC (Window);
   HFONT OldFont = NULL;
   char Buffer [128];
   DWORD Extent;

   MyData->Font = Font;
```

```
if (MyData->Font)
   OldFont = SelectObject (dc, MyData->Font);
GetWindowText (Window, Buffer, sizeof Buffer);
Extent = GetTextExtent (dc, Buffer, strlen (Buffer));

GetWindowRect (Window, &Rect);
MoveWindow (Window, Rect.left, Rect.top,
   LOWORD (Extent) + 4, HIWORD (Extent) + 4, FALSE);

if (OldFont) SelectObject (dc, OldFont);
ReleaseDC (Window, dc);
}
```

Although we don't expect this to happen under a VB control, a window should be prepared to have the *system* font specified in a *WM_SETFONT* message—which means, the parameter that contains the new font handle will, in fact, be NULL. This is accommodated by altering the device context's font only if an actual handle was supplied.

Once the dimensions of the caption are determined (using the call to *GetTextExtent()*), a tad is added on each side for a margin, and *MoveWindow()* is called to resize accordingly.

The only interesting thing about painting the tip window is that, in order to obtain the background and foreground colors, a *WM_CTLCOLOR* message must be sent to allow the text color to be altered, and a background brush to be supplied. Normally this message is sent to a window's parent; but in this case it must be sent to the Tips control itself:

```
static void near pascal OnPaint (LPMYDATA MyData, HWND Window)
   {
   PAINTSTRUCT ps;
   HDC dc = BeginPaint (Window, &ps);
   char Buffer [128];
   RECT Rect;
   HBRUSH Brush, OldBrush = NULL;
   HFONT OldFont = NULL;

   if (MyData->Font)
      OldFont = SelectObject (dc, MyData->Font);
   GetWindowText (Window, Buffer, sizeof Buffer);

   GetClientRect (Window, &Rect);
   Brush = (HBRUSH) SendMessage (MyData->Tool,
      WM_CTLCOLOR, (WPARAM) dc,
      MAKELONG ((WORD) Window, CTLCOLOR_STATIC));
   if (Brush) OldBrush = SelectObject (dc, Brush);
   Rectangle (dc, Rect.left, Rect.top, Rect.right, Rect.bottom);
```

```
SetBkMode (dc, TRANSPARENT);
TextOut (dc, 2, 2, Buffer, strlen (Buffer));

if (OldFont) SelectObject (dc, OldFont);
if (OldBrush) SelectObject (dc, OldBrush);
EndPaint (Window, &ps);
}
```

If a new brush was supplied, we select it into the device context. We then draw the window frame and its text, and then replace the original font and brush, as needed.

The tip window procedure contains no surprises:

```
LRESULT _export FAR PASCAL TipWndProc
    (
    HWND Window,
    UINT Msg,
    WPARAM wParam,
    LPARAM lParam
    )
{
LPMYDATA MyData = (LPMYDATA) GetWindowLong (Window, 0);
LRESULT Result = 0;
switch (Msg)
    {
    case WM_NCCREATE:
        Result = OnNcCreate (Window, (LPCREATESTRUCT) lParam);
        break;
    case WM_NCDESTROY:
        free (MyData);
        break;
    case WM_SETFONT:
        OnSetFont (MyData, Window, (HFONT) wParam);
        break;
    case WM_GETFONT:
        Result = (LRESULT) (int) MyData->Font;
        break;
    case WM_SYSCOLORCHANGE:
        InvalidateRect (Window, NULL, TRUE);
        break;
    case WM_PAINT:
        OnPaint (MyData, Window);
        break;
    case WM_SETFOCUS:
        SetFocus ((HWND) wParam);
        break;
    default:
        Result = DefWindowProc (Window, Msg, wParam, lParam);
    }
return Result;
}
```

MyData is freed when the window is destroyed; the font received in any *WM_SETFONT* message is returned if queried in a *WM_GETFONT* message; and if the system colors are changed by the end user, the window is made to redraw itself. The only other thing is that the tip window refuses to allow the focus to be set to itself, throwing it back to the window losing the focus if the attempt is made.

The registration for this class is self-contained in TIP.C:

```
static WNDCLASS WndClass =
   {
   0,
   TipWndProc,
   0,
   sizeof (LPMYDATA),
   NULL,
   NULL,
   NULL,
   NULL,
   NULL,
   "Tip"
   };

void far pascal RegisterTipClass  (HINSTANCE Instance)
   {
   WndClass.hCursor = LoadCursor (NULL, IDC_ARROW);
   WndClass.hInstance = Instance;
   if (! RegisterClass (&WndClass))
     MessageBox (NULL, "Registration of Tip class failed!",
       "Tip", MB_ICONSTOP);
   }
```

The *RegisterTipClass()* function is prototyped in INTERNAL.H; we've already seen it invoked in the *VBINITCC()* function.

Using the Tips Control

To use the Tips control, simply add the VBX to your list of custom controls, drop one on a form that has some controls for which you'd like to provide user hints, set the Delay property (and, possibly, the ForeColor and BackColor properties, or the AutoColor property). Then, in your form's *Load* event, add hints to the control using its *AddItem* method and the window handle of the associated tool as an index. For example:

```
Sub Form_Load ()
Tips1.AddItem "Cut", cmd_EditCut.hWnd
Tips1.AddItem "Copy", cmd_EditCopy.hWnd
Tips1.AddItem "Paste", cmd_EditPaste.hWnd
End Sub
```

If you wish, you can alter the text of a caption at any time, again using the tool's window handle as an index:

```
Tips1.Captions(cmd_EditCut.hWnd) = "Cut selected circuit"
```

That's all there is to it! Now, there's no excuse for omitting tool tips in your application...even if you *are* writing one for 16-bit release.

PART 4

Microsoft's OLE Control Wizard

What Is This Thing Called COM?   347

Creating a Simple OCX   365

Working with OCX Stock Properties   391

Custom OCX Properties   411

Custom Methods and Events   437

What Is This Thing Called COM?

14

WHEN I TOOK MY seventeen-day Grand Canyon rafting trip, I was one of the lucky ones—I got to go for the entire seventeen days. Most people can't take that much time off, of course; so the rafting company has figured out a way to offer more options, even though there's only one way in and one way out for the rafts. We put in at Lee's ferry, of course. But about a week later, we arrive at Bright Angel Trail and Phantom Ranch, located at the trail's end. Some passengers leave at this point, spending the night at Phantom Ranch and hiking up to the South Rim in the morning. Meanwhile, new folks will have already hiked *down* Bright Angel and are ready to continue on with us.

After about another week, we get to Whitmore Wash. Now, there's no trail out of Whitmore. But there is a helicopter landing pad, and a helicopter ferries passengers and gear between the river and the Bar-10 Ranch on the North Rim. So another set of passengers can leave, and be replaced by yet another set for the final three days.

The three-day passengers tend to be a distinct lot. Although some people really only have a few days to spare, most of these are folks who are trying the Grand Canyon rafting experience for the first time. Maybe they aren't sure they'll like rafting; maybe they aren't sure they'll like camping.

By the time the helicopter was bringing new passengers in to Whitmore Wash, the boatmen were treating me like an adopted brother. So I was able, and happy, to assist in orienting the newcomers. This included showing them how to pack their "dry bags," rubberized sacks that could be sealed so that water can't get in. Each three-day passenger is given one for his or her personal gear, and one for their sleeping gear.

Among the newbies (a computer term I taught the boatmen) were five ladies from "New Yawk," who hastened to assure me they wouldn't need much assistance. "We camp *awl* the time," one woman, Louise, told me. "In the summa, every Friday, this nice young man takes us on his canoe to an island in Lake George and he leaves us alone until Sunday evening. So, we know awl about camping."

In spite of their vast outdoors experience, they hadn't learned to pack appropriately for a three-day trip—their dry bags were so full they couldn't be sealed. I looked into one and found the woman's purse neatly placed at the top. Finally we took the excess stuff and stowed it in the bottom of the baggage boat; then I showed the ladies how to fold and roll the lips of their bags, burping the air out of them as they rolled them down, and finally slipping the end straps through the buckles and tightening them. By the time the last bag was sealed, we were *all* sweating.

That night I was again called to help; the ladies had no idea how to set up their tents—in fact, when I got there, they were trying to erect the tent fly by itself! "I thought you guys went camping a lot," I kidded. "Which of you set up your tent before?"

The ladies looked puzzled, and finally Louise admitted, "It was always just waiting for us on the island." I assume that the "nice young man" had set it up for them before he ferried them over, but apparently they had never questioned it!

The next morning, Louise came moaning to my tent. "Pawl, do you have any Advil? I am *so* sowah!" Well, I'm a programmer; of *course* I have Advil...and Mylanta, as far as that goes. I gave her a couple tabs and watched her wash it down with a swig of "ku-awffee."

What had made her so sore, I wondered? The day before, she had stepped off a helicopter, walked down a short hill and climbed into a raft. I knew she hadn't gone on any hikes. The night before *I* had set up her tent, on a nice, soft, perfect spot.

"I hope this kicks in, soon!" she said. "Befowah I have to face that awful job again!"

"What awful job?" I asked.

She looked at me in amazement. "Why, closing that gawdam dry bag, of course!"

I bring up this whole, sordid story because it illustrates that one can *think* he or she knows all about something, and may even know enough about it to make use of it—but still not know all there is to know. The ladies' limited experience camping hadn't seemed limited to them—and yet, they didn't even recognize the parts of a tent, or that a purse wasn't needed a mile below the surface of the Earth. It hadn't mattered on Lake George. It *did* matter in the Canyon.

Most campers never make it to Grand Canyon. (Of course, most campers can erect their tents, in spite of that.) And most programmers will never need to know how OCXs work under the hood, either. But if you ever *do* find yourself needing to work with them below the Lake George level of complexity, you might find yourself needing an Advil and some "ku-awffee," too. So sit back and keep reading, and I'll try to share what I know.

In Chapter 2, I presented an overview of OCXs—what they're for, and, at an *extremely* high level, how they work—or, at least, what they do. Actually, looking back, I spent more time telling what they *don't* do than what they do! But that was necessary, simply to make up for the huge selling job Microsoft's marketing department has done on the concept.

OCXs are here, however, and we're going to be writing some...so we'd better get down to details, just to provide the backdrop, so you'll have a better idea what is happening inside MFC when your OCX is executing.

Introducing the Common Object Model

When Microsoft first came up with the idea for *COM*, the acronym stood for "Component Object Model." However, it was clear that if the multi-platform, multi-vendor vision of the future was to be achieved, more corporations than Microsoft needed to be involved. Microsoft did, indeed, find other vendors to join in and COM was renamed "Common Object Model" in celebration of that fact.

The purpose of the Common Object Model is to make *all* computer software components—*every single one*—have the same programmatic interface, at least at its base. Put another way, in object-oriented languages like Smalltalk, *all* object classes are derived from a base class called "Object." In the COM view of the world, all software components are derived from a base "class" called COM.

COM is designed to be a "binary standard." That means it is intended to be language independent. In practice, all of the OLE books I've read that cover the COM present only C and C++ examples, as if those were the only computer languages! In reality, COM requires certain features in any language to be used to implement a COM object; specifically, the ability to invoke a function through a pointer. Pascal qualifies, but Basic, COBOL, and FORTRAN do not.

COM objects are accessed through sets of functions called *interfaces*. Although interfaces are supposed to be language-independent, they are designed as if they were C++ classes with **virtual** functions. Thus, to implement them in C you would need to manually code the virtual method table as a **struct** of function pointers. Needless to say, few programmers actually use C to program COM objects.

> In the C++ world, each interface is described as if it were a C++ class. It is important to distinguish that the interface is not the object. Thus, Microsoft convention uses an I prefix for interface classes instead of C, as in IUnknown.

IUnknown is the one interface every COM object *must* implement, or the object won't be a COM object. And, every other interface is *derived* from *IUnknown*, in the C++ class sense. So, a good place for us to start is to take a close look at *IUnknown*.

Introducing the IUnknown Interface

To understand how the COM interface works, the first thing we need to do is locate its declaration. But trying to find *IUnknown*'s declaration is like trying to find your purse at the bottom of a baggage boat. When you look at the set of header files included with Visual C++ 4.0, you'll find one named OLE2.H. This sounds like a good place to start, right? Unfortunately, the declaration isn't located here. Another likely place to look would be in the header file COMPOBJ.H, since COM once stood for Component Object Model. But the only clue this file provides is the **#pragma** producing the message, "WARNING: your code should **#include** objbase.h instead of compobj.h."

The OBJBASE.H header file gets us very close since *IUnknown* is used in some macros in this file, but it isn't declared there. So we must look further. Eventually, you'll discover that I've only told you this much so you'll understand that OLE 2 is *truly* not a technology you can master in a weekend—not necessarily because it's so complex, *really*, but because it has been so over-designed.

When all is said and done, and the preprocessor has had its say and the compile is through, the interface for *IUnknown* has the following structure:

```
class IUnknown
  {
  public:
    virtual long QueryInterface
       (
       long riid,
       void far * far *ppvObject
       ) = 0;
    virtual long AddRef (void) = 0;
    virtual long Release (void) = 0;
  };
```

Understand, I have simplified this greatly. First, none of the parameters is actually **long**; they have been given **typedef**s that *equate* to **long**s. And those double **far** pointers for the *ppvObject* parameter? Each is hidden by a *__RPC_FAR* macro...or maybe it's a **typedef**. I wasn't able to locate its definition.

Further, you won't actually find "class IUnknown" anywhere. That's because "class" has been replaced by the **typedef** "interface," which is defined to mean "struct." (There's a comment explaining that "struct far" is used to guarantee **this** will be a **far** pointer, but of course this point is moot for a flat 32-bit compiler, and the keyword **far** has been commented out of the actual code.) So, rather than the simplified version you see above, the actual code from the header file is:

```
interface IUnknown
    {
    public:
        virtual HRESULT __stdcall QueryInterface(
          /* [in] */ REFIID riid,
          /* [out] */ void __RPC_FAR *__RPC_FAR *ppvObject) = 0;

        virtual ULONG __stdcall AddRef( void) = 0;

        virtual ULONG __stdcall Release( void) = 0;

    };
```

As the consumer of a COM object, you should not care how the object is implemented. On the other hand, if you are *writing* a COM object, you have to *provide* those implementations. So let's see what the three functions do.

First, note that no constructor is provided. That's because an interface is *not* an object, C++ syntax notwithstanding. You have to create your COM object in some other way—a common one is to invoke the *CoCreateInstance()* function. You have to supply something called a *globally unique identifier*, or GUID, and *CoCreateInstance()* will give you back a pointer...not to the object, but to the *IUnknown* interface.

> *You* never *actually get hold of a COM object itself. That's because you have no say-so as to* where *the object actually resides. It may be on your computer, but it could be in a separate memory space. It might be on another computer. It might be on another* planet*. It doesn't matter. You do everything you need to do through the interface.*

The *first* thing you need to do is inform the object that you *have* this interface, which you do by calling *AddRef()*. This increments an internal reference count. Now, why this couldn't be done internally when the interface pointer was obtained, has never been clear to me. That would have been cleaner in an object-oriented sense. In any case, for every time you call *AddRef()*, you must eventually call *Release()*. When the number of calls to *Release()* equals the number of calls to *AddRef()*, the object is free to delete itself, or whatever it does to free up system resources. This technique makes it possible for a single object to provide interfaces, and therefore services, to many different applications, or many parts of the same application, without each consumer having to know about the others.

It's all well and good that you can tell an object, through its *IUnknown* interface, that it's in use and, later, that you're done with it. Still, this functionality isn't terribly useful. That's why the remaining function, *QueryInterface()*, exists. You give it a *REFIID* (which is really another GUID) and, if the interface you've requested is supported by this COM object, you get back a pointer to *it*—and, for gosh sake, don't forget to call *AddRef()* and, later, *Release()*, on the new pointer!

Since an interface is *not* the object itself, you need a way to create an object *before* you can get hold of any of its interfaces, even *IUnknown*. As mentioned, one way is to invoke *CoCreateInstance()*, a global function. Once you have an existing object, you can always make another of its type using the *IClassFactory* interface. This interface is also used by *CoCreateInstance()*; so obviously it is possible, *somehow*, to get an *IClassFactory* interface *before* an object is created—but how to do this is not published information. Nevertheless, all COM objects must support an *IClassFactory* interface as well as *IUnknown*.

As I mentioned in Chapter 2, there is no method defined by COM for enumerating available interfaces. Instead, you have to ask for the one you want and, if it isn't available, you ask for your second choice. The idea was that there would be a relatively small number of published interfaces that everyone would use; but as far as I know, no one has ever published such a list, so everyone who produces a new COM object tends to introduce a new interface. Also, when an existing interface proves inadequate, a new one will replace it—there's no mechanism for specifying interface versions. So we have *IClassFactory* and *IClassFactory2*, an enhanced version of *IClassFactory*. What happens if you need a further enhancement and write *IClassFactory3*...at the same time that someone in another company does the same thing? I shudder to think.

Introducing OLE Automation

The proliferation of interfaces must have seemed unmanageable early on, because soon after OLE 2 was introduced, it was followed by OLE Automation.

OLE 2 and, for that matter, OLE 1, allowed special application types called "servers" to provide support for components called "subdocuments." The idea was that you shouldn't have to write a full word processor, just because your application needs word processing abilities as a minor issue. And users certainly appreciated being able to drop, say, a spreadsheet component into a word processed document (like a business plan). But the server applications often sported complex macro languages, and a whole new type of programmer was created whose forte is making highly specialized applications using these servers as development platforms.

But OLE alone didn't permit one component of the application to control another programmatically. That's where OLE Automation comes in. At the surface, OLE Automation addresses an obvious need—that of programmatic control of OLE objects—but its implementation finds another approach to the interface problem. Instead of generating a new interface for each set of functions, OLE Automation uses *one* interface—*IDispatch*—to solve the problem once and for all—sort of. *IDispatch* allows access to VBX-like properties and methods, and provides a feedback mechanism similar to events, to a consumer. These properties, methods, and events can be enumerated and referenced by name, via yet another interface, *ITypeInfo*. It is customary to use *ITypeInfo* to enumerate the names of all properties, events, and methods, and then give those names to the *IDispatch* interface where they can be translated into *DISPID*s, 32-bit numbers that are cheaper to look up than strings for repeated uses.

OLE Controls

Implemented as a feature of an OLE server, OLE Automation provides support for properties and methods. Thus, a spreadsheet can include an inserted OLE graphic object, which can be programmatically manipulated from the spreadsheet through its macro language.

However, what if the user alters the graphic, either at its source or through the spreadsheet using in-place editing (another OLE 2 feature)? Or, rather, what if the spreadsheet application *needs to know* the graphic has been altered? OLE 2 servers do not provide any way, other than periodic polling of their properties, for a container to know this. When your container needs to be notified of events occurring to the embedded object, an OLE Server isn't good enough...you need an OLE Control.

As you may know, OLE allows servers to be implemented either for separate execution, in which case they will be running their own address space and may be running on an entirely different computer, or as in-place servers. An in-place server is implemented as a DLL: It runs in the same address space as its container. Please note that the container itself does not know, and shouldn't care, whether a server it requests is running separately or in-place. (This allows for executable servers that create an embedded object, and in-place servers that view or play it later.)

> *OLE Controls are* always *written to run in-place. Therefore they can never be run as stand-alone applications (though I don't know why you'd want to, anyway). Typically they are less ambitious than an OLE server. A typical OLE server might be a spreadsheet application that includes charting, reporting, file management, printing, and so on. A typical OLE control might be a grid control that could be the foundation of a spreadsheet—but falls far short of being a spreadsheet, itself.*

There is a special type of COM object called a *collection*. With an OLE collection, many instances of a control (or its data) can be accessed as if they were elements of an array. An OLE collection object can support additional, value-added features; but at its heart it supports adding, locating, accessing, and deleting the objects it contains. These features are provided via the *IEnumVARIANT* interface. I mention this here because many OLE controls, for example those based on the Windows Listbox, can be implemented as collections.

Memory Lights the Corners

Something that has been overlooked in Microsoft's crazed effort to encourage us to move to 32-bit processing, is that Windows 95 and Windows NT's use of a linear 32-bit processing space is far less efficient than Windows 3.1's use of 16-bit space. Windows 95, when running 16-bit applications, does so in a single address space that mimics the Win31 way of doing things: That is, a second copy of an application uses the first copy's code segment. Thus, an application's code is loaded into RAM and occupies RAM only once, no matter how many copies are running. This means, among other things, that the second instance of an application takes less time to start executing than the first. Likewise, a 16-bit DLL is loaded just once and shared by all the applications that need its services.

This is not the case in the 32-bit, linear address space. Each 32-bit application runs in an address space all its own. It is possible for one application to request a shared memory block, but the application loader doesn't do this. The good news is that if one copy of an application trashes its own code, that won't affect other concurrently-running copies of the same application. The bad news is that each copy will occupy memory, requiring more RAM all together; and both copies will take the same amount of time to load. In fact, with page swapping due to the increased memory requirements, the second may take *longer!* That's why Windows 3.1 ran well with 8Mb of memory, while Windows 95 needs at least twice that much memory to run tolerably.

An OLE control's DLL (it usually has an .OCX extension) is typically a bit smaller than an equivalent .VBX—but this is deceiving. In order to run, the OCX requires the services of no fewer than six OLE DLLs plus the MFC DLLs. Thus the first OCX used by any OLE container incurs a substantial overhead in disk space, distribution disks, and setup and application load time. If your application runs in 32-bits, and you allow more than one copy of your app to run at a time, the problem merely becomes worse because each DLL must be loaded separately into the address space of its caller's copy.

Property Types

VBXs support two kinds of properties: standard and custom. The standard properties are pre-implemented; all you have to do is say which ones you want. The custom properties, of course, depend entirely on you for their names, storage characteristics, and implementation.

OCXs extend this idea to include a couple more kinds of property. In addition to custom and standard properties (which are called *stock properties* in OLE), OCXs also have *ambient* and *extended* properties.

The custom properties are set up much as they were in VBXs: You must specify a name for the property and a data type. When creating the control with the OLE Control Wizard (the only sane way to do so), you are also given the option of having the property value stored automatically, or by *set* and *get* functions that you will implement.

Stock Properties

The list of stock properties varies somewhat depending on the version of the OLE Control Wizard you are using. Table 14.1 shows a sample list.

Extended Properties

Now, if you don't see your favorite standard property in this list, don't panic. Some properties that were standard properties in VBXs have been placed in a separated category for OCXs. This category is called *extended properties*, and what makes them distinct from the stock properties is that

Table 14.1 Sample Stock OCX Properties

Stock Property	Description
BackColor, ForeColor	Defines the color to be used in the interior and text or lines of the control, respectively. These properties are similar to their VBX namesakes.
BackStyle	Specifies how text and dotted or dashed lines are to be displayed in the control, Transparent (0) or Opaque (1). Similar to the VBX property of the same name.
Caption, Text	Specifies the text that is the control's label or contents. These two properties are mutually exclusive. They are identical to the VBX properties of the same name.
Enabled	Specifies whether the control can accept keyboard focus. Identical to the VBX property of the same name.
Font	Defines the font to be used in displaying text within this control. This property replaces all the VBX font properties: *FontBold*, *FontItalic*, *FontName*, *FontStrike*, and *FontUnderline*.

these properties are required, and are managed by the container, not by the control. In fact, although the control can obtain the values of these properties, it almost never needs to do so. The list is shown in Table 14.2.

Ambient Properties

The most exciting new properties are the *ambient properties*. The idea is that a control *might* want to change some of these values, but in most cases they can be "inherited" from the container in which they've been placed.

Table 14.2 The Set of OCX Extended Properties

Extended Property	Description
Cancel, Default	Applies to button-type controls; sets the button that will be clicked automatically if the Escape key (Cancel) or Enter key (Default) is pressed. This property is identical to the VBX property of the same name.
Name	Provides the name of the object as given by the container. This property is identical to the VBX property of the same name.
Parent	Identifies the document in which the control is embedded. Controls can use this property to query their own containers.
Visible	Is TRUE if the control is visible. This property is identical to the VBX property of the same name.

For example, how many times have you placed a bunch of label controls on a Visual Basic form (such as an About box), changed the color of the form itself, and then had to laboriously alter the *BackColor* properties of each label to match? With OCX Controls, the *BackColor* ambient property can be used to supply a value to the *BackColor* stock property. If you like, you can even *omit* the stock property, knowing that the control's background color will still be adjustable according to the background color of its container.

Table 14.3 lists the *ambient properties*—and notice the many names that duplicate stock properties.

To retrieve ambient properties, an OLE Control must obtain an interface to its container because ambient properties are *actually* properties of the container, not the control itself! This means that the container *must* be a COM object in its own right...which is why VB4 is an OLE application.

Stock Methods

VBXs have a fairly generous list of available stock methods. The list for OCXs is much smaller, consisting of exactly two: *DoClick* and *Refresh*. *DoClick* simulates a user's mouse click on the control. *Refresh* forces the control to repaint itself.

> *If you wish to implement a collection-like control using the Control Wizard, you'll have to add* AddItem, RemoveItem, *and similar methods yourself. Or, you can write the control from scratch and make it an OLE container by implementing the* IEnumVARIANT *interface.*

Events

As with properties, OLE controls have defined four kinds of event. These are *Request* events, *Before* events, *After* events, and *Do* events. Unlike the four types of properties, however, there is no innate difference among these event types, except for a single argument requirement in two of them.

Request events are those that are triggered before a cancelable operation occurs. In effect, the container is given the chance to cancel this operation. A *Request* event may supply any number of arguments (as any event may), but the final argument is a reference Boolean called *Cancel*. When the event

Table 14.3 The Set of OCX Ambient Properties

Ambient Property	Description
DisplayAsDefaultButton	Button-type controls will read this to learn if they should paint themselves as the default button. (They should be able to get the same information by reading their own *Default* extended property.)
LocaleID	This property allows the control to find out in what country the application in which it's embedded is running.
MessageReflect	If this value is TRUE, messages sent by the control to the container should be automatically reflected back to the container. This is similar to the way the VBX manager sends WM_COMMAND notifications back to a control procedure as VBM_COMMAND messages.
ScaleUnits	This property names the coordinate system being used by the container, for example, "Twips."
ShowGrabHandles	Grab handles are the little thingies that some controls display when they can be moved or resized. If this property is TRUE, and *UIDead* is FALSE, the control should display itself with grab handles.
SupportsMnemonics	If TRUE, the container supports hot keys in labels to allow faster keyboard access to the control.
TextAlign	Text alignment: 0 is default (numbers right justified, text left justified), 1 is left, 2 is center, 3 is right. Full right-and-left justification is specified by a value of 4. Note that these numbers do *not* match the values for the common *TextAlign* property used by many VBXs.
UIDead	In general, will return TRUE if the container's *Enabled* property is FALSE. This allows a container to be disabled and automatically disable all the controls it contains...although why they didn't call this property *Enabled* is not clear to me.
UserMode	This property returns TRUE if the control is being used by an end-user, and FALSE if the form that contains it is in design mode.

is triggered, this argument is given a value of False; however, the event handler can change this to True if the operation the event warns of, is not desired. Although nothing enforces this, we are encouraged to name these events so that the word "Request" is incorporated; for example, *RequestUnload*. *Before* events are fired before processing some external occurrence. For example, the standard Windows edit control generates an *EN_UPDATE* notification each time the contents of the control are about to change, but before the change is actually applied to the control. If you were to use this notification to trigger an event, you might call it *BeforeChange*.

Likewise, *After* events are fired *after* processing has taken place, so they are more of a notification. The *EN_CHANGE* notification, also sent by the Windows standard edit control, is an example of this. If you were use this notification to trigger an event, you might call it *AfterChange*.

Do events are those for which processing has already been implemented, but for which the user/programmer may wish to enhance or replace the implemented behavior. The last argument to such an event is always *EnableDefault*, another Boolean. When the event is triggered, this argument has a value of True. If you wish to replace the original implementation with your own code, just set the argument to False in addition to whatever other handling you do.

Microsoft has encouraged us to use the event type as part of the name: For example, *RequestChange, BeforeChange, AfterChange,* and *DoChange*. I concur with this recommendation. However, they have given us eight stock events and *none* of them follows this convention. The stock events are shown in Table 14.4.

Table 14.4 The Set of OCX Stock Events

Stock Event	Description
Click, DblClick	Triggered when the user clicks any mouse button over the control. The *Click* event is also implemented by some controls to indicate their value has changed—a holdover from VBXs that should *not* have been retained.
Error	Triggered when some asynchronous, external error occurs in your control. This event includes enough arguments for you to make fairly clear to the container what's gone wrong.
KeyDown, KeyUp	Triggered when the user presses or releases a key while this control has the keyboard focus. The key code is passed via a reference argument; your code can change this code to 0 in order to suppress further processing of the keystroke.
MouseDown, MouseMove, MouseUp	Triggered by mouse actions other than clicks, occurring over the control. Unlike the *Click* event, these events include mouse coordinate information.

The VBX/OCX Face-off

There's no doubt that OCXs provide a lot more capability than VBXs. The question is, at what cost do we get this extra power? I set out to test the relative speed of VBXs, 16-bit OCXs, and 32-bit OCXs. I was interested in three things: load time for the respective applications, access time of control properties, and redraw time.

For the first, I wrote a simple loader in C that takes the current time, loads the application (specified on the loader's command line), and calculates and displays the elapsed time:

```
#include <windows.h>

int PASCAL WinMain
    (
    HINSTANCE Instance,
    HINSTANCE Previous,
    LPSTR Command,
    int CmdShow
    )
{
char Buffer[128];
DWORD StartTime = GetTickCount();
WinExec (Command, CmdShow);
wsprintf (Buffer, "%s took %ld milliseconds to start.",
    Command,
    GetTickCount() - StartTime);
MessageBox (NULL, Buffer, "Timed Launch", MB_ICONINFORMATION);
return 0;
}
```

I compiled for 16-bit Windows and called the application **Launch**. To run it, all I have to do is drag an application on top of its name in a Folder or the Explorer.

Next, I designed a custom control that would be simple, to the point, and could be equivalently implemented as a VBX, or an OCX for either 16 or 32-bit execution. This control paints its background white, draws a colored ellipse on top, and has just five properties: *Left, Top, Width, Height,* and *TestMe*—a data sink to test the speed of setting properties.

I won't reproduce the code for the controls here; it's lengthy and most of it is boilerplate anyway—I produced the VBX using VBX Genie, of course, and used the Control Wizard to produce both OCXs. To build a 16-bit OCX, you *must* use Microsoft Visual C++ version 1.52. The Control Wizard that came with earlier versions does not generate OCXs compatible with Visual Basic.

Once installed, it was a simple matter to run Control Wizard, accept the defaults, and generate the OCX skeleton. I then enhanced the *OnDraw()* function to match my VBX, and added the *TestMe* property. (OCXs have size and position properties built-in.)

I built the project with the release libraries, including optimizations, which more closely approximates the way real release controls would be packaged. I told the compiler to aim at 386 or better CPUs, since you can't run Windows 95 or Visual Basic 4 on anything less, anyway.

In theory, you should be able to take your 16-bit OCX and simply recompile under a 32-bit processor to get a 32-bit OCX. I suppose this *was* true when Visual C++ 2.2 was the current version. However, I am now doing 32-bit compiles (when I do them at all!) with Visual C++ 4, and I got a link error when trying to compile the older Control Wizard code. Rather than wrestle with it, I just used the newer Control Wizard to generate an equivalent OCX, copied the drawing code from the 16-bit OCX, and compiled that. The full compile and link for 32-bits took over 15 minutes. (Perhaps I should mention that I *am* running Windows 95 on a 386-40 with 8Mb of memory, far less of a machine than Microsoft recommends. But, still.)

With my three controls compiled, I was ready for my first comparison: file size. All three controls were compiled for release, aimed at 80386 CPUs, and optimized for speed as shown in Table 14.5.

Here the VBX loses—until you realize that the OCXs must be distributed with the massive OLE and MFC DLLs.

Next I created three Visual Basic 4 projects. Each was identical to the others, except for the control that appeared on *Form1*. Each had two small blocks of code. One was attached to a command button, and timed the control's ability to send data to a property:

```
Private Sub Command1_Click()
```

Table 14.5   File Size Comparison of the Three Controls

Control Type	File Size
VBX	31.9 K
16-bit OCX	21.4 K
32-bit OCX	23.0 K

```
Dim StartTime As Date
StartTime = Now
MousePointer = vbHourglass
Dim i As Integer
For i = 1 To 20000
   FaceOff.TestMe = i
Next i
MsgBox "Operation took " + _
   Format$(Now - StartTime, "ss") + _
   " seconds."
MousePointer = vbDefault
End Sub
```

The other resizes the control as the form is resized, allowing for a visual estimation of redraw speed:

```
Private Sub Form_Resize()
Command1.Top = ScaleHeight - (Command1.Height * 1.5)
Command1.Left = ScaleWidth - Command1.Width - 300
FaceOff.Width = ScaleWidth - (300 * 2)
FaceOff.Height = Command1.Top - (300 * 1.5)
End Sub
```

I then started my speed tests. The tests are easy to run; you just drag the name of each VB app to LAUNCH.EXE, note the reported load time, then click the Test button and try resizing the form. I ran the tests on my 386-40 8Mb and my 486-100 8Mb laptop. Microsoft recommends 12Mb for Windows 95, but the people I've talked to agree that 16Mb is much better, and 32Mb is even better than that! Unfortunately, I'm just a poor writer and can't afford machines as powerful as Bill Gates can.

To be sure the loading results weren't skewed by DLLs already loaded, I disabled the Microsoft Office "Fast Start" app, which pre-loads the OLE DLLs, and performed each set of tests on a freshly-booted computer. Anyway, Table 14.6 shows the results for the load test, in seconds. Table 14.7 shows the results for the set property timings.

Table 14.6 The Results of Loading the Three DLLs

Control Type	386-40/8Mb	486-100/8Mb
VBX	14	10.5
16-bit OCX	44	15
32-bit OCX	13*	

*Because the 32-bit app runs in a preemptive multitasking space, the Launcher reported a much shorter time than it actually took for the app to appear. On the 386, for example, it actually took almost a minute.

Table 14.7 The Results for the Set Property Timings

Control Type	386-40/8Mb	486-100/8Mb
VBX	4	1
16-bit OCX	11	3
32-bit OCX	5	

I developed the controls on my desktop 386. When I tried to transport the applications to my laptop (using Setup Wizard) I experienced *another* unpleasant surprise: The 32-bit OCX refuses to self-register! That's because the 32-bit Setup Wizard has its own set of problems, quite separate from the ones we worked around for the 16-bit version. At the time of this writing, after three weeks of research, I have been unable to find out what the problem is. So I'm unable to actually install an application using a 32-bit OCX onto another computer. Hopefully a fix for this problem will be released by the time this books hits the shelves—keep an eye out on the Coriolis Home Page on the Net for latest developments.

The conclusion I come to, to put it bluntly, is that OLE controls are only worth using if you actually need their extra abilities—that would include using them in a 32-bit VB application, of course—and are willing to devote a lot of effort to wrestling with an immature technology. But if you intend to stick with VB4-16, or even VB3 (VB3 apps load a *lot* faster than VB4 apps), you may not need the OLE Control technology at all.

Creating a Simple OCX

15

AS I WAS DOING IT, I knew I shouldn't have done it. It was too late, too dark, and too cold. But there I was, hiking by myself at night, in winter. I had left later than I intended, and arrived at the trailhead too late, and now I was trudging along in the dark. I could barely make out the night-gray sky above the skeletal fingers of the winter trees; but my flashlight prevented me from seeing *anything* except its narrow beam, so I managed to follow the white swath of trail without it.

Stupid, stupid, stupid, I kept thinking to myself. *I should have turned back when I saw it was getting dark. I could've gone back home. I should turn around now!* But I didn't. I made my way along the trail in silence, awed by the hush of the frozen forest. I had been here many times in other seasons; but then the woods had been alive with noise. Now there wasn't a sound anywhere; even the air hung still. The snow was soft and made only the slightest whisper as I waded through it.

Suddenly, I stumbled on a hidden rock and swore in surprise. From above came an odd sound: *crack, crack-crack-crack-crack.* My heart leaped into my throat. I expected to hear a branch crash to the ground, perhaps under the weight of too much snow, but no such crash occurred.

Hesitantly, I resumed my hike. The spot I'd chosen on the topographic map for my campsite shouldn't be much farther ahead. My pack felt unbalanced after my near-fall, and I hiked it up, jostling its contents. A can of soup rang against a pan inside. Instantly, there it was again: *crack, crack-crack-crack-crack.* What could it be?

Even though the sound came from above, I began to think of all the things that lived in these woods. There were deer—what do deer *do* in the winter, anyway? I had seen *Bambi* years ago, but all I could remember was that when spring came along, they danced with skunks and rabbits and fell in love. And bears lived here—that was cool; they hibernated. But what if I woke one up? Wouldn't he be hungry and *really* annoyed?

I suddenly realized that, both times I had heard the strange sound, I had first made a noise of my own. I caught my breath, determined to face whatever it was, and clapped my hands together. *Crack, crack-crack-crack-crack! Crack-crack-crack...!* The sky came alive with the flapping of enormous wings as vultures leapt off their bedroom branches into the air—one per tree. Hungry, maybe; *certainly* annoyed. But vultures wouldn't harm me. I started shaking in relief. I had no idea I'd been so freaked. But it was all right. Winter or not, night or not, it was still the forest I knew fairly well, and I could relax.

Working on your first OCX (OLE control) can be a lot like my nighttime walk in the woods. You know so little—there's so much there, and so much hidden in C++ classes and the COM specifications. Windows was complicated enough, and VBXs had so many moving parts—but at least all those parts were knowable. We are expected to create OCXs without really knowing what the underlying framework is doing, and it's a scary prospect. I can't make OCXs any simpler. But at least I can go with you, figuratively speaking, so you don't have to walk this trail alone.

What we're going to do is create as simple an OCX as we can, using the Control Wizard; and then walk through the generated code. That'll give you a base from which you can add features, and be able to tell the new code generated for the features, from the code that is the bare minimum needed to implement an OCX.

As I've mentioned earlier, there are two types of OCX: 16-bit and 32-bit. The 16-bit OCXs must be created with the Control Wizard that comes with Microsoft Visual C++ 1.52x; earlier versions of Control Wizard appear to work but the resulting OCXs can't actually be used with Visual Basic 4.

32-bit OCXs must be generated by the Control Wizard that comes with Microsoft Visual C++ 2.2 (again, earlier versions don't actually work), or Microsoft Visual C++ 4. Since VC++ 4 is the latest version (as of this writing), that's the one we'll use. And, with it (on a separate, included CD-ROM) is the latest 16-bit version, Visual C++ 1.52c.

Creating a 16-bit OCX

After you have installed Visual C++ 1.52c—and you must request the OLE tools when you do so—you must install the Control Wizard as a separate step. This installation adds Control Wizard to MSVC's *Tools* menu. It doesn't matter if you already have a project opened in the MSVC IDE or not; Control Wizard creates a new project for you. Its main window looks like the one shown in Figure 15.1.

The Project Name entry serves the same purpose as with App Wizard. And, as with App Wizard, the project name is automatically duplicated in the New Subdirectory field. You can revise the name of the new subdirectory if you like, even blanking it out to use an existing directory; but don't try to create a new project in a directory in which an older project already exists. Visual C++ wizards insist on having just one project per directory.

Also note that Visual C++ 1.5x tools, including the Control Wizard, do not understand Windows 95 long file names. The names you see in the

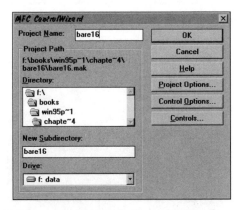

Figure 15.1 Creating a new project with Control Wizard.

Directory list are the 8.3 file name synonyms Win95 presents to 16-bit applications.

Clicking the Project Options button brings up the Project Options dialog as shown in Figure 15.2.

Checking the Context Sensitive Help checkbox encourages Control Wizard to generate a set of files that serve as a head start for online help for the control. These files will be in RTF format, and very few people actually do their help files that way. Still, if you do, this can be a nice head-start.

"External Makefile" is for holdouts who are still running command-line compilers. "Source Comments" will include some helpful comments to the generated files. You'll want to check this, at least on the first few OCXs you write. "License validation" generates both a .LIC file to accompany your project, and code within the project to require its presence. If the control is being used within a runtime environment, it doesn't matter if the .LIC is there or not. However, the control will refuse to be loaded into a design-time environment unless the license file is present. This allows you to write and sell a control and prevent an end-user who buys the application using this control, from developing further applications with it without buying the control itself.

The Control Options dialog, as shown in Figure 15.3, is activated by clicking the Control Options button.

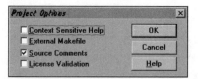

Figure 15.2 Using the Project Options dialog.

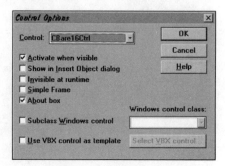

Figure 15.3 Using the Control Options dialog.

At this time there will be just one control in the combo box. Use the Controls button to add more if you wish. "Activate when visible," if checked, tells the eventual control container that the .OCX should be loaded and active whenever this control can be seen. Unchecked, the control behaves more like a non-control OLE server: It will be painted in a default fashion until the user or the application actually causes it to become active. Because of the nature of controls, which are almost always present for the explicit purpose of allowing the user instant response to a user interface interaction, this checkbox is almost always checked. (That is its default value, anyway.)

You have seen the Insert Object dialog box; it is available to any OLE container application and contains a list of OLE object types that may be inserted into the container. Strictly speaking, an OLE control *is* an OLE object. However, it is highly unlikely that the author of a word processing document or the like, will really want to add a button or list box object to the document, no matter how pretty your button or list box is. So, to avoid cluttering up the Insert Object list box, we usually leave the "Show in Insert Object dialog" checkbox unselected.

The meaning of the "Invisible at runtime" checkbox is just as you'd expect. However, you should note that this is a *suggestion*, not anything that is (or can be) enforced. It is up to the container. In most cases, however, the suggestion is followed and if the checkbox is checked, the control will only be painted if the document or form it's on is in design mode.

If you've used Visual Basic, you know how the Frame control works: Unlike the Group box in standard Windows applications, which is merely decorative, the VB Frame actually acts as a container for other controls. Then, if the Frame is disabled, all the controls on it are also disabled; if it is made invisible, so are the controls it contains; if it is moved, all the controls on it move with it; and so on. It's nice to know the ability to write such controls has not been lost with the move to OLE; and checking the "Simple Frame" checkbox enables it.

The About Box provides an easy way for your programmers to check the version and other information you care to supply with your control. End users, of course, never see it. Checking this option will produce the about box files automatically as part of your control. Note that the format of the About Box, when produced by the 16-bit Control Wizard, will be the (now quaint) style favored by Microsoft in Windows for Workgroups' salad days— you may want to modify this.

If your OCX is going to be an improvement on a standard Windows control as seen by the Visual Basic IDE—for example, you want an owner-draw list box, or a scroll bar that allows a range wider than 32K—you can select the underlying Windows control by checking "Subclass Windows control" and selecting it from the "Windows control class" combo box. You can write into the combo box, so if you want to subclass a control you've written or purchased, rather than one of the standard Windows controls, you can do so. (However, you'll have to write code in the control to load the base control's DLL.) Remember, though, that you are writing a 16-bit OCX—and therefore, you can only subclass a 16-bit control. This leaves out the nifty new controls Windows 95 has added for 32-bit applications.

If you have an existing VBX that you'd like to convert into an OCX, the "Use VBX control as template" button will be of enormous help. You'll have to press the "Select VBX control" button to select the VBX, of course. But then Control Wizard will load the VBX, read its *MODEL* structure, and duplicate the control name and properties and events from the VBX. Of course, it cannot copy the *code*—it just provides equivalent support for the names. But this is a substantial portion of the work; and copying over your VBX code for *implementing* those properties and events shouldn't be a very complex job. (Especially if you created your VBX using the VBX Genie, so that the support for each property is coded in a separate function.)

Like VBXs, OCXs can be homes to more than one control. While a multi-control VBX is slightly more efficient than storing one control per VBX, a multi-control OCX can be a *lot* more efficient—especially if it's likely that more than one of the packaged controls will be used by the same application. This is because of the time it takes to load the DLL itself (as detailed in the previous chapter). To describe each of the controls in your OCX, click the Controls button to see the Controls dialog as shown in Figure 15.4.

When the dialog appears, it already contains your first entry—its name is derived from the project name—and the entries in the various text boxes apply to it. To add a control, click the "Add Control" button. The new control name will be the same as the first, with the digit "1" appended. Obviously, this is not intended to be a useful name—plan on changing it. As you click on one entry or another in the list box, the textbox contents will change, always tracking the selected control. If you wish to remove a control, selecting it and clicking the "Delete control" button will do the trick.

The "Short Name" is the name by which the control will be known internally to the OLE subsystem. This includes entries in the System Registry, and

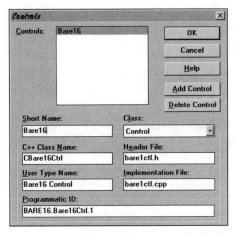

Figure 15.4   Describing the controls using the Controls dialog.

is opposed to the "User Type Name," which is how the control will be labeled when a user queries the system for available OLE controls. The "C++ Class Name" identifies the same entity from the standpoint of the code that will be placed in the "Header file" and "Implementation file" you specify. The combo box labeled "Class" has no other options in it, in spite of the documentation that says otherwise.

The "Programmatic ID" follows the standards of OLE Automation, and identifies the control, first by the name of the OCX in which it resides, and then by yet another variation of its name. The terminating one seems to be a constant; if you add another control, its programmatic ID will also end with the digit "1."

Checking and Changing the Control Settings

As with App Wizard, Control Wizard will display a dialog detailing its intentions, giving you one last chance to reconsider before letting it spew forth the requested project. In this example, where we have gone entirely with default values, the New Control Information dialog looks like the one shown in Figure 15.5.

Do read this information. If you click Cancel now, you'll be back at the Control Wizard dialog, able to modify whatever option you forgot or got wrong. Once you click OK, the only practical way to change any of these options is to go through the entire procedure again, more carefully.

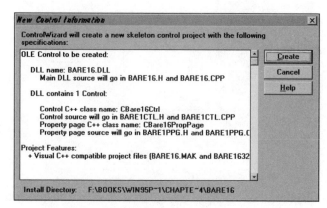

Figure 15.5 Checking the control setting using the New Control Information dialog.

While the Control Wizard is generating files, a small status box appears to let you know the name of each file as it is generated. When it's done—and it doesn't take long—Visual C++ will open the new project for you and you're ready to go.

Your *very first step* is one you will probably *always* forget...so pay attention. On the *Tools* menu, in addition to *Control Wizard*, you'll find an entry labeled, *Make TypeLib*. This required step has been integrated into the 32-bit environment, but here in 16-bits you have to explicitly perform it. What's more, you need to *re*-run it before you compile, after adding properties, events, or methods to one of the controls in this project. The file this step produces is called the Type Library, and it is used to register your control to the OLE subsystem on the computers on which applications using your control will be installed.

Even though every single time but this one, you'll want to make changes to the skeleton Control Wizard generates, it's still a good idea to do a preliminary compile of the project as it is now. That'll give you a chance to verify project settings and directory locations, because if anything is awry it'll generate error messages during the compile or the link.

Creating a 32-bit OCX

The 16-bit Control Wizard, when generating the project files for an OCX, includes a .MAK file for a matching 32-bit OCX. You can spot it because it has the digits "32" appended to the name. For example, the project file for the OCX produced in the previous section was called Bare16.MAK; but there's another file in the same folder called Bare1632.MAK.

Unfortunately, this file is intended for use with Visual C++ 2.2, which is now obsolete. If you load it as a workspace file into Visual C++ 4, it will be converted and everything will look fine—until you try to build the project. It fails during the link step, unable to find a file called OCS30D.LIB. This file is a component of MFC 3, and is included with neither Visual C++ 1.52c nor Visual C++ 4.

Changing the references in BARE1632.MAK from "OCS30" to "OCS40" doesn't seem to make a difference—rebuilding, the linker still asks for the same files. And I was unable to find any place in the IDE where this dependency was indicated.

So it seems that building a 32-bit OCX must be done from scratch. Fortunately, this is not as big a deal as it could be. After all, Control Wizard—the 32-bit version—still does most of the work. And I'll offer a suggestion later in the chapter, for simplifying the task of maintaining source code for both versions.

In Visual C++ 4, Control Wizard is no longer a separate tool. To create an OCX project, you use the *File* menu and choose *New...*, just as you would any other project. The New dialog appears, offering you a choice of new things to make; you simply select Project Workspace and click OK.

It's the New Project Workspace dialog where you say what *kind* of workspace you wish to create—and "OLE ControlWizard" is one of your choices, as shown in Figure 15.6.

In this case, the Create button doesn't yet create the actual project; instead it kicks off the first Control Wizard panel—for this new version of Control Wizard uses the same multi-page approach we took with the Setup Wizard Workaround in Chapter 12. Figure 15.7 shows the updated dialog.

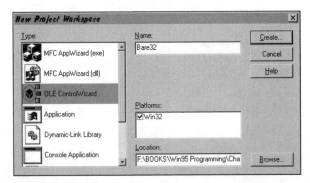

Figure 15.6 Creating a workspace with the New Project Workspace dialog.

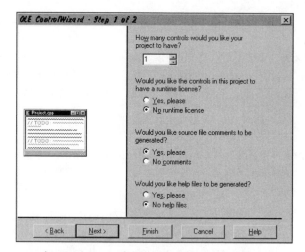

Figure 15.7 Using the OLE ControlWizard dialog.

The choices here are, of course, the same as they were in the 16-bit version. Of interest is the first question: How many controls do you wish to place in this OCX? You now specify this number up front, and it can range from 1 to 99.

There are two interesting things on the next page as shown in Figure 15.8.

The first is that this is your opportunity to modify the default names for control, classes, and files. Clicking the Edit Names button displays the appropriate dialog shown in Figure 15.9.

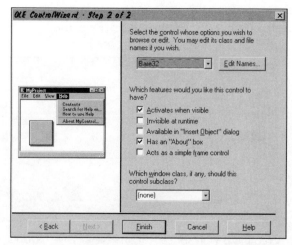

Figure 15.8 Reviewing the second page of the OLE ControlWizard dialog.

Figure 15.9 Using the Edit Names dialog.

Here, finally, is that control over the property page names that the 16-bit Control Wizard didn't provide.

The second interesting thing about the second Control Wizard page is the list of window classes the OLE control can subclass. In addition to the original Windows classes, this list now contains all the new Windows 95 classes as well. Table 15.1 provides the complete list.

When you click the Finish button, as with the 16-bit Control Wizard, you get a last chance to read over your selected options and make sure they are what you want, as shown in Figure 15.10.

Figure 15.10 Checking the New Product Information dialog.

Table 15.1 Window Classes That Can Be Subclassed from the OLE Control

Window Class	Description
BUTTON	The original Windows push button. This class also includes all traditional variations, such as radio (option) buttons, checkboxes, and the group box frame.
COMBOBOX	The traditional combo box in all three variations: simple, drop down, and drop down list.
LISTBOX	The traditional list box with its variations: Single, multiple and extended selection, multi-column, tabular, and so on.
msctls_hotkey32	Available only to 32-bit OCXs, and only in Windows 95 or Windows NT 4.0, this is a window that enables the user to create a hot key. A "hot key" is a key combination that the user can press to perform an action quickly.
msctls_progressbar32	Available only to 32-bit OCXs, and only in Windows 95 or Windows NT 4.0. This is a window that an application can use to indicate the progress of a lengthy operation through the filling of a rectangle with color.
msctls_statusbar32	Available only to 32-bit OCXs, and only in Windows 95 or Windows NT 4.0. This is a horizontal window in a parent window in which an application can display various kinds of status information. This control resembles the MFC *CStatusBar* class, so it should be possible to simulate this in a 16-bit OCX.
msctls_trackbar32	(Also known as a "slider.") Available only to 32-bit OCXs, and only in Windows 95 or Windows NT 4.0. This is a window containing a slider and optional tick marks that sends notification messages to indicate changes in its position.
msctls_updown32	(Also known as "Spin control.") Available only to 32-bit OCXs, and only in Windows 95 or Windows NT 4.0. This is a pair of arrow buttons that the user can click to increment or decrement a value, such as a scroll position or a number displayed in a companion control. Note that Microsoft *still* hasn't officially combined this control with any kind of readout, which is how everyone uses it.
SCROLLBAR	The tradition scroll bar in both its vertical and horizontal flavors.
STATIC	The traditional static control; it can display text *or* an icon.
msctls_SysAnimate32	Available only to 32-bit OCXs, and only in Windows 95 or Windows NT 4.0. This is a window that displays successive frames of an Audio Video Interleaved (AVI) clip during a lengthy operation.

Continued

Table 15.1 Window Classes That Can Be Subclassed from the OLE Control (Continued)

Window Class	Description
msctls_Header32	Available only to 32-bit OCXs, and only in Windows 95 or Windows NT 4.0. This is a resizable button that appears above a column of text, allowing the user to display more or less information in the column.
msctls_ListView32	Available only to 32-bit OCXs, and only in Windows 95 or Windows NT 4.0. This window class is currently undocumented.
msctls_TabControl32	Available only to 32-bit OCXs, and only in Windows 95 or Windows NT 4.0. This sets up buttons that look like the dividers in a notebook or the labels in a file cabinet. By using a tab control, an application can define multiple pages for the same area of a window or dialog box.
msctls_TreeView32	Available only to 32-bit OCXs, and only in Windows 95 or Windows NT 4.0. This is a window that displays a hierarchical list of items, such as headings in a document, the entries in an index, or the files and directories on a disk. Each item consists of a label and an optional image, and each item can have a list of sub-items associated with it.

As before, if this is not *exactly* what you want, click Cancel and make the desired modifications. When you click OK, your project will be generated as shown in Figure 15.11.

At this point, you can do your initial build. This first build takes a *long* time and, depending on how much memory you have in your computer, you may even have to close all other applications and/or restart Windows.

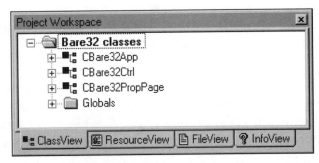

Figure 15.11 Generating the final project.

However, as long as you preserve the various intermediate files, subsequent rebuilds after minor changes such as adding code to the skeleton, take a much shorter time thanks to incremental compiling and linking.

Examining the Code

Since we've just generated two OCXs—one for 16-bit and one for 32-bit—I thought it might be instructive if we examined the code for both, one after the other.

An OCX—as opposed to the controls it contains—is represented by a single module. In this case, the header file for this module is BARE16.H/BARE32.H. Except for the name difference, the contents are identical:

```
// bare16.h : main header file for BARE16.DLL

#if !defined( __AFXCTL_H__ )
   #error include 'afxctl.h' before including this file
#endif

#include "resource.h"        // main symbols

/////////////////////////////////////////////////////////////////////////////
// CBare16App : See bare16.cpp for implementation.

class CBare16App : public COleControlModule
{
public:
   BOOL InitInstance();
   int ExitInstance();
};

extern const GUID CDECL _tlid;
extern const WORD _wVerMajor;
extern const WORD _wVerMinor;
```

It's interesting that the default-generated name for the derived class ends in *App*. You can override this, of course, before Control Wizard generates the code. Most people don't bother, however, because you seldom actually have to work with this code.

The class *COleControlModule*, an extension to MFC version 2.5 (used by Visual C++ 1.52) and a part of MFC 4, encapsulates, as the name states, OLE controls. Only the *InitInstance()* and *ExitInstance()* methods must be overriden in an actual control, as Control Wizard does in BARE16.CPP/BARE32/CPP:

```
// bare16.cpp : Implementation of CBare16App and DLL registration.

#include "stdafx.h"
#include "bare16.h"

#ifdef _DEBUG
#undef THIS_FILE
static char BASED_CODE THIS_FILE[] = __FILE__;
#endif


CBare16App NEAR theApp;

const GUID CDECL BASED_CODE _tlid =
{ 0xbf3c5063, 0x5433, 0x11cf, { 0xb4, 0x27, 0x44, 0x45, 0x53, 0x54, 0x0, 0x0 } };
const WORD _wVerMajor = 1;
const WORD _wVerMinor = 0;
// Bare32.cpp : Implementation of CBare32App and DLL registration.

#include "stdafx.h"
#include "Bare32.h"

#ifdef _DEBUG
#define new DEBUG_NEW
#undef THIS_FILE
static char THIS_FILE[] = __FILE__;
#endif


CBare32App NEAR theApp;

const GUID CDECL BASED_CODE _tlid =
{ 0x8af31f00, 0x54b0, 0x11cf, { 0xb4, 0x27, 0x44, 0x45, 0x53, 0x54, 0, 0 } };
const WORD _wVerMajor = 1;
const WORD _wVerMinor = 0;
```

In each case, one single instance of the *COleControlModule*-derived class
is created. A constant initialized with each module's globally unique ID is
defined; the values differ between each module as they always will. (If
one of these projects were to be regenerated, its GUID would be different
still.) The major and minor versions are also defined as constants, and will
be available throughout the project, since they are (as you saw in the
header file) declared as **extern**s. Please note that these values are *not*
locked to the values of the same name in the VERSIONINFO resource.
Should you have occasion to update the resource, don't forget to update
these constants as well.

Again, except for names, *InitInstance()* and *ExitInstance()* are identical in
the two OCXs:

```
BOOL CBare16App::InitInstance()
{
   BOOL bInit = COleControlModule::InitInstance();

   if (bInit)
   {
      // TODO: Add your own module initialization code here.
   }

   return bInit;
}

int CBare16App::ExitInstance()
{
   // TODO: Add your own module termination code here.

   return COleControlModule::ExitInstance();
}
```

If you wanted to do something special when the OCX was loaded or unloaded—display a banner, perhaps—these are the functions you would modify. Normally you can leave them alone.

OCXs are self-registering (more or less), thanks to functions that do not belong to any classes, but reside in the module implementation file anyway:

```
STDAPI DllRegisterServer(void)
{
   AFX_MANAGE_STATE(_afxModuleAddrThis);

   if (!AfxOleRegisterTypeLib(AfxGetInstanceHandle(), _tlid))
      return ResultFromScode(SELFREG_E_TYPELIB);

   if (!COleObjectFactoryEx::UpdateRegistryAll(TRUE))
      return ResultFromScode(SELFREG_E_CLASS);

   return NOERROR;
}
```

An "Scode" is a structured value that returns, not a simple "failed" or "succeeded," but a whole range of values from "total failure" through "sort of failed" through "more or less succeeded" to "total success." In reality, this complex value is way more information than is required; so the *ResultFromScode()* macro is used to boil it down to a simple TRUE or FALSE.

A similar function can unregister the OCX if necessary:

```
STDAPI DllUnregisterServer(void)
{
   AFX_MANAGE_STATE(_afxModuleAddrThis);

   if (!AfxOleUnregisterTypeLib(_tlid))
      return ResultFromScode(SELFREG_E_TYPELIB);

   if (!COleObjectFactoryEx::UpdateRegistryAll(FALSE))
      return ResultFromScode(SELFREG_E_CLASS);

   return NOERROR;
}
```

The control itself is declared in a pair of files whose names were, of course, derived from the name of the OCX. In real life, you'd probably want to change these; I left them alone to see what we'd get. Because the 16-bit Control Wizard is restricted to 8.3 file names, BARE16CTL.H becomes BARE1CTL.H. The 32-bit Control Wizard permits long file names, so BARE32CTL.H it is. Still, no change in the code:

```
// bare1ctl.h : Declaration of the CBare16Ctrl OLE control class.

/////////////////////////////////////////////////////////////////
// CBare16Ctrl : See bare1ctl.cpp for implementation.

class CBare16Ctrl : public COleControl
{
   DECLARE_DYNCREATE(CBare16Ctrl)

// Constructor
public:
   CBare16Ctrl();

// Overrides

   // Drawing function
   virtual void OnDraw(
         CDC* pdc, const CRect& rcBounds, const CRect& rcInvalid);

   // Persistence
   virtual void DoPropExchange(CPropExchange* pPX);

   // Reset control state
   virtual void OnResetState();

// Implementation
protected:
   ~CBare16Ctrl();
```

```
      DECLARE_OLECREATE_EX(CBare16Ctrl)      // Class factory and guid
      DECLARE_OLETYPELIB(CBare16Ctrl)        // GetTypeInfo
      DECLARE_PROPPAGEIDS(CBare16Ctrl)       // Property page IDs
      DECLARE_OLECTLTYPE(CBare16Ctrl)        // Type name and misc status

  // Message maps
  //{{AFX_MSG(CBare16Ctrl)
      // NOTE - ClassWizard will add and remove member functions here.
      //    DO NOT EDIT what you see in these blocks of generated code !
  //}}AFX_MSG
  DECLARE_MESSAGE_MAP()

  // Dispatch maps
  //{{AFX_DISPATCH(CBare16Ctrl)
      // NOTE - ClassWizard will add and remove member functions here.
      //    DO NOT EDIT what you see in these blocks of generated code !
  //}}AFX_DISPATCH
  DECLARE_DISPATCH_MAP()

  afx_msg void AboutBox();

  // Event maps
  //{{AFX_EVENT(CBare16Ctrl)
      // NOTE - ClassWizard will add and remove member functions here.
      //    DO NOT EDIT what you see in these blocks of generated code !
  //}}AFX_EVENT
  DECLARE_EVENT_MAP()

  // Dispatch and event IDs
  public:
    enum {
  //{{AFX_DISP_ID(CBare16Ctrl)
      // NOTE: ClassWizard will add and remove enumeration elements here.
      //    DO NOT EDIT what you see in these blocks of generated code !
  //}}AFX_DISP_ID
    };
};
```

As is common in Microsoft-generated code, much of the action is hidden in macros. This helps the Control Wizard to avoid making typing mistakes, I suppose. As with App Wizard, it is *crucial* that you follow the advice against modifying certain sections of code. Class Wizard has *no* sense of humor when it comes to your modifying the blocks it owns. Areas that are *not* so marked, you can modify—at your own risk of course. I know from experience that reformatting the code causes no harm. And it's certainly all right to add method prototypes for class functions you intend to add. But I'd advise against *removing* any of the method or property entries Control Wizard generated for you.

The implementation files are BARE1CTL.CPP and BARE32CTL.CPP. They begin by invoking the macro that supports dynamic object creation:

```
// bare1ctl.cpp : Implementation of the CBare16Ctrl OLE control class.

#include "stdafx.h"
#include "bare16.h"
#include "bare1ctl.h"
#include "bare1ppg.h"


#ifdef _DEBUG
#undef THIS_FILE
static char BASED_CODE THIS_FILE[] = __FILE__;
#endif


IMPLEMENT_DYNCREATE(CBare16Ctrl, COleControl)
```

The message map, as with all MFC applications...er, controls...er, *things*—handles the routing of any Window messages or menu commands to the desired object. Of course, in an OLE control, there won't be any messages from menus and the control itself will supply the only window from which messages need to be processed. So this mechanism might seem a tad overkill for the job at hand. Still, this is the way MFC handles messages and Class Wizard seems to like it:

```
/////////////////////////////////////////////////////////////////////////
// Message map

BEGIN_MESSAGE_MAP(CBare16Ctrl, COleControl)
   //{{AFX_MSG_MAP(CBare16Ctrl)
   // NOTE - ClassWizard will add and remove message map entries
   //     DO NOT EDIT what you see in these blocks of generated code !
   //}}AFX_MSG_MAP
   ON_OLEVERB(AFX_IDS_VERB_PROPERTIES, OnProperties)
END_MESSAGE_MAP()
```

The Dispatch Map is conceptually similar to the Message Map. The difference is that it dispatches OLE messages from the interfaces to MFC. In other words, when your control's container sets a property or invokes a method, the Dispatch Map will make sure the right code is executed to satisfy the request:

```
/////////////////////////////////////////////////////////////////////////
// Dispatch map

BEGIN_DISPATCH_MAP(CBare16Ctrl, COleControl)
   //{{AFX_DISPATCH_MAP(CBare16Ctrl)
   // NOTE - ClassWizard will add and remove dispatch map entries
```

```
//    DO NOT EDIT what you see in these blocks of generated code !
//}}AFX_DISPATCH_MAP
DISP_FUNCTION_ID(CBare16Ctrl, "AboutBox", DISPID_ABOUTBOX, AboutBox,
VT_EMPTY, VTS_NONE)
END_DISPATCH_MAP()
```

Events are also managed by OLE through interfaces, but because they are triggered by the control, rather than the control's behavior, there is a separate map for them:

```
/////////////////////////////////////////////////////////////////////////
// Event map

BEGIN_EVENT_MAP(CBare16Ctrl, COleControl)
   //{{AFX_EVENT_MAP(CBare16Ctrl)
   // NOTE - ClassWizard will add and remove event map entries
   //     DO NOT EDIT what you see in these blocks of generated code !
   //}}AFX_EVENT_MAP
END_EVENT_MAP()
```

Supporting Property Pages

You should be familiar by now with the toolbox in Visual Basic, and you know that Visual C++ 4's App Studio has one, too, when designing a dialog box or other form. You know that an OCX, adding to the list of custom controls, shows up in the toolbox. Now, in Visual Basic, the control's properties are listed in a Property box. Visual C++, on the other hand, uses Property Pages, a new type of resource that developers for Windows 95 are encouraged to use.

Property Pages are a set of tabbed forms on a dialog. Each tab has a name for the properties it groups, like "Font" or "Color" or whatever. OLE controls are modified, at design time, by property pages; so there is a structure for their definition:

```
/////////////////////////////////////////////////////////////////////////
// Property pages

// TODO: Add more property pages as needed.  Remember to increase the count!
BEGIN_PROPPAGEIDS(CBare16Ctrl, 1)
   PROPPAGEID(CBare16PropPage::guid)
END_PROPPAGEIDS(CBare16Ctrl)
```

The one page you are supplied by default is named "General;" users will expect that to be the first page on the dialog. There are a couple of stock property pages you can use; any others you will need to design. (We'll do this in the next chapter.)

Supporting the Registration Database

The next block of identifiers contains information that works with the Registration database—a number of GUIDs are required for almost every aspect of your control:

```
/////////////////////////////////////////////////////////////////////////
// Initialize class factory and guid

IMPLEMENT_OLECREATE_EX(CBare16Ctrl, "BARE16.Bare16Ctrl.1",
   0xbf3c5060, 0x5433, 0x11cf, 0xb4, 0x27, 0x44, 0x45, 0x53, 0x54, 0x0, 0x0)


/////////////////////////////////////////////////////////////////////////
// Type library ID and version

IMPLEMENT_OLETYPELIB(CBare16Ctrl, _tlid, _wVerMajor, _wVerMinor)


/////////////////////////////////////////////////////////////////////////
// Interface IDs

const IID BASED_CODE IID_DBare16 =
    { 0xbf3c5061, 0x5433, 0x11cf, { 0xb4, 0x27, 0x44, 0x45, 0x53, 0x54, 0x0,
0x0 } };
const IID BASED_CODE IID_DBare16Events =
    { 0xbf3c5062, 0x5433, 0x11cf, { 0xb4, 0x27, 0x44, 0x45, 0x53, 0x54, 0x0,
0x0 } };
```

Note the reference to _wVerMajor and _wVerMinor, remembering again that these constants' values are independent of those in the VERSIONINFO resource, which is used to actually deploy these OCXs to users' machines.

The various options you specified when creating the control show up next, as coded elements of an array:

```
/////////////////////////////////////////////////////////////////////////
// Control type information

static const DWORD BASED_CODE _dwBare16OleMisc =
   OLEMISC_ACTIVATEWHENVISIBLE |
   OLEMISC_SETCLIENTSITEFIRST |
   OLEMISC_INSIDEOUT |
   OLEMISC_CANTLINKINSIDE |
   OLEMISC_RECOMPOSEONRESIZE;

IMPLEMENT_OLECTLTYPE(CBare16Ctrl, IDS_BARE16, _dwBare16OleMisc)
```

One of those macros in the header file created an *embedded class* in *CBare16Ctrl* or *CBare32Ctrl*, respectively. It is a class factory, required by

OLE to actually create instances of this control. Most of the factory is implemented by macro as well; but one method must be explicitly supplied:

```
//////////////////////////////////////////////////////////////////////
// CBare16Ctrl::CBare16CtrlFactory::UpdateRegistry -
// Adds or removes system registry entries for CBare16Ctrl

BOOL CBare16Ctrl::CBare16CtrlFactory::UpdateRegistry(BOOL bRegister)
{
  if (bRegister)
    return AfxOleRegisterControlClass(
      AfxGetInstanceHandle(),
      m_clsid,
      m_lpszProgID,
      IDS_BARE16,
      IDB_BARE16,
      FALSE,                       //  Not insertable
      _dwBare16OleMisc,
      _tlid,
      _wVerMajor,
      _wVerMinor);
  else
    return AfxOleUnregisterClass(m_clsid, m_lpszProgID);
}
```

Remember, here we are registering the control; the registration code we saw a few pages back was for registering the *OCX*. See, it's the NRA's worst nightmare: *Everything* gets registered.

Now we get to the code that you may actually find yourself modifying. First, there's the control's constructor and destructor:

```
//////////////////////////////////////////////////////////////////////
// CBare16Ctrl::CBare16Ctrl - Constructor

CBare16Ctrl::CBare16Ctrl()
{
  InitializeIIDs(&IID_DBare16, &IID_DBare16Events);

  // TODO: Initialize your control's instance data here.
}


//////////////////////////////////////////////////////////////////////
// CBare16Ctrl::~CBare16Ctrl - Destructor

CBare16Ctrl::~CBare16Ctrl()
{
  // TODO: Clean up your control's instance data here.
}
```

As usual in these things, you allocate any special resources your control needs in the constructor, and de-allocate them in the destructor.

The *OnDraw()* function serves the same purpose as its namesake in any *CWnd*-derived class in MFC: It has the job of painting the control on demand. You should always do all of your control's painting here. *OnDraw()* is invoked *whenever* painting is required—not just on screen, and not just for an active control. The implementation of *OnDraw()* that Control Wizard gives you simply draws an ellipse within a rectangle. You will certainly want to replace this code in a real control! But, for now, that's adequate:

```
/////////////////////////////////////////////////////////////////////////////
// CBare16Ctrl::OnDraw - Drawing function

void CBare16Ctrl::OnDraw(
        CDC* pdc, const CRect& rcBounds, const CRect& rcInvalid)
{
   // TODO: Replace the following code with your own drawing code.
   pdc->FillRect(rcBounds,
CBrush::FromHandle((HBRUSH)GetStockObject(WHITE_BRUSH)));
   pdc->Ellipse(rcBounds);
}
```

Just as MFC supplies functions for automating the transfer of information from object variables to dialog box controls and back again, so Control Wizard supplies functions for populating and reading property pages:

```
/////////////////////////////////////////////////////////////////////////////
// CBare16Ctrl::DoPropExchange - Persistence support

void CBare16Ctrl::DoPropExchange(CPropExchange* pPX)
{
   ExchangeVersion(pPX, MAKELONG(_wVerMinor, _wVerMajor));
   COleControl::DoPropExchange(pPX);

   // TODO: Call PX_ functions for each persistent custom property.
}
```

As you add properties to your control, you'll want to update the property page template and then add code here to actually make sure the values are transferred to and from the control. (Again, we'll get some practice doing this when we start working with property pages in the next chapter.)

Many things in the OLE universe just happen, without us normal mortals really knowing why. Sometimes, for example, a running OLE control must be able to reset itself to initial values. The *OnResetState()* method accommodates this need:

```
///////////////////////////////////////////////////////////////////////
// CBare16Ctrl::OnResetState - Reset control to default state

void CBare16Ctrl::OnResetState()
{
   COleControl::OnResetState();   // Resets defaults found in DoPropExchange

   // TODO: Reset any other control state here.
}
```

Again, as you add properties to your control, you'll want to give them initial values here—rather than in the constructor, which, of course, is executed only once for each control.

If you requested an About box of Control Wizard, as we did in this example, you'll find a method for displaying it:

```
///////////////////////////////////////////////////////////////////////
// CBare16Ctrl::AboutBox - Display an "About" box to the user

void CBare16Ctrl::AboutBox()
{
   CDialog dlgAbout(IDD_ABOUTBOX_BARE16);
   dlgAbout.DoModal();
}
```

That's the last function in this file. All that remains is a comment:

```
///////////////////////////////////////////////////////////////////////
// CBare16Ctrl message handlers
```

Class Wizard will append message handlers here as you request them.

You may have noted that, except for class names and GUIDs, *everything in the 16-bit and 32-bit versions of this control is identical.* However, since you can't make *truly* identical 16-bit and 32-bit controls—the GUIDs *must* be different, or there will be registration conflicts—you can't simply use the same files for both versions, anyway. What you *can* do is put the actual code in a *separate* file, and **#include** it into appropriate places in each project. For example,

```
void CBare16Ctrl::OnDraw(
        CDC* pdc, const CRect& rcBounds, const CRect& rcInvalid)
{
#include ".\common\ondraw.inc"
}
```

This **#include** directive will look in the COMMON folder that lives in the same directory as the current project's folder. It implies a structure like the one shown in Figure 15.12.

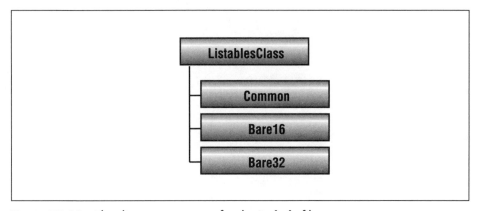

Figure 15.12 The directory structure for the **include** files.

There's another file that implements the property page dialog, but I'm going to defer looking at it until the next chapter, when we start working with control properties. Meanwhile there's one more pair of files that's significant, and they always have the same names: STDAFX.H and STDAFX.CPP. These files do not contain any actual code. Instead, the .CPP simply **#includes** the .H file, and *that* **#includes** all the standard MFC header files. (The "AFX" is a holdover from MFC's original name, "Application Frameworks"—a name they couldn't use because Borland released a product by that the same name shortly before MFC was released.) STDAFX.H is the file that makes the precompiled headers work. You'll note that when you do a full build, STDAFX.CPP is always compiled first and separately—also, that it takes the most time. It's time well spent, however, because all the subsequent implementation files can reuse the precompiled header information.

I hope you've found this little tour of the generated code enlightening...and non-threatening. Although the underlying OLE subsystem is enough to terrify the most seasoned hiker, MFC really does succeed in taming it. And being familiar with the Control Wizard-produced, MFC code makes modifying it much more like a walk along a summer trail than a nighttime trek through the winter woods.

Working with OCX Stock Properties

16

SOMETIMES YOU GET TO THE POINT where you just *have* to do things yourself if you want to get them done right. For example, take the locating of a portable toilet.

Everything taken into the Grand Canyon must be taken out—there are *no* exceptions. So when a group of 24 passengers and six boatmen raft through it, interesting logistics come into play regarding the handling of, shall we say, personal wastes.

The problem has been solved by the handy customization of medium-sized ammunition cans. These "ammo cases" are waterproof, almost exactly the height of a chair seat, and come equipped with sealable lids and carrying handles. Add a couple of heavy-duty trash bags for lining and a toilet seat bolted to a wooden frame that fits perfectly into the top of an open ammo can, and *voilà!* You have the centerpiece of the most beautiful bathroom you've ever seen. All that's left is deciding where, exactly, to put it.

That's normally the job of the baggage boatmen. But in our first week in the Canyon, we began to suspect we were being made the, er, butt of jokes; because every night the porta-potty seemed to be located in harder and harder places to get to. One night it was placed in the midst of rocks we had to climb over; the next it was on a low cliff; once it was hidden in a thicket of tamarisk trees. After one guy fell into the river at night trying to find it, I decided to take matters into my own hands and find a proper spot for the thing.

We were camping at a place called Ledges, named after the shale slabs that it was made of. It was the first place we'd camped that *wasn't* a sandy beach. There were no stands of trees, and no convenient side canyons, so this was going to be a challenge. However, I spotted, at one end of the camp, a place where some of the higher ledges had broken off some time in the previous centuries. These slabs of shale had shattered and stood on end, forming a perfect screen for the little bathroom-sized nook I found right at the waters' edge.

The boatman accompanying me raised an eyebrow but set up the porta-potty where I suggested. What a beautiful spot! Hidden completely from camp, the waters of the Colorado rushed past one's feet, sure to encourage the most stubborn sitter to relax. Ledges is located at one side of a gorge, where the river narrows and sheer rock walls rise on either side. It's also at a bend, so my little bathroom somehow had a cozy, intimate feel to it, in spite of the grandeur and the fact that the nearest wall was about 100 feet away.

I was so pleased with my job of placement that I talked about it all evening. I thought about it that night, how pretty the rock walls would look in the morning with the fresh light of the new sun setting them aglow. I couldn't wait to use it. And, when dawn finally came and I got to enjoy the fruits of my handiwork, sure enough! It was as beautiful and peaceful as I had thought—for about five minutes.

This trip was made in October, and ours was one of the very few expeditions on the river...one of the few, but not by any means the *only* one. As I sat there in the morning air, I saw a kayaker paddle into sight, from around the upstream bend. And then another...and another...until a whole school of them lined up, waiting for instructions before tackling the rapids just downstream.

Now, Miss Manners suggests that, when unexpectedly faced with someone doing something normally not done in public, one should simply pretend not to see. Unfortunately, these guys didn't appear to have read Miss

Manners' advice column, because I was immediately entertained by every feeble bit of toilet humor known to man: "Don't forget to flush!" "Have enough paper?" "That book any good?" All I could do was grin good-naturedly and hope they went on their way...*before* anyone else used the porta-potty and discovered my "perfect" location wasn't so perfect, after all.

> *When you get to the point that you have to do things yourself...make damned certain you really* do *do the job better than it was being done before. If it's not, people* will *notice...and they will probably* not *keep quiet about it.*

Designing a Better List Box

It's hard to think you can't improve on the Visual Basic list box, though. The built-in, Windows list box has so many really neat abilities, like tab stops and owner-draw abilities, that are masked when Visual Basic steps in between. And, since we've got to figure out something useful to do while learning how to write OLE controls, why not improve on the VB list box?

In this chapter, we're going to focus on implementing OCX stock properties. We'll do so by adding them to three different (but related) controls in the same OCX. The three controls, when completed, will each support a listbox feature missing from the Visual Basic list boxes. The first, TabList, will be a regular text list box, but will support the setting of tab stops for columnar information. The second, ImageList, will display a list of images instead of, or with, text. And the third, DrawList, will support owner-draw abilities from the Visual Basic development environment.

Sound like fun? Good! So let's get started.

Start the 16-bit Control Wizard and name the project "Listbxs" (we are limited to eight characters, of course). The New Subdirectory field repeats this value by default; but I'll change it to "Chap16," as shown in Figure 16.1.

The placement of the Control Options... button and the Controls... button is odd, because really you should click the bottom one first. That brings up the dialog that lets you define all the controls this OCX will house, as shown in Figure 16.2.

After defining the three controls, you click the Control Options button, as shown in Figure 16.3.

Figure 16.1 Creating a new project.

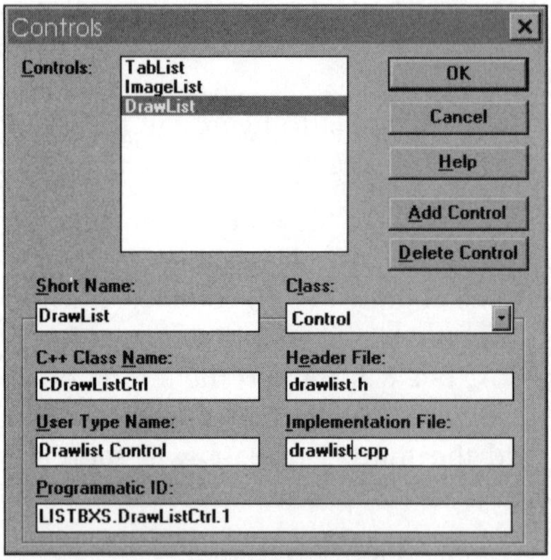

Figure 16.2 Selecting controls for the OCX control.

The important thing in this dialog is to be certain that all three controls subclass the Windows listbox control. After those changes have been made, you are ready to generate the project. When this is done, don't forget to run the Make Typelib tool (as described in the previous chapter). You can then perform a test compile.

Before you do, however, you may wish to alter the default bitmaps for the tools. Control Wizard generates plain gray boxes with the letters "OCX" on them—identical for each of the controls in the OCX. That's going to make them hard to tell apart; so I created the set shown in Figures 16.4, 16.5, and

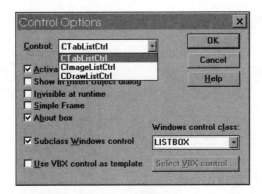

Figure 16.3 Using the Control Options dialog.

Figure 16.4 The TabList button.

Figure 16.5 The ImageList button.

Figure 16.6 The DrawList button.

16.6. You'll note that OCX button bitmaps, unlike VBX button bitmaps, do not require a beveled border—the OCX container's toolbox will supply that.

Taking TabList for a Dry Run

Once it's compiled, you can try out the new OCX controls. Start VB4-16 (the 16-bit version of Visual Basic 4) and choose the *Tools..Custom Controls* command. The list of registered controls will appear, but your new OCX won't be there—it isn't yet registered. OCXs are self-registering, however; so all you have to do is load it once. You do that by pressing the Browse button and locating your new OCX. (Remember that Visual C++ is producing LISTBXS.DLL—we'll give it the .OCX extension manually as a final step before release.) After locating and selecting the DLL, the Custom Controls dialog will appear similar to the one in Figure 16.7.

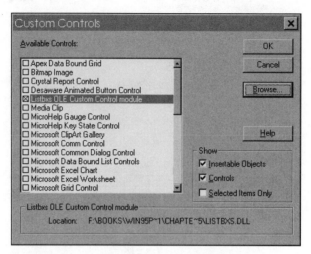

Figure 16.7 The Visual Basic Custom Controls dialog.

Once registered, the control will continue to appear in this dialog until and unless it is unregistered (a task that requires deleting nine entries from the Registration Database).

By the way, if you happen to try to load a 16-bit control into 32-bit Visual Basic, you will get a simple and unhelpful message stating that it was "unable" to load your control. If you've installed both VB4-16 and VB4-32, remember that the association with files of a .VBP extension (Visual Basic project files) will be to the last version you installed. You can modify the extensions using the Explorer's *Options..File Types* dialog. For example, since I do most of my work in 16-bits, I altered the **open** verb to refer to VB4-16, and added an **open 32-bits** verb for those other times.

A Glimpse of a Hidden Control

Once the LSTBXS OCX has been added to your list of tools, the three new bitmaps will immediately appear in your toolbox, from which you can add them to a form. However, when you do so, you may at first think nothing has happened; because although you can "draw" the new control, at design time you see nothing but the resizing handles—and, if you deselect the new control, even those vanish.

But the control is really there. And, if you run the project, you'll see that the control really does paint itself as an empty list box...*at runtime only.* A further clue arises from the fact that the list box has no border.

We've created these three controls and compiled them...*without specifying any properties.* Now, we do get some properties by default; you can see them listed in the VB properties box when you select the control. But all of those are "ambient" properties, managed by the container, like the position and size properties. *BorderStyle* isn't one of those, because its border is something a control must manage for itself.

To add *BorderStyle*, and any of several other stock properties to the controls, you must turn to Visual C++'s Class Wizard. Choose the OLE Automation page, and be sure the control to which you want to add properties is listed in the Class Name combo box. (We'll be adding properties to all three controls, but you have to go through the full set of motions for each one.) Click the Add Property... button. The dialog shown in Figure 16.8 will appear.

As mentioned in the previous chapter, the External Name combo box is pre-loaded with a list of available stock properties; and *BorderStyle* is one of them. All three controls in this OCX should have the stock properties shown in Figure 16.9 added.

Now, if you were to compile right now, these controls would *not* show up in the VB properties box. Why not? Simply because they haven't been regis-tered! Once again, you must run the *Tools..Make Typelib* command, *before* compiling. You have to do this *every* time you add a new property, event, or method to your OLE control. (Visual C++ 4, the 32-bit compiler, will do this automatically.) Once the type library is up-to-date, the new properties will be added to the Registration Database the next time the OCX is loaded; and the *BorderStyle* property will show up in the properties box as desired.

However, its default value is 0—that is, no border. How can we change that?

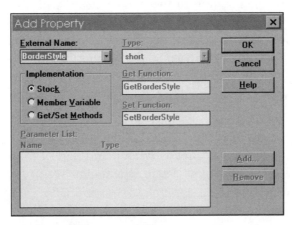

Figure 16.8 Using the Add Property dialog.

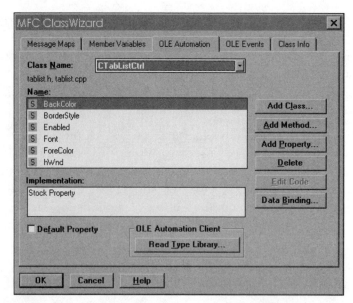

Figure 16.9 Stock properties for the Enhanced Listbox control.

Setting Default Property Values

The stock properties are managed automatically by base classes you can't directly manipulate. So how can you change a default value of a stock property?

Strictly speaking, you can't. However, you *can* alter the default for a specific *control*. All you have to do is set the property to the desired value when the control is first created.

Don't confuse the creation of the control itself, with the constructor of the C++ object *representing* the control. There's a method, *OnResetState()*, that is invoked whenever a control needs to be reset, for whatever reason—and one reason is its initial creation. So that leaves the question...how do you set *any* stock property values?

If you'll refer back to Figure 16.8, you'll note that the stock property *BorderStyle* has a pair of "get" and "set" functions listed. The function names are disabled; they can't be changed. That's because these *are* stock properties; and those functions, already written and part of the base class, are how the properties are managed. There is a similar set of functions for each of the stock properties.

So, to make the *BorderStyle* property default to 1 (fixed single), all you have to do is add one line of code to the already-existing *OnResetState()* method for each of the three controls:

```
void CTabListCtrl::OnResetState()
    {
    // Invocation of base method supplied by Control Wizard
    COleControl::OnResetState();
    // Specific default property values set by you
    SetBorderStyle (1);
    }
```

After compiling, if you add a TabList control to a VB form, by default it will appear as a simple black frame. It *still* doesn't look like a list box at design time...or, indeed, like anything much at all. And yet, if you try, you'll find the list box does show up at runtime. What's happening here?

If you'll check out TabList's *OnDraw()* function, you'll see that Control Wizard has generated the following code:

```
void CTabListCtrl::OnDraw(
        CDC* pdc, const CRect& rcBounds, const CRect& rcInvalid)
{
    DoSuperclassPaint(pdc, rcBounds);
}
```

The function *DoSuperclassPaint()* is responsible for seeing that the subclassed listbox control paints itself when needed...but, for some reason, it is *not* considered "needed" at design time. That means we'll have to add alternate drawing instructions for design mode.

The regular VB listbox control paints itself as a white rectangle at design time, its control name displayed in its upper left-hand corner. We can mimic this behavior with the following code, our first try at painting an OLE control at design time:

```
void CTabListCtrl::OnDraw(
        CDC* pdc, const CRect& rcBounds, const CRect& rcInvalid)
    {
    if (AmbientUserMode())
        DoSuperclassPaint(pdc, rcBounds);
    else
        {
        CBrush * OldBrush =
            pdc->SelectObject ((HBRUSH) GetStockObject (WHITE_BRUSH));
        pdc->Rectangle (rcBounds);
        pdc->TextOut (rcBounds.left, rcBounds.top,
            AmbientDisplayName());
        pdc->SelectObject (OldBrush);
        }
    }
```

The inherited method *AmbientUserMode()* returns TRUE if the control is being used in a running application; FALSE if it is being used to design one. *AmbientDisplayName()* retrieves the name of the control if the container supports this property—as Visual Basic 4 does.

Both of these functions are examples of accessing *ambient properties*. I described these a couple of chapters ago, but perhaps seeing them in use will bring the concept home for you. Just as the TabList control is an OLE object embedded in a container, with properties of its own that the container might need to set or query, so does the *container* have properties the control might need to query. Such properties are *ambient* properties. Usually they are used to allow controls to blend in with the container on which they lie; but some ambient properties, like the two just mentioned, are available for other purposes—like providing different appearance or behavior depending on whether the control is in design mode. And, in design mode, our new control now looks as you see it in Figure 16.10.

An ambient property is why we have to replace the original brush with a stock brush: The device context given to us in the *OnDraw()* method has already had selected into it, a brush of the ambient background color (at design time). Neither this brush nor its color is affected by the value of the *BackColor* stock property. To be more designer-friendly, we'll have to explicitly set the brush to the desired *BackColor*. That makes our second stab at the *OnDraw()* code look like this:

```
void CTabListCtrl::OnDraw(
      CDC* pdc, const CRect& rcBounds, const CRect& rcInvalid)
  {
  if (AmbientUserMode())
    DoSuperclassPaint(pdc, rcBounds);
  else
    {
    CBrush Brush (TranslateColor (GetBackColor()));
    CBrush * OldBrush =
      pdc->SelectObject (&Brush);
    pdc->Rectangle (rcBounds);
    pdc->SetTextColor (TranslateColor (GetForeColor()));
    pdc->TextOut (rcBounds.left, rcBounds.top,
      AmbientDisplayName());
    pdc->SelectObject (OldBrush);
    }
  }
```

The nested call to *TranslateColor()* is required because OLE doesn't use COLORREFs—it uses an almost undocumented data type called *OLE_COLOR*. This data type is 32-bits wide, just like a COLORREF, but its internal format

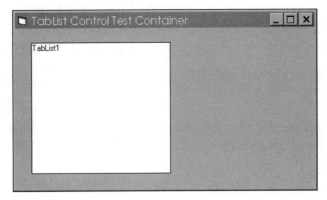

Figure 16.10 The TabList control in design mode.

is more similar to the Visual Basic color representation. Interestingly, while *TranslateColor()* has been provided, there doesn't seem to be an analogous function to derive a COLORREF from an OLE_COLOR!

When the designer explicitly changes the control's background color, the effect is seen immediately on the design-time rectangle. However, at run-time it has no effect! That's because there is no built-in code to communicate the altered colors to the underlying list box. We have to do that, ourselves.

The message a parent receives when a child is about to paint itself, as you'll recall from our VBX work, is WM_CTLCOLOR. When requested, Class Wizard provides the following handler:

```
HBRUSH CTabListCtrl::OnCtlColor(CDC* pDC, CWnd* pWnd, UINT nCtlColor)
{
    // TODO: Add your message handler code here and/or call default

    return COleControl::OnCtlColor(pDC, pWnd, nCtlColor);
}
```

Obviously, the base implementation doesn't do anything useful. We have to replace this behavior, supplying a background brush and altering the text colors. That means, we have to *own* a background brush—making one a member variable of each of our enhanced listbox control classes:

```
class CTabListCtrl : public COleControl
{
    ⇓
    ⇓
// Implementation
protected:
```

```
~CTabListCtrl();
CBrush * Brush;

⇓
⇓
};
```

The pointer must receive a NULL value in the constructor (which I do
properly, in the member initialization area, rather than the function body as
the generated comment suggests):

```
CTabListCtrl::CTabListCtrl()
  : Brush (NULL)
  {
  InitializeIIDs(&IID_DTabList, &IID_DTabListEvents);

  // TODO: Initialize your control's instance data here.
  }
```

Choosing a Tissue Color

We don't actually *create* the brush in the constructor; that would be too easy.
Actually, the problem is that the *BackColor* value isn't yet available when the
control is being constructed. It becomes available in time to be used when
OnResetState() is invoked—but it will have been initialized to the container's
ambient *BackColor* property, and the probably isn't what you want.

An OLE_COLOR is, essentially a COLORREF, but with some extra abilities.
You may recall from Chapter 4, that a COLORREF is a four byte structure in
which the lowest-order byte represents a red value, the next lowest green,
and the second highest, blue. The high-order byte is unused.

However, in an OLE_COLOR, the byte *is* used. If, for example, the top bit is
one, then the low-order byte is assumed to be an index into the system
color table (that's the table you access through the *GetSysColor()* API call).

Producing an initial OLE_COLOR value isn't hard. A COLORREF can be
used directly, if you like. (That's why no one at Microsoft bothered to write
an explicit conversion function—one wasn't needed.) You can also use the
system colors as long as you **or** them with 0x80000000.

So, before creating that brush, we first provide initial values for the *BackColor*
and *ForeColor* properties. In this case, we want to use *COLOR_WINDOW*
and *COLOR_WINDOWTEXT*, respectively, to mimic the default colors of the
Windows Listbox control:

```
void CTabListCtrl::OnResetState()
  {
```

```
// Invocation of base method supplied by Control Wizard
COleControl::OnResetState();
// Specific default property values set by you
SetBorderStyle (1);
SetBackColor (0x80000000 | COLOR_WINDOW);
SetForeColor (0x80000000 | COLOR_WINDOWTEXT);
delete Brush;
Brush = new CBrush (TranslateColor (GetBackColor ()));
}= new CBrush (TranslateColor (GetBackColor ()));
}
```

If there was a brush already allocated, it is deleted. (It is always safe to use the **delete** operator on a NULL pointer.) We must also remember to delete the brush, if there is one, in the control's destructor:

```
CTabListCtrl::~CTabListCtrl()
    {
    delete Brush;
    }
```

However, the important thing is to delete the old brush, and create a new one, when the *BackColor* property is *first loaded*, and when it has *changed*.

All properties are loaded during execution of the control's *DoPropExchange()* member function. That is, custom properties are loaded there; stock properties are loaded during execution of the base version of *DoPropExchange()*, which is invoked first. So, any time after that, we can discard whatever old brush there might be, and create a fresh one in the correct color:

```
void CTabListCtrl::DoPropExchange(CPropExchange* pPX)
    {
    ExchangeVersion(pPX, MAKELONG(_wVerMinor, _wVerMajor));
    COleControl::DoPropExchange(pPX);

    // TODO: Call PX_ functions for each persistent custom property.

    delete Brush;
    Brush = new CBrush (TranslateColor (GetBackColor ()));
    }
```

We also need to be responsive to real-time changes of the *BackColor* value. Since that's a stock property, we don't have access to the actual code that is invoked to effect the change. However, there is a **virtual** function, *OnBackColorChanged()*, that we can override. We have to manually add the declaration to the header file:

```
class CTabListCtrl : public COleControl
{
    ⇓
    ⇓
```

```
// Implementation
protected:
  ~CTabListCtrl();
  CBrush * Brush;
  virtual void OnBackColorChanged(void);
  ⇓
  ⇓
};
```

And we have to manually add the function to the implementation file, too (Class Wizard can't assist in this):

```
void CTabListCtrl::OnBackColorChanged(void)
  {
  delete Brush;
  Brush = new CBrush (TranslateColor (GetBackColor ()));
  }
```

Now we can implement the *OnCtlColor()* handler, after getting Class Wizard to add it to the class declaration and the message map:

```
HBRUSH CTabListCtrl::OnCtlColor(CDC* pDC, CWnd* pWnd, UINT nCtlColor)
  {
  pDC->SetTextColor (TranslateColor (GetForeColor ()));
  return (HBRUSH) Brush->m_hObject;
  }
```

You'd think this would work, right? That's all it took to implement this feature for VBXs. But it doesn't work here! However, don't panic. This wasn't a wasted effort; we're just not done yet.

If you'll recall from our work with VBXs, subclassed controls send messages to their parent windows. The WM_CTLCOLOR message is one such. In a VBX, the VBX manager, which is supplying the form window on which the control is placed, "reflects" these messages back to the control procedure. It's simple, it's neat, and it works.

So, of course, the OLE designers had to find another way to do it. When an OLE control subclasses a standard control, OLE provides a special reflector window for it. In theory, you could monitor messages to the reflector window yourself, and handle any that were of interest (such as WM_CTLCOLOR).

But even *that* is a simplification of what really happens, because some containers might, someday, prefer to reduce system overhead by a minuscule amount, by providing their *own* reflector windows!

So a new set of message map entries has been added to accommodate reflected messages, whoever might be reflecting them. Class Wizard doesn't know about these, so you have to write them in yourself (very carefully, *outside of* the Class Wizard comments). First you place the prototype in the class declaration:

```
class CTabListCtrl : public COleControl
{
    ⇓
    ⇓
// Implementation
protected:
    ~CTabListCtrl();
    CBrush * Brush;
    virtual void OnBackColorChanged(void);
    LRESULT OnOcmCtlColor(WPARAM wParam, LPARAM lParam);
    ⇓
    ⇓
};
```

The "Ocm" stands for OLE Command Message, or something like that. You also have to add a macro to the message map itself, in the implementation file:

```
BEGIN_MESSAGE_MAP(CTabListCtrl, COleControl)
    //{{AFX_MSG_MAP(CTabListCtrl)
    ON_MESSAGE(OCM_COMMAND, OnOcmCommand)
    ON_WM_CTLCOLOR()
    //}}AFX_MSG_MAP
    ON_OLEVERB(AFX_IDS_VERB_PROPERTIES, OnProperties)
    ON_MESSAGE(OCM_CTLCOLOR, OnOcmCtlColor)
END_MESSAGE_MAP()
```

These messages aren't "cracked" for you; all the handlers have identical calling sequences in which the only arguments are *wParam* and *lParam*. We could actually put the working code there. But I decided to go ahead and crack the messages, and then send them to the proper handler myself:

```
LRESULT CTabListCtrl::OnOcmCtlColor(WPARAM wParam, LPARAM lParam)
    {
    return (long) (LPVOID)
      OnCtlColor (CDC::FromHandle ((HDC) wParam),
        CWnd::FromHandle ((HWND) LOWORD(lParam)),
        (int) HIWORD(lParam));
    }
```

Since *OnCtlColor()* expects MFC object arguments, like a *CDC* and a *CWnd*, we accommodate it using the static *FromHandle()* member functions of each class. These functions return temporary objects, so we don't have to worry about deleting them explicitly.

Now a compile and test will show a rectangle whose background and text colors can be changed at both design and run times.

Using the Stock Font Property

One of the stock properties we added to our new controls was the *Font* property. This one property replaces all the VBX font properties, such as *FontBold, FontName, FontSize,* and so on.

After our experience with the *BackColor* and *ForeColor* properties, you'd probably expect actually making the *Font* property to be an equal hassle. Fortunately, this is not the case. There *is* an *OnFontChanged()* virtual function, but the base implementation does exactly what you'd want it to do: Send the underlying control window a *WM_SETFONT* message. That takes care of runtime; so that leaves us with the single task of obtaining and using that font when we are drawing the design-time representation of our controls.

The function we want, built into *COleControl*, has the unlikely name of *SelectStockFont()*. This function turns object-oriented programming on its head, since it is a member of *COleControl* yet places the new font into the device context passed it as an argument. Still, it works. So here's our final *OnDraw()* variation for this chapter:

```
void CTabListCtrl::OnDraw(
      CDC* pdc, const CRect& rcBounds, const CRect& rcInvalid)
   {
   if (AmbientUserMode())
     DoSuperclassPaint(pdc, rcBounds);
   else
     {
     CBrush * OldBrush = pdc->SelectObject (Brush);
     pdc->Rectangle (rcBounds);
     CFont * OldFont = SelectStockFont (pdc);
     pdc->SetTextColor (TranslateColor (GetForeColor()));
     pdc->TextOut (rcBounds.left, rcBounds.top,
       AmbientDisplayName());
     pdc->SelectObject (OldBrush);
     pdc->SelectObject (OldFont);
     }
   }
```

Setting Up the Property Pages

If, while testing the new controls in Visual Basic, you happened to bring up the dialog box associated with the word "(Custom)" in the Properties box, you got your first glimpse of a raw property page, looking much like Figure 16.11.

Every control gets a skeleton property page like this. It's your job to fill it in. And don't say, "I'll just skip it—after all, Visual Basic's properties box does the job just fine." The whole point of writing OCXs is to use them in containers *other than* Visual Basic—otherwise, we could just stick with the faster and easier-to-write VBXs. Property pages are *supposed* to be the way all future objects will have their design-time attributes modified; it won't surprise me if a future version of Visual Basic doesn't even *have* a properties box.

But we're not going to fill in that general page right now. We'll hold off until a later chapter, after we've defined our custom properties, and we can do them all on the same page. However, we *can* add two more pages for some of our stock properties.

There are *three* stock property pages we get for free: one for fonts, one for colors, and one for pictures. We won't need the picture page (yet), but we do have a *Font* property and two color properties that could take advantage of these ready-to-go pages.

The stock property pages are added manually to a structure in each control's implementation file. The structure looks like this when first generated by Control Wizard:

```
BEGIN_PROPPAGEIDS(CTabListCtrl, 1)
   PROPPAGEID(CTabListPropPage::guid)
END_PROPPAGEIDS(CTabListCtrl)
```

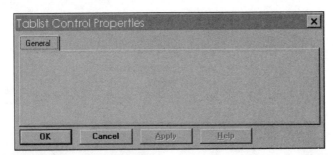

Figure 16.11 An empty property page.

The second parameter to the *BEGIN_PROPPAGEIDS* macro is a count of entries. When you add an entry, either stock or custom, be sure to increment this count! With the two pages added, the structure is modified thus:

```
BEGIN_PROPPAGEIDS(CTabListCtrl, 3)
  PROPPAGEID(CTabListPropPage::guid)
  PROPPAGEID(CLSID_CColorPropPage)
  PROPPAGEID(CLSID_CFontPropPage)
END_PROPPAGEIDS(CTabListCtrl)
```

No further effort (other than a compile) is required! Amazingly, the Fonts property page automatically links to the *Font* stock property (and any other font properties you might have!) and makes it work, as seen in Figure 16.12.

Regarding the Colors property page, seen in Figure 16.13, there's good news and there's bad news. The good news is that, like the font property

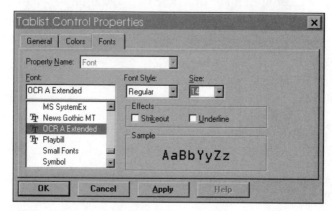

Figure 16.12 The Font property page.

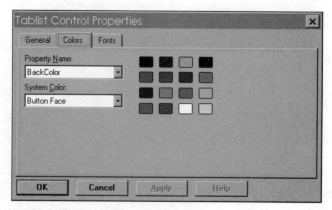

Figure 16.13 The Colors property page.

page, the color property page automatically links to *any* color properties you have, stock or not. The bad news is, this has to be the ugliest, most ineffectual color choice dialog in the history of the known Universe. Where's the pretty color palette we're used to from the Common Dialogs? Still, what did you expect for nothing? —And, perhaps, it will be replaced in the near future by a more attractive one.

Moving Along

After the kayakers finally went on their way, I returned to camp somewhat chagrined that my "perfect" spot for a porta-potty had its flaws, nonetheless. Still, that didn't mean the situation was hopeless. A few modifications—like moving the ammo case behind one of the shale slabs—would provide more privacy without spoiling the view too much. Whenever you set out to make something new, it usually requires more than one attempt.

Currently, our listbox controls need a lot of work. The stock properties we added in this chapter are helpful; but we need a way to get data into and out of the list boxes. Custom properties and methods are needed to accomplish this. In the next chapter we'll add some custom properties to our improved listbox controls.

The view will get better, I promise!

Custom OCX Properties

17

A FTER THE PORTA-POTTY EXPERIENCE in the Grand Canyon, you'd think I'd never want to *see* a kayak again. But I had the chance to paddle one just a few months later—near Key West—and I took it.

Mosquito Coast is the uninviting name of the outfitters in Key West who arranged the expedition to the keys' backcountry. Key West, itself, is well populated; but the keys near it are not. So, after a relatively brief van ride along US 1, we came to our put-in point and got into our kayaks.

These were not the enclosed kayaks you usually see, the ones where your first lesson is how to roll over without drowning. These were slightly broader and therefore more stable, and open on top so you just sit there and paddle with the double-bladed oar. It's amazing; I'm hardly an athlete, but with a minimum of effort you can send the little craft skittering over the water.

Our destination was a little group of mangrove islands that had anchored themselves near Cow Key. We paddled over maybe half a mile of open Gulf water to get to them. The water is shallow, between five and ten feet deep—less in some places—and the mangroves root directly into the salty bottom. There is no "dry" land for them.

Now, you'd think this would be a pretty inhospitable place for a tree. But the mangrove tree starts life as a seed that drifts along the shallow bottom until it nudges against something—anything. If that relative security lasts long enough, it sends out shoots that anchor it still further. You can call this the tree's gestation; its birth comes when it finally grows tall enough to break out into the air, where it grows leaves and starts looking more like a tree than a spiny piece of seaweed.

Usually, the "something" the seed nudges against is the root system of another, more mature mangrove tree. So the mangroves tend to grow in clumps and form "islands" with no surface. Sometimes, in a hurricane, the entire island will be dislodged from its anchorage and float until the storm subsides, at which time it sends down new roots and takes up housekeeping in the new location, looking none the worse for wear.

This is much as we hope to accomplish with the Extended Listbox controls we began in the previous chapter. We've ripped the standard list box from the usual platform, and transplanted it into an OLE control. (Actually, *three* controls: TabList, ImageList, and DrawList.) Now our job is to make sure that, like the re-anchored mangrove forests, these transplanted list boxes can fit seamlessly into their new home. And the way we do this is by adding *custom properties*.

Introducing Custom Properties

As with VBXs, an OCX custom property is simply one that you, the OCX developer, write. Where possible, you should reuse property names borrowed from other controls (though there is nothing enforcing this). Reusing the name doesn't provide you with the implementation, however. You really do have to make this a custom job, which means you have both the freedom to be as creative as you like, and the responsibility to not surprise your end users with unexpected effects.

Since we are mimicking the Listbox control, as a starting off point, we should check to see what properties it makes available. The Visual Basic Properties box provides the list shown in Figure 17.1.

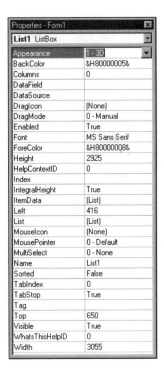

Figure 17.1 Listbox properties.

Of this list, many of the "properties" are ambient or stock properties. When they are subtracted from the list, we are left with the custom properties presented in Table 17.1 that must be implemented.

Clearly, the list presented in Table 17.1 is not a trivial one. And yet, it's not as much work as it seems, either; because most of these properties are actually implemented by the list box itself. All we have to do is pass them through the OCX to the underlying code. So let's start with those.

Starting with the Roots

Each of the standard Windows controls has support for certain attributes, which are set by including certain bit flags when the underlying window is created. I call these "root properties." They are also called "pre-create" or "pre-hWnd" properties. In the case of the Listbox control, they include whether the list box resizes itself according to the height of items it contains, whether items in the list box should be sorted automatically, and so on. These root properties are particularly easy to make available to the OCX interface. For listbox-derived controls, they are *Columns, IntegralHeight, MultiSelect,* and *Sorted.*

Table 17.1   Custom Properties to Be Implemented

Property	Description
Appearance	Provides a choice of two alternate draw methods: *Flat* (the original Windows 3.1 style) or *3-D* (the snazzier Windows 95 style). The documentation states that this property is "not available to 16-bit OCXs."
Columns	Allows for multi-column list boxes. We'll implement this differently for TabList than for ImageList and DrawList.
DataField, DataSource	We will not implement these data-aware properties.
IntegralHeight	This property specifies whether the Listbox will resize itself vertically so that only an even number of list items will be visible.
ItemData	This "shadow array" parallels the List property, allowing you to attach data items to each list item that will follow the list item even if it is moved due to sorting, inserting, or deleting a previous item.
List	The default property of the Listbox; this array provides access to each item in it.
ListCount	Available only at run-time, this property reveals the number of elements in the List array.
ListIndex	Available only at run-time, this property can be read to find out which element of *List* is selected, or written to, to programmatically *set* the current selection.
MouseIcon, MousePointer	These properties allow the designer to specify a non-standard mouse pointer for the list box. We will omit support for these seldom-used properties.
MultiSelect	Specifies one of three levels of multiple selection allowed on this listbox: single selection only, the old-style (Windows 2.1) multiple selection, or the more modern extended selection.
NewIndex	Can be read at design time only to find which element in the list was most recently added. (If the list box is sorted, figuring out this value without benefit of this property can be tricky.)
SelCount	This property is most useful in a multi-selection list box. Available only at run-time, it reveals the number of currently-selected items.
Selected	This array property, available only at run-time, can be queried to find out which item or items in *List* are currently selected.
Sorted	Specifies whether the list box will automatically sort items as they are entered.
Text	This shortcut property is equivalent to *List(ListIndex)*. It is read-only and available only at run-time.
TopIndex	This property can be used to read or set the index of the item in *List* that is the currently top-most visible item in the list box. It is available only at run-time.

IntegralHeight and *Sorted* are each of type BOOL. These are easy to add because each can be implemented as a "member variable," meaning that MFC will manage the getting and setting of the values for you. Sure, you'll want to know when one of these values is set; but there's a notification function that is automatically generated as well.

The next property is *Columns,* a **short** that states the number of columns in the list box—its default value is one. For the ImageList and DrawList controls, it, too, can be a member variable and you should add it now. However, for reasons we'll explain in a few pages, the TabList control requires *Columns* to be a "get/set" property; we'll add it to that control shortly.

Like the stock properties in the previous chapter, these properties are added by Class Wizard, after clicking on the OLE Automation tab. Figure 17.2 shows the *Sorted* property being added. Please note that I have *not* accepted the pseudo-Hungarian name of "m_sorted" for the member variable. (The only Hungarian name I've ever *really* liked was "Zsa Zsa," anyway.)

After adding these properties to the TabList control, an inspection of its code reveals a few changes. The first is that two variables and two functions have been added to the class declaration (three, including *Columns,* for DrawList and ImageList), as well as dispatch IDs for the properties:

```
class CTabListCtrl : public COleControl
{
    ⇓
    ⇓
// Dispatch maps
    //{{AFX_DISPATCH(CTabListCtrl)
    BOOL IntegralHeight;
    afx_msg void OnIntegralHeightChanged();
    BOOL Sorted;
    afx_msg void OnSortedChanged();
    //}}AFX_DISPATCH
    DECLARE_DISPATCH_MAP()

    afx_msg void AboutBox();
    ⇓
    ⇓
// Dispatch and event IDs
public:
    enum {
    //{{AFX_DISP_ID(CTabListCtrl)
    dispidIntegralHeight = 1L,
    dispidSorted = 2L,
    //}}AFX_DISP_ID
    };
};
```

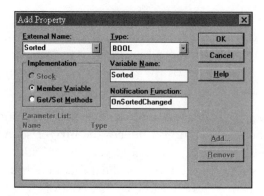

Figure 17.2 Adding the Sorted property.

The remaining changes are in the implementation file, beginning with the dispatch map:

```
BEGIN_DISPATCH_MAP(CTabListCtrl, COleControl)
  //{{AFX_DISPATCH_MAP(CTabListCtrl)
  DISP_PROPERTY_NOTIFY(CTabListCtrl, "IntegralHeight", IntegralHeight, _
    OnIntegralHeightChanged, VT_BOOL)
  DISP_PROPERTY_NOTIFY(CTabListCtrl, "Sorted", Sorted, OnSortedChanged, _
    VT_BOOL)
  DISP_STOCKPROP_BORDERSTYLE()
  DISP_STOCKPROP_BACKCOLOR()
  DISP_STOCKPROP_ENABLED()
  DISP_STOCKPROP_FONT()
  DISP_STOCKPROP_FORECOLOR()
  DISP_STOCKPROP_HWND()
  //}}AFX_DISPATCH_MAP
  DISP_FUNCTION_ID(CTabListCtrl, "AboutBox", DISPID_ABOUTBOX, AboutBox, _
    VT_EMPTY, VTS_NONE)
END_DISPATCH_MAP()
```

The *DISP_PROPERTY_NOTIFY* macros state the name of the property, the name of the data member in which it is to be stored, the name of the notification function, and the data type.

These variables receive their default values, as well as having their stored values serialized, in the *DoPropExchange()* function. Oddly, Class Wizard does *not* write this code for you, although the information required is all known to it. Apparently it was felt that a property with a persistent value would be the exception, rather than the norm. (Why couldn't that have been a check mark on the Class Wizard's Add Property dialog?) Anyway, the actual functions to perform the serialization are simple enough to code. There's a whole list of ones you can use; they all begin with *PX_*, followed by the data type (I'm showing the DrawList version here, so you can see the *Columns* property serialized as well):

```
void CDrawListCtrl::DoPropExchange(CPropExchange* pPX)
   {
   ExchangeVersion(pPX, MAKELONG(_wVerMinor, _wVerMajor));
   COleControl::DoPropExchange(pPX);

   PX_Bool (pPX, "IntegralHeight", IntegralHeight, TRUE);
   PX_Bool (pPX, "Sorted", Sorted, FALSE);
   PX_Short (pPX, "Columns", Columns, 1);

   delete Brush;
   Brush = new CBrush (TranslateColor (GetBackColor ()));
   }
```

All three of these properties must be specified to the Windows Listbox control, *before* the list box is actually created. This is done by modifying the window style flags in the *PreCreateWindow()* function:

```
BOOL CDrawListCtrl::PreCreateWindow(CREATESTRUCT& cs)
   {
   cs.lpszClass = _T("LISTBOX");
   if (Columns > 1)
      cs.style |= LBS_MULTICOLUMN;
   if (! IntegralHeight)
      cs.style |= LBS_NOINTEGRALHEIGHT;
   if (Sorted)
      cs.style |= LBS_SORT;
   return COleControl::PreCreateWindow(cs);
   }
```

It is possible for one of these properties to be set even at run-time. If this happens, the original control must be destroyed and recreated with the new values. We make sure this happens in each of the notification functions (the highlighted lines are the ones I added):

```
void CTabListCtrl::OnIntegralHeightChanged()
   {
   RecreateControlWindow();
   SetModifiedFlag();
   }

void CTabListCtrl::OnSortedChanged()
   {
   RecreateControlWindow();
   SetModifiedFlag();
   }
```

Implementing Enumerated Properties

The fourth of those pre-create properties, *MultiSelect*, is a little trickier than the first three, simply because users are accustomed to seeing its values as strings: "Single," "Multiple," and "Extended," even though the values are actually stored as numeric values—usually, 0, 1, and 2, respectively.

Giving a VBX control what we always called "enumerated properties" was simple. All you had to do was supply the enumeration list when you defined the property. It's a lot more complicated in OLE controls (why are you not surprised?) but the toughest part is finding any documentation. Thus, make sure you mark this section because you'll be using it as a reference in the months to come.

With OLE controls, an "enumerated" property is actually made of the same data types as any other property. What makes it special, is that you supply strings by which the allowed values can be represented—and that, in turn, implies a limited number of permitted values.

If your control will have any enumerated properties, you must override three functions inherited from *COleControl*. Class Wizard won't help you do this; you have to type in the function prototypes yourself. The three functions are *OnGetPredefinedStrings()*, *OnGetPredefinedValue()*, and *OnGetDisplayString()*:

```
class CTabListCtrl : public COleControl
{
    ⇓
    ⇓
// Dispatch maps
    //{{AFX_DISPATCH(CTabListCtrl)
    BOOL IntegralHeight;
    afx_msg void OnIntegralHeightChanged();
    BOOL Sorted;
    afx_msg void OnSortedChanged();
    short MultiSelect;
    afx_msg void OnMultiSelectChanged();
    //}}AFX_DISPATCH
    DECLARE_DISPATCH_MAP()

    virtual BOOL OnGetPredefinedStrings (DISPID DispID,
        CStringArray* Strings,
        CDWordArray* Cookies);
    virtual BOOL OnGetPredefinedValue (DISPID DispID,
        DWORD Cookie,
        VARIANT FAR* Value);
    virtual BOOL OnGetDisplayString (DISPID DispID,
        CString & String);
```

```
    ⇓
    ⇓
// Dispatch and event IDs
public:
    enum {
    //{{AFX_DISP_ID(CTabListCtrl)
    dispidIntegralHeight = 1L,
    dispidSorted = 2L,
    dispidMultiSelect = 3L,
    //}}AFX_DISP_ID
    };
};
```

Each of the three functions takes, as its first parameter, a "dispatch ID." You can see these IDs defined as part of the class in the above code fragment; the functions use them to identify for which property they are being invoked. All three functions are designed to accommodate enumerated and non-enumerated properties; they simply return FALSE if they are invoked for a non-enumerated property.

OnGetPredefinedStrings() is invoked when the system needs the names of the full set of enumerations for a given property. You are supposed to fill a supplied array with pointers to the strings that represent the allowed values. Rather than treat the array as an indexed one, so that element number 2, say, is represented by the number 2, you must *also* fill a separate array with "cookies"—that's apparently a technical term, brought to us by the same folks who invented "burgermeister" and "thunk." String number two is then associated with "cookie" number two, and you'll be given that "cookie" back later when the system wants to refer to that same enumeration.

To implement this properly, the strings should be stored in the resource pool's string table. I've added the three strings, as shown in Figure 17.3.

ID	Value	Caption
IDS_TABLIST	1	Tablist Control
IDS_TABLIST_PPG	2	Tablist Property Page
IDS_IMAGELIST	3	Imagelist Control
IDS_IMAGELIST_PPG	4	Imagelist Property Page
IDS_DRAWLIST	5	Drawlist Control
IDS_DRAWLIST_PPG	6	Drawlist Property Page
IDS_TABLIST_PPG_CAPTION	101	General
IDS_IMAGELIST_PPG_CAPTI	103	General
IDS_DRAWLIST_PPG_CAPTIO	105	General
IDS_SINGLE	200	Single
IDS_MULTIPLE	201	Multiple
IDS_EXTENDED	202	Extended

Figure 17.3 Enumerations in the String Table.

We also have to add a data member to contain each of them to the class declaration. I nested them further in a **struct**, to avoid any chance of name conflicts:

```
class CTabListCtrl : public COleControl
{
    ⇓
    ⇓
    struct tag_MultiSelect_Values
        {
        CString Single;
        CString Multiple;
        CString Extended;
        } MultiSelect_Values;
    ⇓
    ⇓
};
```

The MFC *CString* class doesn't have a string table constructor, but it does have a *LoadString()* method we can invoke:

```
CTabListCtrl::CTabListCtrl()
    : Brush (NULL)
    {
    InitializeIIDs(&IID_DTabList, &IID_DTabListEvents);

    MultiSelect_Values.Single.LoadString (IDS_SINGLE);
    MultiSelect_Values.Multiple.LoadString (IDS_MULTIPLE);
    MultiSelect_Values.Extended.LoadString (IDS_EXTENDED);
    }
```

With that initialization behind us, we can (finally!) look at *OnGet-PredefinedStrings()* in action:

```
BOOL CTabListCtrl::OnGetPredefinedStrings (DISPID DispID,
    CStringArray* Strings,
    CDWordArray* Cookies)
    {
    switch (DispID)
        {
        case dispidMultiSelect:
            Strings->Add (MultiSelect_Values.Single);
            Cookies->Add (0);
            Strings->Add (MultiSelect_Values.Multiple);
            Cookies->Add (1);
            Strings->Add (MultiSelect_Values.Extended);
            Cookies->Add (2);
            return TRUE;
        }
    return FALSE;
    }
```

As directed, it returns FALSE unless *DispID* happens to be the one assigned to the *MultiSelect* property. In that case, the three enumeration strings are added to the *Strings* array; and the associated values are added to the *Cookies* array in the same order. (If the two arrays are both order-dependent—and they are—why couldn't the string index have been used instead of the separate "cookie" array? Possibly because then there'd have been no excuse to add the word "cookie" to the official MFC lexicon, I guess.)

The *OnGetPredefinedStrings()* function will be invoked when the full list of enumerations is needed, for example, when the property's possible values are about to be displayed in the Properties box. When the user *selects* one of them, the *OnGetPredefinedValue()* function will be invoked:

```
BOOL CTabListCtrl::OnGetPredefinedValue (DISPID DispID,
    DWORD Cookie,
    VARIANT FAR* Value)
  {
  switch (DispID)
    {
    case dispidMultiSelect:
      Value->vt = VT_I2;
      Value->iVal = (short) Cookie;
      return TRUE;
    }
  return FALSE;
  }
```

Amazingly, "cookies" aren't intended to be the actual values; they are merely another link in the seemingly endless chain of indirection. However, I deliberately made the "cookie" array elements equal to the desired, associated enumeration values.

The *Value* argument is a pointer to a VARIANT, a **union** that is not indexed in the Visual C++ 1.52c online help, but has the following structure:

```
typedef struct FARSTRUCT tagVARIANT VARIANT;
typedef struct FARSTRUCT tagVARIANT VARIANTARG;

typedef struct tagVARIANT {
  VARTYPE vt;
  unsigned short wReserved1;
  unsigned short wReserved2;
  unsigned short wReserved3;
  union {
    unsigned char bVal;
    short iVal;
    long lVal;
    float fltVal;
```

```
      double  dblVal;
      VARIANT_BOOL  bool;
      SCODE scode;
      CY    cyVal;
      DATE date;
      BSTR bstrVal;
      IUnknown  FAR*   punkVal;
      IDispatch  FAR*  pdispVal;
      SAFEARRAY  FAR*  parray;
      unsigned char  FAR *  pbVal;
      short FAR* piVal;
      long  FAR*  plVal;
      float  FAR*pfltVal;
      double  FAR*  pdblVal;
      VARIANT_BOOL  FAR* pbool;
      SCODE  FAR*pscode;
      CY FAR* pcyVal;
      DATE  FAR* pdate;
      BSTR  FAR*  pbstrVal;
      IUnknown FAR*  FAR*ppunkVal;
      IDispatch FAR*  FAR*  ppdispVal;
      SAFEARRAY FAR* FAR*  parray;
      VARIANT  FAR* pvarVal;
      void  FAR*  byref;
   };
};
```

I know *I'm* impressed! I think the only data type they've left out is "pointer
to a novel by Dickens." You must set the VARTYPE element *vt* to advise
what you're sending. In the case of the *MultiSelect* property, which is
defined as a **short,** we make the above assignment to the *iVal* member, and
state the data type by assigning *VT_I2* to the *vt* member. (There is, of course,
a full set of **#define**s, one for each possible data type.)

The final function of the set of three is *OnGetDisplayString()*. This is called
when the system needs to know the current value of a property, but wishes
to display it as the appropriate enumeration:

```
BOOL CTabListCtrl::OnGetDisplayString (DISPID DispID,
    CString & String)
  {
  switch (DispID)
    {
    case dispidMultiSelect:
      switch (MultiSelect)
        {
        case 0:
          String = MultiSelect_Values.Single;
          break;
        case 1:
```

```
                String = MultiSelect_Values.Multiple;
                break;
            case 2:
                String = MultiSelect_Values.Extended;
                break;
            }
        return TRUE;
        }
    return FALSE;
    }
```

That leaves us, almost as an afterthought, with the internal management of the *MultiSelect* property. The notification function is just like the first three:

```
void CTabListCtrl::OnMultiSelectChanged()
    {
    RecreateControlWindow();
    SetModifiedFlag();
    }
```

And the code added to *PreCreateWindow()* is similar to that servicing the other three, as well (the new code is highlighted):

```
BOOL CTabListCtrl::PreCreateWindow(CREATESTRUCT& cs)
    {
    cs.lpszClass = _T("LISTBOX");
    if (! IntegralHeight)
        cs.style |= LBS_NOINTEGRALHEIGHT;
    if (Sorted)
        cs.style |= LBS_SORT;
    if (MultiSelect == 1)
        cs.style |= LBS_MULTIPLESEL;
    else if (MultiSelect == 2)
        cs.style |= LBS_EXTENDEDSEL;
    return COleControl::PreCreateWindow(cs);
    }
```

Finally, we must add an entry to *DoPropExchange()*:

```
void CTabListCtrl::DoPropExchange(CPropExchange* pPX)
    {
    ExchangeVersion(pPX, MAKELONG(_wVerMinor, _wVerMajor));
    COleControl::DoPropExchange(pPX);

    PX_Bool (pPX, "IntegralHeight", IntegralHeight, TRUE);
    PX_Bool (pPX, "Sorted", Sorted, FALSE);
    PX_Short (pPX, "MultiSelect", MultiSelect, 0);

    delete Brush;
    Brush = new CBrush (TranslateColor (GetBackColor ()));
    }
```

Don't forget to run *Tools..Make Typelib* before compiling, since you've added properties. But, once you do, you should be able to start Visual Basic and see the new properties, including the enumerations for the *MultiSelect* property.

Sending Down Shoots

The next set of properties we'll implement are those *already implemented* by the underlying Windows Listbox control. To make them work, we just have to send a message to the control. In this section we'll implement three properties: *ListCount, ListIndex,* and *TopIndex.* The data type of all three is **short** and none of the three should appear in the design-time Properties box.

This type of property is implemented using Get and Set functions, because the OLE control does not, itself, need to store this data at its own level—nor would it be useful if it did. Instead, the OLE control is acting in these instances as a medium, a channel through which the information flows. Figure 17.4 shows Class Wizard's Add Property dialog as it adds one of these properties. Note that I have blanked out the Set function value, since this is a read-only property. (It follows that you would blank out the value of the Get function value for a write-only property.)

As it happens, none of these three properties is persistent; so we don't need to add any code to the *DoPropExchange()* function. All we need to do is send messages to the underlying window, one for each of the Get and Set functions.

Sending a message to the underlying control is about as simple as it can be. Remember, your new OLE control class is derived from the *COleControl* class, which is ultimately derived from *CWnd.* The *CWnd* class has a

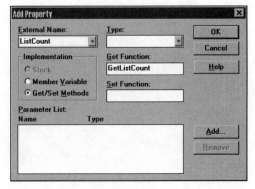

Figure 17.4   Adding a read-only Get/Set property.

SendMessage() member, used to send messages to itself. Its *wParam* and *lParam* arguments each default to zero, if you don't supply values for them. So, to implement *GetListCount()*, for example, all we need is one line of code:

```
short CTabListCtrl::GetListCount()
   {
   if (AmbientUserMode())
      return (short) SendMessage (LB_GETCOUNT);
   else
      {
      ThrowError (CTL_E_PERMISSIONDENIED, IDS_NOSHOW);
      return NULL;
      }
   }
```

> *AmbientUserMode() returns TRUE if the control is working in a running application, and FALSE if a form is being designed. To prevent a property from appearing in a container's Properties box, simply throw any error from its Get function.*

The member function, *COleControl::ThrowError()* that does the job for us, uses standard exception handling. (I know, C++ exception handling is only simulated in Visual C++ 1.52c, but the simulation is adequate to do the trick here.) This function should only be used when an error occurs during a set or get of a property; there's a stock *Error* event you can fire at other times.

There are two variants of *ThrowError()*. One takes a stringtable ID as the second parameter; the other takes a pointer to a local string. Even though we have to provide a resource string (*IDS_NOSHOW*) with the error, in this particular case the text will never be seen and the user will be unaware there was an "error." Personally, I like the VBX technique of simply setting a "no show" flag better. But no one asked me.

When the system tries to load this property value into the Properties box at design time, an error will occur—Visual Basic doesn't care what the error is—so read-only properties never show up in the box. At run-time, if the program tries to assign a value to this property, the *set not supported* error will be triggered.

TopIndex can be read from, again only at run-time:

```
short CTabListCtrl::GetTopIndex()
   {
```

```
if (AmbientUserMode())
   return (short) SendMessage (LB_GETTOPINDEX);
else
   {
   ThrowError (CTL_E_PERMISSIONDENIED, IDS_NOSHOW);
   return NULL;
   }
}
```

We have a new requirement in setting *TopIndex*, in that we mustn't allow the container to set it to a value out of range for the available indexes. This is going to be a recurring theme, so I've added a little helper function:

```
BOOL CTabListCtrl::IsValidIndex (short TestIndex)
   {
   return ((TestIndex > -1) &&
      (TestIndex < (short) SendMessage (LB_GETCOUNT)));
   }
```

Using this function, *SetTopIndex()* becomes simple to code:

```
void CTabListCtrl::SetTopIndex(short NewValue)
   {
   if (IsValidIndex (NewValue))
      {
      SendMessage (LB_SETTOPINDEX, NewValue);
      SetModifiedFlag();
      }
   else
      ThrowError (CTL_E_INVALIDPROPERTYVALUE,
         IDS_INVALIDPROPERTYVALUE);
   }
```

ListIndex is just slightly trickier, not because of OLE, but because list box controls behave a little differently depending on whether they are set for single or multiple selection. If single selection and one item is selected, *ListIndex* returns the index of that item (if no item is selected, it returns a -1). In a multiple selection list box, *ListIndex* returns the index of the item contained within the focus rectangle, whether or not that item is actually selected:

```
short CTabListCtrl::GetListIndex()
   {
   if (AmbientUserMode())
      {
      if (MultiSelect)
         return (short) SendMessage (LB_GETCARETINDEX);
      else
         return (short) SendMessage (LB_GETCURSEL);
      }
   else
      {
```

```
      ThrowError (CTL_E_PERMISSIONDENIED, IDS_NOSHOW);
      return NULL;
      }
   }

void CTabListCtrl::SetListIndex(short NewValue)
   {
   if ((IsValidIndex (NewValue)) ||
       ( (! MultiSelect) && NewValue == -1))
      {
      if (MultiSelect)
         SendMessage (LB_SETCARETINDEX, NewValue);
      else
         SendMessage (LB_SETCURSEL, NewValue);
      SetModifiedFlag();
      }
   else
      ThrowError (CTL_E_INVALIDPROPERTYVALUE,
         IDS_INVALIDPROPERTYVALUE);
   }
```

Seed Properties

There are some properties whose values are set by some action of the
control, and so can be read, but not written to—just as once the DNA has
been deposited into a mangrove seed, it cannot be further modified. Strictly
speaking, the *ListCount* property is one of these. However, the internal
maintenance of this property happens with no effort on our part. This is not
true of the *NewIndex* property.

At the list box control level, there *is* no such property. However, whenever
an item is added or inserted into the list box, the messages that accomplish
this, return the index of the new item. Since setting a property cannot return
a value, we have to save that index; reading the artificial *NewIndex* property
allows the container to obtain it.

When we add the *NewIndex* property to the controls, we'll have to make it a
get/set property, because OLE can't maintain it. We still need to make the value
a data member of the class, however; so we have to type in its definition:

```
class CTabListCtrl : public COleControl
{
  /
  /
private:
  short NewIndex;
  /
  /
};
```

The property's default value is -1; this is not a persistent property, so it need not have a presence in *DoPropExchange()*. However, it must receive this default value in *OnResetState()*:

```
void CTabListCtrl::OnResetState()
  {
  /
  /
  NewIndex = -1;
  }
```

Returning the value when requested is trivial; if it weren't a "no show" property, it could be accomplished in one line:

```
short CTabListCtrl::GetNewIndex()
  {
  if (AmbientUserMode())
    return NewIndex;
  else
    {
    ThrowError (CTL_E_PERMISSIONDENIED, IDS_NOSHOW);
    return NULL;
    }
  }
```

NewIndex is a read-only property, so it has no Set function.

Since the argument *NewValue* (originally called *nNewValue* by Class Wizard) isn't used, I've removed its name from the function header to avoid getting warnings of unused arguments, which some compilers generate.

The *ListIndex* property follows this same pattern:

```
short CTabListCtrl::GetListIndex()
  {
  if (AmbientUserMode())
    {
    if (MultiSelect)
      return (short) SendMessage (LB_GETCARETINDEX);
    else
      return (short) SendMessage (LB_GETCURSEL);
    }
  else
    {
    ThrowError (CTL_E_PERMISSIONDENIED, IDS_NOSHOW);
    return NULL;
    }
  }

void CTabListCtrl::SetListIndex(short NewValue)
  {
```

```
if ((IsValidIndex (NewValue)) ||
    ( (! MultiSelect) && NewValue == -1))
  {
  if (MultiSelect)
     SendMessage (LB_SETCARETINDEX, NewValue);
  else
     SendMessage (LB_SETCURSEL, NewValue);
  SetModifiedFlag();
  }
else
   ThrowError (CTL_E_INVALIDPROPERTYVALUE,
      IDS_INVALIDPROPERTYVALUE);
}
```

Strings and Things

The next property we'll implement is the *Text* property. This is interesting because it's the first string property we've worked with.

When you use Class Wizard to add the *Text* property, it will allow you to make it a stock property. Usually, that's what you want. However, the stock *Text* property exposes the window's caption, and a list box's caption is about as useful as a carport on a mangrove island. So we have to implement this property as a custom, get/set property. And, since the *Text* property is read-only, you must delete the name of the Set function to make it so.

Whether stock or custom, the data type of the *Text* property is frozen at *BSTR*. Fortunately, the MFC *CString* class already provides conversion functions to this data type. In fact, Class Wizard's skeleton code places a *CString* variable there for you, and returns the value from it correctly. All you have to do is put something meaningful in the string.

In our case, that "something meaningful" will be the text of the currently selected (single-selection) or last-clicked (multi-selection) item in the list:

```
BSTR CTabListCtrl::GetText()
  {
  if (AmbientUserMode())
    {
    short i = GetListIndex();
    CString s;
    if (i > -1)
      {
      short Length = (short)
         SendMessage (LB_GETTEXTLEN, (WPARAM) i);
      SendMessage (LB_GETTEXT,
         (WPARAM) i,
         (LPARAM) (LPSTR) s.GetBuffer (Length));
      s.ReleaseBuffer (Length);
```

```
        }
    return s.AllocSysString();
    }
else
    {
    ThrowError (CTL_E_PERMISSIONDENIED, IDS_NOSHOW);
    return NULL;
    }
}
```

The *SelCount* property returns the number of currently selected items in the list. It's usually implemented as a read-only property; but in an OCX we can be more subtle than that, allowing an assignment of zero (to deselect all items) but throwing an error if any other value is supplied:

```
short CTabListCtrl::GetSelCount()
    {
    if (AmbientUserMode())
        {
        if (MultiSelect)
            return (short) SendMessage (LB_GETSELCOUNT);
        else
            return (short) (SendMessage (LB_GETCURSEL) > -1) ? 1 : 0;
        }
    else
        {
        ThrowError (CTL_E_PERMISSIONDENIED, IDS_NOSHOW);
        return NULL;
        }
    }

void CTabListCtrl::SetSelCount(short NewValue)
    {
    if (NewValue == 0)
        {
        if (MultiSelect)
            SendMessage (LB_SETSEL, FALSE, MAKELPARAM (-1, 0));
        else
            SendMessage (LB_SETCURSEL, (WPARAM) -1);
        SetModifiedFlag();
        }
    else
        ThrowError (CTL_E_INVALIDPROPERTYVALUE,
            IDS_INVALIDPROPERTYVALUE);
    }
```

One Tree, Many Branches

As our adventure in custom properties continues, we find we have no less than three array properties to implement.

Array properties are, admittedly, awkward to handle in VBXs. Fortunately OLE controls have solved that particular problem, by making it just one aspect of a broader problem: Accessing properties with arguments.

If you think about it, programmatically specifying a one-dimensional array element looks an awful lot like a method invocation with one argument. So, the logic goes, why not treat them the same? And, as a side benefit, you can create a multi-dimensional array, which is something VBXs never quite managed before they were disowned.

We can start with the *List* property which, as you know, provides access to each item in the listbox. You use Class Wizard as usual, but when adding the new property you click on the Add... button near the Parameter List listbox. That brings up the Add Property Parameter dialog, as shown in Figure 17.5.

When Class Wizard generates the Set and Get functions, it will include an *Index* parameter of type **short**:

```
BSTR CTabListCtrl::GetList(short Index)
   {
   if (IsValidIndex (Index) || Index == -1)
      {
      CString s;
      if (Index > -1)
         {
         short Length = (short)
            SendMessage (LB_GETTEXTLEN, (WPARAM) Index);
         SendMessage (LB_GETTEXT,
            (WPARAM) Index,
            (LPARAM) (LPSTR) s.GetBuffer (Length));
         s.ReleaseBuffer (Length);
         }
      return s.AllocSysString();
      }
   else
      {
      ThrowError (CTL_E_INVALIDPROPERTYVALUE,
         IDS_INVALIDPROPERTYVALUE);
      return NULL;
      }
   }
```

Figure 17.5 Adding a property parameter.

Note that we didn't bother to check for *AmbientUserMode()*. You are probably used to the *List* property not showing up in the Properties box of Visual Basic 3. But that's okay; any request for an element will trigger the "Invalid property value" error when no items are in the list box, and *any* error prevents the property from showing up in the Properties box.

Setting the *List* property means replacing an existing item—something the underlying list box control doesn't support. We can still make it happen, though, by storing the requested index's item data, deleting the item, inserting the new one at the same location, and restoring the item data. Notice that this function also resets the *NewIndex* property:

```
void CTabListCtrl::SetList(short Index, LPCTSTR NewValue)
   {
   if (IsValidIndex (Index))
      {
      DWORD ItemData = SendMessage (LB_GETITEMDATA,
         (WPARAM) Index);
      SendMessage (LB_DELETESTRING, (WPARAM) Index);
      NewIndex = (short) SendMessage (LB_INSERTSTRING,
         (WPARAM) Index, (LPARAM) NewValue);
      SendMessage (LB_SETITEMDATA, (WPARAM) NewIndex, ItemData);
      SetModifiedFlag();
      }
   else
      ThrowError (CTL_E_INVALIDPROPERTYVALUE,
         IDS_INVALIDPROPERTYVALUE);
   }
```

Speaking of the item data, it is accessed through the control's *ItemData* array property:

```
long CTabListCtrl::GetItemData(short Index)
   {
   if (IsValidIndex (Index))
      return SendMessage (LB_GETITEMDATA,
         (WPARAM) Index);
   else
      {
      ThrowError (CTL_E_INVALIDPROPERTYVALUE,
         IDS_INVALIDPROPERTYVALUE);
      return NULL;
      }
   }

void CTabListCtrl::SetItemData(short Index, long NewValue)
   {
   if (IsValidIndex (Index))
      {
      SendMessage (LB_SETITEMDATA,
```

```
         (WPARAM) Index, NewValue);
      SetModifiedFlag();
      }
   else
      ThrowError (CTL_E_INVALIDPROPERTYVALUE,
         IDS_INVALIDPROPERTYVALUE);
   }
```

That leaves us with the *Selected* property. This property is implemented
directly by the Listbox control, but *only* when that control has been created
with one of the multiple selection styles set. That means we'll have to
supply just a bit of extra code to hide that difference from the user of our
controls:

```
BOOL CTabListCtrl::GetSelected(short Index)
   {
   if (IsValidIndex (Index))
      if (MultiSelect)
         return (BOOL) SendMessage (LB_GETSEL, (WPARAM) Index);
      else
         return (BOOL) (SendMessage (LB_GETCURSEL) == Index);
   else
      {
      ThrowError (CTL_E_INVALIDPROPERTYVALUE,
         IDS_INVALIDPROPERTYVALUE);
      return NULL;
      }
   }
```

In a multiple-selection list box, determining if a given entry in the list box is
currently selected is the object of the *LB_GETSEL* message. In a single
selection list box, you have to find out the current selection and compare it
against the queried *Index.*

Assigning a value to the *Selected* property is slightly more complex, because
that value may be intended to either select or *deselect* the indexed item:

```
void CTabListCtrl::SetSelected(short Index, BOOL NewValue)
   {
   if (IsValidIndex (Index))
      {
      if (MultiSelect)
         SendMessage (LB_SETSEL, (WPARAM) NewValue,
            MAKELPARAM (Index, 0));
      else if (NewValue)
         SendMessage (LB_SETCURSEL, (WPARAM) Index);
      else
         SendMessage (LB_SETCURSEL, (WPARAM) -1);
      SetModifiedFlag();
      }
```

```
else
  ThrowError (CTL_E_INVALIDPROPERTYVALUE,
    IDS_INVALIDPROPERTYVALUE);
}
```

Using an index of -1 with the *LB_SETCURSEL* message deselects the current item, whatever it is.

You Say You Want to Derive a Control...?

With the exception of the *Columns* property, which we've not yet implemented for the TabList control, we've treated all three controls the same...a task which, I'm sure, you found a bit tedious at times.

In the next chapter, we're going to add the individual features that will distinguish each of these three controls from the others. But, meanwhile, you're entitled to ask: Why did we have to do this? Isn't this supposed to be C++ with object-oriented programming? If so, why couldn't I just write *one* generic listbox control class, then derive the three real controls from it?

Well, you *can*...but there are a number of steps you must go through to accomplish this, because neither Control Wizard nor Class Wizard provides any support in this matter.

First, you need to locate the *BEGIN_MESSAGE_MAP* macro in the implementation file for your base class, and remove the entry:

```
ON_OLEVERB(AXS_IDS_VERB_PROPERTIES, OnProperties)
```

If you don't, the container will list the properties for your derived class *and* the base class—in other words, inherited properties will be listed twice.

Next, if the base class isn't intended to be used by itself (it's an "abstract" class), you should change its *UpdateRegistry()* function to simply return TRUE. This prevents the base class from being registered and therefore showing up in the list of controls in this OCX. You'll have to do the same for the base class' property page registration, too.

In the base class' constructor, you'll need to remove the call to *InitializeIIDs()*, which caches type information for the base class; otherwise there will be a memory leak when your OCX is unloaded because the cached information will not be freed.

You'll also have to dive into the project's .ODL file—*very* carefully—and comment out the information to the base class. The .ODL file is the object description, and it is modified whenever you run the *Tools..Make Typelib* utility, which you must do whenever you add or remove a property, event, or method. So you'll have to add checking the .ODL file to that chore, to make sure your comments haven't reverted to code.

You'll need to find the base class' *DoPropExchange()* member function, and delete the line:

```
ExchangeVersion(pPX, MAKELONG(_wVerMinor, _wVerMajor));
```

That's because your derived class or classes will call this explicitly, and an attempt to call it twice will generate one of those assertion boxes.

While you're thinking of the *DoPropExchange()* function, be sure to go into the derived classes' version of this and change the entry:

```
COleControl::DoPropExchange(pPX);
```

so that their base class is called instead of the grandparent class.

Now, those code changes are the easy part. Much tougher is the further modification you must make to the .ODL file. You'll have to manually update the property, event, and method dispatch IDs. This is not a trivial task, because the dispatch ID is not a simple number. Basically, it is divided into two halves. The LOWORD is the distance from the top of the dispatch map, one-based. The HIWORD is the distance of the map from the most-derived class, zero-based. Worse, the DISPIDs for events are handled differently than they are for properties and events.

What I'm saying is, even though repeating your code three times seems tedious, it's actually less work and less prone to mistakes than trying to use object-derivation...suggesting, again, that OLE controls were less than thoroughly thought out.

Now, if I haven't talked you out of this, let me refer you to MFC Technical Note #39, which describes *exactly* how to figure out those dispatch IDs.

The Appearance Property

A property we made no attempt to implement was the *Appearance* property. This is a stock property for 32-bit OLE controls, but is unavailable for 16-bit controls. Why can't we just implement it manually?

If we were not writing a control derived from an existing Windows control class, we could, easily. We would lose the *BorderStyle* property and replace it with *Appearance*, an enumerated property with two choices: "Flat" and "3-D." Based on which choice was picked, we'd just paint our *own* borders...a simple rectangle, or the beveled edges of a three-dimensional shape.

The problem is, since we *did* derive from a control class, there's no place left to draw the bevels. As an OLE control, we are not permitted to draw outside of our own boundaries...and the OLE control subsystem does the job of sizing the control. Our boundaries are the subclassed boundaries.

You can take another approach: You can, instead of deriving from a control class, make a window of that class a *child window* of the control. You can then make the child any size you like, including making it a little smaller than the OLE control to allow room for the border. In such a case, you would create the child window without a border of its own, since the OLE control is responsible for painting the border (thin or 3-D, as desired).

You'd probably make an object of the child window class (*CListbox*, in this example) a property of the control. Instead of using *SendMessage()*, you'd be able to use the object methods of that class, which might actually be easier. And messages from the child would go directly to the OLE control window, which would be its parent, simplifying the message map hassles we had to go through.

The down side is that there will be an extra window in the system, which is a bit of extra overhead. You have to decide whether support for the *Appearance* property, which is really the only benefit, is worth it.

Paddling On

In our next chapter, we'll add those properties to TabList, ImageList, and DrawList to make each of them unique. I've separated this task from the present chapter, simply because these details will involve more Windows-type programming than OLE-type programming. So, if you are just skimming for OLE control details, you can skip the next chapter. On the other hand, if you are reading to develop these useful controls, read on!

18 Custom Methods and Events

L ET ME TAKE YOU on a kayaking trip through a mangrove island.

As I described, the mangroves are rooted *below* the surface of the water, so there's no surface. However, the roots don't coalesce into a trunk until they just about get to the water line, and they all intertwine so there *is* a surface of sorts, if you happen to be a squirrel or a lizard. For a human to venture in there would be madness—he or she would quickly get so entangled in the maze extrication might well be impossible.

Although from a distance the islands appear to be solid, they are in fact not even contiguous. Each is threaded with open water that looks much like a web of interconnecting streams on a conventional island. It is through those "streams" that we kayak.

Even those streams are not without their peril, however. Many of them end abruptly, in a root-choked cul-de-sac. Even when they aren't actually blocked, mangrove limbs, intertwined overhead, may gradually approach the water level so closely that, no matter how far backwards you bend, passage is impossible. And the streams wind and twist so that you can never tell what's coming up—never know whether the trail you follow will pan out, or entrap you in a web of branches so tightly you have to jump out and pull your craft out of them...if you can.

Like mangrove islands, OLE controls also look solid...until you approach them. They look fresh and green and exciting. And they *are* exciting...but not in the way you'd like, if you work for a living and have to face deadlines.

Now, I could have just told you that two chapters ago...but I wanted you to have this experience, in the safe confines of a book, that might save you from a workplace disaster in the cutthroat confines of your place of employment. So, let's look at what we're trying to do with the enhanced Listbox controls.

First, they are based on a solid foundation in the form of the standard Windows list box. This is a tool we've used, literally, for years; it's been used directly, as a child control-within-a-control, and within VBXs. All we've asked to do with it is add tabs and columns, and use the owner-draw facility to display pictures or allow the VB programmer to do so. This is not a big thing; in many of my beginning Windows programming classes, I have my students do an owner-draw list box project.

But programming an OLE control, even one based on a solid child window class, puts one up against a web of classes, functions, and interfaces that makes the twisted roots of a mangrove island look like a sandy beach. And so, I lead you on into the thicket, as we attempt to leave the trivial accomplishments behind and complete our three OLE controls.

Frankly, all mangroves look alike to me. But if you know your mangroves, you can tell them apart by their leaf size, branch shapes, and so on.

Our three list boxes are also intended to appear quite similar—our implementing the preceding identical sets of properties helps ensure that. But they are *not* truly identical, and we are now ready to being distinguishing between them.

Specializing the TabList Control

The TabList control is intended to display multiple columns of data, in which each text item is expected to contain some number of tab characters.

As you may know, a normal list box displays these characters as little black blotches. That's because the *LBS_USETABSTOPS* style isn't usually set. For our TabList control, we'll set it as shown here:

```
BOOL CTabListCtrl::PreCreateWindow(CREATESTRUCT& cs)
   {
   ⇓
   ⇓
   cs.style |= LBS_USETABSTOPS;
   return COleControl::PreCreateWindow(cs);
   }
```

That's all it takes to make the list box align tab characters to its default tab stops. These stops are positioned at every 32 dialog base units, or about eight characters apart. That's probably not what you'll want. So we have to provide a way to set custom tab stops.

We already have a *Columns* property. Previously we implemented it according to its usual rules, which works fine for the DrawList and ImageList controls. But, for the TabList control only, we'll remove that code from *PreCreateWindow()* so we can use the value for a different purpose:

```
BOOL CTabListCtrl::PreCreateWindow(CREATESTRUCT& cs)
   {
   cs.lpszClass = _T("LISTBOX");
// if (Columns > 1)
//    cs.style |= LBS_MULTICOLUMN;
   ⇓
   ⇓
   cs.style |= LBS_USETABSTOPS;
   return COleControl::PreCreateWindow(cs);
   }
```

That purpose, of course, is to determine how many elements are in our new *TabStops* array. (There will be one fewer tabs than columns.) Please note the distinction between this custom property and the *TabStop* extended property, managed by the container.

As an array, the *TabStops* property is added to the control as shown in Figure 18.1.

We could store these tab stops in a managed, MFC array. But that really seems like overkill to me. I can't imagine there'd ever be more than, say, 32 tab stops in a single list box. So I'm going to implement storage for this property as a simple, in-line array:

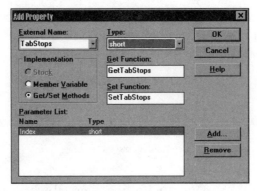

Figure 18.1 Adding the *TabStops* property.

```
class CTabListCtrl : public COleControl
{
   ⇓
   ⇓
private:
   short NewIndex;
   enum { MaxTabStops = 32 };
   short TabStops[MaxTabStops];
   ⇓
   ⇓
};
```

That gives us the expected form for the *get* function:

```
short CTabListCtrl::GetTabStops(short Index)
   {
   if (Index >= 0 && Index < (Columns - 1))
      return TabStops[Index];
   else
      {
      ThrowError (CTL_E_INVALIDPROPERTYARRAYINDEX,
         IDS_INVALIDINDEX);
      return 0;
      }
   }
```

However, when the user sets the value, we not only need to store it—we need to send it to the list box control:

```
void CTabListCtrl::SetTabStops(short Index, short NewValue)
   {
   if (Index >= 0 && Index < (Columns - 1))
      {
      TabStops[Index] = NewValue;
      ResetTabs();
      }
```

```
  else
     ThrowError (CTL_E_INVALIDPROPERTYARRAYINDEX,
        IDS_INVALIDINDEX);
  SetModifiedFlag();
  }
```

I moved the sending of the LB_SETTABSTOPS message to a separate function, because it also needs to be sent if the number of columns changes.

Columns, you remember, was implemented as a member variable of the DrawList and ImageList controls. We need to make it a *get/set* function of the TabList control, however. That means adding it to the class declaration as a property (it's a **short**). Its *get* function is trivial:

```
short CTabListCtrl::GetColumns()
  {
  return Columns;
  }
```

However, we must not let the user set *Columns* any higher than 33 (one greater than the number of elements in the *TabStops* array):

```
void CTabListCtrl::SetColumns(short NewValue)
  {
  if (NewValue > 0 && NewValue <= (MaxTabStops + 1))
    {
    Columns = NewValue;
    ResetTabs ();
    SetModifiedFlag();
    }
  else
     ThrowError (CTL_E_INVALIDPROPERTYARRAYINDEX,
        IDS_INVALIDINDEX);
    }
```

The *ResetTabs()* function is interesting because it must perform a conversion. List box tab stops are in dialog base units, but a Visual Basic developer is going to want to make the specification in twips. Even so, not all containers of your OLE control may be Visual Basic, and other development environments may use other coordinate systems.

Moreover, the Windows API function *GetDialogBaseUnits()* returns the base unit sizes for the *system* font, not necessarily the font being used in the dialog.

The OLE CDK provides a few tools to help. The algorithm isn't terribly complex, but it does contain three blocks of code:

```
void CTabListCtrl::ResetTabs (void)
  {
  if (Columns > 1)
    {
    CFontHolder FontHolder = InternalGetFont ();
    TEXTMETRIC TextMetrics;
    GetFontTextMetrics (&TextMetrics, FontHolder);
    WORD DlgWidthUnits = TextMetrics.tmAveCharWidth / 4;
    WORD DlgHeightUnits = TextMetrics.tmHeight / 8;

    int TabStopsX [MaxTabStops];
    POINTL HiMetricPoint;
    POINTF ContainerPoint;
    ContainerPoint.y = 0;
    SIZE ListboxPoint;
    CWindowDC dc (CWnd::FromHandle ((HWND) GetHwnd ()));
    for (int i = 0; i < MaxTabStops; i++)
      {
      ContainerPoint.x = TabStops[i];
      ContainerPoint.y = 0;
      TransformCoords (&HiMetricPoint, &ContainerPoint,
        XFORMCOORDS_POSITION |
        XFORMCOORDS_CONTAINERTOHIMETRIC);
      ListboxPoint.cx = (int) HiMetricPoint.x;
      ListboxPoint.cy = (int) HiMetricPoint.y;
      dc.HIMETRICtoDP (&ListboxPoint);
      TabStopsX[i] = ListboxPoint.cx;
      }

    SendMessage (LB_SETTABSTOPS,
      MaxTabStops, (long) (LPSTR) TabStops);
    }
  }
```

In the first block, we obtain the control's font and derive a pseudo-dialog-units-sort of value from it. In the second, we run through each of the tab stops in the array, converting it from himetric coordinates to the dialog coordinates the list box will understand. Finally, we send the converted coordinates to the base list box.

Since the list box control is nice enough to do all the columnizing for us, we need add no further properties to this control. The one thing that would be nice if we are to *test* it, would be a way to get stuff *into* the list box.

On the Class Wizard dialog, under the OLE Automation tab, we can add methods as well as properties to a control. The procedure is very similar; in fact, it turns out that properties and methods differ more in concept than in implementation. The biggest difference is in how the container provides access; most will assign values to a property using an assignment operator, while methods will be exercised using a function or procedure call-like syntax. But all of that is window dressing. Underneath, they are the same.

So, we can add our first method, *AddItem*. And here we come to brick wall number one: We'd like to mimic the *AddItem* method used by VBXs, which allow an optional second parameter. However, OLE Controls do not support optional arguments. And they do not permit anything analogous to "overloaded" methods. So we'll either have to omit the second parameter (which specifies an index for insertions), require it, or write *two* methods with different names (*AddItem* and *InsertItem*, for example). That last one is my preferred solution; but we only need *AddItem* for now.

When adding a method we must specify any arguments by name and by type. *AddItem* requires one argument, *Item*, whose data type is *BSTR*. It is *not* a class. A *BSTR* is similar to a standard C-style string, except that it is preceded by a length. That value is located at a negative offset from the address, so *BSTR*s can be used as C-strings in many contexts.

Class Wizard will generate the appropriate dispatches for *AddItem*, so that the following function is generated and all we have to do is fill it in:

```
void CTabListCtrl::AddItem(BSTR FAR* Item)
    {
    SendMessage (LB_ADDSTRING, 0, (LPARAM) (LPVOID) Item);
    SetModifiedFlag();
    }
```

Next, in order to mimic a true list box control, we'll want to add support for events like click, double-click, and so on. Events are what separate OLE controls from other OLE servers. As with properties, there are stock events and custom events. Adding stock events is so trivial, I'll leave you to experiment with that on your own. It's the custom events that are interesting. However, the adventure with custom events begins with the ImageList control.

Specializing the ImageList Control

The ImageList's specialty is displaying, not text, but collections of pictures. OLE provides a surprising amount of very sophisticated support—and then, stops just short of what we need.

Earlier you saw me use the *CFontHolder* class. I didn't really say anything about it. But there's also a *CPictureHolder* class, and the two have a lot in common. That's because their innards are inextricably tangled with the web of OLE, and fonts and pictures are actually accessed through OLE interfaces, rather than directly.

Such a distancing might seem at first to be a good idea. After all, both fonts and pictures are intended to be displayed more often than they are intended to be mucked about with. The extra level does get in the way when you *do* want to fiddle with a font—modify it, for example. And many applications exist that perform various transformations on bitmaps. But as long as the level-of-indirection provides access to those abilities, and makes the more common uses simpler, who cares? —Well, *we* will. But I'll come to that.

In the ImageList control, the *List* property is an array of pictures, rather than of text. That means, when it is added by Class Wizard, the data type must be specified as *LPPICTUREDISP*.

Many controls have a *single* picture property—in fact, there is a *stock* picture property, and a stock property page to support it. You can also make custom picture properties, which require a get/set implementation (rather than member variable). If you have these, then adding the highlighted line to your list of property pages will provide a very nice, free manner of supplying access to it (don't forget to increment the page count in the *BEGIN_PROPPAGEIDS* macro):

```
BEGIN_PROPPAGEIDS(CTabListCtrl, 4)
    PROPPAGEID(CTabListPropPage::guid)
    PROPPAGEID(CLSID_CColorPropPage)
    PROPPAGEID(CLSID_CFontPropPage)
    PROPPAGEID(CLSID_CPicturePropPage)
END_PROPPAGEIDS(CTabListCtrl)
```

As with the stock font property page, the picture page automatically latches on to any of your picture properties...*as long as they aren't array properties.* That's consistent, though, since array properties can't be loaded at design time.

If you wished to manage the picture property yourself, you could add a *CPictureHolder* data member to your control class. However, we need an array of them; and the ImageList control is based on a list box, so we can use *it* to store the values for us.

See, an owner-draw list box uses the same *LB_ADDSTRING, LB_DELETESTRING,* and so on, messages that a regular list box uses. The difference is—in spite of the message name—that, instead of supplying a pointer to a string buffer, you give it *any* 32-bit value you like. That 32-bit value can as easily be a pointer to an object as anything else.

To make ImageList *be* an owner-draw list box, we only have to set one of two flags in the *PreCreateWindow()* function:

```
BOOL CImageListCtrl::PreCreateWindow(CREATESTRUCT& cs)
  {
  cs.lpszClass = _T("LISTBOX");
  if (Columns > 1)
    cs.style |= LBS_MULTICOLUMN;
  if (! IntegralHeight)
    cs.style |= LBS_NOINTEGRALHEIGHT;
  if (MultiSelect == 1)
    cs.style |= LBS_MULTIPLESEL;
  else if (MultiSelect == 2)
    cs.style |= LBS_EXTENDEDSEL;
  cs.style |= LBS_OWNERDRAWFIXED;
  return COleControl::PreCreateWindow(cs);
  }
```

Those flags are *LBS_OWNERDRAWFIXED* for fixed-height items, and *LBS_OWNERDRAWVARIABLE* if the various items in the list box will be of different sizes.

ImageList has an *AddItem* method, just like TabList. However, in ImageList's case, the method takes a *LPPICTUREDISP* argument. This is where we initially create and deliver to the underlying list box, a *CPictureHolder* object:

```
void CImageListCtrl::AddItem(LPPICTUREDISP Item)
  {
  CPictureHolder * NewItem = new CPictureHolder;
  NewItem->SetPictureDispatch (Item);
  NewIndex = (short) SendMessage (LB_ADDSTRING,
    0, (LPARAM) (LPVOID) NewItem);
  SetModifiedFlag();
  }
```

Rather than create it on the stack, we use the **new** operator and assign the result, temporarily, to a pointer. Initially the *CPictureHolder* object does *not* hold any pictures. You can make an "empty" picture with the *CreateEmpty()* method. However, we want to create a picture from the argument passed to this function. That's what the *SetPictureDispatch()* method does for us. Once prepared, we can give the pointer to the underlying list box for management, using the *LB_ADDSTRING* message.

Now that it's in there, the *get* function can retrieve it as needed:

```
LPPICTUREDISP CImageListCtrl::GetList(short Index)
  {
  if (IsValidIndex (Index))
    {
    CPictureHolder * NewItem;
    SendMessage (LB_GETTEXT,
      (WPARAM) Index, (LPARAM) (LPVOID) &NewItem);
    return NewItem->GetPictureDispatch();
    }
  else
    {
    ThrowError (CTL_E_INVALIDPROPERTYVALUE,
      IDS_INVALIDPROPERTYVALUE);
    return NULL;
    }
  }
```

The *LB_GETTEXT* message retrieves the 32-bit value from the list box, and places it in the *CPictureHolder* pointer we thoughtfully provided for that purpose. The *GetPictureDispatch()* method will return the *LPPICTUREDISP* value the container needs.

You might wonder why I didn't use the *LB_GETITEMDATA* message to retrieve that value, as is done in some examples. It's true that an owner-draw list box duplicates the 32-bit value supplied by *LB_ADDSTRING* in the item data for that index. However, that's just a copy. And our ImageList control has an *ItemData* array property, just like TabList; so it's possible that copy will be overwritten.

In fact, you can see this done in the *set* function for *List*:

```
void CImageListCtrl::SetList(short Index, LPPICTUREDISP NewValue)
  {
  if (IsValidIndex (Index))
    {
    DWORD ItemData = SendMessage (LB_GETITEMDATA,
      (WPARAM) Index);
    CPictureHolder * NewItem;
    SendMessage (LB_GETTEXT,
      (WPARAM) Index, (LPARAM) (LPVOID) &NewItem);
    delete NewItem;
    SendMessage (LB_DELETESTRING, (WPARAM) Index);
    NewItem = new CPictureHolder;
    NewItem->SetPictureDispatch (NewValue);
    NewIndex = (short) SendMessage (LB_INSERTSTRING,
      (WPARAM) Index, (LPARAM) (LPVOID) NewItem);
    SendMessage (LB_SETITEMDATA, (WPARAM) NewIndex, ItemData);
    SetModifiedFlag();
    }
  else
```

```
    ThrowError (CTL_E_INVALIDPROPERTYVALUE,
      IDS_INVALIDPROPERTYVALUE);
}
```

SetList() is invoked when the user wants to replace one picture with another. List boxes have no support for this operation; you have to delete the item and then insert the new one in its place. Doing this loses whatever item data value might have been set for the original item, however. So, in the above code, we first *preserve* the item data, make the swap, then restore it.

Now that we have the data safely managed by the list box, how and when do we draw it?

You've already seen (in Chapter 16) how messages (like *WM_CTLCOLOR*) are "reflected" back by the OLE system, from the underlying control, to the OLE control class. Owner-draw list boxes also generate messages that should be reflected back. They are *WM_COMPAREITEM* (used if the listbox is sorted, to determine in what order items should be added), *WM_MEASUREITEM*, to determine how much room the items need for display, and *WM_DRAWITEM*, to actually do the painting. Each of the messages is accompanied by an entire structure especially designed for the purpose; *lParam* points to this structure.

When the list box has the *LBS_OWNERDRAWFIXED* style, it sends a *WM_MEASUREITEM* message to its parent just once, when it is first created. That's because all the items are supposed to be the same size, so why keep asking? If the list box has the *OWNERDRAWVARIABLE* style, however, *WM_MEASUREITEM* messages will be sent to the parent for every entry.

As we did with *WM_CTLCOLOR*, to handle these messages we have to go through two steps. First, add standard message handlers as if we were the parent window. Second, add the entries to the message map for "ocm" messages:

```
BEGIN_MESSAGE_MAP(CImageListCtrl, COleControl)
  //{{AFX_MSG_MAP(CImageListCtrl)
  ON_WM_CTLCOLOR()
  ON_WM_DRAWITEM()
  ON_WM_MEASUREITEM()
  ON_MESSAGE(OCM_COMMAND, OnOcmCommand)
  //}}AFX_MSG_MAP
  ON_OLEVERB(AFX_IDS_VERB_PROPERTIES, OnProperties)
  ON_MESSAGE(OCM_CTLCOLOR, OnOcmCtlColor)
  ON_MESSAGE(OCM_DRAWITEM, OnOcmDrawItem)
  ON_MESSAGE(OCM_MEASUREITEM, OnOcmMeasureItem)
END_MESSAGE_MAP()
```

The two named functions, *OnOcmDrawItem()* and *OnOcmMeasureItem(),* you'll have to write, which means adding their prototypes to the class declaration. When that's done, you can write the actual code, which just does the basic message cracking:

```
LRESULT CImageListCtrl::OnOcmMeasureItem (WPARAM wParam,
    LPARAM lParam)
  {
  OnMeasureItem ((int) wParam, (LPMEASUREITEMSTRUCT) lParam);
  return 0;
  }

LRESULT CImageListCtrl::OnOcmDrawItem (WPARAM wParam,
    LPARAM lParam)
  {
  OnDrawItem ((int) wParam, (LPDRAWITEMSTRUCT) lParam);
  return 0;
  }
```

You'd think that measuring the area a picture wishes to take up would be trivial; but now we come to a second brick wall: The *CPictureHolder* class offers no means of querying the picture it holds, to find out what size it would like to be. Now, it's true that metafiles size well and Windows 95 does a beautiful job of resizing bitmaps—much better than Windows 3.1 ever did. Still, most graphics have an ideal size...and we have no way of finding out what that is.

So, instead of measuring the graphic, we have no recourse but to respond to the *WM_MEASUREITEM* message with an arbitrary size:

```
void CImageListCtrl::OnMeasureItem(int nIDCtl,
    LPMEASUREITEMSTRUCT lpMeasureItemStruct)
  {
  lpMeasureItemStruct->itemWidth = 80;
  lpMeasureItemStruct->itemHeight = 60;
  }
```

Since the *WM_MEASUREITEM* message requests measurements in device coordinates (pixels), the above values would allow ten graphics across, and ten high, on a medium-resolution screen.

When the *WM_DRAWITEM* message arrives, it's time to actually draw the thing:

```
void CImageListCtrl::OnDrawItem(int nIDCtl,
    LPDRAWITEMSTRUCT lpDrawItemStruct)
  {
```

```
if ((int) lpDrawItemStruct->itemID > -1)
    {
    CDC * dc = CDC::FromHandle (lpDrawItemStruct->hDC);
    CPictureHolder * Item;
    SendMessage (LB_GETTEXT,
        (WPARAM) lpDrawItemStruct->itemID,
        (LPARAM) (LPVOID) &Item);
    RECT ImageRect;
    ImageRect.top = lpDrawItemStruct->rcItem.top;
    ImageRect.left = lpDrawItemStruct->rcItem.left;
    ImageRect.bottom = ImageRect.top + 60;
    ImageRect.right = ImageRect.left + 80;
    Item->Render(dc, &ImageRect,lpDrawItemStruct->rcItem);
    }
}
```

It's important to realize that these messages come in *even when the list box is empty*. That's why we have to test to make sure the item being requested is valid. (A request for an empty list box has an *itemID* of -1.) Other flags in the *DRAWITEMSTRUCT* let you know whether the item being drawn is currently selected, and whether the list box currently has the input focus—most applications draw items differently in each of those cases. For our purposes, the above code will let us see if any of this is working at all.

Once we've retrieved the *CPictureHolder* item, we can draw it simply by invoking its *Render()* method. *That's* a lot easier than wrestling with bitmaps ever was!

And yet, when we test, we discover it doesn't work right. I wrote a test program, placed three Image controls on it (pre-loaded with bitmaps), and loaded the list box with the images using this code:

```
Private Sub Command1_Click()
ImageList1.AddItem Image1.Picture
ImageList1.AddItem Image2.Picture
ImageList1.AddItem Image3.Picture
End Sub
```

When run, I got the effect seen in Figure 18.2.

As you can see, the ImageList control is displaying the three images—but one, almost, on top of the other. In fact, each is displaced by the exact height of one line of text...as if the ImageList had been a standard list box.

Further debugging revealed brick wall number three: In this version of MFC and the OLE Control Development Kit, the "reflector" window *doesn't reflect* WM_MEASUREITEM *messages!* Apparently they simply (and accidentally) left it out of a **switch** statement. With the *MEASUREITEMSTRUCT*

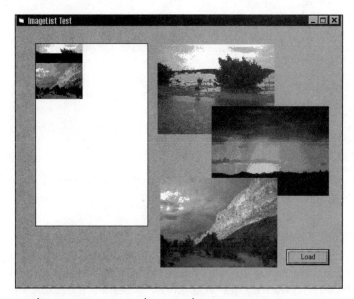

Figure 18.2 The ImageList Control not working.

unaltered by a handler, the item height and width are never set...*and there's nothing you can do about it!*

Now, presumably, another release of the 16-bit Visual C++ (version 1.52d, perhaps?) will fix this flaw. But, in the meantime, the simple task of implementing an OLE control based on an owner-draw list box simply can't be done. (Note that, using the alternative method described in the previous chapter, of making the list box a child window rather than subclassing it, would not have this problem. But it's tough to have to start from scratch—remember, Control Wizard will not step in and let us modify what it's generated—at the seventh hour of a due project. Especially when everything was done as the documentation says it's to be!)

So, for this project, ImageList is "done"...pending release of a bug-fix from Microsoft.

Implementing Custom Events

Since the *WM_MEASUREITEM* method doesn't work, we can't really finish the DrawList control, either. But, since that's the showcase for implementing custom events, let's look at it anyway.

The idea is to convert the *WM_COMPAREITEM*, *WM_DRAWITEM*, and *WM_MEASUREITEM* messages into events that the container can respond to.

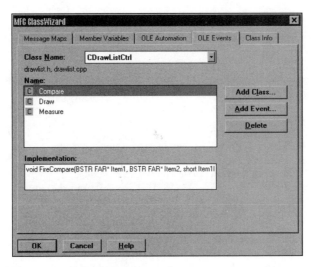

Figure 18.3 Class Wizard's OLE Events tab.

Adding events to a project requires use of the Class Wizard and its OLE Events tab, as seen in Figure 18.3.

To add an event, click the Add Event button. As with properties, there is no "edit event" button, so you've got to make certain you've got it right, or you'll have to delete the errant event and try again. Figure 18.4 shows the Add Event dialog.

Again, as with property arguments, be certain you know in advance what arguments you want and in what order you want them. You can't change them later, except by deleting the entire event and starting over.

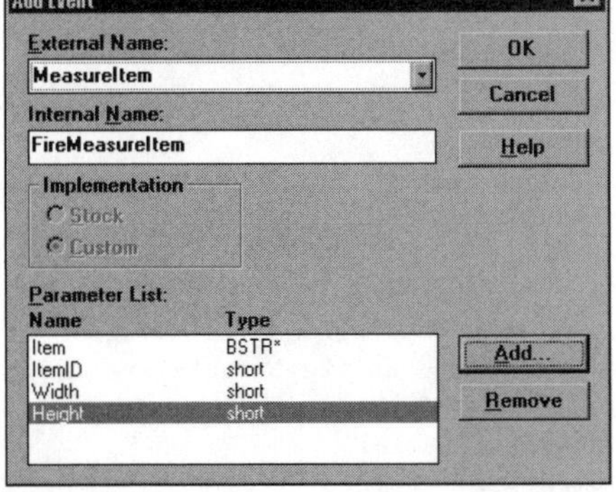

Figure 18.4 Adding an event.

Once you've added your events, you'll find the class declaration has been modified:

```
class CDrawListCtrl : public COleControl
{
    ⇓
    ⇓
// Event maps
    //{{AFX_EVENT(CDrawListCtrl)
    void FireDraw(OLE_HANDLE DC, BSTR FAR* Item,
        short x, short y, short Width, long Height, short ItemIndex)
        {FireEvent(eventidDraw,EVENT_PARAM(VTS_HANDLE
        VTS_PBSTR  VTS_I2  VTS_I2  VTS_I2  VTS_I4  VTS_I2),
        DC, Item, x, y, Width, Height, ItemIndex);}
    void FireCompare(BSTR FAR* Item1, BSTR FAR* Item2,
        short Item1Index, short Item2Index, short FAR* Comparison)
        {FireEvent(eventidCompare,EVENT_PARAM(VTS_PBSTR
            VTS_PBSTR  VTS_I2  VTS_I2  VTS_PI2),
            Item1, Item2, Item1Index, Item2Index, Comparison);}
    void FireMeasure(BSTR FAR* Item, short ItemIndex,
        short FAR* Width, short FAR* Height)
        {FireEvent(eventidMeasure,EVENT_PARAM(VTS_PBSTR
        VTS_I2  VTS_PI2  VTS_PI2), Item, ItemIndex, Width, Height);}
    //}}AFX_EVENT
    DECLARE_EVENT_MAP()
    ⇓
    ⇓
};
```

These are **inline** functions, so you won't find any matching code in the implementation file. The only "real" function is *FireEvent()*, but its somewhat obscure calling sequence has been masked by the infinitely-friendlier generated functions *FireCompare()*, *FireDraw()*, and *FireMeasure()*.

As with ImageList, DrawList has implemented functions for dealing with these three messages when they arrive. The difference is in the internal code. Where ImageList actually did the drawing, DrawList defers each of these operations to the container. For example, the *OnCompareItem()* function looks like this:

```
int CDrawListCtrl::OnCompareItem(int nIDCtl,
        LPCOMPAREITEMSTRUCT lpCompareItemStruct)
    {
    short Result;
    BSTR Temp1 = GetList (lpCompareItemStruct->itemID1);
    BSTR Temp2 = GetList (lpCompareItemStruct->itemID2);
    FireCompare (&Temp1, &Temp2,
        lpCompareItemStruct->itemID1,
        lpCompareItemStruct->itemID2,
        &Result);
    SysFreeString (Temp1);
    SysFreeString (Temp2);
```

```
return Result;
}
```

Although the DrawList control is an owner-draw control like ImageList, its *List* array property is expected to contain strings. (The developer can use these strings or the numeric *ItemData* array property, to decide what to draw.) The *GetList()* function (implemented as in TabList) returns a *BSTR* string. But *FireCompare()* insists on having a *pointer* to a *BSTR*. And so we must assign the return value from *GetList()* to temporary variables, so we can pass their addresses.

When *FireCompare()* is invoked, execution here will freeze while the container's handler for the *Compare* event executes.

GetList(), I remind you, invokes *CString::AllocSysString()* to return this *BSTR*. When it is called by the system, we don't have to worry about whatever is to become of the string thus allocated. However, when *we* call it, we must release those strings—as *SysFreeString()* does.

OnDrawItem() is coded similarly:

```
void CDrawListCtrl::OnDrawItem(int nIDCtl, LPDRAWITEMSTRUCT lpDrawItemStruct)
  {
  BSTR Temp = GetList (lpDrawItemStruct->itemID);
  FireDraw ((OLE_HANDLE) lpDrawItemStruct->hDC,
    &Temp,
    lpDrawItemStruct->rcItem.top,
    lpDrawItemStruct->rcItem.left,
    lpDrawItemStruct->rcItem.bottom -
      lpDrawItemStruct->rcItem.top,
    lpDrawItemStruct->rcItem.right -
      lpDrawItemStruct->rcItem.left,
    lpDrawItemStruct->itemID);
  SysFreeString (Temp);
  }
```

And so is *OnMeasureItem()*, with the added thrill of needing yet another couple of temporary values to aid in the conversion between one data type and another:

```
void CDrawListCtrl::OnMeasureItem(int nIDCtl, LPMEASUREITEMSTRUCT
lpMeasureItemStruct)
  {
  BSTR Temp = GetList (lpMeasureItemStruct->itemID);
  short Width, Height;
  FireMeasure (&Temp,
    lpMeasureItemStruct->itemID,
    &Width,
    &Height);
  SysFreeString (Temp);
```

```
lpMeasureItemStruct->itemWidth = Width;
lpMeasureItemStruct->itemHeight = Height;
}
```

(Of course, as with the ImageList control, this function will never be called until compiled with a fixed version of MFC.)

Caught In the Thicket

So here we are, three chapters into designing our own OCX...and we've hit enough brick walls to require a fresh start. And there's no guarantee that the new start will be successful, either!

OLE, as I've said, is a proposed solution for the problem of application inter-communication, that *needs* solving. And someday it will probably get there. But it's not ready yet. Think of OLE as something that, someday, will be worth a great deal to you to have been playing with all this time...sort of like collecting baseball cards or comic books. But if you try to make a living at it *today*, you are apt to tear out your hair trying it.

One thing I should mention: A lot of the problems we've experienced in these last few chapters go away when you approach them from the 32-bit world of Visual C++ 4.0. But the premise of this book was to show you how to make the most of the world in which your *customers* live, not the ivory tower in which Bill Gates lives. And, in that world, VBXs still seem to be the most viable choice.

But don't stop *playing* with OCXs! It's clearly possible to write them; there are a few out there. But it's also clearly *very difficult* to write them: When we were preparing the CD-ROM for this book, we wanted to include as many shareware and demo OLE controls as possible—and found very few out there. Meanwhile, new VBXs show up on the online services almost every day...and their download counts are high, showing that there is still a great deal of interest in them.

OLE is an exciting technology, and it's an exciting and, yes, challenging time to be a part of it. The convenience of the *CPictureHolder* class, for example, may not make up for the things it *can't* do—but the abilities it's missing, will probably be added. And *then* it'll be a heck of a tool! The same goes for the other components that make up OLE.

Just remember, programming Windows was also once the activity of hobbyists. And, if you started into playing with Windows back then, aren't you glad you did?

A Few Notes on the Tools

MOST BOOKS ON PROGRAMMING focus specifically on a single computer language. Some focus on a particular vendor's compiler for one language! In that, this book is quite unusual; its focus is Windows programming, and includes sample code in no fewer than three programming languages: C, C++, and Visual Basic.

This isn't just an attempt to make everyone happy or confuse everyone either! I firmly believe that the days of the one-trick programmer—whether that trick is C++, C, assembly, or whatever—are permanently behind us. So are the days of the programmer who can focus exclusively on applications or on tools—the so-called "applications programmer" and the "systems programmer." Today's tools may well have become more powerful than ever before, but with that power comes the responsibility to know how to use them productively and, even, safely.

With that in mind, I had the after-thought that it might be worth sharing a few personal comments and observations regarding the tools I worked with in writing the code for this book.

Visual C++ 1.52c

The majority of code in this book is in C or C++. While I made some attempt to compile some of it using the Borland compiler, Visual C++ 1.5x was the primary tool.

Visual C++ 1.52 was the version I did most of my development with, including the development of the VBX++ class library. While I was writing the last few chapters, Visual C++ 1.52c was released and I switched to that, not expecting any side-effects.

Then, a seeming disaster occurred: My hard disk crashed. I had, of course, been backing up my files regularly with Windows 95 Backup. In fact, since I'd been installing new software on a weekly basis, I was backing up my entire set of four logical drives each week. Boy, did I pat myself on the back when that disk crashed, until I tried to actually *restore* from the backup tapes. On each attempt, a message box appeared warning that a "serious" memory error had occurred, and I should re-install Windows 95 Backup! (Which I did once, to no avail.) I finally was able to restore from a smaller backup that was months old...better than nothing, but not much. I then had to re-create the book code by copying the code examples from the book files (which, thank God, I had been sending to my publisher).

To be sure I had gotten it right, I of course had to re-test. And VBX++ didn't work!

I finally discovered the problem: The new version of Visual C++ wasn't mapping data segments the same way the older version had. Remember, the *MODEL* structure includes **near** pointers to various strings which are assumed to reside in the same data segment as the structure itself. This had been true with Visual C++ 1.52, but was no longer. So the disk crash turned out not to be a disaster at all; I would never have re-tested "working" code and you'd have gotten it—in non-working form—on the accompanying CD-ROM. (Except that you'd have never known there was a problem if you didn't have the very *latest* version of the compiler.)

There are a couple of lessons here, both of which show up my own tendency to be optimistic:

- Don't assume a new backup program works just because it *appears* to. *Making* a backup tape is the *easy* part! It's the *restore* step that's hard. And, clearly, a limited test of a few files won't reveal problems that show up only with a massive backup.

- Don't assume a "minor" upgrade of a compiler will behave just like the previous version, only better. Unfortunately, my experience has shown that vendors cannot be trusted to report every change in behavior; and not every change is benign in every situation.

Borland C++ 4.5

Where possible (in other words, with VBXs), I tested with Borland C++ 4.5. Borland was once king of the compilers, so it was a disappointment to find that, in every case, Borland's emitted code was larger than that produced by Microsoft Visual C++ 1.52c. Borland's compile times are still impressive, though if you're doing 32-bit work, Visual C++ 4.0 can give it a run for its money (mostly because of incremental compiling).

Borland 4.5 does not include anything like the OLE Control Wizard, so I didn't attempt to use it for the OLE Control code.

Visual Basic 4

Visual Basic *3* was possibly the most exciting new language product I've ever worked with. When VB4 came out, I was immediately impressed with its expanded abilities, most notably user-defined classes.

But—and it's a big "but"—VB4's *runtime* is an OLE server...and that means, no 16-bit VB app, no matter how trivial, can be distributed without including two disks' worth of OLE DLLs.

This is disturbing. Microsoft is basically passing the job of preparing end-users' computers for OLE, on to *us*. (The nightmare of incompatible OLE DLLs for Windows 3.1 vs. Windows 95 was covered in Chapter 11.) Even if you don't like OLE and don't believe in it, you are forced to help distribute it—at your own expense—for the privilege of using VB4's user-defined classes.

A lot of the other programmers I've talked to have decided not to put up with this. Some are sticking with VB3 (which is still and always will be an excellent tool), and some are jumping ship and turning to Borland's Delphi.

Of course, many have shrugged their shoulders, accepting this as "the price we must pay." (I'm one of these.) If you decide to stick with VB3, though, remember that you *can* write user-defined objects: We just *call* them VBXs.

The Compiler du Jour

A few days after I finished the book, Borland announced the release of Borland C++ 5.0. I mention this because by the time you purchase this, Borland C++ 5.0 will have been out for a while. (For that matter, Visual C++ 1.52d or 1.52z may be "current"!) It takes a certain amount of time to write a book like this, and vendors have been releasing new versions of their tools literally faster than we can keep up.

When I wrote *Windows Programming Power with Custom Controls*, I included detailed instructions on how to make each of the code examples compile. It didn't matter; with every new, minor, compiler release, some piece or other of the code would break or produce a bizarre warning from one compiler or another. Readers didn't hesitate to write and complain.

But the problem wasn't with my *code*—it was that the readers weren't familiar enough with the tools they used to know what warnings were benign, or what new option needed tweaking to make the code work as it had with older versions.

> *COBOL programmers can afford the luxury of working with a stable, mature tool; unfortunately, we can't. Each of the compiler vendors has had stable, mature tools but in the never-ending search for profits they've "fixed" what wasn't broken time and again. And we little programmers are tossed about like flotsam on a storm-tossed sea, trying desperately to stay afloat.*

There's no way around it: By the time you get this book, some of the code will probably need adjusting to compile cleanly with the current crop of tools. I'll post updates to Coriolis' Web site, of course (http:\\www.coriolis.com). But nothing will substitute for your becoming knowledgeable about your own tools. In fact, the code that *doesn't* compile cleanly could be doing you a bigger favor than the code that does; because it shows up changes in the compiler that you might not have discovered on your own.

Combination VBX/OCXs

B

I N PREPARING THIS BOOK, especially while studying the OLE Controls (so I could explain them better!), I realized that there is no reason why a single DLL couldn't do double-duty as a VBX/OCX.

To pull this off, you'll have to make the OCX your primary goal. However, in each of your *get* and *set* and notification functions, and your method invocations, instead of putting the code right there, call another function. *That* function's arguments should *not* be MFC classes—that is, use the OLE control handler to crack the MFC and OLE classes down to their C elements, call the sub-function, then if the sub-function returns any values, build them back into the appropriate MFC handlers.

After you've completed and tested the OLE control, use VBX Genie to generate an equivalent VBX in C—same properties and events. Methods, as we know, are limited to the pre-defined few; implement an *Action* property to substitute for the rest of them. And then, again, don't directly implement the get or set functions; instead call the worker functions described in the last paragraph.

When compiled and linked together, you'll have a single DLL with both OLE and VBX hooks. When the DLL is loaded, the OLE self-registering mechanism will kick in. VB4 won't be able to avoid "seeing" the DLL as an OCX, because those are the hook functions it tries first. However, VB3, which doesn't know about OCXs, will try the VBX hooks and will find them. And either path will cause the common core functions to actually implement the properties and methods.

(Events will have to be fired knowing which mechanism is active, using either *VbFireEvent()* or *COleControl::FireEvent()*. You could add an *IsVBX* argument to your worker functions so they'd know which to do.)

If you choose to implement your dual control over a base window class (with attention to the problems we experienced doing that in OLE controls, in Chapter 18), instead of registering the base class in a *LibMain()* function, you must do it in the OCX module's class. Remember, also, that you'll have to distribute the OLE DLLs with your OCX, even when it's only going to be used as a VBX for a while. The DLL itself will be an OLE server, and will require those other DLLs to load.

Using this technique might require a little more work, but not too much; and it would allow you to maintain and distribute a single DLL even when your customer base hasn't yet settled on a single version of Visual Basic, much less Windows.

Using the Companion CD-ROM

LIKE ALL GOOD WRITERS, I guess I've saved the best stuff for last. Included with this book you'll find a companion CD-ROM jam-packed with all of the source code and tools featured in this book as well as an assortment of other leading development tools and controls for Windows programmers. The OCX revolution is just beginning to take off but there is an emerging supply of sample OCXs and other goodies to help you master the work of moving to OCXs and the 32-bit world.

Let's start be looking at how the CD-ROM is organized.

How the CD-ROM IS Organized

I hate it when I buy a book that comes with a CD-ROM only to find that the CD is a big maze to unravel. Since a number of directories and software are stored on the CD, I've provided Table C.1 to help you navigate. All of the source code for the book is included in the subdirectories withinn the SOURCE directory.

Using the Source Code

As I stated, the source code is in the SOURCE directory. If you are looking for code from a particular chapter just locate the appropriate subdirectory within the SOURCE directory. In Appendix A you'll find a set of notes about how the source code was created and tips about using different C++ compilers. Compiled version of all of the controls are provided on the CD-ROM, but the source code is also available for you to examine and customize. (And of course I hope you do!)

Using the Tools

In the TOOLS directory you'll find an assortment of icon editing and manipulation software including:

Table C.1 Main Directories on the Companion CD-ROM

Directory	Description
CONTROLS	This directory contains a number of OCX and VBX controls you can use and experiment with for building 16- and 32-bit applications. Here you'll find over 100 controls—everything from printer controls to database engines.
DEMOS	This directory contains an assortment of Windows development tools, examples, and other goodies to help you develop Windows applications.
SOURCE	This is the directory you'll probably use the most. It contains all of the source code for the controls and utilities presented in the book. A subdirectory is provided for each chapter that contains code examples.
TOOLS	For this directory, I've provided some useful Windows development-related utilities including icon editing and manipulation software, compression and encryption software, and so on.
WINDOWS	Last but not least, this directory contains Windows tools needed to run VB programs—runtime Libraries.

- Paint Shop pro (16 and 32-bit) graphics package that gives Photoshop a run for its money.

- Microangelo—an incredible app for programmers that gives its users great control over icons and glyphs. (Windows 95 version only.)

- Icon manager—a great tool for changing icons for applications right from the File Manager (16-bit and Windows NT only). It allows icons to be easily moved, copied, and organized into files. It can also read and write icons in all popular file formats that contain icons including ICO, DLL, EXE, ICL, and ICA. Icon Manager will install icons into Program Manager directly using Dynamic Data Exchange.

- Icon Studio for creating and manipulating icons (16-bit and Windows NT only). It works as a stand-alone app and as an add-on to Icon Manager

You'll also find some other useful tools including:

- Anti Virus Software from McAffee and ThunderByte

- Compression and encryption software including Winzip and Drag 'n Zip

- Programmer's File Editor (PFE), which is a very helpful and powerful file editing program that was designed with programmers in mind

Using the Sample Custom Controls

In the CONTROLS directory you'll find some very useful OCX and VBX controls—all ready for you to drop into your Windows applications. The types of controls provided include printer controls, database engines, graphics and animation, controls, and others. Here are some highlights:

- HTML browser control which allows you to create your own custom Web browser

- Internet connectivity controls

Using the Demo Software

In the DEMO directory you'll find demonstration packages from some of the biggest custom control makers in the industry including:

- Accusoft
- Apex
- Desaware
- Distinct
- Dolphin
- Farpoint

Index

16-bit OCXs, 367
32-bit OCXs, 367
3D Controls OCX, 278
#include, 59, 388

—A—

About box, 41, 44, 274, 369, 388
About property, 41
Access time of control properties, 361
Accessing ambient properties, 400
Accessing properties with arguments, 431
Action property, 310
Activate event, 210
Add Event button, 451
Adding a new tool, 250
Adding custom C++ components to a VB
    app, 54
Adding individual colors, 72
Adding objects to Visual Basic, 18
Adding one color to another, 71
AddRef(), 352
Addresses
    descriptor, 11
    real, 10
    structure, 145
Advanced button, 256
After events, 360
AFX, 389
Aggregation, 198
Aligning tab characters, 439
Ambient properties, 357, 397
AmbientUserMode(), 425
ANSI standards, 88
API, Declare statements, 287
API Text Viewer applet, 253
App Expert, 235
App Studio, 20, 224
App Wizard, 235
Appearance property, 435

append, 100
Applications
    code, separating, 224
    compound, 25
    concurrently-running, 356
    load time, 361
    pages, 271
    server, 353
Arguments, name and type, 443
Array index, 322
Array properties, 431
Arrays
    multi-dimensional, 431
    order-dependent, 421
    tab stops, 439
Assigned addition operator, 101
Assigning an object to itself, 96
AutoColor, 332
Automatic bit-storage, 307

—B—

BackColor, 329
Background brush, 401
Base class, 434
Before events, 358
Bevels, 436
Binary/text conversion, 104
Bitmaps
    default, 394
    monochrome, 75
    resizing, 448
Black box within a black box, 17
Boolean data type, 150
boolproperty, 150
BorderStyle, 397
Borland
    App Expert, 235
    battles with Microsoft, 88

Resource Workshop, 224
WinSight, 251
Borland C++ compiler options, 117
Borland Resource Workshop, 20
Brace function, 248
Brush class, 73
BRUSH.CPP, 73
Brushes, 74
Building a 32-bit OCX from scratch, 373
Busy flag, 207
Button
About, 274
Back, 274
Exit, 274
Finish, 274, 288
Next, 273
owner-draw, 318

—C—

C language, disadvantages, 52
C programmers, 8
C++ language
benefits, 18, 53
encapsulation, 53
exception handling, 425
functions, 25
interfaces, 350
name mangling, 122
private properties, 190
version 4.0, 240
writing OCXs, 53
Cancelling an operation, 358
Captions, retrieving, 328
CASE, 169
Case sensitive comparisons, 97
Case sensitive link options, 256
CaseSensitive property, 95
Casts, 104
Catching and dispatching messages, 308
CDK, 15
CD-ROM, included files, 282
Changing a control's background color, 401
Changing control settings, 371
Checking assignments, 96
Checking for pre-existing installations, 242
Child window, 436
Class factory, 385

Class inheritance, 187
Class library, 7
Class Wizard
adding properties, events,
and methods, 27
modification, 382
skeleton code, 429
Classes
color component, 67
control, 112, 139
derived, 146, 197
event, 112
flag, 198
GDI, 56
listable, 187
model, 111, 117
naming, 55
operators, 60
property, 112, 142
range, 100
stand-alone, 114
string, 89
text, 88
types, 111
vendor-free text, 88
Clear, 326
Clear(), 93
clientcontext, 84
Clients
application replacement, 10
backward compatibility needs, 9
CmDialog control, 18
Code
determining if 16-bit or 32-bit, 13
reusable, 4
segment descriptor, 13
Code scripts, 225
Code template, 171
CodeGenerator, 230
Coding a C++ VBX library, 111
Coding a code generator, 177
Coding a reusable progress bar, 278
Coding the methods, 322
COleControl, 418
COleControlModule, 379
Collection of arguments, 217
Collections, 189, 289, 355, 358
Color class, 65
Color component classes, 67

colorproperty, 152
COLORREF, 65
Colors
    system, 329
    property page, 408
Columns
    list box, 415
    user-set, 441
COM, 24, 26, 350
Comm control, 19
Common Dialog DLL, 299
Common Dialog VBX, 300
Common Object Model. *See* COM
Comparing OCX and VBX performance, 362
Comparing OCXs to VBXs, 26
Comparing text strings, 96
Compiler options, 115
Component Object Model, 350. *See also*
  COM
Components
    building, 170
    history, 5
    power of software, 4
    reusable, 24
    Setup Wizard Workaround, 268
CompuServe, 262
Computer-Aided Software Engineering. *See*
  CASE
Concatenation operation, 100
const char *, 105
Constants, 187, 315
Constructor, 91, 113, 126, 398
Container
    inheritance, 357
    model, 112
    properties, 400
    unordered, 140
Context Sensitive Help checkbox, 368
Context-sensitive help, 47, 313
Control block, 17
Control class, 112, 139
Control Development Kit. *See* CDK
Control Options... button, 393
Control procedure, 128
Control procedures, 35
Control Wizard
    creating a project, 27
    don't remove method or property

    entries, 382
    generating OCXs, 362
    producing a skeleton OCX, 14
    setting up custom properties, 356
    warning, 27
Controls
    "back-panel", 7
    adding methods, 442
    adding properties, 442
    as objects, 18
    changing defaults to set a property, 398
    child window, 436
    CmDialog, 18
    Comm, 19
    constructor, 386
    description, 6
    destructor, 386
    Directory, 287
    Drive, 287
    File, 288
    Frame, 369
    frequently-used reference, 418
    graphical, 15, 136
    hardware, 6
    ImageList, 443
    maintaining other controls, 319
    number of properties, 157
    OLE, 354
    owner-draw list box problem, 450
    painting, 387
    property access time, 361
    re-creating, 417
    registering, 386
    SSPanel, 278
    subclass list box, 399
    TabList, 438
    Timer, 18
    tips, 318
    visibility, 18
    Windows attributes, 413
Controls... button, 393
Converting VBXs to OCXs, 21
Cookies, 419
Copy constructor, 63
Copyright, 184
Creating a 16-bit OCX, 367
Creating a 32-bit OCX, 372
Creating a new MSVC project, 243

Creating a new project in Borland C++, 255
Creating a vendor-free text class, 88
Creating a vendor-free Windows class library, 56
Creating compound documents, 25
CurrentPage, 273
Custom controls
    encapsulation, 7
    placing an address, 145
    skeleton, 15
    standard Windows, 8
    VBX, 5
Custom events, 216, 450
Custom properties, 207, 412
Custom-named methods, 21
customproperty, 151
CWnd, 424

—D—

Data types, converting VB, 308
Data-less objects, 19
DDE, 23
Declarations
    forward, 323
    IUnknown, 351
Declare, 253, 287
De-selecting a required standard property, 203
Design decisions, 54
Designing a code generator, 170
Designing a main form, 271
Designing an interface, 177
Designing and writing VBXs, 14
Destructor, 91, 127
Determining if code is 16-bit or 32-bit, 13
Determining the current selection in a list box, 433
Developer dilemma when choosing tools, 9
Development, speeding, 10
Device context, 57
DEVICE.CPP, 78
Dialogs
    converting coordinates, 442
    Find, 300
    Open, 299
    repetitive coding, 298
    Replace, 300
    Save, 299
    tabs, 384
    Tools, 251
Directory control, 287
Disclaimer text, 275
Dispatch ID, 419, 435
Dispatch map, 383
Dispatch(), 131, 147
Display function, 291
Dithered brush, 76
Dividing text, 107
Do events, 360
DoClick, 358
DoPropExchange(), 403
Drawing, 79
DrawList, 452
Drive control, 287
Duplicate declaration errors, 114
Dynamic Data Exchange. *See* DDE

—E—

Elements
    color, 165
    one-dimensional array, 431
    removing, 142
    subscripted, 99
    user interface, 209
    VbData structure, 229
Empty list box, 449
Encapsulation, 7, 17
Endless chain of indirection, 421
Endless recursion, 207
enum, anonymous, 38, 143
Enumerated properties, 418
Enumerating available interfaces, 353
enumproperty, 152
Equivalence operators, 98
Error number, 253
Event class, 112
EVENTINFO, 39
Events
    Activate, 210
    After, 360
    arguments, 218
    Before, 358
    compared to properties, 158
    custom, 216, 450

defining, 8
Do, 360
Initialize, 215
Request, 358
standard class-based, 159
trigger, 384
using type as part of the name, 360
Events page, 214
Extended Listbox controls, 412
Extended properties, 356
External Name combo box, 397

—F—

Field assignments, 124
File control, 288
File names contrasted with module names, 268
Files
    Borland's Open and Save dialogs, 299
    header, 89, 114
    header files list, 31
    help, 45
    .INI file, 240
    long names, 367
    .MAK file, 244
    module definition, 48
    names, 268
    .ODL file, 435
    resource script, 47
    template, 233
    testing for existence, 270
    text format, 188
    .VBP files, 396
    version, 396
Find, 300
FindApplication, 249
FindIndex(), 322
FindReplace control, 305
FindText(), 302
Flags, 196, 229, 301
floatproperty, 156
Font handle, 339
Font property, 406
Fonts property page, 408
ForeColor, 329
Forms
    CodeGenerator, 230

combobox's command button, 211
in VB4, 208
initializing, 179
modal, 213
Frames, 272
FromHandle(), 405
Functions
    Brace, 248
    Display, 291
    Expand, 281
    FindIndex(), 322
    get, 424
    GetVersion(), 270
    helper, 309, 426
    hook, 30
    lookup, as a subscript, 99
    method-handling, 323
    OnDraw(), 387
    overloaded, 147
    property, 191
    set, 424
    virtual, 25, 123, 131
Future of OLE, 454

—G—

Garage software, 299
GDI, 55, 57, 78
GDI class library, 80
GDT, 11
Generating code, 226
Generating distribution disks, 262
Genie, 172, 271
Get, 192
GetPrivateProfileString(), 240
GetVersion(), 270
Global descriptor table. *See* GDT
Globally unique identifier. *See* GUID
Gradient control, 162
GRADIENT.VBX, 165
Graphical controls, 136
Group properties, 201
GUID, 352, 388

—H—

Half-object-oriented programming, 74
Handlers, default, 135

Header files, 89, 114
Headers, precompiled, 114
Help, 313
HelpContextID, 314
Helper class, 89
High-order nybble, 307
HIWORD, 435
Hook functions, 30

#include, 59, 388
IClassFactory, 25
IClassFactory2, 25
IDE, 30, 170, 236
IDE search paths, 241
IDispatch, 26, 354
ImageList control, 443
Images, 449
Implementing OCX stock properties, 393
Implementing tool tips, 318
Implementing VBX++, 114
Incremental development, 4
Indirection, 11
Inheritance, 187
IniData control, 186
Initial build, 377
Initial node, 256
Initialize event, 215
Initializer, 197
In-place editing, 354
Installation problems, 262
InstallTool, 238
Instantiated model objects, 123
Integrated Development Environment. *See*
  IDE
Intel 80x86 chips, 10
Interdependencies between methods and
  properties, 222
Interfaces
    designing first, 177
    enumerating available, 353
    IClassFactory, 25
    IClassFactory2, 25
    IDispatch, 26
    IUnknown, 25
    language-independent, 350
    programmatic, 350
    typedef, 351

Internal reference count, 352
INTERNAL.H, 31
Internationalization, 15
Invisible at runtime, 369
IsDlgButtonChecked, 256
Item data, 432
ITypeInfo, 354
IUnknown, 25, 350

Keyword Dim, why not to use, 190

Language of choice, 18
LDT, 11
Let, 192
Levels of indirection, 444
LibMain(), 122
Line continuation character, 186
Linear address space, 355
List boxes
    basis of OLE controls, 438
    better, 393
    coordinates, 442
    determining current selection, 433
    draw styles, 447
    empty, 449
    loading, 193
    multiple selection, 426
    multi-selection, 196
    owner-draw, 446
    properties, 202
    tab characters, 439
List of registered controls, 395
Listable classes, 187
Lists, index, 38
Load event, 179
Loading a property from disk, 312
loadstring(), 94
Local descriptor table. *See* LDT
Long file names, 248, 367
Lookup function as a subscript, 99
Lower case, 107
LOWORD, 435
Low-order nybble, 307
LSTBXS OCX, 396

—M—

Macros, 382
Marshaling layer between 16-bit and 32-bit applications, 27
Member variable, 415
memset(), 94
Message map, 383
Messages
    catching and dispatching, 308
    cracking, 142, 405, 448
    default handlers, 36
    dispatching mechanism, 324
    handlers, 53
    help, 46
    in an empty list box, 449
    MFC handling, 383
    ocm, 405, 447
    reflected, 447
    separating, 130
    special, 129
    subclass controls, 404
    switches, 35
Methods
    Clear, 326
    coding, 322
    compared to properties, 442
    custom, brick wall, 443
    custom-named, 21
    default, 192
    defining, 7
    handler, 137
    names, 81
Methods page, 220
MFC
    cookie, 421
    usefulness, 24
    writing OCXs, 26
Microsoft
    App Studio, 224
    App Wizard, 235
    battles with Borland, 88
    class library, 7
    Control Development Kit, 30
    Dialog Editor, 20
    MSVC 1.5x, 242
    technology, 23
    VBX obsolescence, 5

Visual C++, 27
Microsoft Foundation Classes. See MFC
Minus operator, 102
Modal form, 213
Model class, 111, 117
Model page, 304
MODEL.CPP, 122
Models
    list of instantiated objects, 123
    tracking properties, 157
Modifying default names for control, classes, and files, 374
Modules
    code, 269
    names, 268
Mouse fly-bys, 335
MSBASIC forum, 262
Multi-control OCXs, 370
Multiplication operator, 103

—N—

Name mangling, 122
Naming properties, 16
NewIndex property, 427

—O—

Object linking and embedding. See OLE
Object-oriented programming. See OOP
Object-oriented thinking, 20
Objects
    assigning characters to text, 155
    assigning to itself, 96
    COM, 352
    control, 139
    data-less, 19
    internal (hidden) parts, 105
    naming, 55
    rectangle, 84
    reference count, 220
    self-registering, 26
    Text, 90, 105
    text, storing a standard C-style string in, 93
    tool tips container, 318
    whether is in use, 353
ObjectWindows, 14, 54

OCXs
    background, 6
    building 16-bit, 361
    can be derived from VBXs, 21
    compared to VBXs, 6, 26
    comparing code to VBXs, 378
    complexity, 6
    converting to VBXs, 21
    custom properties, 412
    disk space overhead, 356
    memory leak, 434
    multi-control, 370
    problems, 454
    property types, 356
    registering, 385, 395
    "secret" standard, 21
    self-registering, 380
    speed test, 361
    stock properties, 393
    types, 367
    under the hood, 349
    unregistering, 381
    wave of the future, 26
    writing is difficult, 454
    written in C++, 53
OLE
    controlling objects program-
        matically, 354
    controls, 354, 358, 438
    controls, when to use, 364
    definition, 6
    DLLs, conflicting, 263
    DLLs, location, 286
    enumerated property, 418
    frequently used reference, 418
    future, 454
    interfaces, 444
    object types list, 369
    original, 24
    proposed solution, 454
    standard for OLE 2, 13
OLE Automation, 353
OLE Command Message. *See* Messages, ocm
OLE_COLOR, 400, 402
OnAction(), 310
OnCreate(), 307
OnDraw(), 387
One-time-only trick of processing a file, 114

OnMouseMove(), 335
OnNcCreate(), 39
OnNcDestroy(), 39
OnResetState(), 387
OOP, 17, 201, 434
Operators
    append, 100
    assigned addition, 101, 141
    assigned subtraction, 142
    assignment, 95
    comparison, 97
    delete, 403
    equivalence, 98
    minus, 102
    multiplication, 103
    new, 445
Optional parameters, 193
Options for tabs, 178
Overloaded versions of Store(), 92

—P—

Padded resources, 232
PageCount, 272
Pages
    Events, 214
    Methods, 220
    Model, 196
    Project, 183
    Property, 384, 407
    setting options, 271
    tab, 182
    Version, 184
paintcontext, 83
Painting an OLE control at design time, 399
Parentheses, use of, 184
Passthrough procedures, 191
Pens, 76, 165
Persistent value in a property, 416
Petzold, Charles, 298
pictureproperty, 155
Pictures
    measuring area, 448
    replacing, 447
Placing text on a device context, 82
Placing text within a rectangle, 82
Point class, 59
POINT.CPP, 59

Pointers
    data type, 422
Pointers to custom property structures, 38
Portable GDI Library, 59
Powell, John Wesley, 3
Precompiled headers, 114
Pre-create properties. *See* Root properties
PreCreateWindow(), 445
Pre-hWND properties. *See* Root properties
Pre-setup, 268
Prime form, 179
Private properties, use of, 190
Procedures
    control, 35
    pop-up window, 44
Producing the required installation files, 284
Programmers
    mediocre, 169
Programming
    object-oriented, 17
    structured, 8
Programs
    assembling from components, 4
    testing, 108
Progress bar, 278
Project page, 183, 303
Projects
    intial build, 377
    new, 243
Properties
    About, 41
    already implemented by Windows
      Listbox control, 424
    ambient, 357, 397, 400
    array, 145, 147, 431, 444, 453
    artificial NewIndex, 427
    AutoColor, 332
    compared to events, 158
    compared to methods, 442
    constructors invoked, 127
    custom, 207, 356, 412
    custom, data type, 207
    custom, encapsulated, 160
    custom, list, 413
    data type, 113
    default values, 149
    defining, 7
    enumerated, 418
    extended, 356

    font, 406
    group, 201
    hWnd, 319
    implemented in code, not storage, 194
    inherited from the base class, 60
    inherited, listed twice, 434
    loading from disk, 42
    module contrasted to class, 189
    names, 412
    naming, 16
    non-enumerated, 419
    page, 201
    persistent value, 416
    read-only, 425
    required, 201
    setting, 327
    setting and retrieving, 40
    setting flags, 16
    standard, 143, 203, 356
    static instatiations, 126
    stock, 356, 444
    storing to disk, 42
    string, 429
    tag, 183
    values affected by messages, 142
    when to protect, 190
Properties box, 412
Properties page, 201
propertieslist, 156
Property class, 112
Property classes, 142
Property page, 407
Property pages
    description, 384
    modifying, 375
    populating, 387
Protected mode, 11

—Q—

QueryInterface(), 353

—R—

range class, 100
Raw property page, 407
Reading VB4 files, 189
Real addresses, 10

Re-creating controls, 417
Rectangle class, 62
Redraw time, 361
Reference count, 220
Refresh, 358
Registering models, 123
RegisterWindowMessage(), 302
Registration Database, 385. *See* System Registry
Release(), 352
Releasing strings, 453
Removing a substring from text, 102
Repeating code, 53, 171
Replace, 300
ReplaceText(), 302
Replacing one picture with another, 447
Repopulating a collection, 218
Request events, 358
Resource pool, 224, 419
Resource script, 224
Resource script file, 47
Resource Workshop, 224
Retesting an index, 148
Retrieving a caption, 328
Retrieving ambient properties, 358
Reusable About box, 274
Right and left shift operators, 72
Root properties, 413
Royal Road to VBXs, 16
Running servers in place, 355

Scode, 380
Seed properties, 427
Self-installing IDE tools, 235
SendKeys, 249, 255
Servers
    in-place, 355
Set, 192
Setting and retrieving property values, 40
Setting and retrieving values in VB4, 191
Setting flags for properties, 16
Setting properties, 327
Setting stock property values, 398
Setting up a project, 264
Setup Wizard
    file compression, 266
    filler lines, 267

how it works, 264
    problem, 364
    problems with installation, 262
    tracking required files, 282
    workaround, 268
Setup Wizard Workaround, 276, 285
SETUP.EXE, 264
SETUP.LST, 264, 266
SETUP1.EXE, 267
Sheridan 3D Controls OCX, 278
Sheridan Software, 181
Short name, 370
Size class, 62
Smalltalk, 350
Software Artistry, 169
Software component. *See* Components
Solid color, 76
Speed tests, 363
Speeding development, 10
SSPanel, 278
SSTab control, 181
Stand-alone classes, 114
Standard assignment statements, 60
standardevent, 159
Statements, Declare, 253
STDAFX.CPP, 389
STDAFX.H, 389
Stock brush, 400
Stock picture property, 444
Stock properties, 356
Store(), 92
strcmp(), 96
String class, 89
String manipulation, 234
String properties, 429
stringtable constructor, 420
Structured programming, 8
Subclasses, 319
Subclassing, 324, 370
Subdirectories, 367
Subdocuments, 353
Subscripted text, 99
Substitutions, 225
Supported IDEs, 236
SWDEPEND.INI, 265, 282
System colors, 329
System Registry, 26, 370
System resources, for OCXs, 6
systemcolor, 70

—T—

Tab control, 181
TabList control, 438
TabStops property, 439
Tag property, 183
TAL, 4
Tandem computers, 4
Terminator, 197
Test for equivalence, 60
Test program, 85
Testing your methods in OOP, 108
Text boxes, programmatic changes, 187
Text class, 88
Text object, 90
Text property, 429
textproperty, 153
Timer, 335
Timer control, 18
Tip window, 338
Title case, 107
Tool tips, 318
ToolNumber, 242
Triggering an event, 159
Truncating text, 106
TurnPage, 273
Twips, 441
Type Library, 372

—U—

Union, 421
Unloading custom property forms, 214
Unregistering an OCX, 381
Updating the type library, 397
Upper case, 107
Use of event type as part of the name, 360
User-defined collection, 189
User-defined resources, 224
Using the Tips control, 342

—V—

VB list box, 393
VBData structure, 306
VBINITCC(), 30, 122
VBM_SETPROPERTY, 309
VBRUN300.DLL, 20

VB-style strings, 145
VBTERMCC(), 30, 122
VBX code generator, 170
VBX Genie, 54, 172, 178, 236, 303, 319
VBX skeleton, 29
VBX++, 111
VBXGEN.INI, 180
VBXHELP.C, 43
VBXs
    add objects to Visual Basic 3, 18
    background, 5
    can function as OCXs, 8
    compared to OCXs, 6, 26
    comparing code to OCXs, 378
    converting to OCXs, 21, 370
    description, 30
    designing and writing, 14
    early effects on Windows development, 5
    ease of design, 14
    language for writing, 18
    must be 16-bit DLLs, 178
    no custom methods, 40
    property types, 356
    provide control for data-less objects, 19
    reusable, 24
    shortcomings, 5
    skeleton, 29
    speed test, 361
    standard, 14
    structure, 30
    why they will be used a long time, 8
    writing on top of existing windows, 16
    writing to meet triple standards, 19
VBXs aren't dead yet, 9
VBXs teach OOP, 17
Version combo box, 181
Version mismatch problems, 158
Version page, 180, 184
VERSIONINFO, 379
virtual destructor, 91
Virtual functions, 123
Visibility of controls, 18
Visual Basic
    adding objects, 18
    success, 5
Visual Basic 4.0, 174, 223
Visual C++, 115, 361
Visual enhancement, 162
VISUAL.C, 30, 32, 229, 320

—W—

WaitCursor, 180
Well-designed VBX standard, 14
WEP(), 32
White, Georgie, 4
Wildcard, 288
WINAPI.BAS, 253
Window
    generic, 16
    handle, 250
    ID, 252
    listing onscreen, 251
    pop-up, 44
    procedures, 6
    reflector, 404
    reflector, problem, 449
    sizing automatically, 338
    standard, 20
    subclassing, 324
    tip, 319, 338
Windows
    controls, 6
    development changes, 5
    GDI, 57
    messages, 6, 53
    platforms in use, 262
    standard class with VBX, 16
    stockroom, 74
    third-party programs, 5
    window procedures, 6
Windows 95
    16-bit code support, 10
    apparent bug, 287
    classes, 375
    inefficient use of 32-bit processing
      space, 355
    OLE DLLs are not backward compatible,
      263
    property pages, 172
Windows Exit Procedure. *See* WEP()
Windows NT, inefficient use of 32-bit
  processing space, 355
*Windows Programming Power with Custom
Controls*, 29
WinSight, 251
WM_CTLCOLOR, 330, 401
WM_KEYDOWN, 314
WM_NCCREATE, 339
WM_SETFONT, 406
Writing a skeleton custom control, 15
Writing VBXs on top of existing
  windows, 16